Understanding Law

Understanding Law

Skills and Sources for Students

Bobby Vanstone

LONGMAN
LONDON AND NEW YORK

Addison Wesley Longman Limited
Edinburgh Gate
Harlow
Essex CM20 2JE
United Kingdom
and Associated Companies throughout the world

First published 1998

ISBN 0-582-31720-7

British Library Cataloguing-in-Publication Data
A catalogue record for this book is available from the British Library

Set by 35 in 10.5/12pt Baskerville
Printed in Great Britain by Henry Ling Ltd., at the Dorset Press, Dorchester, Dorset.

Contents

Acknowledgements

I would like to thank the many students I have taught, especially for the questions they ask. I have discussed some of the material in this book with my sixth form students at Hagley RC High School and thank them for their patience, their humour and their contribution to the process of authorship.

I am very grateful to Liz Sherratt, a long-term colleague and mentor, who read the manuscript in draft and made many helpful comments.

The publishers are grateful to the following for permission to reproduce copyright material:

Butterworth & Co Ltd for extracts from *SENTENCING AND CRIMINAL JUSTICE* by Andrew Ashworth, 2nd ed. 1995 and from the article 'Appointment by Invitation' by Josephine Hayes in *NEW LAW JOURNAL* Vol 147 No 6787, p. 520; Her Majesty's Stationery Office for extracts from *HANSARD* 15 January 1998, *LAW COMMISSION REPORTS*, a) *HCP* 171 95/96 and b) *CM*2646 and the *ROYAL COMMISSION ON CRIMINAL JUSTICE, CM*2263; The Editor of The Legal Executive Journal and the author Sir Peter Graham, for an extract from his article 'The Parliamentary Counsel Office' in *THE LEGAL EXECUTIVE JOURNAL*, October 1993.

We have been unable to trace the copyright holders of *JUDGING JUDGES* by Simon Lee, 1989, and would appreciate any information which would enable us to do so.

About this book

THE SKILLS

We find out what the law is from *primary materials*: statutes and cases, and from *secondary materials*: textbooks, learned articles, reports of Commissions. Unfortunately, both kinds of materials are sometimes difficult to understand. Difficult, not impossible. What I hope to do in this book is to give you an opportunity to read materials from a wide range of sources, to help you to understand what you are reading and to relate it to things you know already or will be learning about soon. I also aim to develop the skills you will need in study of law and those that are necessary for examination success.

Vocabulary

The first block to understanding is often vocabulary. Lawyers are well known for using a long word when a short one would do. In this book I have printed the words that might give you problems in **bold**. A meaning for each such word is given in the glossary at the back of the book. It is unlikely that I have always guessed correctly which words you will find difficult – so do use a dictionary for any word you don't know that I haven't spotted.

Summary

The next step is usually to make a summary of what you have read. This is always useful as an aid to memory and a knowledge of any piece of material in this book will impress examiners if you use it appropriately – so it is a good idea to make your own notes and keep them with other notes on the same topic. A summary has to be in your own words. If you find yourself copying anything but the tiniest quotation, you have probably not understood what you are reading and should read it again.

Analysis

Students have to develop skills of analysis – that is, the ability to read a piece and reach conclusions about what it means. You will find many examples of several different arguments within one piece of material. Try listing the arguments for and against a particular proposition.

Evaluation

One of the higher-order skills expected of students is that of evaluation. Once you have listed arguments, you are engaging in evaluation when you decide which are the strong and which the weak points and what the best solution would be in the case or situation being considered. This is a difficult skill to develop and I have provided a lot of practice throughout the book. Do remember that there is no such thing as a right answer: there are only poor arguments and good arguments.

Application

Once you know what the law is, you will usually be required to apply it in a given situation. Again, I have provided practice in application: usually by asking you to consider alternative solutions to that chosen by a judge or to decide what decision might be appropriate if the facts were slightly different.

You will find some questions headed 'Connections'. Their purpose is to demonstrate that the subject does not exist in little boxes. We learn it as if it does, in order to make it manageable, but you will improve your understanding by considering how each part relates to the whole. Whenever you are reading legal material it is a good idea to note in passing the points that are interesting in different contexts from that for which you are doing the particular piece of reading. You will find the Connections questions more useful as you progress through your course and if you find a particular question incomprehensible, just put it to one side and come back to it at a later stage in your course. These questions will prove particularly useful during revision.

Verbal skills

Lawyers need good verbal skills. Few of us are born with them: they come with practice. If you develop better verbal skills through your study of law, you will find them of help whatever you do for a living. I have provided plenty of discussion material and some more formal oral work to help you. Remember that the key to success in oral work is the same as for written work: preparation.

Preparing for examinations

Finally, you are almost certainly preparing for a written examination. I have provided written exercises to help you but the larger contribution is probably the provision of a wide variety of written material for you to consider. Most of the material in this book is very well written. It is interesting to compare the written styles of the pieces. Be a critical reader: is this person making him or herself clear? Are any arguments properly supported by evidence or authority, as appropriate? Particularly if you find a piece helpful, why not get the whole document from your library and read some more of it? What is it that makes it so effective? When a piece of written work is less successful, why is this so? Sharpen your critical faculties on other people's attempts to communicate, then home in on your own written work and decide how it might be improved.

I have suggested topics for discussion and things to write about, things to do by yourself and things to do in a group. The more you *do*, the more you will understand; the more you understand, the more you will remember. If you are working by yourself, you can still learn a lot from the 'Discuss' questions: try listing arguments for and against and finding material to support both points of view.

This is not a textbook. It does not cover the whole of any law syllabus. You will need to use a textbook to find a complete picture of any topic. This book will, however, help you to understand the law and it will lay a foundation that will help you to learn a lot more law.

The sources

I have used a range of sources in this book and I hope you will want to look at some of them in full and find other sources for yourself. A University Law Library is the best place to look but if you do not have access to this you should talk to your local library staff. Reference libraries in large towns and cities may well carry most or all of these sources and even the smallest local library can obtain any of these things for you through the national network for a very modest fee – my local library charges 60p per document.

Cases

The cases are all from the All England Law Reports, published by Butterworths. You will find that they are widely available. The citation after the names tells you where to find the case: so, *Duport Steels v Sirs* [1980] 1 All ER 529 means that you will find the case at page 529 of volume 1 for the year 1980. If you are using a different set of law reports, be aware that the case is likely to be in the same volume or a slightly later or earlier one – so this one might be in the last 1979 volume of some reports, or in the second 1980 volume.

Statutes

Statutes are published in volumes by year. Many libraries carry annotated versions which contain useful notes written by an expert in the subject-matter. You will also find looseleaf books containing all the statute law on a particular topic together with notes on the law.

White Papers and Law Commission reports

White Papers and Law Commission reports are available from the Stationery Office, which has bookshops in several cities. Publications are listed in the catalogue in your local library, and more and more is becoming available on the Internet.

Finally, do enjoy using this book. Law is an imperfect, living, fascinating study.

Table of Cases

Table of Statutes

Table of Legislative Provisions

European Legislation

Hong Kong Legislation

PART ONE

Introduction to Part One

The materials in this part of the book are concerned with the way in which the law is made, some of the people who make decisions as to what the law is and whether it applies to the case before them, and some wider issues about how disputes should be handled and what should be done with people convicted of criminal offences.

I have drawn on a wide range of material in the hope that you will do so too when you want to pursue an issue further or research something not covered in this book. I have to commend to you the services of your local library. Mine has been able to obtain documents for me from libraries all over the country for a very modest fee. More and more information is now available on the Internet too.

It is, of course, one thing to have access to written material and quite another to understand it. The questions at the end of each section are designed to help you understand but there is no short cut and I hope you will enjoy reading, thinking, drafting answers and grappling with the material.

1 Sources of law

There are three major sources of law: the European Union, Parliament and judicial precedent. They rank in that order, so when a lawyer needs to know what the law is, the first question is whether the European Union has made any rules on the subject; if not, has Parliament? If neither the EU nor Parliament has made law, it is necessary to find out whether the point has been decided by a court.

1.1 EUROPEAN LAW

The European Union makes law on matters connected with business, but there are large areas of English law unaffected by the EU. On the other hand, if the EU has made law on a matter, then that is the law.

It took a very long time for lawyers and others to adjust to the idea that the supreme power to make law in certain areas had passed from Parliament to the institutions of the EU. The constitutional implications of membership were discussed in *Blackburn v Attorney-General* [1971] 2 All ER 1380. While Britain was negotiating to join the Common Market (as the EU was then called), Mr Blackburn brought an action against the government, claiming that they had no right to surrender Parliament's right to make law. Lord Denning gave judgment in the Court of Appeal:

> Much of what Mr Blackburn says is quite correct. It does appear that if this country should go into the Common Market and sign the **Treaty of Rome**, it means that we will have taken a step which is irreversible. The **sovereignty** of these islands will thenceforward be limited. It will not be ours alone but will be shared with others. Mr Blackburn referred us to a decision by the European Court of Justice, *Costa v ENEL* in February 1964, in which the court in its judgment said:
>
> > '. . . the member-States, albeit within limited spheres, have restricted their sovereign rights and created a body of law applicable both to their nationals and to themselves.'

> Mr Blackburn points out that many regulations made by the European Economic Community will become automatically binding on the people of this country; and that all the courts of this country, including the House of Lords, will have to follow the decisions of the European Court in certain defined respects, such as the construction of the treaty.
>
> I will assume that Mr Blackburn is right in what he says on those matters. Nevertheless, I do not think these courts can entertain these actions . . . We take no notice of treaties until they are embodied in laws enacted by Parliament, and then only to the extent that Parliament tells us . . . Mr Blackburn acknowledged the general principle, but he urged that this proposed treaty is in a category by itself, in that it diminishes the sovereignty of Parliament over the people of this country. I cannot accept the distinction. The general principle applies to this treaty as to any other. The treaty-making power of this country rests not in the courts, but in the Crown; that is, Her Majesty acting on the advice of her Ministers. When her Ministers negotiate and sign a treaty, even a treaty of such paramount importance as this proposed one, they act on behalf of the country as a whole. They exercise the **prerogative** of the Crown. Their action in so doing cannot be challenged or questioned in these courts.
>
> Mr Blackburn takes a second point. He says that, if Parliament should implement the treaty by passing an Act of Parliament for this purpose, it will seek to do the impossible. It will seek to bind its successors. According to the treaty, once it is signed, we are committed to it irrevocably. Once in the Common Market, we cannot withdraw from it. No Parliament can commit us, says Mr Blackburn, to that extent. He prays in aid the principle that no Parliament can bind its successors, and that any Parliament can reverse any previous enactment . . . We have all been brought up to believe that, in legal theory, one Parliament cannot bind another and that no Act is irreversible. But legal theory does not always march alongside political reality. Take the Statute of Westminster 1931, which takes away the power of Parliament to legislate for the dominions. Can anyone imagine that Parliament could or would reverse that statute? Take the Acts which have granted independence to the dominions and territories overseas. Can anyone imagine that Parliament could or would reverse those laws and take away their independence? Most clearly not . . . What are the realities here? If Her Majesty's Ministers sign this treaty and Parliament enacts provisions to implement it, I do not envisage that Parliament would afterwards go back on it and try to withdraw from it. But, if Parliament should do so, then I say we will consider that event when it happens. We will then say whether Parliament can lawfully do it or not.

Mr Blackburn's argument seems finally to have been vindicated by the decisions in the *Factortame* cases. This is a saga about fishing rights that began during the 1970s and developed into British anxiety about Spanish fishermen owning British vessels and then using British fishing quotas. To prevent this, Parliament passed the Merchant Shipping Act 1988, which provided that 75 per cent of the shareholders and directors of a company owning British fishing vessels must be British. The validity of that Act was challenged by the owners of fishing boats that were deprived of their right to fish as a result of this legislation. Their argument was that the Act was of no effect because it was contrary to the Treaty provisions on freedom of movement of capital within the EC: eventually, they won. During the course of the many cases involved, Lord Bridge gave a judgment in *Factortame Ltd v Secretary of State (No 2)* [1991] 1 All ER 70:

> Some public comments on the decision of the Court of Justice, affirming the **jurisdiction** of the courts of member states to override national legislation if necessary to enable **interim relief** to be granted in protection of rights under Community law, have suggested that this was a novel and dangerous invasion by a **Community institution** of the sovereignty of the United Kingdom Parliament. But such comments are based on a misconception. If the supremacy within the European Community of Community law over the national law of member states was not always inherent in the EEC Treaty it was certainly well established in the **jurisprudence** of the Court of Justice long before the United Kingdom joined the Community. Thus, whatever limitation of its sovereignty Parliament accepted when it enacted the European Communities Act 1972 was entirely voluntary. Under the terms of the 1972 Act it has always been clear that it was the duty of a United Kingdom court, when delivering final judgment, to override any rule of national law found to be in conflict with any **directly enforceable rule of Community law**. Similarly, when decisions of the Court of Justice have exposed areas of United Kingdom statute law which failed to implement Council directives, Parliament has always loyally accepted the obligation to make appropriate and prompt amendments. Thus there is nothing in any way novel in according supremacy to rules of Community law in those areas to which they apply and to insist that, in the protection of rights under Community law, national courts must not be inhibited by rules of national law from granting interim relief in appropriate cases is no more than a logical recognition of that supremacy.

European legislation

European Union legislation takes different forms and is different in nature from UK legislation. Each form of legislation begins with a statement of its purpose and judges have regard to this when determining what the legislation means. The major treaty is the Treaty of Rome 1957. It begins with a list of the original signatories, who were the Heads of State of the six founder members, and continues:

> Determined to lay the foundations of an ever closer union among the peoples of Europe,
>
> Resolved to ensure the economic and social progress of their countries by common action to eliminate the barriers which divide Europe,
>
> Affirming as the essential objective of their efforts the constant improvement of the living and working conditions of their peoples,
>
> Recognising that the removal of existing obstacles calls for concerted action in order to guarantee steady expansion, balanced trade and fair competition,
>
> Anxious to strengthen the unity of their economies and to ensure their harmonious development by reducing the differences existing between the various regions and the backwardness of the less favoured regions,
>
> Desiring to contribute, by means of a common commercial policy, to the progressive abolition of restrictions on international trade,
>
> Intending to confirm the solidarity which binds Europe and the overseas countries and desiring to ensure the development of their prosperity, in accordance with the principles of the Charter of the United Nations,
>
> Resolved by thus pooling their resources to preserve and strengthen peace and liberty, and calling upon the other peoples of Europe who share their ideal to join in their efforts,
>
> Have decided to create a European Economic Community . . .

The Treaty then lays out the principles and policies of the EU. An example that has given rise to much litigation is Article 119:

> Each Member State shall during the first stage ensure and subsequently maintain the application of the principle that men and women should receive equal pay for equal work.
>
> For the purpose of this Article, 'pay' means the ordinary basic or minimum wage or salary and any other considerations, whether in cash or in kind, which the worker receives, directly or indirectly, in respect of his employment from his employer.
>
> Equal pay without discrimination based on sex means:
>
> (a) that pay for the same work at piece rates shall be calculated on the basis of the same unit of measurement;
> (b) that pay for work at time rates shall be the same for the same job.

Treaty provisions *automatically* become part of the law of member states.

More detail is provided by Directives. Directives do not become part of the law of Member States, they are instructions to the Member States to change their law, if necessary, so that the law in all Member States becomes the same within a given time limit. In 1975 the Council passed a Directive designed to harmonise the law of Member States on equal pay. Like the Treaties, Directives begin with a preamble setting out their purpose and citing the Article on which they are based. This Directive, 75/117 (the 117th directive of 1975) includes in its preamble:

> Whereas implementation of the principle that men and women should receive equal pay contained in Art. 119 of the Treaty is an integral part of the establishment and functioning of the common market;
>
> Whereas it is primarily the responsibility of the Member States to ensure the application of this principle by means of appropriate laws, regulations and administrative provisions; . . .
>
> Whereas it is desirable to reinforce the basic laws by standards aimed at facilitating the practical application of the principle of equality in such a way that all employees in the Community can be protected in these matters;
>
> Whereas differences continue to exist in the various Member States despite the efforts made to apply the resolution of the conference of the Member States of 30 December 1961 on equal pay for men and women and whereas, therefore, the national provisions should be approximated as regards application of the principle of equal pay . . .

The body of the Directive then provides:

> *Article 1* The principle of equal pay for men and women outlined in Art. 119 of the Treaty, hereinafter called 'principle of equal pay', means, for the same work or for work to which equal value is attributed, the elimination of all discrimination on grounds of sex with regard to all aspects and conditions of remuneration . . .
>
> *Article 2* Member States shall introduce into their national legal systems such measures as are necessary to enable all employees who consider themselves wronged by failure to apply the principle of equal pay to pursue their claims by judicial process after possible recourse to other competent authorities.
>
> *Article 3* Member States shall abolish all discrimination between men and women arising from laws, regulations or administrative provisions which is contrary to the principle of equal pay . . .
>
> *Article 5* Member States shall take the necessary measures to protect employees against dismissal by the employer as a reaction to a complaint within the undertaking or to any legal proceedings aimed at enforcing compliance with the principle of equal pay . . .

The UK response to this was to **implement** the Equal Pay Act but difficulties arose with the concept of 'equal value'. In *Pickstone v Freemans* [1988] 2 All ER 803 the House of Lords considered the problem:

> Lord Keith of Kinkel:
>
> My Lords, under the Equal Pay Act 1970, as brought into force with amendments on 29 December 1975, a woman employee could claim **parity**

of pay with a male employee in the same establishment only where she was employed on like work with the man or where she was employed on work rated as equivalent with that of the man. That was the effect of s 1(1) and (2) of the Act . . . By virtue of s 1(5) a woman's work could only be rated as equivalent with that of a man in her job if his job had been given an equal value, according to certain criteria, on a job evaluation study. A job evaluation study could not be carried out otherwise than with the consent of the employer.

The EC Commission took the view that this state of the law did not comply with the obligation of the United Kingdom government to implement art 119 of the EEC Treaty, **enjoining** application of the principle that men and women should receive equal pay for equal work, together with EC Council Directive 75/117 (the equal pay directive) adopted by the Council on 10 February 1975. The Commission accordingly applied to the Court of Justice of the European Communities for a declaration that the United Kingdom had failed to **obtemper** this obligation in respect that it had not adopted measures enabling women to obtain equal pay for equal work in circumstances where there had been no job evaluation study. . . .

The United Kingdom government took steps to correct the defect in its equal pay legislation identified in the judgment of the European Court. Section 2(2)(a) of the European Communities Act 1972 provides:

> 'Subject to Schedule 2 to this Act, at any time after its passing Her Majesty may by Order in Council, and any designated Minister or department may by regulations, make provision – (a) for the purpose of implementing any Community obligation of the United Kingdom, or enabling any such obligation to be implemented, or of enabling any rights enjoyed or to be enjoyed by the United Kingdom under or by virtue of the Treaties to be exercised . . .'

Schedule 2 to the Act contains general provisions as to subordinate legislation, including in para 2(2) a provision making subject to **annulment** by resolution of either House of Parliament any statutory instrument containing regulations made without a draft having been approved by resolution of each House.

So the Secretary of State for Employment made a draft which was introduced as the Equal Pay (Amendment) Regulations 1983, SI 1983/1794, in the House of Commons on 29 July 1983 and in the House of Lords on 5 December 1983. Both Houses approved the draft albeit, in the case of the House of Lords, subject to a reservation. Quotations from the speech of the Under Secretary of State for Employment, **initiating** the debate in the House of Commons, are to be found in the speech of my noble and learned friend Lord Templeman. . . .

In the present case the respondent, Mrs Pickstone, who is employed by the appellant employers as a 'warehouse operative', claims that her work as such is of equal value with that of a man, Mr Phillips, who is employed in the same establishment as a 'checker warehouse operative', and who is paid £4.22 per week more than she is paid. However, it happens to be the fact that one man is employed in the establishment as a warehouse operative doing the same work as Mrs Pickstone. The employers maintain that the existence of this fact precludes Mrs Pickstone from claiming equal pay with Mr Phillips under s 1(2)(c) of the 1970 Act as amended [by the Equal Pay (Amendment) Regulations 1983], notwithstanding that she may be performing work of equal value with his and notwithstanding that the difference in pay may be the result of discrimination on grounds of sex.

This argument is based on the words in para (c) 'not being work in relation to which paragraph (a) or (b) above applies'. The employers say that the work on which Mrs Pickstone is employed is work to which para (a) applies because it is like work with a man in the same employment, namely the one male warehouse operative. So Mrs Pickstone's work does not qualify under para (c).

The question is whether the exclusionary words in para (c) are intended to have effect whenever the employers are able to point to some man who is employed by them on like work with a woman claimant within the meaning of para (a) or work rated as equivalent with hers within the meaning of para (b), or whether they are intended to have effect only where the particular man with whom she seeks comparison is employed on such work. In my opinion the latter is the correct answer. The opposite result would leave a large gap in the equal pay provision, enabling an employer to evade it by employing one token man on the same work as a group of potential women claimants who were deliberately paid less than a group of men employed on work of equal value with that of the women. This would mean that the United Kingdom had failed yet again fully to implement its obligations under art 119 of the Treaty and the equal pay directive and had not given full effect to the decision of the European Court in *EC Commission v UK* Case 61/81 [1982] ECR 2601. It is plain that Parliament cannot possibly have intended such a failure. The draft regulations of 1983 were presented to Parliament as giving full effect to the decision in question. The draft regulations were not subject to the parliamentary process of consideration and amendment in committee, as a Bill would have been. In these circumstances and in the context of s 2 of the European Communities Act 1972 I consider it to be entirely legitimate for the purpose of ascertaining the intention of Parliament to take into account the terms in which the draft was presented by the responsible minister and which formed the basis of its acceptance. The terms in which it was presented to the House of Commons are set out in the speech of my noble and learned friend Lord Templeman. Much the same was said before the House of Lords. There was no suggestion that the exclusionary words in para (c) were intended to apply in any other situation than where the man selected by a woman complainant for comparison was one in relation to

> whose work para (a) or para (b) applied. It may be that, in order to confine the words in question to that situation, some necessary implication falls to be made into their literal meaning. The precise terms of that implication do not seem to me to matter. It is sufficient to say that the words must be **construed purposively** in order to give effect to the manifest broad intention of the maker of the regulations and of Parliament. I would therefore reject the appellant's argument. . . .

Regulations become part of UK law as soon as they come into force. For example, Regulation 1251/70 provides for the right of workers to remain in a Member State after having been employed in that State, a more detailed application of the principle of freedom of movement of workers set out in Article 48 of the Treaty. The Regulation is part of the law of all Member States but Directive 64/221, which provides a set of rules by which nationals of Member States can be denied a right of entry to another Member State on grounds of public policy, public security or public health, sets out the basis on which each State can make its own law and gives six months for them to do so.

Check your understanding

Can you explain the meaning of the words and phrases in **bold** type in the passages? Are there any other words you need to look up in a dictionary? What is a job evaluation study (referred to in *Pickstone v Freemans*)?

Discuss

1 It was argued for the Crown in *Blackburn v Attorney-General* that Mr Blackburn had no *locus standi*; that is, he had insufficient personal interest in the subject-matter to bring a court action. Why do we have a rule that a litigant must have *locus standi*? Do you consider Mr Blackburn to have had a sufficient personal interest? If the Court of Appeal decided he did not, who might?

2 Compare what Lord Denning was saying at the end of the excerpt from *Blackburn v Attorney-General* with the decision of the courts on the validity of the Merchant Shipping Act 1988. Did Parliament 'go back on [the Treaty] and try to withdraw from it'? Does the decision in *Factortame* have implications for any future Parliament which passes an Act purporting to withdraw Britain from the EU?

3 Compare the style of the excerpts from the Treaty and Directive with the style of the Crime (Sentences) Act 1997 (see p. 79). What is the point of the preambles in the European legislation?

4 Why does the EU concern itself with issues like equal pay and maximum working hours? What have they to do with economic union?

Write

1 Explain what is meant by the doctrine of Parliamentary sovereignty.

2 Summarise the excerpt from Lord Keith's judgment in *Pickstone v Freemans*. Take care to use your own words: if you use any of his phrases, remember to put them inside quotation marks.

Connections

1 *Blackburn v Attorney-General* is concerned with constitutional law, which is a branch of public law. Distinguish between public law and private law and make a list of the areas of law that fall into each category.

2 In *Pickstone v Freemans* the House of Lords used Hansard to decide what Parliament had intended. Lord Templeman's speech in *Pickstone v Freemans* contains quotations from the responsible Minister when he opened the debate on the Equal Pay (Amendment) Regulations. There is a reference to an excerpt from Hansard at p. 10. Until the decision in *Pepper v Hart* (1993), courts did not use Hansard. Consider the arguments for and against its use. Why do you think the House of Lords 'broke the rules' and used Hansard in *Pickstone v Freemans*?

3 When you have looked at the chapter on statutory interpretation, you may like to consider what approach to statutory interpretation the House of Lords was adopting in *Pickstone v Freemans* and why.

4 Judges bear in mind the desirability of having legal rules similar to those of other Member States of the EU. The Law Commission Report on Privity of Contract, at para 3.8 (see p. 243), also makes this point.

1.2 PARLIAMENTARY LAW MAKING

Parliament consists of two Houses: the House of Lords and the House of Commons. The House of Commons is the more important, being the elected chamber and more powerful. It can, by exercising powers under the Parliament Acts of 1911 and 1949, make law without the consent of the House of Lords but this is very rare and, as the War Crimes Act 1991 illustrates, not to be recommended.

The War Crimes Bill was designed to allow prosecution in Britain of people believed to have committed murder in concentration camps in

Eastern Europe during the Second World War. As they were not British citizens and the crime was not committed on British territory they could not, as the law stood, be prosecuted in British courts. The House of Lords, whilst recognising the desirability of convicting murderers, rejected the Bill on the pragmatic grounds that after fifty years it would not be possible to hold fair trials. The House of Commons overruled the House of Lords' objections and the Bill became an Act. There have, at the time of writing, been few attempts to prosecute under the Act and no convictions.

The Crown has a purely formal role in the legislative process: all Acts require the Royal Assent, but this is never withheld.

Drafting

The subject has its own vocabulary. Each Act begins as a **Bill**, drafted by **Parliamentary Counsel to the Treasury**, who are trained lawyers. The way in which they work is described by Sir Peter Graham KCB, QC in the following passage taken from an article he wrote for the *Legal Executive Journal* of October 1993:

> *Drafting a Bill*
> When the appropriate Cabinet Committee has given approval to a department's bid for a Bill, instructions are prepared in the department for sending to the Parliamentary Counsel Office. The nearest – though perhaps not very close – **analogy** would be instructions to Counsel prepared by a firm of Solicitors with a view to the drafting of a complex commercial agreement.
>
> When the instructions arrive in the Office, the First Parliamentary Counsel assigns them to one of his senior colleagues. The Office works in pairs so that each senior member is assisted by a junior member. Accordingly, in practice, two sets of the relevant instructions are provided and from then on the 'team' charged with the instructions deals directly with the department concerned. Obviously the preparation of a Bill may take a matter of days, weeks or months depending upon the subject matter and the size of the Bill which is proposed.
>
> During the course of the preparation period, there will be many exchanges of correspondence, several meetings (always held in the Parliamentary Counsel Office) and a number of drafts. Eventually, a draft will be agreed between Counsel concerned and the department, but that process is not as leisurely as might appear from that proposition. This is because every Bill has a date at which it is to be considered by the Cabinet Committee responsible for authorising the introduction of the Bill into the House of Commons or the House of Lords.
>
> After introduction of a Bill, the team responsible for its preparation become responsible for the preparation of any government amendments which may be required. The team will also discuss the grouping of amendments

(government and opposition) with the officials of the House of Commons and, if asked by those officials, will furnish advice on amendments tabled otherwise than by the government. In these latter respects, the members of the Parliamentary Counsel Office adopt a completely **non-partisan** stance: indeed, their relationship with the officials of both Houses is one of ***uberrimae fidei***. Thus, it may occur that the government wants to table an amendment which, for technical reasons, would be outside the rules of one House or the other. In such a case the Office will advise the government that it cannot proceed as it wishes.

Rules

The rules of the House of Commons (more than those of the Lords) are in many respects very technical and it is one of the functions of Parliamentary Counsel Office to ensure that every government Bill complies with those rules. Thus, for example, Bills involving the expenditure of public money cannot proceed beyond second reading without an appropriate money resolution. It is the function of the Office to prepare the appropriate motion for a money resolution. Much more complex considerations arise in the context of Finance Bills. Suffice to say that the Budget Resolutions, on which the Budget debate takes place, are drafted by the Parliamentary Counsel in charge of the Finance Bill.

Role of Counsel

As a general principle, the individual Parliamentary Counsel do not specialise in any particular branch of statute law, but, because of the demands of the annual Finance Bill, the practice has developed whereby one of the senior Counsel takes charge of the Finance Bill for a period of four or five years. The junior member of his team will, however, change at least once during that period because it is important that all the juniors have experience of Finance Bill work. In practice, at least two teams of Counsel will be involved on the Finance Bill in the three months before Budget day and it is not unknown for a third or fourth team to have to be brought in nearer to Budget day to deal with specific topics.

At any one time, at least four of the Counsel are on secondment to the Law Commission where they draft consolidation Bills and participate in the law reform programme of the Law Commission. In this latter respect, those on secondment take an active part in the law reform programme as well as preparing the draft Bills which accompany Law Commission reports.

It is sometimes asked whether it would not be more efficient to have draftsmen permanently attached to specific departments. While it is true that some departments, for example the Home Office, legislate almost every **session**, the work load is uneven and there are several departments which only rarely legislate.

Accordingly, permanent attachment is impractical on those grounds alone. There are far more important reasons for keeping the draftsmen separate

> from the departments. In particular, the draftsmen are able, by their direct access to the **Law Officers** on points of law, to ensure that a powerful Secretary of State does not legislate in a way which might infringe the liberties of the subject without clearance by the Law Officers. Moreover, the collegiate nature of the Parliamentary Counsel Office ensures not only an excellent ***esprit de corps*** but also a continuous exchange of ideas and information which helps to preserve the **cohesiveness** of the statute book.

The government is responsible for most Bills and may have sought opinions on its proposals by issuing a **Green Paper** or a **White Paper** before the Bill is drafted. For example, before making radical changes in the Legal Aid system, the government issued a Green Paper called *Legal Aid: Targeting Need* in 1995. It was followed by a White Paper, *Striking the Balance*, in 1996. The excerpt from that White Paper (see p. 64) illustrates that Green Papers are consultative documents, whereas White Papers are statements of, and rationales for, government policy.

Similarly, the Crime (Sentences) Act 1997 was preceded by a White Paper, *Protecting the Public*. The material on sentencing (p. 79) demonstrates how the proposals in the White Paper are translated into legislation.

The Law Commission has a duty to keep the whole of the law under review. It is very influential in law reform. The Law Commission generally produces a report with a draft Bill annexed to it, so that all Parliament has to do is to debate the Bill. The Law Commission also produces Consultation Papers which contain a thorough review of the existing law, proposals for reform and requests for comment from interested parties. The Law Commission then takes comments into account when producing its final report and making recommendations for reform.

Debating

Bills are debated in Parliament. The **First Reading** is the formal introduction of a Bill to the House. The major debate is the **Second Reading**, during which it is decided in principle whether to change the law. The detailed provisions are considered during the **Committee Stage**, conducted by a small number of MPs who have some knowledge of the subject-matter of the Bill. Membership of the committee is balanced to reflect the membership of the House of Commons – so, when there is a Labour government with a substantial majority, all committees have a substantial Labour majority.

After the Committee Stage, the Bill comes back to the House for the **Report Stage**, at which amendments proposed by the Committee are considered by the House. Amendments are often welcomed by the government, as sensible proposals to improve the operation of the Act, but this stage can also be an opportunity for discussion of less welcome suggestions.

The excerpt that follows gives a flavour of what a debate in the House of Commons is like. It comes from Hansard, the daily **verbatim** record of proceedings in Parliament. This debate took place on 15 January 1997, during the Report Stage of the Crime (Sentences) Bill:

New clause 14

CORPORAL PUNISHMENT

—(1) Where a person of not less than 14 years of age is convicted of an imprisonable offence, the court by or before which he is convicted may make an order that he shall be subject to corporal punishment.

(2) The Secretary of State shall, by statutory instrument, subject to annulment in pursuance of a resolution of either House of Parliament, make rules for the administration of the sentence of corporal punishment. – *[Mr Marlow.]*

Brought up, and read the First time.

Mr Tony Marlow (Northampton, North): I beg to move, That the clause be read a Second time. I tabled the new clause with the support, after a short trawl, of 29 of my hon. Friends. I am committed to the powers and sovereignties of the House and, in general, I do not believe that any international involvements or commitments should stand in the way of the House doing what it believes to be right for this country in this country.

It may seem to some bloodthirsty, even Neanderthal, to propose anything as mediaeval as the reintroduction of **corporal punishment**, but unfortunately – as everyone in the House must know – most of our citizens, especially the law abiding, the old, the poor and defenceless, are daily threatened by an escalating savagery and barbarism that is much more bloodthirsty and Neanderthal than corporal punishment while their tormentors, who so readily and callously destroy peace of mind and quality of life, have nothing to fear. As we all know, crime – particularly hooligan crime – is getting worse. As yet, no effective solution has been proposed, still less enacted.

It is fine for us in this place who, by and large, have a good standard of living. We are privileged, and we have a choice as to the area in which we live. We are cocooned in our relative prosperity. But for many of our constituents, life is hell. It is different out there. If hon. Members had to live in the intimidatory conditions imposed upon many of our constituents, we would be less precious, less squeamish and less elitist in our approach to the problem. As the problem has worsened, we have wrung our hands – but otherwise looked away.

We have a duty that for too long we have neglected. We need to make an urgent impact, and to do that we must be imaginative. We must break away from the parrot cries – one of which we heard earlier from the hon. Member for Knowsley, North (Mr Howarth) – about the need for better rates of detection. Of course we need better rates of detection, which will help. But we need effective deterrents – deterrents that truly deter. We need effective treatments – treatments that reform. By no stretch of the imagination are either of those available yet.

I recommend two approaches. First, for those who have gone off the rails for the first time, I recommend the **judicious** development of a system of outward bound training. Those who, perhaps, have had a bad start in life or who have taken a wrong turning can be sent on a course into the mountains to work with and take responsibility for others as part of a team. They can be challenged and, perhaps, they will succeed. If they satisfy the rigorous training conditions, they can pass out with an award of esteem. For many of our confused and alienated young, such a scheme could establish a basis of purpose and confidence in their lives on which they could build to become useful and satisfied citizens, rather than being sucked deeper into a vortex of criminal sub-culture.

Those who are more hardened and contemptuous of society – and only them – I would threaten with the new clause. Corporal punishment should be made available to the courts in place of imprisonment, with a system of corporal punishment introduced later by statutory instrument. At whom would I target this punishment? Basically, anti-social youth – the mugger, the ram-raider, the vandal, the graffiti artist, the hooligan, those who seek to intimidate potential witnesses and the tin-pot Napoleons who seek the admiration of their peers by ever more outrageous behaviour.

Why should we apparently seek to turn back the pages of history? I believe that our first duty is to safeguard the quality of life of many of our citizens whose lives have been made miserable by these malcontents. I believe that no current deterrent or penalty is effective, and I do not believe that any Member of this House can honestly say that corporal punishment would not be a deterrent. I do not believe any historical analysis that suggests that corporal punishment fell into disuse when it was last available because nobody wanted to use it as it was not effective. However, circumstances at that time were different from those of today. At that time, we had a disciplined society – now we do not. Corporal punishment would have a great effect on criminal patterns of behaviour. Bullies are also cowards.

I do not envisage corporal punishment as a daily occurrence, and some judges and magistrates may be reluctant to impose it. In most of our cities the cane could be kept in the cupboard, but threats – along with reports of the circumstances of its occasional use – would be sufficient for it to work. Some hon. Members may feel that such a proposal is out of date – even barbaric. They have had more than a generation to prove their case and to suggest alternative remedies. They have manifestly failed.

Mrs Elizabeth Peacock (Batley and Spen): Does my hon. Friend agree that we are often told that there is no evidence to suggest that corporal punishment would work, and we are asked why we propose it? Does he further agree that there is no real evidence to suggest that corporal punishment would not work as a deterrent?

Mr Marlow: Common sense, our experience of history and evidence from other countries in, for example, the Middle East – although I am not suggesting that we follow the line taken in the Middle East – suggest that such policies are a deterrent.

Mr Elfyn Llwyd (Meirionnydd Nant Conwy): Has the hon. Gentleman studied the effect of secure training orders on young people? The Government introduced those orders only recently. Is he saying that they have already failed?

Mr Marlow: I am not saying that any particular course of action or proposal from the Government has failed, but everyone would agree that the levels of crime – particularly hooligan crime – and disruption on some of our poorer estates are much greater than those of the past. We have a continuing social problem and although some measures are doing some good, we have not solved the problem yet.

Without the reintroduction of corporal punishment, we will not satisfy the needs of our constituents – whatever pious hopes we have and however liberal we might feel. Something has to be done. The present system is not working and we do not have a solution yet. My final point is that a truth – an unpleasant truth, but a truth nevertheless – that has been proved by history is, sadly, that civilisation cannot be maintained without an element of barbarism to protect it.

. . .

Mr Warren Hawksley (Halesowen and Stourbridge): I support the new clause. I have argued for corporal punishment on many occasions and I am pleased to do so again. Last year, I introduced a **ten-minute Bill** that attracted more support than I had expected. I served on the **Standing Committee** on the Bill now under discussion, but I did not table an amendment. However, in 1984, I believe, on the Criminal Justice Bill, there was a whole day's debate on an amendment that I had tabled on the subject. It is an important subject, about which our constituents are concerned. They believe that corporal punishment would be a deterrent, and to my mind that is extremely important.

The Isle of Man has already been mentioned, and my hon. Friend the Member for Batley and Spen (Mrs. Peacock) asked in an intervention whether there was a case against corporal punishment. Before I tabled my amendment in 1984, I visited the Isle of Man to see what the position was. At that time, the law was still on the statute book there, but was not being used.

I was told by the chief constable on the island that when crowds came over from Liverpool and Manchester for football matches, people arriving in the harbour at Douglas would invariably ask his officers on the gates whether it was true that there was still corporal punishment on the island. When they were told that that was indeed the case, the response was, 'Don't worry, Guv, we won't cause any trouble while we're here.'

Corporal punishment is a deterrent, and that was demonstrated on the Isle of Man. I strongly believe that we should reintroduce it here. The

Opposition will no doubt suggest that it is degrading and that the European Court of Human Rights would say the same. When we talk of degradation, we should think of the victims, and how degrading it is for them.

There has been another change since 1984, because the Government have been questioning the powers of the European Court of Human Rights. When the renewal came up, serious doubts were expressed, whereas I remember that when I asked the then Prime Minister in 1980 whether she would withdraw our signature from the Convention, she said no. I believe that the time is coming when the court will take so different a view from ours on what the law should be that we will withdraw from it.

On the categories of offenders on whom the courts should be able to impose such punishment, I believe that they should include youngsters who attack elderly people and mug them for only a few pounds. I believe that their treatment of those elderly people is a degrading act, and that corporal punishment would be of great advantage in such cases. When it was known that a court was prepared to order such punishment to be carried out, there would soon be a reduction in such crimes. Even if some **benches** were initially nervous of introducing it, other benches would quickly prove that it was working as a deterrent. It is with great pleasure that I support the new clause.

Mr A J Beith (Berwick-upon-Tweed): It is no part of the case against the reintroduction of corporal punishment to deny that some young people are **recalcitrant**, that their crimes against those more vulnerable and weaker than themselves are horrible and that the state has found it difficult to determine a satisfactory system to punish them or to teach them the error of their ways, but the facts did not support the **contention** that corporal punishment can be brought back to fill that gap.

The experience of the use of corporal punishment in this country was not the glowing success that is implied by the supporters of the new clause. Corporal punishment has proved ineffective in the fight against crime: when it was available for robbery with violence, before its abolition in 1948, three separate Government surveys found that offenders who underwent it committed more subsequent crimes than similar offenders who received other sentences.

. . .

Reintroduction would contravene our international obligations under the European Convention on Human Rights, as was clear from the 1978 Tyrer case and from our experience in relation to the Isle of Man. Those who have begun to try to persuade the Government that we should withdraw from the convention should have regard to the fact that we subscribe to it not simply to set a standard against which to judge what happens here, but to assist in upholding of human rights in countries throughout Europe. To withdraw from the convention would be to withdraw our support for the upholding of human rights in all respects, and that would be an extremely bad step for Britain to take.

Reintroduction would also create problems in relation to the medical professions and the law. A medical practitioner would have to be present when corporal punishment was administered, which would contravene the World Medical Association's 1975 Tokyo declaration, which laid down that doctors should not participate in, or be present at, any procedure during which 'cruel, inhuman or degrading treatment' is used.

. . .

Mr John Townend (Bridlington): . . . Ten or 15 years ago, it would have been inconceivable that 12, 14 or 15-year-olds would be capable of stealing not one but five, 10 or 15 cars. I cannot help but believe that it would be far better for them, and far more effective, if they were given six strokes of the cane the first time they were caught, rather than being warned or freed to steal more cars and to put their lives and those of many others at risk.

Mr Andrew Mackinlay (Thurrock): The hon. Gentleman referred to the explosion of crime in the past 10 or 15 years. Has it occurred to him that one of the hallmarks of the Thatcher–Major period is the creation of a selfish society, in which avarice is at the forefront? Among the consequences of the Government's policies in a range of areas are the growth in crime and the lowering of values.

The Minister of State, Home Office (Mr David Maclean): This has been a short but interesting debate. . . .

I am not satisfied that corporal punishment would, in practice, be a useful punishment today, or that we should seek to provide for it in the Bill. It is now almost 40 years since corporal punishment was abolished as a sentence of the court. My hon. Friends argue that corporal punishment would be a deterrent. If it were to act as a deterrent, it would have to be used regularly, predictably and immediately. Frankly, I do not believe that that would be the case.

. . . Corporal punishment has a role to play for parents who administer sensible discipline to their children owing to the immediacy of the infliction of the punishment on the youngster who is doing wrong. Judicial flogging in the cool light of day after many months, or, I suspect, years later after dozens of appeals – as in some of the cases in the United States – would not be an effective deterrent.

Sir Ivan Lawrence (Burton): Does my right hon. Friend agree that, if we were able to use corporal punishment in schools – as we always did – it would not be necessary to have judicial corporal punishment, which he condemns?

Mr Maclean: That is an entirely different area, into which I will not stray, because we have a lot of other business to conduct. No doubt, a philosophical debate on the merits of corporal punishment at all levels of society – in schools, by parents on their children or judicial flogging – would be an interesting occasion at some point, but I do not want to get into that at the moment.

. . . I will not now debate the merits or demerits of Britain's signing the convention. We are party to it and the British Government have no proposals to withdraw from it at the present moment. That means that we are bound by the European Court of Human Rights, which ruled in 1978 in the Tyrer case, which involved a birching on the Isle of Man, that such punishment was incompatible with article 3 of the convention. It found that the birching imposed on Tyrer constituted degrading punishment within the meaning of article 3 and emphasised that it considered corporal punishment to be 'institutionalised violence', with the individual being 'treated as an object in the power of the authorities'.

6.30 pm

Mrs Peacock: I am listening carefully to my right hon. Friend, but what about the almost institutionalised violence that many elderly people suffer in their own homes? Rightly, they and their relatives believe that some pain should be inflicted on the young people who cause that damage.

Mr Maclean: Such violence is deplorable, which is why we have increased the penalties for those who commit it. Clauses 1, 2 and 3 propose some of the most dramatic action taken since the war to deal with habitual, persistent and violent criminals. Clause 1 introduces automatic life sentences for the most violent criminals. Clause 2 proposes seven-year sentences for the evil people who peddle drugs. Clause 3 deals with persistent burglars who terrorise people by their activities. My hon. Friend supported those measures. The Opposition could not make up their mind, but one day I hope that they may vote for them. That is the action that we are taking. Such penalties, the increasing numbers in prison and our success in getting crime down over the past three years mean that the policies of imprisonment have worked. We will continue those policies.

Mr Michael: The Minister had a difficult row to hoe in responding to the debate, but he should not have misrepresented our position on the Bill. We have made it clear that we want consistency and **progression of sentencing** in our courts so that appropriate sentences are given, particularly to repeat offenders. We have explained the best methods to achieve that, especially in Monday's speech by the Shadow Home Secretary.

New clause 14 is a diversion from the serious debates in which we have been seeking to make the Bill more effective and improve its consistency. We will return to some of those important issues when this new clause has been dealt with. The Minister rightly referred to it as whistling in the wind. We oppose it and will vote against it, if it is put to a vote.

Mr Marlow: By leave of the House, I have the greatest respect for my right hon. Friend the Minister, particularly for the massive and good work that he is doing in his current job. Although his arguments might convince a minority in this House, beyond the Home Office insiders and professionals, he would not begin to have an audience outside it. He said that the prospect of prison is a deterrent, but it manifestly is not for the people for whom corporal punishment would be appropriate. Violence, hooliganism,

> vandalism, graffiti and the mugging of old ladies are going on apace and are increasing day by day. Prison is there as a deterrent, but it is not working and we need something else.
>
> My right hon. Friend the Minister made several arguments. First, the European convention on human rights is not supported by and is not an acceptable argument to Conservative Members. It has to go. We have a Government in our own country and we have to decide in our own Parliament. We ran the affairs of a third of the world until 30 or 40 years ago. Surely we are allowed to govern ourselves now. Cannot we make our own decisions? We are a mature democracy.
>
> Secondly, the Minister said that it would be months before sentences were carried out. That is not an argument against corporal punishment but against the judicial system. Vandals and hooligans should be in court on Tuesday and punished on Wednesday; if they do it again on Thursday, they should be back on Friday.
>
> My right hon. Friend knows in his heart and in his bones that there is a massive problem out there. He is doing what he can, but the new clause is a weapon that we could use. If he is uncertain whether it will be successful, we could use it for a trial period and suck it and see.
>
> My right hon. Friend has listened to the arguments and we have had a good debate. It is my intention – the large number of my colleagues in the House reveals that it is also their intention – to give the subject an airing. It is time that we started to fight back and moved to defend the people who are suffering. We are all right; we have a privileged life style, but many of our constituents are suffering and we are not doing enough to help them.
>
> I see no purpose in pushing the new clause to a vote, but this is the beginning and its time will come.
>
> I beg to ask leave to withdraw the motion.
>
> *Motion and clause, by leave, withdrawn.*

The **Third Reading** is an opportunity to make minor changes which tidy the Bill, rather than altering anything of substance.

A Bill has **clauses** and **sub-clauses**, which become **sections** and **sub-sections** when the Bill has passed through all its stages and become an Act (see excerpts below). Detailed provisions of the Act are put at the back in **schedules**. See the Crime (Sentences) Act 1997 at p. 79 for an example of what an Act looks like.

Delegating

Not all legislation is by way of statute. Parliament often gives power to other bodies to make law. This is known as **delegated legislation**. A good example of how this works is to be found in the Civil Procedure Act 1997.

The Act provides for procedural rules to be made but provides for them to come into force by way of delegated legislation:

> s 3(1) Rules made and allowed under section 2 are to—
>
> (a) come into force on such day as the Lord Chancellor may direct, and
> (b) be contained in a statutory instrument to which the Statutory Instruments Act 1946 is to apply as if it contained rules made by a Minister of the Crown.
>
> (2) A **statutory instrument** containing Civil Procedure Rules shall be subject to annulment in pursuance of a resolution of either House of Parliament.

Section 4(2) contains very wide powers for the Lord Chancellor to 'amend, repeal or revoke any enactment to the extent he considers necessary or desirable in consequence of

> (a) section 1 or 2, or
> (b) Civil Procedure Rules'
>
> and sub-section (5) of that section provides:
> 'No order may be made under subsection (2) unless a draft of it has been laid before and approved by resolution of each House of Parliament.'

The Act also provides that it is to come into force on a day, or separate days for different provisions, appointed by the Lord Chancellor by statutory instrument. This is a very common provision in Acts and it is important to realise that just because Parliament has passed an Act, the law has not necessarily changed. The Act has to be brought into force and this is often delayed in order to give time for systems to be set up. The Civil Procedure Act 1997, for example, provides for a Civil Procedure Rules Committee to be set up and for that Committee to make rules; it also provides for an advisory body, the Civil Justice Council, to advise the Lord Chancellor. By giving power to the Lord Chancellor to implement the Act in stages, the Act makes it possible to choose to take advice first, or to get the system up and running before appointing the Council.

Check your understanding

1 Make sure you have mastered the vocabulary of the subject, the words in **bold** in the explanatory material.

2 Can you explain the meaning of other words and phrases in **bold** type? Are there any other words you need to look up in a dictionary?

3 What does Mr Marlow mean, in his opening speech, by 'international involvements or commitments [that] stand in the way of the House doing what it believes to be right for the country in this country'?

Discuss

1 Look at the Civil Procedure Act 1997, s 3(2) and s 4(5). They refer to two different procedures for creating statutory instruments. How do these procedures differ and why do you think each was chosen for the particular purposes of these two sections of the Act?

2 Why do governments issue Green Papers? Why do they issue White Papers? Can you find evidence to demonstrate that either of these activities is a necessary and effective part of the legislative process?

3 Mr Marlow would introduce a system for corporal punishment by statutory instrument. Do you think this would have been an appropriate way to do it?

4 Look at the passage from Hansard and find the formal phrases used in debate by MPs; for example, look at how they refer to each other. Why is it done this way? Do you think it is a good idea?

5 Is this a good standard of debating? How might individual MPs have improved their case? Look at what is said about value-laden language at p. 67. Can you find value-laden language here? Is it used appropriately?

6 Much of the evidence used in the debate is **anecdotal**. Find some examples. Do you consider anecdotal or statistical evidence to be more effective in debate?

7 Organise your own debate on a controversial issue. Make sure each side uses evidence in argument and, before you begin, agree a set of rules about conducting a debate.

Write

Do some research into a piece of legislation of your choice. For example, were there any cases which drew attention to a gap or defect in the law? Was the Act preceded by a White Paper? Did the Law Commission influence its introduction or draft the Bill? Then, with reference to the specific Act, write an outline of the process by which Parliament makes law.

Reading

Larger reference libraries may keep Hansard, in which the debates relating to legislation are recorded. This is, however, very unwieldy. *Keesing's Contemporary Archives* gives a summary of the passage of major pieces of legislation and is likely to be available in a greater number of libraries.

Connections

1 Look at the excerpts from Law Commission work elsewhere in this book.

2 Compare what is said about sentencing policy in the debate with the material on sentencing at p. 68.

3 Professor Simon Lee says, in his book *Judging Judges* (see p. 40), 'The good communicator presumably tailors the message according to the audience'. Who do you think the MPs engaged in this debate intended their audiences to be? Did they communicate effectively?

4 There is mention in the debate of the European Convention on Human Rights. How does the Convention affect Parliament's power to make law?

1.3 STATUTORY INTERPRETATION

Many cases hinge on whether a particular word or phrase in a piece of legislation applies to facts of the case. It is for the judges to decide on that meaning and they have traditionally done so by following the literal approach, giving the words their plain, ordinary, grammatical meaning. The reason for this approach was explained by Lord Diplock in *Duport Steels v Sirs* [1980] 1 All ER 529:

> My Lords, at a time when more and more cases involving the application of legislation which gives effect to **policies** that are the subject of bitter public and parliamentary controversy, it cannot be too strongly emphasised that the British Constitution, though largely unwritten, is firmly based on the **separation of powers**: Parliament makes the laws, the judiciary interpret them. When Parliament legislates to remedy what the majority of its members at the time perceive to be a defect or a **lacuna** in the existing law (whether it be the written law enacted by existing statutes or the unwritten common law as it has been **expounded** by the judges in decided cases), the role of the judiciary is confined to **ascertaining** from the words that Parliament has approved as expressing its intention what the intention was, and to giving effect to it. Where the meaning of the statutory words is plain and **unambiguous** it is not for the judges to invent fancied ambiguities as an excuse for failing to give effect to its plain meaning because they themselves consider that the consequences of doing so would be **inexpedient**, or even unjust or immoral. In controversial matters such as are involved in industrial relations there is room for differences of opinion as to what is expedient, what is just and what is morally justifiable. Under our Constitution it is Parliament's opinion on these matters that is **paramount**.

An alternative approach to interpretation is to consider what Parliament was trying to achieve and then to read the disputed word or phrase in the light of the underlying purpose. What word could be plainer in its meaning than 'road'? Quite a few words really. I may think I know what a road is, but in different contexts it might include different things.

This was the problem for the Court of Appeal in *Cutter v Eagle Star* [1997] 2 All ER 311. C was injured in a fire in a car owned by X and insured with E. The fire was caused by fumes from lighter fuel that had leaked from a container left in the car by X. C obtained judgment against X: s 151 of the Road Traffic Act 1988 makes the insurance company responsible for paying the damages awarded. At the time of the incident, the car was in a car park. Eagle Star would be liable, under s 145(3)(a) of the Road Traffic Act 1988, if the injury to C was caused by or arose out of *the use of the vehicle on a road.* The point to be decided was, therefore, the meaning of 'road'.

Beldam LJ:

> Section 192(1) provides: '. . . "road", in relation to England and Wales, means any highway and any other road to which the public has access . . .'. As might be expected in a Road Traffic Act, the word 'road' occurs many times. It appears in sections creating offences, sections imposing duties on drivers and sections providing for traffic regulation in general. The definition provided in s 192 has thus to do duty in many different circumstances . . .
>
> The definition is clearly intended to include roads which are not highways but to exclude roads to which the public do not have access. There are, therefore, two separate questions: (i) is the place in question a road? (ii) If it is a road, do the public have access to it?

Beldam LJ adopted the words of Lord Widgery CJ in *Cox v White* (1976) with regard to the second question: '. . . any road may be regarded as a road to which the public have access upon which members of the public are to be found who have not obtained access either by overcoming a physical obstruction or in defiance of prohibition **express or implied**.' He continued:

> The present case requires the court to focus on the first question, whether the car park or any part of it can be considered a road having regard to its layout, its physical characteristics and the type of use made of it . . .
>
> The origin of the definition of 'road' in s 192 of the 1988 Act can be traced to the Motor Car Act 1903, an Act introduced for the protection of the public. Section 1 created the offences of driving a motor car on a public highway recklessly, negligently or at a speed or manner which was dangerous to the public. It further required a person driving a motor car to stop and give his name and address if an accident occurred to any person owing to the presence of a motor car on the road.

Section 20 of the 1903 Act provided:

> (1) . . . The provisions of this Act and of the principal Act shall apply in the case of a roadway to which the public are granted access, in the same manner as they apply in the case of a public highway.

A more comprehensive Act for the protection of the public was the Road Traffic Act 1930, which, as its **long title** proclaims, was—

> 'An Act to make provision for the regulation of traffic on roads and of motor vehicles and otherwise with respect to roads and vehicles thereon, to make provision for the protection of third parties against risks arising out of the use of motor vehicles . . .'

It is to be noticed that s 14 of that Act created an offence of driving a motor vehicle on common land, moorland or other land of whatsoever description (not being land forming part of a road), or any road being a bridleway or footway, though it was not an offence to drive a vehicle on land within 15 yards of a road provided it could lawfully be driven on the road and was driven on the land only for the purpose of parking the vehicle.

I should also refer to s 15 of the 1988 Act which, in creating the offence of driving or attempting to drive or being in charge of a motor vehicle under the influence of drink or drugs, did not confine the offence to a road. The offence could be committed on a road or other public place.

Part II of the 1930 Act made provision for **compulsory third party insurance**. Section 36(1)(b) was the **precursor** of s 145(3)(a) of the 1988 Act. Section 121 defined 'road' to mean 'any highway and any other road to which the public has access, and includes bridges over which a road passes'; a definition which has been carried down in successive Road Traffic Acts and into s 192 of the 1988 Act. The draughtsman, by adopting this definition, obviously intended to combine in one definition the highway in s 1, the road in s 6 and the roadway in s 20 of the 1903 Act. In my view, 'roadway' denotes any way used for the passage of vehicles and I would so interpret the word 'road' in s 192 . . .

The origin of the provision in s 151 of the 1988 Act requiring an insurer to meet a judgment obtained in respect of a compulsorily insurable risk was s 10 of the Road Traffic Act 1934, passed when it had become clear that such a measure was necessary in certain circumstances to secure that the victims of accidents actually received the compensation awarded to them. Taken in the context of the legislation as a whole, I consider that the definition in s 192 should be given a meaning consistent with the intention to protect the public and to secure compensation for third parties injured or caused damage by the use of motor vehicles. I would give the definition a broad rather than a confined meaning to achieve the declared aim of the statute . . .

Beldam LJ then reviewed several cases in which the issue had been whether a car park was a 'road'. The cases were concerned with giving guidance to magistrates in reaching a decision on the issue and were not particularly conclusive. He continued:

> It seems to me that in these judgments and the judgment in the present case, too great an emphasis was placed on seeking to answer the question: is the car park a road? I consider the question would more correctly be posed by asking: is there within the car park a roadway? In the present case, I think that there is within the Great Hall car park a roadway, ie a way marked out for the passage of vehicles controlled by conventional traffic signs and markings and regularly used by members of the public seeking a car parking space. The risk of accidents causing injury arising out of the use of cars on this roadway is scarcely less than on any other road. Members of the public, whether driving vehicles or leaving and returning on foot to them or merely walking through the car park could as easily be injured as in many of the open air car parks I have mentioned. There are, moreover, many other situations in which cars may be driven on defined routes over open spaces or land when attending sporting events or other entertainment.
>
> The fact that the car is being driven to or from a parking space as opposed to using the way through the field or area in question as a route from one road to another, ought not, in my opinion, to decide whether or not an injured person is paid the compensation for which he has obtained judgment. Nor, for example, ought it to decide whether, if an accident occurs, a driver is under a duty to produce his insurance details and to give his name and address.

In argument, reference had been made to amendments to the Road Traffic Act 1988 so that some offences could be committed not only on a road but also in any other public place.

> These extensions, introduced as a result of widespread concern about the scope of the Road Traffic Act offences, were part of the recommendations of the Road Traffic Law Review set up on 31 January 1985 under the chairmanship of Dr Peter North. In ch 8 of its report, Road Traffic Law Review Report (HMSO 1988), the review considered whether bad driving offences should be limited to conduct on a road. In para 8.2 the review pointed out that there was a difference in the definition of road between England and Wales on the one hand, and Scotland on the other and said:
>
>> 'In England and Wales it does not include, for example, driving in a car park, on a garage forecourt or on a private square. In other words, there is a range of public places, to which drivers may have access with their vehicles, which fall outside the scope of these bad driving offences.'

> In para 8.6 the review recorded the opinion of the Director of Public Prosecutions that the definition of 'road' . . . was both unclear and too narrow and that it was essential that the definition of 'road' should be replaced by words which included unmade-up roads, private roads, car parks and parks adjacent to public houses.
>
> These statements from so distinguished a review panel might lend support to a suggestion that the definition of 'road' in s 192 of the 1988 Act could not include a car park of any kind. But, as I have attempted to show, that is not the **construction** hitherto put on the definition in s 192 . . .
>
> For these reasons, I would hold that the areas in the Great Hall car park in Tunbridge Wells marked out for the passage and parking of vehicles were within the definition of 'road' in s 192 of the 1988 Act. The injury sustained by the appellant was one which arose out of the use of a motor vehicle on a road and the respondent is bound under s 151 to meet the judgment.

The literal and purposive approaches are often regarded as being mutually exclusive – if you apply one it would be incorrect to apply the other – and certain to yield different results. Of course, this is not true if Parliament has succeeded in saying exactly what it means. This point is nicely illustrated in the Court of Appeal's decision in *Jones v Tower Boot Company* [1997] 2 All ER 406. J, a 16-year-old, was employed by T as a last operator for about five weeks. During that time he was racially abused and assaulted by two fellow employees: the assaults included burning him with a hot screwdriver. He resigned and claimed damages from T on the basis that they were responsible for the discriminatory conduct of their employees.

Waite LJ:

> When an industrial tribunal is considering whether, for the purposes of s 32(1) [Race Relations Act 1976] any conduct complained of does or does not amount to a 'thing done by a person in the course of his employment', is the tribunal bound to answer that by reference to: (a) the words 'course of employment' in the sense in which they are employed in everyday speech; or (b) the principles laid down by case law for the establishment of vicarious liability by an employer for the torts committed by an employee during the course of his employment?
>
> That is an issue of widespread importance. The fact that the mechanism of the relevant sections of the 1976 Act is matched exactly by corresponding provisions in the Sex Discrimination Act 1975 means that the issue needs to be resolved in relation to all acts of harassment on the grounds of race or sex which occur in an employment context.
>
> Two principles are, in my view, involved. The first is that a statute is to be construed according to its legislative purpose, with due regard to the result which it is the stated or presumed intention of Parliament to achieve

and the means provided for achieving it (the purposive construction); and the second is that words in a statute are to be given their normal meaning according to general use in the English language unless the context indicates that such words have to be given a special or technical meaning as a term of art (the linguistic construction). It will be convenient to deal with those separately.

The purposive construction

The legislation now represented by the Race and Sex Discrimination Acts currently in force broke new ground in seeking to work upon the minds of men and women and thus affect their attitude to the social consequences of difference between the sexes or distinction of skin colour. Its general thrust was educative, persuasive, and (where necessary) **coercive**. The relief accorded to the victims (or potential victims) of discrimination went beyond the ordinary remedies of damages and an injunction – introducing, through **declaratory powers** in the court or tribunal and recommendatory powers in the relevant commission, provisions with a proactive function, designed as much to eliminate the occasions for discrimination as to compensate its victims or punish its perpetrators. These were linked to a **code of practice** of which courts and tribunals were to **take cognisance**. Consistently with the broad front on which it operates, the legislation has traditionally been given a wide interpretation . . . There is no indication in the 1976 Act that by dealing specifically with the employment field, Parliament intended in any way to limit the general thrust of the legislation.

A purposive construction, accordingly, requires s 32 of the 1976 Act (and the corresponding s 41 of the 1975 Act) to be given a broad interpretation. It would be inconsistent with that requirement to allow the notion of the 'course of employment' to be construed in any sense more limited than the natural meaning of those everyday words would allow.

The linguistic construction

Mr Buckhaven's argument is attractively simple. Vicarious liability is a doctrine of tortious liability which has been applied by the common law to the employment context. Part III of the 1976 Act applies expressly to discrimination in the employment field. The two fields are the same. Words and phrases that have acquired a familiar and particular meaning through case law applied to employers' liability in the former context must, therefore, have been intended by Parliament to have the same meaning when applied to employers' liability in the latter context.

Mr Robin Allen QC, while acknowledging that there is a broad conceptual similarity between the employers' responsibility that applies in both contexts, submits that substantial differences emerge when vicarious liability in tort is analysed and contrasted with the statutory scheme of which s 32 forms part. The employer's authority, for example, is a crucial element in vicarious liability in tort, as evidenced by the statement in *Salmond and Heuston on the Law of Torts* (20th edn, 1992) pp. 456–457:

> 'A master is not responsible for a wrongful act done by his servant unless it is done in the course of his employment. It is deemed to be so done if it is either (1) a wrongful act authorised by the master, or (2) a wrongful and unauthorised way of doing some act authorised by the master.'

That is to be contrasted with the position under s 32(1) of the 1976 Act, where all actions by a person in the course of employment are attributed to the employer 'Whether or not . . . done with the employer's knowledge or approval'. Mr Allen points to other distinctions, such as the greater range of remedies available under the statute (including damages for injury to feelings), than those available in tort against an employer at common law, and the total absence from the concept of vicarious liability in tort of any provision corresponding to the reasonable steps defence under s 32(3).

I am persuaded that Mr Allen's submission is to be preferred, and that there is here no sufficient similarity between the two contexts to justify, on a linguistic construction, the reading of the phrase 'course of employment' as subject to the gloss imposed on it in the common law context of vicarious liability.

Check your understanding

Can you explain the meaning of the words and phrases in **bold** type? Are there any other words you need to look up in a dictionary?

Discuss

1 What approach is Beldam LJ taking in *Cutter v Eagle Star* in interpreting the word 'road'?

2 Beldam LJ says he is giving 'road' 'a broad rather than a confined meaning'. What would have been the consequences for C if he had chosen the narrower meaning?

3 Is there any evidence to suggest that the Court of Appeal has gone beyond interpretation of the law and entered into law making in deciding these cases? Having regard to what Lord Diplock said in *Duport Steel v Sirs*, what approach do you think he might have taken if he had been deciding *Cutter*

v Eagle Star and *Jones v Tower Boot* and what reasons would he have given for his decisions?

4 Lord Diplock speaks of 'the majority of [Parliament's] members at the time'. Does this mean that judges have to apply the literal approach to ascertain the intention of the individuals who voted in favour of the legislation? Is this possible? Is this what the Court of Appeal did in *Cutter v Eagle Star?*

Write

1 Write a note of *Cutter v Eagle Star* in your own words, being careful to include the facts, the decision and the reasons for the decision.

2 Consider the argument that the Court of Appeal in *Cutter v Eagle Star* was giving effect to the intentions of Parliament. By what means may a court determine what Parliament's intentions were?

Connections

1 The Court of Appeal refers to the Road Traffic Law Review Report. Look for references to the work of other bodies elsewhere in judgments throughout the book.

2 Compare the decision in *Cutter v Eagle Star* with that in *Nettleship v Weston* (1971) in which the standard of care expected of a learner driver was held to be the same as that expected of an experienced driver.

3 Compare the drafting style of EC legislation (see pp. 7 and 9) and UK legislation (see pp. 24 and 79). The approach to interpretation is necessarily affected by the style used. What features of the EC style encourage a purposive approach?

4 Look at the material from *Sweet v Parsley* (p. 140) in which the principles of statutory interpretation are discussed.

5 All the following cases, from elsewhere in this book, involve points of statutory interpretation. Look at them and consider what rules and approaches the judge is using:

R v Miller (p. 94)
R v Cunningham (p. 104)
R v Caldwell (p. 105)
R v Preddy (p. 110)
R v Gateway Foodmarkets Ltd (p. 146)
Roles v Nathan (p. 210)
Fisher v Bell (p. 219)
Smith v Eric S Bush (p. 272)
Pickstone v Freemans (p. 9)

1.4 JUDICIAL PRECEDENT

If there is no European law and no statute on a point of law, it is decided by the judge who hears the case in which the point arises. He or she is obliged to follow the decisions made by more senior judges in previous cases. This is the principle of ***stare decisis.*** You need to understand the **hierarchy of courts** and the expressions ***ratio decidendi*** and ***obiter dicta*** in order to understand how precedent works.

Examples of the way precedent works are provided in the chapters on crime, contract and tort. Judges follow a fairly consistent format. Look at Lord Diplock's judgment in *Miller*, p. 94 and note that:

1 He gives a brief account of the facts.
2 He identifies the relevant law.
3 He explains the law.
4 He applies the law to the facts.
5 He comes to a conclusion about whether an offence has been committed.

As the facts of cases are never completely identical, precedent relies on **reasoning by analogy**. This skill is also vital to students in answering problem-style questions. For a simple example of how reasoning by analogy works, look at Lord Denning's judgment in *Lewis v Averay* (p. 262). He takes two previous cases, one with very similar facts, one with what appear at first to be less similar facts, and identifies what those cases have in common with the case he is considering. He comes to the conclusion that the three cases are so similar in their basic essentials that they ought to be governed by the same rule. Similarly, it is settled law that in a case where a plaintiff seeks damages for economic loss there must be foreseeability of the loss, proximity between the parties and it must be fair, just and reasonable to hold that the defendant owed the plaintiff a duty of care. In *Spring v Guardian Assurance* (p. 166), Lord Woolf considered the case of an ex-employee who had suffered a loss because his former employer had given a bad reference which was untrue. He applied the three requirements to a set of circumstances to which they had not been applied before and found that the loss was foreseeable, that there was sufficient proximity between the parties and that it was fair, just and reasonable to hold the employer responsible for the employee's loss.

In *Hedley Byrne v Heller* (1963) Lord Devlin explained what happens when the analogy becomes stretched to its limit: 'An existing category grows as instances of its application multiply, until the time comes when the "cell divides"' – see p. 163.

Judges will refer to a range of sources when deciding what the law is. Often a judge will refer to the arguments put by **counsel**: see, for example: *R v Brown & Others* (1993) (p. 89), *R v Caldwell* (1981) (p. 119) and *Williams v Roffey Brothers* (1990) (p. 226). Judges usually confine their decisions within the scope of the arguments put to them, so the role the barristers play is very important in forming the law, but in *White v Jones* Lord Goff, at p. 167, introduces a point not made by counsel.

Each case has within it a *ratio decidendi*, the reason for the decision the judge reached. It is this reason that is binding on courts hearing similar cases. The judge does not say, 'here is the reason for my decision': he leaves it to judges in later cases to decide what the precise *ratio* is. In *Murphy v Brentwood* at p. 154, Lord Keith gives a narrow *ratio* for the case of *Donoghue v Stevenson*: 'the carelessly manufactured product should be intended to reach the injured consumer in the same state as that in which it was put up with no reasonable prospect of intermediate examination . . .' The proposition that everyone owes a duty of care to his or her 'neighbour' might be described as a wide *ratio* of the same case.

Judges quite often look at the law in other jurisdictions when they are trying to decide what the law in England and Wales should be. In *Hedley Byrne v Heller* Lord Reid referred to American and South African cases. For another example of this, look at *DPP v Majewski* (1976) (p. 116).

Judges also refer to the work of academic lawyers when trying to ascertain what the law is. The work of Professor Sir John Smith is often cited in criminal cases – see *R v Preddy* (1996) as an example. For a less flattering view of academic opinion, see Lord Goff in *Hunter v Canary Wharf* (1997) (p. 192). There are frequent respectful references to the work of the Law Commission.

The major source, however, for determining what the law is when there is no legislative source is the judgments of other judges in earlier cases. Sometimes there are copious references to earlier cases, forming a useful account of the law for students. For example, look at Lord Lane's judgment in *Nedrick* (1986) (p. 102), which provides an excellent history and explanation of the law on intention.

If a judge does not agree with a previous decision which appears to be binding on him, he will *distinguish* it. That is, he will find a material difference in the facts of the precedent and the facts of the case before him and say that, therefore, the present case is not analogous to the precedent. An example of a judge doing this is Judge Havery QC in *Capital and Counties v Hampshire* at p. 176. Interestingly, he did not strictly have to distinguish, as the decision in question was also one of a High Court judge sitting alone.

Other examples of distinguishing can be found in *Frost v Chief Constable of South Yorkshire Police* (1997) (p. 181) and *Thornton v Shoe Lane Parking* (1971) (p. 266). When a judge is distinguishing he is saying that there is a material difference between the case before him and the case that one side in the dispute says binds him. Look at what Lord Denning has to say in *Lewis v Averay* (1971) (p. 264) about the danger of taking distinguishing too far.

It is very important to note where the decisions were made and, therefore, which courts will be bound by which decision. The power a court has depends on its place within the hierarchy of courts. The House of Lords is the most powerful court within the UK. It usually follows its own previous decisions, in the interests of certainty and stability, but occasionally it will decide that a previous House of Lords decision was wrong. The House of Lords reserved the right to change its mind in this way in the Practice Statement of 1966. This decision is never taken lightly, and in *Murphy v Brentwood* (1990) (p. 154) Lord Keith gives the matters he considers relevant in deciding whether to overrule the decision in *Anns.*

Of particular interest is the decision in *Luc Thiet Thuan* (1996) (p. 134) in that it is a Privy Council decision, so not binding on courts in the English system. The binding decision on this aspect of the law is, therefore, *Thornton (No 2)* (1996), a decision of the Court of Appeal. There are, however, many examples of decisions of the Privy Council that have been adopted and become the leading case on a particular point: see *Wagon Mound (No 1)* (1961) (p. 188), for example.

Even though a High Court judge sitting by himself (as opposed to sitting with others in a Divisional Court) does not create a binding precedent, judgments by single High Court judges can be very influential. If a similar issue comes before the Court of Appeal or the House of Lords at a later date, the judgment of a High Court judge may be regarded as highly persuasive.

Check your understanding

1 Can you explain the meaning of the words and phrases in **bold** type?

2 One of the worst faults in examination candidates is the citation of case names to support an argument without any reference to the facts or decision in the case cited. Although this account of precedent is short, there is a lot of work here as you must follow up all the references in order to understand the point being made.

Discuss

1 For each of the cases cited, *how* does this case illustrate a feature of the system of precedent?

2 In the case of *Miller* (p. 94), what is *ratio* and what is *obiter*?

Write

1. Read the judgment in *Miller* (p. 94) and classify its contents into the five areas identified at p. 34 above.
2. Choose another judgment from this book and analyse it in the same way.
3. Take an example of a problem-style question from a textbook or a past examination paper. (A problem-style question is one that sets out a situation and asks you to decide whether X is liable or whether A has committed an offence.) Structure an answer to it using areas 2–5 (the question itself gives you area 1).

Connections

As you read cases in Part Two of the book as part of your study of substantive areas of law, look at what the judge is doing in terms of the system of precedent. What sources is he using? Does he distinguish? Does he express disapproval of a case, while acknowledging that it binds him?

2 People

2.1 THE JUDICIARY

Judges are chosen from among solicitors and barristers. They begin by acting as part-time Recorders, doing some judicial work while they continue in practice. If they discover they do not like the work or they are no good at it, they simply do not renew their contracts (or they are not renewed).

One can apply to become a circuit judge and vacancies are periodically advertised in the press, but until very recently the Lord Chancellor invited lawyers to become High Court judges. This system is the subject of the following article by Josephine Hayes, published in *New Law Journal*:

> The Association of Women Barristers has, for a number of years, been arguing that the present system of appointments to the High Court and appellate courts of England and Wales is flawed. Appointments are not made upon application, but by invitation only, following a private consultation process among the legal great and good: the taking of secret soundings. This is a weakness in the system because the range of candidates in the system is restricted to candidates *already known to those making the recommendations*. Indeed, invitations to join the judiciary have been issued to presumed candidates who turn out not to have wanted the job; rather a waste of recruitment effort. (By contrast, in a more normal recruitment system which invites applications, generally by advertisement, the range of candidates is determined by the candidates themselves in choosing to apply.)
>
> Since the system's operation is secret, not surprisingly the available information on how it works is rather imprecise. However, it is known that the existing judges of the High Court, Court of Appeal and House of Lords are consulted by the Lord Chancellor, and I suggest it is a fair assumption that their comments are of special importance and weight when considering the suitability of candidates for judicial posts.
>
> In recommending candidates, judges would be able to comment only on lawyers whom they know. Which lawyers would they know better than barristers from their old chambers? Thus one **hypothesis** regarding the workings (and failings) of the judicial appointments system is that judges

tend to recommend barristers from their own chambers for appointment to the High Court Bench . . .

The Association studied appointments over a period from 1986 to 1996 and gathered data relating to the 104 appointments made during that time.

. . . It was found that of the 104 appointments made, 70 (67.3%) came from a set of chambers of which at least one ex-member was on the Bench during the assumed consultation period. In other words, only 34 of the new judges (32.7%) were appointed from chambers which did not already have an ex-member on the Bench . . .

The total number of judges in the High Court, Court of Appeal and House of Lords has been gradually rising. At the beginning of 1986, there were approximately 100 judges; this figure rose to about 140 by October 1996. The 104 appointees, from a pool of almost 8,800 barristers, during this period thus replaced over two thirds of the judges, yet came from roughly the same chambers as those they replaced.

The results of the above study can be accounted for in various ways and their significance is, of course, debatable. Some might discount them altogether on statistical grounds: the numbers dealt with are small.

The **predominance** of a few favoured sets of chambers does not appear simply to reflect large size and hence a large pool of potential candidates. Arguably, it reflects the excellent judicial qualities of members of those sets, due to the high calibre of their recruits. However, this argument cannot be proven, given the imperfection of the procedures whereby individuals are identified and assessed. The imperfections of the identification procedure has already been mentioned: I refer to the restriction of the pool of candidates to those whom the appointors happen to know. The imperfection of the assessment procedure is that there is a **dearth** of information, and no general agreement, as to the defining **criteria** used for identifying excellent judicial potential, so that it is impossible to assess how effectively the system works.

By comparison with systems of judicial appointments abroad, our system is still a curious **anachronism**. Solicitors, who comprise by far the greater part of the divided legal profession, are still not, in practice, treated as a significant source of High Court talent. The relationship between Bar and Bench is close and exclusive, and, as the Association of Women Barristers' study demonstrates, the relationship between a small number of sets of chambers and the succession to the Bench is even closer. '**Self-selecting oligarchy**' is an accurate description . . .

The question of who the judges are is closely related to their suitability for the job they do. As Josephine Hayes points out elsewhere in her article, the public do not usually hear about decisions of higher courts. Thus, criticism of the judges is often limited to comments on what circuit judges or Recorders have said during criminal trials. There is, however, considerable academic comment on the work of senior judges. A very readable assessment is offered by Professor Simon Lee in his book *Judging Judges*:

> Fairy tales, noble dreams and nightmares have long bedevilled attempts to judge judges . . . judges have the opportunity to make law. That function is of such fundamental importance to our democracy that judges can, and should, expect informed criticism. Retired Law Lords trundle on to television and radio to say how they would have decided differently. Academics flit across the television screen trying to explain what happened. But all too often the judges' critics fail to construct an appropriate framework within which to judge judges. They fall prey to the fairy tales, dreams and nightmares.
>
> The fairy tale was exposed by Lord Reid, the leading Law Lord of the 1960s and early 1970s:
>
> > 'Those with a taste for fairy tales seem to have thought that in some Aladdin's cave there is hidden the Common Law in all its splendour and that on a judge's appointment there descends on him knowledge of the magic words Open Sesame. Bad decisions are given when the judge has muddled the password and the wrong door opens. But we do not believe in fairy tales any more.'
>
> The most sophisticated **embellishment** of this fairy tale has been described as a Noble Dream. That was Professor Hart's assessment of Professor Dworkin's theory of adjudication. Dworkin argues that there is always one single right answer embedded in the principles which underlie the law. This seems **implausible** but Dworkin has developed his argument so as to emphasize that Aladdin's role is more creative than merely **incanting** Open Sesame. There are indications that some British judges are beginning to take Dworkin's rights thesis seriously. In particular, he has argued that judges should concentrate on principles and ignore policy arguments and some judges have begun to adopt that **rhetoric** . . .
>
> More cynical observers of judicial decision-making do not believe in fairy tales, nor do they indulge in Noble Dreaming. Instead they suffer, according to Hart once again, from Nightmares. Their nightmare is that judges have complete freedom to make the law as they think fit. A British variation on this approach goes further to say that the judges use their discretion to further their own **class interest** in the name of the **public interest**. Professor John Griffith of the London School of Economics (LSE) is the most famous academic to imagine this recurring nightmare . . .
>
> The basic idea of the fairy tale is, as we have seen, that the judge conjures up the answer to any legal problem through some magic formula. The words used are not 'Open Sesame' but 'the rules of statutory interpretation' and 'the rules of precedent'. The leading authority on the so-called rules of statutory interpretation, the late Professor Sir Rupert Cross, has described these fairy tales in recounting his experience as a tutor:

'Each and every pupil told me that there were three rules – the literal rule, the golden rule and the mischief rule, and that the Courts invoke whichever of them is believed to do justice in the particular case. I had, and still have, my doubts, but what was most **disconcerting** was the fact that whatever question I put to the pupils or examinees **elicited** the same reply. Even if the question was What is meant by "the intention of Parliament"? or What are the principal extrinsic aids to interpretation? back came the answers as of yore: "There are three rules of interpretation – the literal rule, the golden rule and the mischief rule." I was as much in the dark as I had been in my student days about the way in which the English rules should be formulated.'

The fairy tale of statutory interpretation therefore begins with the 'literal' rule according to which judges interpret a statute by giving the words their plain meaning. This is useless advice in controversial cases because there may be no single plain meaning. The next 'rule' is the 'golden rule' according to which judges should apply the plain meaning unless that produces an absurdity. But what is absurdity? On to the mischief rule which states that judges should look to the purpose behind the Act. Yet again, there is plenty of room for doubt as to what the mischief was.

Moreover, which rule should one prefer in the event of conflict? Suppose the plain meaning conflicts with the purpose behind the Act, should judges defer to Parliament's wording or Parliament's intention? Or should the judges just choose what *they* think makes most sense?

Sometimes, Parliament has not spoken at all on a legal area. The 'common law' of judicial decisions therefore is all the judge has in the way of pre-existing legal text to guide the current decision. The judge might feel freer to depart from the thrust of that past law, as contrasted with cases of statutory interpretation. Since the common law will be contained in perhaps more than one judgment, or in more than one form within the same judgment, and since the earlier case might be different from the present one, the judge will feel that he has a more creative role. He is not presented with a single **canonical** text as in a statute. He has more room for manoeuvre in deciding exactly what the 'precedent' says. And he can perhaps claim that the precedent does not apply. Moreover, the rules of the game allow him sometimes to overrule the precedent whereas the judge is always expected to pay at least lip-service to Acts of Parliament.

The fairy-tale doctrine of precedent, therefore, begins with the notion that the earlier case is divided into two parts, its *ratio decidendi* (the reason for the decision) and the *obiter dicta* (the incidental remarks of the judge which were not necessary for the decision and so are not binding on future judges). In real life, of course, this fairy tale collapses. *Obiter dicta* are often very important indeed. Even if we focus on the ratio of a case, there are great uncertainties in determining what *is* the ratio. Later judges might well interpret the ratio in different ways. If the judges are split in the result and if the majority judges give different explanations of their conclusions, it will be difficult indeed to extract a ratio from the judgments. One should not exaggerate these difficulties – **headnote**-writers in the press law reports and in the official law reports always manage to summarize the cases succinctly and their accuracy is seldom questioned. But determining the ratio is not the only creative task for a judge who is trying to decide what the pre-existing law suggests as the answer to his present case.

For, even if the ratio is clear, a judge has further tricks of his trade available before he has to apply it. He might 'distinguish' or 'overrule' the precedent. There is some disagreement on what it means to distinguish a case. The standard view seems to be that you distinguish a precedent by identifying some material difference between the facts in the two cases, so that the earlier precedent does not apply to the present case. Others say that is hardly very surprising. If the cases are not alike, then the force of the **adage** that like cases should be treated alike has no application. The cases are unalike, so obviously the earlier decision is not a relevant precedent. They suggest that distinguishing means something more significant, namely that distinguishing a case involves *changing* the precedent. The judge in the later case is narrowing down the rule in the earlier decision, by restricting its sphere of application, but he must do so in such a way that would still justify the same result in the first case. Of course, the headnote at the top of the report of the old case remains the same and some would say that a later judge cannot change the ratio of the earlier decision. But even they would admit that a later judge can change the importance of the earlier precedent by undermining its logic or narrowing its sphere of application.

Distinguishing in either sense is a power which all courts will possess but its power is limited. It only allows judges to restrict the impact of earlier cases, not to expand them. In contrast, the power of overruling is possessed by fewer judges but to greater effect. The rules as to who should follow whom when they can find no way of distinguishing are as follows. Courts should follow higher courts. The High Court therefore follows the Court of Appeal and the Court of Appeal follows the House of Lords. This makes sense if one believes that the better judges **gravitate**, or rather **levitate**, to the top of the judicial hierarchy and if they have more time for reflection on points of law. But does a court have to follow an earlier decision at its own level? The High Court does not have to follow itself. The Court of Appeal is supposed to follow itself except in rare circumstances. The House of Lords used to claim that it was bound by its earlier decisions but has now freed itself through a Practice Statement in 1966 so that it can overrule itself. If there is anything more obvious than the Griffith fallacy, it is the Dworkin fallacy that judges do not make law, given this Practice Statement which clearly envisages the senior judges departing from their earlier decisions. Even if there are no 'gaps' in the law because, as Dworkin believes, there are principles underlying the law, that does not mean that judges never make law. Making law is not just about settling unsettled issues. The Law Lords undoubtedly can make law through the technique of overruling their own previous decisions, in effect by unsettling settled law.

The power of overruling, therefore, is judicial law-making at its most powerful. But in other circumstances, judicial law-making will appear in more subtle forms. Judges can shield behind fairy tales by claiming they are only interpreting statutes or only following precedent. But the reality is that in hard cases they have considerable scope for creativity. They can use different canons of construction to reach different results as to what a statute means. They decide for themselves what is a precedent and whether they will **circumvent** it . . .

. . . Judges, or at least the top appellate judges, have a creative role. They are influenced in their exercise of discretion by such factors as statutes, precedents, principles of the common law, their sense of justice, their sense of the community's sense of justice, the desire to settle the instant dispute, a wish to explain their decision consistently with the expectations of the legal profession so that it can be used as a precedent, the esteem of their peers, and so on.

. . . these can most usefully be reduced to three factors:

1 past law, precedents and statutes;
2 present and future consequences;
3 judicial perception of their own role.

The first factor is the most likely to be explicitly addressed in a judgment. The second factor is approached more coyly. Counsel tend to look for a precedent with the 'right' policy factors in it, thus sneaking consideration of the future into the balance by **ostensibly** referring to the past. I should stress at this point that how counsel argue a case is obviously of the greatest importance to how the judges decide it. Alan Paterson's study of the Law Lords has demonstrated this. But this **truism** is often forgotten by commentators who rush in to criticise the judges when it is in many ways the barristers who have determined the nature of the legal argument. If we are to have more **candid** judgments, we need more candid arguments by counsel. As for the third factor, it seems to me that the legitimacy and degree of creativity in the judicial function must depend on what other institutions of the state are doing. When Parliament was unrepresentative of the people in the eighteenth and nineteenth centuries, the judges did not need to feel hesitant about stepping into the law-making role. In the twentieth century, however, our notions of democracy in the UK suggest that the courts should **defer** to Parliament. In the twenty-first century, or perhaps even now, the fact that Parliament is overburdened may mean that the pendulum should swing back towards judges filling the vacuum. . . .

We would be foolish . . . to believe that the written verdicts provide the whole story. What is not said is often as important as what is said. And what the judges do is as important as what they say.

It has to be said that judicial speeches are not in any event models in the art of communication. Part of this is attributable to the legal profession's general tendency to use **convoluted** language in order to maintain a mystique. Part of it is perhaps because the judges are unsure of their audiences – are they addressing the litigants, their lawyers, other lawyers, academics, the media, the public, posterity, or simply one another. The good communicator presumably tailors the message according to the audience. Many diverse audiences make this a difficult but not impossible task.

Check your understanding

1 Can you explain the meaning of the words and phrases in **bold** type?

2 What are the 'fairy tale', the 'Noble Dream' and the 'Nightmare' views of the way judges make decisions?

3 What is Professor Lee's view of the way judges *should* reach their decisions?

Discuss

1 Choose a House of Lords or Court of Appeal judgment from anywhere in this book and analyse the approach being taken. Can you see evidence of attention to principles? Is policy involved? Does the judge acknowledge that there is a policy decision to be made?

2 Vacancies for High Court judges are now advertised. Do you consider this will change the way they are chosen? Does it address any of the problems identified in Josephine Hayes' article?

Connections

1 Consider the range of communicators whose work is used in this book: judges, journalists, civil servants, academics, MPs. Find examples of good and bad communication and explain why you regard each example as good or bad.

2 Compare what Professor Lee says about the 'fairy tales' of statutory interpretation with the reality of its practice in the cases listed at p. 33. Do the same with what he says about precedent and the examples used in the section of this book on judicial precedent.

2.2 JURIES

The jury is an ancient institution. It began as a body of local people who could be relied upon to know what was happening in their area and to tell the travelling judges who came to hold courts. It is now a body of people chosen from the adult population to hear evidence and decide questions of fact. In civil cases juries are rare but, if they are used, they decide on the amount of damages to be awarded, as well as whether the plaintiff or the defendant should succeed.

Research into juries is rendered very difficult by s 8(1) of the Contempt of Court Act 1981, which provides: '. . . it is a contempt of court to obtain, disclose or solicit any particulars of statements made, opinions expressed, arguments advanced or votes cast by members of a jury in the course of their deliberations in any legal proceedings.'

Juries in criminal cases

The Royal Commission on Criminal Justice (the Runciman Commission) reported in July 1993. Some of its findings on juries are set out below.

Juries

52. As we have said in chapter one, we believe that it should be possible for properly authorised research to be carried out into the way in which juries reach their verdicts and we have recommended that section 8 of the Contempt of Court Act 1981 be amended accordingly. Given, however, the presumption that juries will remain the arbiters of fact at criminal trials in the Crown Court in England and Wales, our recommendations have been designed to ensure that, within the existing trial framework, the issues are presented to them in the clearest possible way. In this section, we consider the best means of presenting the issues to the jury before it retires, together with the arrangements for summoning, selecting, and **vetting** jurors, whether any special arrangements are needed to ensure a racial balance among jurors, and related matters.

(i) Selection of jurors

53. The initial summoning of jurors is done at random from the names of electors on the **electoral register**. This seems the best available means of ensuring that juries reflect the composition of the population as a whole. Although complaints are made that people may wrongly be omitted from the electoral register, no one has identified a convincing alternative means of selecting jurors. We would urge electoral registration officers to take every possible step to ensure that the electoral rolls are comprehensive and include everybody who ought to be included. This is important for the

purpose of securing jurors who are properly representative of the general population. It is also particularly important to continue and expand present efforts to persuade people from the ethnic minority communities to register.

54. When the jury summonses have been issued, many will be returned pleading various reasons for being unable to sit on a jury on the dates in question. These excuses may or may not be accepted. Jurors themselves seem to accept that a certain amount of pressure on them to serve is reasonable; the Crown Court Study shows that 92% of those jurors who had tried and failed to have themselves excused jury service thought that their requests had been dealt with fairly. Where the reasons given are acceptable, we do not suggest that they be overridden in the interests of ensuring a representative sample at all costs. We do, however, recommend that, unless there is a **statutory bar** on the person serving, every effort is made to offer alternative dates at a time that will be more convenient or that gives an adequate opportunity to rearrange his or her affairs in order to leave time for the jury service to be performed.

[The *Crown Court Study* referred to was one of 22 pieces of research commissioned by the Royal Commission. It was conducted by Professor Michael Zander and Paul Henderson.]

55. We have been told that some of the catchment areas from which potential jurors are drawn for individual courts produce an inadequate geographical spread with the result that people are selected to serve on a jury who live close to each other or know each other and may also be known to the defendant. This can be difficult to avoid if jurors are not to be asked to travel unreasonable distances and if **contiguous** parts of the electoral register are used. We recommend, however, that jury summoning officers take whatever steps are practicable to keep to a minimum the risk that individual jurors sitting on the same jury will be known to each other or to the defendant. At the larger court centres this should be possible by using widely separated parts of the electoral register.

56. One likely disincentive to people serving as jurors is the present rate of financial loss allowance that is offered to them.[1] This seems to us wholly inadequate to compensate for loss of earnings in most cases, especially for those who are self-employed. We recommend that the rates be reviewed as a matter of urgency.

---

[1] *Financial loss allowance*

(a) Where the period of time over which earnings or benefit are lost or additional expense is incurred is not more than four hours, the sum of £20.70.

(b) Where the period of time is more than four hours, the sum of £41.40 for each day of the trial.

(c) Where a juror has served on more than ten days, for each day over the tenth the sum may exceed that specified above but must not exceed £77.00 for each further day of the trial.

57. Certain people are ineligible to serve on juries for various reasons. We do not feel that we have any strong basis to recommend any changes to the present position except in one area. We do not see why clergymen and members of religious orders should not be eligible for jury service and recommend that they should be removed from the list of the ineligible. On the other hand, where practising members of a religious sect or order find jury service to be incompatible with their tenets or beliefs, that should entitle them to be excused jury service and we recommend accordingly.

58. Certain people are disqualified from serving as jurors on the grounds of their criminal record. The main categories are those who have ever been sentenced to life imprisonment, detention at Her Majesty's pleasure, or to more than five years' imprisonment; those who have served any period of imprisonment or have received a suspended sentence or a community service order during the previous ten years; and those who have been placed on probation during the previous five years. It is thus possible for a person to sit on a jury while on bail for an offence that is similar to the one for which the defendant is to be tried. Also a person may sit on a jury after a conviction for a criminal offence, provided that the sentence has not been served during the previous ten years (or five years if placed on probation).

59. We are not convinced that these rules are the best that could be devised but before changing them there needs in our view to be proper research into their possible influence on jury verdicts. If such research were to show that defendants with criminal convictions played an improper role in jury deliberations, that might be a basis for changing the current rules. Research might, however, show that, contrary to general belief, the role played by jurors with prior criminal convictions is indistinguishable from the role played by any other category of juror. We recommend that suitable research be conducted once the amendment to section 8 of the Contempt of Court Act 1981 that we have proposed has been made. The only change that we at present recommend is the disqualification from serving on a jury of any person who is on bail.

60. Whatever the precise definition is to be, it is important that the jury summons clearly identifies the categories of people who are disqualified on the grounds of their criminal records and that there are efficient arrangements for checking on any who may be tempted to ignore their disqualification. At present there is a system of sample checks but the Association of Chief Police Officers have told us that there have been substantial shortfalls in the number of checks made. This is either because courts are not submitting their quotas of names on the prescribed sample basis or because the information given is insufficient to enable a search of the records to be made. The Association has suggested that, once the new national criminal record system is running as an independent agency, the routine screening of jurors for criminal convictions should be arranged direct with the agency by the courts themselves. We agree and so recommend. In addition, we

recommend that the form sent to potential jurors should require the juror to affirm that he or she does not have a disqualifying conviction and that he or she understands that this may be checked and that a prosecution may follow if false information is given.

61. Although the initial summoning of persons from the electoral rolls is done on a random basis, several factors may affect that randomness by the time a jury is selected. The rules on eligibility and disqualification that we have already mentioned are relevant factors, as are the various reasons that people may advance for wishing to be excused jury service on a discretionary basis. It may for example be that some women find it more difficult to serve as jurors on account of domestic commitments. The Crown Court Study did in fact find that women were slightly underrepresented on juries compared with what might have been expected. Comparison with the 1991 census, however, indicates that on a national basis ethnic minority groups were not seriously underrepresented. Non-white jurors made up 5% of jurors as compared with 5.9% of the total population.

62. We are reluctant to interfere with the principle of random selection of juries. We are, however, anxious that everything possible should be done to ensure that people from the ethnic minority communities are represented on juries in relation to their numbers in the local community. The pool from which juries are randomly selected would be more representative if all eligible members of ethnic communities were included on the electoral roll. Even if this were to be achieved, however, there would statistically still be instances where there would not be a multi-racial jury in a case where one seemed appropriate. The Court of Appeal in *Ford* held that race should not be taken into account in selecting juries. Although we agree with the court's position in regard to most cases, we believe that there are some exceptional cases where race should be taken into account.

63. We have therefore found very relevant a proposal made to us by the Commission for Racial Equality (CRE) for a specific procedure to be available where the case is believed to have a racial dimension which results in a defendant from an ethnic minority community believing that he or she is unlikely to receive a fair trial from an all-white jury. The CRE would also like to see the prosecution on behalf of the victim be able to argue that a racial dimension to the case points to the need for a multi-racial jury. In such cases the CRE propose that it should be possible for either the prosecution or the defence to apply to the judge before the trial for a selection of a jury containing up to three people from ethnic minority communities. If the judge grants the application, it would be for the jury bailiff to continue to draw names randomly selected from the available pool until three such people were drawn. We believe that, in the exceptional case where compelling reasons can be advanced, this option, in addition to the existing power to order that the case be transferred to another court centre, should be available and we so recommend. However, we do not envisage that the new procedure should apply (as proposed by the CRE) simply because the

defendant thinks that he or she cannot get a fair trial from an all-white jury. The defendant would have to persuade the judge that such a belief was reasonable because of the unusual and special features of the case. Thus, a black defendant charged with burglary would be unlikely to succeed in such an application. But black people accused of violence against a member of an extremist organisation who they said had been making racial taunts against them and their friends might well succeed.

64. The CRE considered whether the judge should have power to order that the three jurors from ethnic minority communities should come from the same ethnic minority as the defendant or victim. They concluded, however, that this would be impracticable. While this may be so, we believe that it should be open to the defence or prosecution to argue the point and to the judge to be able to order in appropriate cases that one or more of the three jurors should come from the same ethnic minority as the defendant or the victim. We so recommend.

The Royal Commission then considered guidance and assistance to jurors and made further recommendations:

- During long trials, court hours might be staggered to allow jurors some time off 'during normal working hours to see to their personal business'. The court day would begin earlier or finish later to make up these hours.
- The explanatory video shown to jurors should be brought up to date, to include an explanation that pre-trial discussions and preparatory hearings may have taken place 'in order to narrow down and clarify the issues for [the jury's] benefit'. The video should also explain why a judge intervenes during a trial: 'in order to prevent irrelevant questioning or argument by counsel, to protect witnesses, to clarify the issues, and to keep the case broadly within any timetable that may have been agreed. It is most important that jurors should not regard such interventions as indicating bias on the part of the judge towards one side or the other.'
- Judges should explain to jurors that they may make notes and should recommend that they do so. It should be standard procedure to supply writing materials for jurors.
- Judges should consider giving juries summaries of agreed written evidence, such as medical reports, and, in lengthy cases, written summaries of evidence given orally. Charts and tables should be used where they would assist in presenting complicated facts to jurors.
- Before the jury in a complex, lengthy or serious trial retires, the judge should consider giving jurors written guidance on the law and, perhaps, 'a written list of the questions they need to address in the course of their deliberations, with written guidance on the bearing that the various possible answers are likely to have on the verdict'.

- Legal argument about, for example, admissibility of evidence should take place before the trial, to avoid the necessity for sending the jury out during the trial.
- Research should be undertaken to decide whether literacy or comprehension tests should be given to jurors to test their ability to understand the issues.

Royal Commissions have been described by cynics as a device for avoiding dealing with problems. This Royal Commission was set up after the emergence of several miscarriages of justice that were allegedly caused by defects in the criminal justice system. Many of its recommendations were implemented: for example, the creation of the Criminal Cases Review Commission.

Juries in civil cases

In some civil cases juries decide on the amount of damages that a successful plaintiff should receive. In *Thompson v Commissioner of Police of the Metropolis* [1997] 2 All ER 762 the Court of Appeal considered the guidance that judges should give to juries in arriving at a figure. The case was concerned with two appeals from awards by juries. Miss Thompson had been assaulted by police as they tried to put her in a cell. The police had then prosecuted her for assault and fabricated evidence against her. She sued for malicious prosecution and the jury awarded £1,500 general damages and £50,000 exemplary damages. Mr Hsu was awarded £20,000 general damages and £200,000 exemplary damages after officers forced their way into his house, assaulted and racially abused him, arrested him and placed him in a cell and then removed property from his house.

Lord Woolf MR:

> In a number of recent cases members of the public have been awarded very large sums of exemplary damages by juries against the Commissioner of Police of the Metropolis for unlawful conduct towards them by the police. As a result these two appeals have been brought by the Commissioner. The intention is to clarify the directions which a judge should include in a summing up to assist the jury as to the amount of damages, particularly exemplary damages, which it is appropriate for them to award a plaintiff who is successful in this type of action. As similar appeals are pending any guidance given by us on this subject should influence the outcome of those appeals in addition to providing guidance for the future. . . .

Lord Woolf explained that the Court of Appeal issues guidelines on the amount of damages to be awarded in particular types of case. Most awards of damages are made by judges but in the few types of case where damages are awarded by a jury:

> there are only two situations in which the Court of Appeal can normally interfere with an award of damages by a jury. The first is where the jury's award is totally disproportionate to the subject matter of the award or is otherwise wholly **erroneous**. Different expressions appear in the authorities to describe what constitutes a wholly erroneous award, but they are all intended to indicate that the award must be clearly wrong and that there is a heavy onus on the appellant who alleges that an award should be set aside on this ground. The second situation is where the summing up is defective in a way which constitutes a misdirection unless the misdirection does not result in any miscarriage of justice. In general litigants are entitled to have an adequate direction given to the jury as to the issues which the jury have to decide, the principles of law which are relevant to those issues, an indication of the respective cases of the parties on those issues and, when appropriate, the effect in law of evidence which has been given. This general approach applies equally to issues as to damages as it does to issues as to liability.

Lord Woolf noted that in *Cassell v Broome* [1972] 1 All ER 801 Lord Hailsham explained why guidance given to juries by judges is limited:

> The first, and paramount, consideration in my mind is that the jury is, where either party desires it, the only legal and **constitutional** tribunal for deciding libel cases, including the award of damages. I do not think the judiciary at any level should substitute itself for a jury, unless the award is so manifestly too large . . . that no sensible jury properly directed could have reached the conclusion . . . The point is that the law makes the jury and not the judiciary the constitutional tribunal, and if Parliament had wished the roles to be reversed in any way, Parliament would have said so at the time of the Administration of Justice (Miscellaneous Provisions) Act 1933 . . . It may very well be that, on the whole, judges, and the legal profession in general, would be less generous than juries in the award of damages for defamation. But I know of no principle of reason which would entitle judges, whether of appeal or at first instance, to consider that their own sense of the **proprieties** is more reasonable than that of a jury, or which would entitle them to **arrogate** to themselves a constitutional status in this matter which Parliament has deliberately withheld from them, for **aught** we know, on the very ground that juries can be expected to be more generous on such matters than judges.

Whilst judges nowadays receive a great deal of guidance and assistance in reaching the correct figure, juries in defamation cases have had little guidance and the result has been disproportionately high sums in defamation actions (awarded by juries) when compared with damages for personal injuries (awarded by judges). In *John v MGN Ltd* [1996] 2 All ER 35, Bingham MR commented:

> A series of jury awards in sums wildly disproportionate to any damage conceivably suffered by the plaintiff has given rise to serious and justified criticism of the procedures leading to such awards. This has not been the fault of the juries. Judges, as they were bound to do, confined themselves to broad directions of general principle, coupled with **injunctions** to the jury to be reasonable. But they gave no guidance on what might be thought reasonable or unreasonable, and it is not altogether surprising that juries lacked an instinctive sense of where to pitch their awards. They were in the position of sheep loosed on an unfenced common, with no shepherd. While the Court of Appeal reaffirmed the fundamental soundness of the traditional approach in *Sutcliffe v Pressdram Ltd* [1990] . . . , the court did in that case recommend trial judges to draw the attention of juries to the purchasing power of the award they were minded to make, and of the income it would produce . . . This was thereafter done, and juries were reminded of the cost of buying a motor car, or a holiday, or a house. But judges were still constrained by authority from steering the jury towards any particular level of award.

Lord Woolf noted that s 8 of the Courts and Legal Services Act 1990 and RSC Ord 59, r 11(4) give the Court of Appeal jurisdiction to order a new trial if a jury has awarded damages that are 'excessive or inadequate' or to substitute an amount of damages that seems proper to the Court of Appeal and then considered the approach taken by the Court of Appeal to this new power and the matter of when aggravated and exemplary damages are appropriate:

> It is when the jury has to consider whether there should be an award of aggravated damages as additional compensation that the award in this class of case is more analogous to that in defamation proceedings. As the Law Commission point out in their admirable consultative paper *Aggravated, Exemplary and Restitutionary Damages* (Consultation Paper No 132 (1993)) para 2.17 ff there can be a penal element in the award of aggravated damages. However, they are primarily to be awarded to compensate the plaintiff for injury to his proper pride and dignity and the consequences of his being humiliated. This injury is made worse for the plaintiff because it is more difficult to excuse when the malicious motives, spite or arrogance are on the part of the police . . .
>
> It is when the jury make an award of exemplary damages that the similarity of this class of action with defamation is closest. However, a factor justifying the award of exemplary damages, which in defamation actions makes consistency in the proper amount to award less likely, is that often the award is to prevent a newspaper profiting from the libel by increasing its circulation. This element of profiting from your tort is almost invariably absent from this class of action. In addition, as the defendant is usually a chief officer of police, the personality of the defendant will not

usually be significant in determining what the appropriate level of **punitive** damages should be. While the conduct calling for the award of exemplary damages may differ it is to be hoped that it will be rare indeed for most senior officers in the force to be in any way implicated.

The fact that the defendant is a chief officer of police also means that here exemplary damages should have a lesser role to play. Even if the use of civil proceedings to punish a defendant can in some circumstances be justified it is more difficult to justify the award where the defendant and the person responsible for meeting any award is not the wrongdoer, but his 'employer'. While it is possible that a chief constable could bear a responsibility for what has happened, due to his failure to exercise proper control, the instances when this is alleged to have occurred should not be frequent. There is also a greater problem of awarding exemplary as well as aggravated damages in the class of action under consideration because the very circumstances which will justify the award of aggravated damages are probably the same as those which make it possible to award exemplary damages. This accentuates the risk of a double counting. At least in defamation proceedings there is the additional factor of the defendant profiting from the libel which provides the independent justification for the award of exemplary damages.

We have already referred to what was said in his judgment in *John's* case by Bingham MR as to the effect of excessive awards of damages in defamation cases on the public perception of civil justice. In this category of case the reaction could understandably be stronger since the excessive awards are being paid out of public money (though police forces other than the Metropolitan do take out insurance) and could well result in a reduction in the resources of the police available to be used for activities which would benefit the public. The Law Commission's Consultation Paper to which we have already made reference considers whether the power to award aggravated and exemplary damages should be abolished. The Law Commission's provisional views expressed in their consultation paper is that the power should be retained. However, it is counter-productive to give juries an impossible task. It must at present be very difficult for a jury to understand the distinction between aggravated and exemplary damages when there is such a substantial overlap between the factors which provide the sole justification for both awards. The extent to which juries fluctuate in the awards which they make (which the present appeals demonstrate) indicated the difficulties which they have. On the other hand there are arguments which can be advanced to justify the retention of the use of juries in this area of litigation. Very difficult issues of credibility will often have to be resolved. It is desirable for these to be determined by the plaintiffs' fellow citizens rather than judges, who like the police are concerned in maintaining law and order. Similarly the jury, because of their composition, are a body which is peculiarly suited to make the final assessment of damages, including deciding whether aggravated or exemplary damages are called for in this area of litigation and for the jury to have these important tasks is an important safeguard of the liberty of the individual citizen.

As the Court of Appeal has usually the responsibility for determining the level of damages when it allows an appeal its decisions should indicate what is the appropriate level for damages in these actions. A standard will be established with which jury awards can be compared. This will make it easier to determine whether or not the sum which the jury has awarded is excessive. To not provide juries with sufficient guidance to enable them to approach damages on similar lines to those which this court will adopt will mean the number of occasions this court will be called on to intervene will be undesirably frequent. This will be disadvantageous to the parties because it will result in increased costs and uncertainty. It will also have adverse consequences for the reputation of the jury system. It could be instrumental in bringing about its demise. . . .

The guidance that should be given

While there is no formula which is appropriate for all cases and the precise form of a summing up is very much a matter within the discretion of the trial judge, it is suggested that in many cases it will be convenient to include in a summing up on the issue of damages additional directions on the following lines. As we mention later in this judgment we think it may often be wise to take the jury's verdict on liability before they receive directions as to **quantum**.

(1) It should be explained to the jury that if they find in the plaintiff's favour the only remedy which they have power to grant is an award of damages. Save in exceptional situations such damages are only awarded as compensation and are intended to compensate the plaintiff for any injury or damage which he has suffered. They are not intended to punish the defendant.

(2) As the law stands at present compensatory damages are of two types: (a) ordinary damages which we would suggest should be described as basic, and (b) aggravated damages. Aggravated damages can only be awarded where they are claimed by the plaintiff and where there are aggravating features about the defendant's conduct which justify the award of aggravated damages. (We would add that in the rare case where special damages are claimed in respect of some specific **pecuniary loss** this claim should be explained separately.)

(3) The jury should be told that the basic damages will depend on the circumstances and the degree of harm suffered by the plaintiff. But they should be provided with an appropriate bracket to use as a starting point. The judge will be responsible for determining the bracket, and we envisage that in the ordinary way the judge will have heard submissions on the

matter from counsel in the absence of the jury . . . Though this is not what was proposed in the case of a defamation action in *John*'s case, submissions by counsel in the absence of the jury are likely to have advantages because of the resemblance between the sum to be awarded in false imprisonment cases and ordinary personal injury cases, and because a greater number of precedents may be cited in this class of case than in a defamation action. We therefore think it would be better for the debate to take place in the absence of a jury.

(4) In a straightforward case of wrongful arrest and imprisonment or malicious prosecution the jury should be informed of the approximate figure to be taken as the correct starting point for basic damages for the actual loss of liberty or for the wrongful prosecution, and also given an approximate ceiling figure. It should be explained that these are no more than guideline figures based on the judge's experience and on the awards in other cases and the actual figure is one on which they must decide.

(5) In a straightforward case of wrongful arrest and imprisonment the starting point is likely to be about £500 for the first hour during which the plaintiff has been deprived of his or her liberty. After the first hour an additional sum is to be awarded, but that sum should be on a reducing scale so as to keep the damages proportionate with those payable in personal injury cases and because the plaintiff is entitled to have a higher rate of compensation for the initial shock of being arrested. As a guideline we consider, for example, that a plaintiff who has been wrongly kept in custody for 24 hours should for this alone normally be regarded as entitled to an award of about £3,000. For subsequent days the daily rate will be on a progressively reducing scale. . . .

(8) If the case is one in which aggravated damages are claimed and could be appropriately awarded, the nature of aggravated damages should be explained to the jury. Such damages can be awarded where there are aggravating features about the case which would result in the plaintiff not receiving sufficient compensation for the injury suffered if the award were restricted to a basic award. Aggravating features can include humiliating circumstances at the time of arrest or any conduct of those responsible for the arrest or the prosecution which shows that they have behaved in a high-handed, insulting, malicious or oppressive manner either in relation to the arrest or imprisonment or in conducting the prosecution. Aggravating features can also include the way the litigation and trial are conducted. . . .

(9) The jury should then be told that if they consider the case is one for the award of damages other than basic damages then they should usually make a separate award for each category. (This is contrary to the present practice but in our view will result in greater transparency as to the make-up of the award.)

(10) We consider that where it is appropriate to award aggravated damages the figure is unlikely to be less than £1,000. We do not think it is possible to indicate a precise arithmetical relationship between basic

damages and aggravated damages because the circumstances will vary from case to case. In the ordinary way, however, we would not expect the aggravated damages to be as much as twice the basic damages except perhaps where, on the particular facts, the basic damages are modest.

(11) It should be strongly emphasised to the jury that the total figure for basic and aggravated damages should not exceed what they consider is fair compensation for the injury which the plaintiff has suffered. It should also be explained that if aggravated damages are awarded such damages, though compensatory and not intended as a punishment, will in fact contain a penal element as far as the defendant is concerned.

(12) Finally the jury should be told in a case where exemplary damages are claimed and the judge considers that there is evidence to support such a claim, that though it is not normally possible to award damages with the *object* of punishing the defendant, exceptionally this is possible where there has been conduct, including oppressive or arbitrary behaviour, by police officers which deserves the exceptional remedy of exemplary damages. It should be explained to the jury: (a) that if the jury are awarding aggravated damages these damages will have already provided compensation for the injury suffered by the plaintiff as a result of the oppressive and insulting behaviour of the police officer and, inevitably, a measure of punishment from the defendant's point of view; (b) that exemplary damages should be awarded if, but only if, they consider that the compensation awarded by way of basic and aggravated damages is in the circumstances an inadequate punishment for the defendants; (c) that an award of exemplary damages is in effect a windfall for the plaintiff and, where damages will be payable out of police funds, the sum awarded may not be available to be expended by the police in a way which would benefit the public (this guidance would not be appropriate if the claim were to be met by insurers); and (d) that the sum awarded by way of exemplary damages should be sufficient to mark the jury's disapproval of the oppressive or arbitrary behaviour but should be no more than is required for this purpose.

(13) Where exemplary damages are appropriate they are unlikely to be less than £5,000. Otherwise the case is probably not one which justifies an award of exemplary damages at all. In this class of action the conduct must be particularly deserving of condemnation for an award of as much as £25,000 to be justified and the figure of £50,000 should be regarded as the absolute maximum, involving directly officers of at least the rank of superintendent.

(14) In an appropriate case the jury should also be told that even though the plaintiff succeeds on liability any improper conduct of which they find him guilty can reduce or even eliminate any award of aggravated or exemplary damages if the jury consider that this conduct caused or contributed to the behaviour complained of.

The figures given will of course require adjusting in the future for inflation. We appreciate that the guideline figures depart from the figures frequently awarded by juries at the present time. However, they are designed to establish some relationship between the figures awarded in this area and those awarded for personal injuries. In giving guidance for aggravated damages we have attached importance to the fact that they are intended to be compensatory and not punitive although the same circumstances may justify punishment.

The correctness of the awards in these cases

In the case of Mr Hsu: the award of £20,000 as compensation including aggravated damages is not a figure with which the court would interfere. Beside the physical injuries he sustained, the consequences for Mr Hsu have been more serious than they would otherwise have been because of his underlying condition. It is in relation to the exemplary damages that the appeal obviously must succeed because of the approach already indicated. There was unprovoked violence in connection with an arrest which took place at Mr Hsu's home. There were a number of officers involved. However, the whole incident was over in a matter of hours and there is already an award of aggravated damages which has to be taken into account. The figure we regard as appropriate is £15,000. So Mr Hsu recovers £35,000 in total. This should suffice to demonstrate publicly the strongest disapproval of what occurred and make it clear to the commissioner and his force that conduct of this nature will not be tolerated by the courts.

In the case of Miss Thompson: . . . we do consider the compensatory damages in this case of £1,500 totally out of line. We bear in mind this lady's initial arrest was lawful but we consider for the subsequent unlawful conduct continuing for seven months we would award £10,000 plus a like sum of aggravated damages and £25,000 exemplary damages (total £45,000). This is marginally less than the total award of the jury but when considering whether to allow the appeal we are concerned with the total award. We will not therefore allow the commissioner's appeal as the jury retain a **margin of appreciation** so this court will not intervene unless the difference as to amount is greater than this.

As to the other appeals which are awaiting determination, we draw the parties' attention to the arrangements which can be made by this court for assistance by way of alternative dispute resolution. We would hope that the guidance we have provided should enable the appeals to be settled without difficulty by the parties themselves, but if they are not we would hope that the parties would seek the assistance of ADR from the court before proceeding with the appeals. If they do not this may be an appropriate matter to be considered when determining the order for costs which should be made.

Check your understanding

Can you explain the meaning of the words and phrases in **bold** type?

Things to do

1 There is a lot of information about juries contained in the excerpt from the Royal Commission's report. Make yourself a set of brief notes about the way juries are selected, the guidance they receive and the problems of juries in fraud trials. Compare your notes with the account of this material in one or two textbooks and make any additions to your notes that you find helpful. For example, in para 57 mention is made of people ineligible for jury service: your notes should include a list of categories of people who are ineligible, excused as of right, excusable and disqualified. Then summarise the recommendations the Royal Commission makes. The Royal Commission's recommendations on guidance to juries have already been summarised for you: you may like to use this summary as a model for your own summary.

2 Go to your local Crown Court and watch a jury trial. Do the jurors make notes, do they ask questions, do they appear to understand what is going on? Does the judge explain things to the jury in a helpful way? What is the gender, racial and age mix of the jury?

3 The Royal Commission made considerable use of the Crown Court Study in coming to its recommendations for changes in connection with juries. The quality of what that Study produced will have been determined to a large extent by the quality of the questionnaires: it is important to ask the right questions. Imagine that you are conducting a Research Study for a Royal Commission. Choose your own topic: it might be the use of legal aid in criminal cases, the sentencing powers of magistrates, the small claims procedure in county courts, an issue of substantive law – anything you like. Decide what you need to know and who you are going to ask to complete your questionnaire and then draft some questions. There might be different groups of people you want to ask about your topic. You will probably want to ask different questions of different people – so you will need several questionnaires.

Discuss

1 Imagine that s 8 of the Contempt of Court Act has been repealed in such a way as to permit research into juries. What would you like to know about how juries reach their decisions? How might researchers find these things out?

2 Is the decision in *Thompson* a policy decision, or is it based on well-established legal principles? Look at what is said in the material on judges about policy decisions (p. 43). At 12(c) on p. 56, Lord Woolf appears to be saying that jurors should consider a policy issue. Is this a policy issue? If it is, is it appropriate to involve juries in policy?

3 What was the 'traditional approach' to advising juries on the amount of damages to be awarded? How was this justified?

4 Why does Lord Woolf regard the traditional approach as unsatisfactory?

5 Arrange a debate: 'This House considers the use of juries in civil cases to be an anachronism and calls for its abolition.'

6 Look at 13 on p. 56. Why should exemplary damages be larger if senior officers are involved?

Write

Write a brief description of a rule of law, a rule of practice and a guideline, giving an example of each.

Connections

1 Consider what Lord Woolf says at p. 53 about the vicarious liability of a chief constable for improper behaviour and compare it with the vicarious liability of an employer for his employee's acts or omissions that cause physical injury. Do you think he is right to say the former is more difficult to justify?

2 Consider the cases of *AB v South West Water Services* (p. 215) and *Surrey CC & Mole DC v Bredero Homes* (p. 275) on the issue of quantum of damages and its relationship with the conduct of the defendant.

3 Note that in *Thompson* Lord Woolf is advocating the use of ADR. Where else did he do so?

4 Look at what Lord Pearce says in *Sweet v Parsley* (p. 144) about jurors' ability to understand differing standards of proof and their tendency to apply 'common sense'.

3 Systems

3.1 CIVIL DISPUTE RESOLUTION

Civil cases are those which are concerned with disputes between two or more individuals. They often arise from accidents, from contractual arrangements or from the breakdown of marriages.

The courts

Most civil actions are settled before they get to court but the cost and delay involved in taking a case to court prompted the government to commission a report from Lord Woolf on *Access to Justice*. Having produced an interim report in 1995, he reported in 1996 and recommended a new 'fast track':

> Section II, Chapter 2, Fast Track: General
>
> 1. In my interim report I recommended the establishment of a new fast track for straightforward cases not exceeding £10,000 in value. I recommended a strictly limited procedure designed to take cases to trial within a short but reasonable timescale with fixed costs that would be known in advance so that litigants could estimate their maximum liability for costs even if unsuccessful. I envisaged that the greater certainty of the procedure and the costs would encourage the development of legal expenses insurance because it would provide certainty to solicitors and to insurance companies and would enable the Legal Aid Board and other bulk purchasers of legal services to make better use of their resources.
> 2. The fast track was welcomed by the Lord Chancellor. He has asked me to develop detailed procedures and a costs structure for the fast track. This I hope has been achieved thanks to the extremely valuable help of the Fast Track Working Group.
> 3. Other jurisdictions, in particular the United States, Canada and Australia, have introduced limited procedures and tracking for straightforward cases. I have examined some of these in operation and been sent valuable

material on others. The Inquiry's academic consultant has conducted a survey. Experience elsewhere has been generally positive although some systems are still at an early stage. My approach has many common features with those but is more radical in that it involves a fixed costs regime.

4. The working group included practitioners nominated both by the professional bodies and the Advice Services Alliance (which covers a wide range of advice centres and law centres). The practitioners on the working group are representative of those who litigate in the civil courts and have experience of a wide range of cases, including personal injury, building and construction, disputes over goods and services, housing disrepair and other housing cases.

5. An issues paper circulated in January 1996 consulted on proposals for the fast track procedures. I and members of the Inquiry Team have discussed the proposals with interested organisations and many individuals. The Inquiry Team has had detailed discussions with representatives of small businesses and the issues paper has been circulated, thanks to the Department of Trade and Industry Small Business Unit, to many of the leading business representatives via bodies such as the Institute of Directors and the Alliance of Independent Retailers and Businesses.

6. The Consumers' Association recommended that the fast track procedure should apply to cases up to £15,000. They said:

> 'This would enable more, relatively straightforward disputes relating to, for instance, building works (home extensions and improvements), to be covered by the procedure. We are aware of many consumer complaints that fall into this category but where the risk of liability for disproportionately high legal costs makes litigation an impractical option for all but the wealthy and/or brave.'

The National Consumer Council (NCC) commented:

> 'Broadly the NCC feels that a fast track could provide lower cost access to justice for fairly straightforward cases of moderate value. In order to ensure that this more rough and ready justice is in fact just, the new proposals need to conform to the basic principles. These are fairness and accessibility, responsiveness to objectives, equality and balance; supported by active case management, adequate resourcing, information and consultation and a non-adversarial approach.'

7. The Law Society and the Bar have been extremely constructive in their contributions. They have submitted a number of very helpful papers to the Inquiry. Their response and that from the profession and consumers, both individuals and businesses, has been overwhelmingly positive. In addition, the Department of Trade and Industry, which has circulated my interim report through its consultative bodies and information channels, has reported overwhelming enthusiasm among business on the proposals for the fast track and on case management generally.

8. The Law Centres Federation, while it did not accept that any link existed between the complexity of a case and its value, did accept that there was a relationship between the costs of the case and the benefit to the client. It commented:

> 'It is clear that a privately paying client would not consider it reasonable that the total cost of the claim should be more than the value of the claim itself in most cases. Given the "person of moderate means" test applied by the Legal Aid Board then the position is likely to be very much the same for legally aided clients.'

9. The Law Society in its response to my interim report supported my outline proposals for the fast track in principle but said:

> 'The Society has continued to support the principle of the fast track provided the procedures are not so curtailed as to discourage settlements and lead to more trials and/or lead to rough justice. The Society also supports proportionality between what is at issue between the parties and the procedures and costs.'

10. The Society also suggests that 'a number of factors, not only monetary value, need to be taken into account when deciding the appropriate track for an action'.

11. There are nonetheless a minority who consider that the whole concept of the fast track is wrong in principle and a greater number who, while supporting the proposals in principle, are concerned about the detail. The issues of principle which were raised relate first to the scope of the fast track and the criteria by which cases are included or excluded and secondly to the concept of proportionality.

12. The fast track is intended to cover the majority of defended actions within the monetary band £3,000–£10,000. All personal injury cases up to £10,000 will be included except where the claimant is a litigant in person and opts for a claim below £3,000 to be dealt with under the small claims procedure. The fast track will also deal with non-monetary claims such as injunctions, **declarations** and orders for **specific performance** which are not suitable for the small claims procedure and do not require to be dealt with on the multi-track. Since the fast track is for defended actions, debt actions, fixed date possession and return of goods actions will not be affected by these proposals unless a substantive defence is filed.

13. The new procedures should enable defended cases up to £10,000 to be progressed fairly within the fast track. Some respondents to the issues paper, notably the Bar, have suggested that all cases should be allocated to the fast track by a given case type, rather than as a result of a presumption based on monetary value. As against this, many respondents have pointed out that all types of cases have the potential to be simple or complex. It is preferable to establish criteria which can be applied to all types of cases and which will enable parties to identify, and the court to decide, whether

or not a case is suitable for handling within the 'no frills' procedure of the fast track. . . .

Chapter 20 The New Rules

1. It is part of my remit to produce a single body of rules of court to replace the existing Rules of the Supreme Court and County Court Rules. A draft set of rules is published at the same time as this report. It constitutes the main core of general rules which in my opinion will be needed to support the new arrangements for civil justice. It is intended to form the basis of consultation with all relevant interests.
2. I set myself five specific objectives for the rule-making exercise:

(a) to identify the core propositions in the rules and to cut down the number of interconnecting provisions which are used;
(b) to provide procedures which apply to the broadest possible range of cases and to reduce the number of instances in which a separate regime is provided for a special type of case;
(c) to reduce the size of the rules and the number of propositions contained in them;
(d) to remove **verbiage** and to adopt a simpler and plainer style of drafting;
(e) to give effect to the **substantive** reforms which I am proposing.

3. Genuine access to justice requires people to be able to understand how the legal procedure works. The procedure, working properly, is a vital guarantee that justice will be done; that it can be seen to work properly helps to ensure that justice will be seen to be done.
4. Given the size of the existing rules, reducing the amount of material in them is obviously desirable in itself. However, reduction of the amount of specialised material in favour of greater reliance on general rules also serves the broader purpose of emphasising the similarities between different types of jurisdiction rather than their differences. In the past the fragmentation of civil justice has undermined its claims to equal treatment with criminal justice in such matters as resources. It has also made civil justice substantively less efficient. My proposals overall are directed towards reversing these features. New rules of broader application will support the new policy. Greater reliance on broader propositions makes it easier for users of civil procedure to keep in mind the objects of the procedure. It reduces complexity and so makes the system more amenable to actual users and more acceptable to ordinary citizens, whether litigants or not. It should reduce the learning and processing costs of courts and lawyers.
5. To help carry forward the work on the new rules, I set up a small working group. It incorporated judicial, consumer and lay advisory viewpoints. The role of the group has been to advise on the preparation of instructions to the draftsman and to comment on the drafts as they were prepared. It has made an enormous contribution to the work, for which

> I am immensely grateful. To my knowledge, this is the first time on which representatives of consumer and advice organisations have been directly involved in the preparation of rules of court. I recommend that they should have a permanent role as a counterbalance to the professional legal viewpoint in the new rule-making committee which will be needed to enact the combined rules.

The cost

The issue of how the civil dispute system works is intimately concerned with what it costs and, therefore, with the extent to which litigation should be state funded. This material is therefore best considered in association with the problem of financing legal work.

Litigants who can afford to pay solicitors' and barristers' fees from their own pockets are often large companies or wealthy individuals. For the rest of society, the cost of using lawyers is always going to be a first consideration when deciding whether to bring or defend a civil action. For nearly fifty years it was considered normal for the poorest members of society to have their legal costs paid by the government, through the legal aid fund. The cost of this provision has risen to the extent that governments of whatever party have recognised a need to reconsider how civil legal work should be funded.

In July 1996 the Conservative government published a White Paper, *Striking the Balance*. It began:

> This paper sets out how the Government has decided to reform the legal aid system in England and Wales. The changes are summarised in Annex A.
>
> The Government published a consultation paper, *Legal Aid – Targeting Need*, in May 1995. There was a great deal of interest in the proposals, and over 200 individuals and bodies responded. An analysis of their comments and views is in Annex B.
>
> The Green Paper set out the weaknesses of the existing legal aid system in England and Wales, and made proposals for its reform as part of the Government's overall strategy to improve access to justice through a co-ordinated programme to:
>
> - simplify the law;
> - make court procedure quicker, simpler and cheaper, and costs more predictable;
> - encourage the use and development of alternatives to courts and lawyers for resolving problems and disputes; and
> - improve the arrangements for providing publicly-funded legal services.
>
> The changes to the legal aid scheme that the Government has decided to make are **radical**. Nothing less will do. Our aim is to improve the balance

between competing and conflicting interests. The Government has to decide how much to spend on legal aid and on other vital public services, such as health and education. The needs of people who require help with the cost of legal services must be balanced against the rights of their **unassisted opponents**, and of victims and witnesses, to fair treatment. Then there are the interests of the taxpayer in ensuring that public spending is controlled, and that money is not wasted on undeserving cases but is made to go as far as it can to meet genuine need.

The Government's reforms will also achieve a new and better balance in the way legally-aided help is obtained. Control of the size of the legal aid budget will be matched with the ability to target priority needs and deserving cases. Pressures for lower costs will be balanced by new safeguards to promote quality. The need to provide a greater choice of services and better access to them will be balanced against the need to ensure that those who give the service are skilled and **competent**.

Balancing interests and policy objectives is never easy and is rarely popular because few people get everything they want. Yet it is what mature and responsible government is all about, and it is at the heart of these reforms.

Our proposals will fundamentally change the way publicly-funded legal services are provided. Legal aid will gradually become a scheme where most services are provided through bulk contracts with fixed prices. But it will be a flexible scheme that will allow us to adapt the way we obtain legal services as demand, legal problems and the services themselves develop.

The White Paper noted that the cost of legal aid had doubled during the previous five years and concluded that 'Tinkering at the edges will not be good enough'. It proposed a range of reforms:

. . . the Government has concluded that radical change is needed:

- to provide effective means of controlling overall costs;
- to encourage efficiency, while maintaining quality;
- to target the available resources on the most appropriate and cost-effective services and the most deserving cases; and
- to promote fair treatment for all concerned, and discourage irresponsible behaviour such as driving up an opponent's costs.

Reform

1.17 The Government intends to meet these objectives by making five main changes. These are:

- replacing the present open-ended approach to resources with **pre-determined budgets** that can be allocated to meet local demand within national priorities;
- extending the scheme to new types of providers and services;

- introducing contracts between providers of services and the Legal Aid Board for specified services of defined quality at an agreed price;
- a new test for deciding whether civil cases should be given legal aid. This will target available resources on the most deserving cases; and
- changing the rules governing financial conditions to increase the potential liability of assisted persons to contribute to their own and, in civil cases, their opponents' **costs**.

1.18 The Legal Aid Board will have the major responsibility for making the reforms happen, by making contracts with providers of legal services.
1.19 The Government intends to widen the reach of legal aid to provide a broader and more flexible range of services. Solicitors and barristers in private practice will continue to play the largest role. But advice agencies, salaried lawyers, mediators and others will also be included. As a result, legal aid will, in principle, be capable of providing any help that can either:

- prevent court proceedings or questions that would demand a legal solution from arising, or
- promote their settlement or other disposal, in accordance with the law and in a way that will produce an enforceable result.

The form of that help will range from information about available services and initial advice and assistance, to various kinds of more substantial service, including mediation and help preparing and presenting court cases.
1.20 Chapter 2 explains how the Government intends to get better control over spending by fixing budgets in advance for criminal, civil and family legal aid, and how we will target appropriate services and deserving cases.
1.21 Chapter 3 explains that the Government intends to take a flexible approach to obtaining services, but that most will be bought under contracts. Contracting for specified services at agreed prices will help to control total spending and target priority areas, and will enable the Legal Aid Board to insist on efficiency, effectiveness and quality in selecting providers.
1.22 We will address concerns about fairness by increasing the potential liability of legally-aided people to pay something towards their own and their opponents' costs. Chapter 4 sets out our plans for financial eligibility for civil and family legal aid, and the financial conditions that will apply when it has been granted.
1.23 Chapter 5 describes the Government's proposals for criminal legal aid in more detail. It shows how we plan to design the administration of legal aid in criminal cases to fit the proceedings better, and therefore to be more efficient.
1.24 Chapter 6 deals with implementation. The new scheme will be flexible so that it can adapt to prevailing circumstances, continue to make the best of the available resources, and meet the public's varying needs in a fast-changing world. We intend to proceed carefully and learn by experience

as we implement the policy. For this reason, and because we do not yet know when we will be able to introduce legislation to make some of the changes, Chapter 6 does not go beyond setting out a broad implementation programme.

A Labour government came into power in May 1997 and announced an integrated review of legal aid and civil justice. In October 1997 the Lord Chancellor addressed the Law Society and explained that from the following April there would be no civil legal aid for cases involving claims for damages. These would be financed on a conditional fee basis: that is, the solicitor gets no fee if the case is lost but a higher fee than would be normal if the case is won. The solicitor's basic fee is paid by the losing side; the additional fee is paid out of the damages. If the case is lost, the client has to pay the solicitor's **disbursements** and the other side's costs.

It is possible to insure against losing but the premium may vary from several hundred to several thousand pounds, depending on the nature of the claim. Medical negligence cases are notoriously difficult and there is, at the time of writing, concern over whether potential plaintiffs in such cases would be able to afford the insurance premium and the medical reports that are necessary before such an action can be brought.

These proposals leave Legal Aid to finance criminal defence and civil cases where damages are not the object – such as family cases concerning children.

Check your understanding

1 Can you explain the meaning of the words and phrases in **bold** type?

2 What is the 'fast track system'?

3 Documents that are concerned with making arguments one way or the other often contain value-laden language. That is, the words a writer uses are chosen to influence the way the reader perceives the facts. Look at the passages and find examples of value-laden language. There is nothing wrong with value-laden language, provided you know when you are using it and can recognise its use by someone else.

Discuss

1 What evidence can you see in the extracts from *Access to Justice* and *Striking the Balance* that there has been a process of consultation before the final report and the White Paper, respectively, were issued? Why is consultation considered to be a good thing?

2 What is meant by 'proportionality' in discussing the relationship between damages and costs? Why might there be concern if this was the only criterion used to decide how an issue would be dealt with?

3 Why did Lord Woolf include representatives of consumer and advice organisations in his working group? Do you agree that this was a good idea?

4 Describe the features that a good civil dispute system should possess. Which of these do you regard as essential and which dispensable if they prove costly?

5 What are the advantages and disadvantages of the Legal Aid system as it has existed from 1948 to 1998? Would the reforms proposed in *Striking the Balance* have been preferable to the expansion of conditional fees?

Write

1 Summarise Lord Woolf's arguments for changing the court rules.

2 Describe the different methods that may be used to finance a civil action.

3 Find an example of value-laden language from the passages above, from elsewhere in this book or from an article in a newspaper or legal journal. Rewrite the arguments presented in the passage in an objective style.

4 Consider the way in which *you* would fund civil litigation and present your ideas in the style of para 1.17 of *Striking the Balance*. Write yourself some notes on the reasons for each of your reforms so that you could explain and defend them in discussion with others.

Connections

1 Legal Aid is the responsibility of the Lord Chancellor. What other responsibilities and powers does he have within the legal system?

2 A very large part of the legal aid budget goes on criminal work. What reforms might be made to that provision? Why are changes of the kind being advocated for civil work not appropriate in criminal cases?

3.2 SENTENCING

A defendant who has pleaded guilty or been found guilty is sentenced by the magistrates or the judge. The maximum fine or sentence of imprisonment is laid down by Parliament but, subject to that maximum, the court has a wide discretion as to what sentence should be passed.

The court will consider:

- the offence(s): the normal sentence for this offence, any factors that make the offence more or less serious;
- the offender: his or her past record and present circumstances – whether the defendant has a settled job and home, for example;
- guidance from the Court of Appeal.

It would be reasonable to say that deciding on sentencing policy is an issue for government, dealing with individual cases is for the courts of first instance and ensuring a consistent approach is the job of the Court of Appeal. Friction occurs from time to time because these roles necessarily overlap and sentencing is a politically sensitive issue.

The Criminal Justice Act 1991 laid down some policy on when a sentence of imprisonment should be passed:

> 1 (1) This section applies where a person is convicted of an offence punishable with a custodial sentence other than one **fixed by law**.
> (2) Subject to subsection (3) below, the court shall not pass a custodial sentence on the offender unless it is of the opinion—
>
> (a) that the offence, or the combination of the offence and one or more offences associated with it, was so serious that only such a sentence can be justified for the offence; or
> (b) where the offence is a violent or sexual offence, that only such a sentence would be adequate to protect the public from serious harm from him.
>
> (3) Nothing in subsection (2) above shall prevent the court from passing a custodial sentence on the offender if he refuses to give his consent to a **community sentence** which is proposed by the court and requires that consent . . .

In his book *Sentencing and Criminal Justice*, Andrew Ashworth considers the arguments for using alternatives to imprisonment in sentencing:

Chapter 9.2 The Principle of Restraint in the Use of Custody

. . . there is now widespread international assent to the principle of restraint in the use of imprisonment. Resolution VIII of the Eighth United Nations Congress on the Prevention of Crime and the Treatment of Offenders (1990) states in paragraph 5(e) that 'imprisonment should be used as a sanction of last resort'. The **Council of Europe** has likewise declared a policy of encouraging the use of non-custodial sentences and reserving custodial sentences for the most serious types of offence. Chapter 3 of the 1990 White Paper on *Crime, Justice and Protecting the Public* also pointed in the same general direction, but without ever **enunciating** the principle.

How ought the principle to be stated? Would it be right to proclaim it as a pillar of English sentencing policy? What are the arguments in its favour?

For the present, it is sufficient to state the principle as one which argues for the use of non-custodial instead of custodial sentences, and which argues for shorter rather than longer custodial sentences. The UN declaration, which refers to imprisonment as a sanction of last resort, is an inferior formulation because it implies that custody may justifiably be used for someone who persistently commits minor offences. Brief consideration is given here to four supporting arguments – doubts about the reformative potential of custody, doubts about its preventive effect, humanitarian concerns, and the proportionality argument. The discussion concludes with an examination of the arguments in favour of abolishing imprisonment.

(a) Doubts about the Reformative Potential of Penal Institutions

These doubts have been longstanding. Earlier this century Alexander Paterson, one of the most influential of Prison Commissioners, declared that 'it is impossible to train men for freedom in a condition of capitivity'. By 1977 the mood of **scepticism**, encouraged by the works of criminologists, had found its way into the official publication on *Prisons and the Prisoner* [published by the Home Office]:

> 'Experience in recent years has led increasingly to scepticism about the compatibility of rehabilitation in this traditional, **paternalistic** form with the practicalities of day-to-day life in custody. The **coercion** which is inherent in a custodial sentence and the very nature of "total institutions" tend to direct the whole of the inmates' individual and group energies towards adjustment to the austerely unnatural conditions; towards alienation from authority; and thus towards rejection of any rehabilitative goals towards which the staff may be working.'

Notwithstanding this, the Home Office persisted with the rhetoric of rehabilitation; and . . . the May Committee (1979) argued for a new concept of 'positive custody'. Conditions in the prisons in recent years – the emphasis on security in the late 1960s and the 1970s, the gross overcrowding and deteriorating prison estate in the 1980s, not to mention the riots of 1990 – have made such **aspirations** virtually impossible to attain. The White Paper of 1990 **conceded** the point. 'Nobody now regards imprisonment, in itself, as an effective means of reform for most prisoners . . . however, the majority of prison staff try to inject a positive purpose into the regime, prison is a society which requires virtually no sense of responsibility from prisoners.' It is this last point which looms large in present government philosophy: that prison conditions are so artificial, in that prisoners 'do not have to find a job and do not have to look after their families', that they generate a 'culture of dependence'.

The 1990 White Paper concluded that prison 'can be an expensive way of making bad people worse'. That, however, takes the matter somewhat further. It is one thing to argue that prisons are rarely able to rehabilitate the offenders whom they contain. It is another thing to argue that they may make matters worse. What is the evidence?

The Woolf Inquiry [The Woolf *Inquiry into Prisons*, which reported in 1991] declared that 'it is now generally accepted that, particularly with young offenders, there is a risk that a custodial sentence, instead of making it less likely that the offender will offend again, increased that danger'. This statement is weakened by its vague reference to 'a risk', but it is clear that Woolf LJ and Judge Tumim intended it in a stronger sense which echoes the 1990 White Paper: 'imprisonment provides many opportunities to learn criminal skills from other inmates'. No criminological study has been constructed to test whether prison causes crime by facilitating the spread of criminal know-how, but there are research findings which show that a person is more likely to be reconvicted, the more custodial sentences he has served (Walker, 1985). Moreover, there may be psychological and social consequences of imprisonment. The degradation of being stripped of one's possessions on entry to prison; the social, sexual and other deprivations entailed by the prison regime; the **stultifying** effect of prison regimes; the difficulty of reintegration into society – all these might be expected to affect many prisoners psychologically. Nigel Walker shows that much of the evidence for these effects is anecdotal and descriptive rather than rigorously tested, and more applicable to long-term than other prisoners. His contention is that there is virtually no evidence that these effects, even if they do occur, persist long after the prisoner's release. The drift of Walker's argument is to criticise the tendency of some to exaggerate the unwanted side-effects of custody. His **critique** leaves unexplained the finding of David Farrington and Chris Nuttall (1980) that those who had spent most of their sentences in overcrowded prisons had reconviction rates higher than expectation. In overall terms the reconviction rates following prison are similar to those for most forms of community sentence: prison is neither significantly better, nor significantly worse.

(b) Doubts about the Preventive Effect of Custody

The present [at the time of writing, 1995] Home Secretary, Michael Howard, has proclaimed that 'prison works'. This can hardly be a reference to deterrence or to rehabilitation, since the reconviction figures within two years give no cause for encouragement in that respect. It may be true to say that 'prison works' because it succeeds in incapacitating almost all prisoners (except the very few who escape) for the duration of their sentences. But this hardly seems a persuasive basis for penal policy, since (a) it is a short-sighted kind of effectiveness when so many of the prisoners then reoffend when they are released; (b) it is especially short-sighted in view of the Home Secretary's commitment to **austerity** in prisons rather than to more progressive policies; and (c) the impact of keeping these offenders in prison is slight in terms of additional security for the ordinary citizen since . . . fewer than 3% of offences result in conviction, and many of those [convicted] are not sentenced to imprisonment. It follows that the threat to a citizen's safety and security is not likely to be diminished significantly by imprisoning 50,000 rather than 40,000 people. When in the United States the National Academy of Sciences investigated the **incapacitative effect** of imprisonment on the crime rate, they found it to be marginal. It is therefore clear that the preventive effects of custody are frequently over-estimated.

(c) Humanitarian Concerns

The arguments just considered are tied to **efficacy**. Prison appears rather ineffective at rehabilitating or deterring many of the offenders who experience it. However, 'effectiveness' in terms of crime control is unlikely to provide the major justification for imprisonment, which has come to be regarded as a basic social institution in the last 150 years. David Garland argues that 'like all complex institutions, the prison simultaneously pursues a number of objectives and is kept in place by a range of forces'. It may have a **symbolic** and general **deterrent** function. We have seen that its incapacitative effects are limited to the duration of the sentence for those **incarcerated**. And it is commonly regarded as the most punitive way in which modern society ought to deal with criminals. It is not, therefore, instrumental in a single sense, and arguments for restraint in its use must take a wider sweep. A fourth argument is that prison constitutes such a severe **abridgement** of a person's ordinary rights that it should for that reason be kept to a minimum.

The humanitarian line of argument manifests itself in different forms. It has sometimes been argued that imprisonment should be used less because the prisons are overcrowded. There is some logic in this: a given number of months' incarceration in overcrowded conditions may be as punitive as a longer period in less unpleasant conditions. It coheres with respect for human rights, and in the United States the constitutional rights of inmates have been invoked to limit the number of inmates held in certain prison systems (Rutherford, 1988). But it is essentially a temporary argument, which does not relate to the inevitable pains of imprisonment. Overcrowding could be removed by a massive programme of prison building. If we suddenly had fifty or sixty thousand prison places available, the principle of restraint in the use of imprisonment would be **impotent** if reliant on this particular argument. Another form of the humanitarian argument is that conditions in English prisons in the 1980s and 1990s have been and are so deficient in basic respect for the dignity and well-being of inmates that custody must be used less. In view of the continuing overcrowding in local prisons, it seems inevitable that their conditions will amount to 'inhuman or degrading punishment' contrary to article 3 of the European Convention on Human Rights for some time to come (Evans and Morgan, 1992), and it is right that such conditions should be inflicted on as few people as possible, if any. Indeed, strictly interpreted, it is an argument for the immediate enactment of the Woolf Committee's prison capacity constraint. If the current proposals, by senior judges and others, to enact the European Convention into English law were to come to fruition, English judges might find themselves in the same position as some US judges, having the power either to close certain prisons or at least to require them to admit only a given number of prisoners. As an argument for restraint, this is tied to **contemporary** prison conditions and does not yield a general argument for restricting the use of custody.

A more compelling line of reasoning stems from the inevitable pains of imprisonment. Of course it must be related to an actual prison system rather than a **hypothetical** one. Perhaps, therefore, the crucial question would be: if all the prison reforms proposed by Woolf had been implemented, would there still be a case for the principle of restraint? In favour of an affirmative answer, one can cite the fact that custody entails a deprivation of freedom of movement, which is one of the most basic rights. Loss of that right takes away the freedom to associate with one's family and friends, and separates one from home and also open society. Prison also involves, in almost all regimes, deprivation of the ability to make many decisions about one's day-to-day life. It is therefore a severe restriction on ordinary human liberties, far above those imposed by most non-custodial sentences. These considerations suggest that custody should not be used without some special reasons, and should be reserved for the most serious cases of lawbreaking. In particular, they suggest that custody should not simply be seen as the top rung of a ladder which starts with discharges and fines, and runs upward through probation, curfews and community service orders. The imposition of a custodial sentence restricts liberty to a far greater degree than any other sentence, and for that reason should require special justification.

(d) The Proportionality Argument

A further argument for restraint in the use of custody derives from **proportionality**. In principle, custodial sentences should be reserved for those offences which are serious enough to justify the deprivation of liberty. We will see, when discussing s 1(2)(a) of the 1991 Act . . . , that the courts have not succeeded in respecting this principle. At a theoretical level it is possible to grade forms of punishment according to their relative severity, and to argue that for certain crimes any custodial sentence, or a custodial sentence of a given length, is plainly disproportionate. So, in relating to a run-of-the-mill shop theft to a value of £50 or £100, one could argue that the harm done by the offender to the interests of the victim or the public cannot fairly be compared to the deprivations imposed on the offender by a sentence of, say, six months' imprisonment. That argument becomes even stronger when account is taken of the poor conditions in which such short sentences are typically served in English prisons. The same argument can be developed more generally to place proportionality constraints on resorting to custodial sentences.

(e) Restraint or Abolition?

The above arguments for restraint might be stiffened in order to present a case for abolishing prisons altogether. After all, little has yet been said in favour of prisons as an essential part of the penal system, and some authors such as Thomas Mathieson have campaigned for abolition. Would anything of value be lost if there were no prisons? Many would argue that an underlying general deterrent would be lost, and that lawbreaking would increase if offenders knew that in no circumstances could they be incarcerated. That **assertion** is largely unproven, and there is little evidence that reductions in the level of prison use have produced increased in offending, although that is not quite the same thing. Another counter-argument is that prison will always be necessary for the incapacitation of a relatively small number of dangerous offenders. The evidence on incapacitation is hardly encouraging, but as often said some persistent violent or sexual offenders would present a tremendous risk if allowed to remain in the community. How would the abolitionists deal with these points? Their answer would be grounded in fundamental social reforms which would remove the inequalities which seem associated with much offending; in devising new methods of containing even serious and unpredictable offenders in the community and altering attitudes towards offending; and in greater commitment to victim work (Mathieson, 1990). Some would go further and propose a restorative approach to criminal justice, which would break free from the present emphasis on state prosecution and punishment (eg Wright, 1991).

Whether abolition could be realised without social catastrophe must be a matter for **conjecture**. It seems to be quite unreal as a practical aim in the foreseeable future in most Western nations, if only because the alternative strategies of widespread social reform or completely restorative systems of criminal justice seem unlikely to occur on the required scale. Thinking people who are concerned about criminal justice should be aware of the arguments, but it is more realistic to consider ways of reducing reliance on imprisonment . . .

In April 1996 the government issued a White Paper, *Protecting the Public,* which made out a case for increased use of imprisonment in certain circumstances:

Chapter 11 MANDATORY MINIMUM PRISON SENTENCES FOR DRUG DEALERS

11.1 The Government proposes that the court should be required to impose a mandatory minimum prison sentence of 7 years on offenders aged 18 or over who are convicted of drug trafficking offences involving class A drugs and who have two or more previous convictions for similar offences, unless there are genuinely exceptional circumstances. The courts would, of course, retain the discretion to impose higher sentences in appropriate cases.

11.2 Chapter 4 described the Government's comprehensive strategy on tackling drugs. Severe deterrent sentences for those who deal in hard drugs are an essential element of this strategy. The Government has increased the maximum penalties for trafficking offences involving class A drugs to life imprisonment – but the dealers need to know that if they continue offending they will on conviction automatically go to prison for a very long time. This is what the new proposals are designed to achieve.

11.3 The key elements of the Government's proposal are as follows:

- it will apply to drug trafficking offences involving class A drugs excluding simple possession and offences relating to the proceeds of drug trafficking. The principal offences covered by the proposal are therefore:
  - offences of production, supply and possession for supply of class A drugs (sections 4 and 5 of the Misuse of Drugs Act 1971);
  - an offence of assisting in or inducing the commission outside the UK of an offence relating to a class A drug which is punishable under a corresponding law (section 20 of the 1971 Act);
  - offences of importing or exporting a class A drug (section 3 of the 1971 Act);
  - offences of manufacturing or supplying certain substances useful for manufacturing controlled drugs or using a ship for illicit traffic in class A drugs contrary to the Criminal Justice (International Co-operation) Act 1990;
  - an offence of conspiracy to commit any of those offences under s 1 of the Criminal Law Act 1977;
  - an offence of attempting to commit any of those offences under s 1 of the Criminal Attempts Act 1981;
  - an offence of inciting another person to commit any of those offences, whether under section 19 of the 1971 Act or at common law; and
  - aiding, abetting, counselling or procuring the commission of any of those offences;
- any previous convictions for relevant offences will count as qualifying convictions, including convictions as a young offender, convictions prior to commencement and convictions which are 'spent' under the Rehabilitation of Offenders Act 1974;
- the mandatory minimum sentence must be imposed where the third qualifying conviction, which triggers the mandatory penalty, relates to an offence which was committed after commencement. The offender must also have been at least 18 years old when he or she committed the final qualifying offence (although not necessarily the first two);
- the three qualifying convictions must relate to separate court appearances. Each of the qualifying convictions must relate to an offence

committed after the previous conviction. This means that if an offender with no previous convictions was convicted of three drug trafficking offences at one court appearance, or two offences at one appearance and a third on a separate occasion, that would not trigger a mandatory minimum sentence;

- where an offender is liable to a mandatory sentence, the court will be required to impose a sentence of at least 7 years. However, the mandatory minimum sentence is just that: a minimum. The court will retain the discretion to impose a higher sentence in appropriate cases;
- the court will also have discretion not to pass the mandatory minimum sentence in genuinely exceptional cases. This is intended to allow for occasional quite unforeseeable circumstances where it would plainly be unjust and unnecessary to impose the mandatory sentence. But it should be emphasised that this provision will be designed to cover only genuinely exceptional cases – it will certainly not be open to the courts to set aside the mandatory sentence merely because it is higher than the sentence they would otherwise have been minded to impose. The court will be required to explain what were the exceptional circumstances which justified setting aside the mandatory sentence; and
- if an offender who has already received a mandatory sentence is convicted of a fourth or subsequent offence, which was committed after the mandatory sentence was imposed, he or she will receive a further mandatory sentence. In such cases it may be appropriate for the court to consider imposing a higher sentence than the mandatory minimum.

11.4 The White Paper *Tackling Drugs Together* charts a comprehensive strategy for attacking the drugs problem in England over the period 1995–98. Good progress is being made – arrests, convictions and drug seizures all bear witness to ever more effective enforcement against those involved in the supply and trafficking of drugs. But the police and Customs also need the full support of the courts. We are determined that those who persist in trading in human misery and ruined lives should get the punishment they richly deserve – a very long prison sentence. The Government's new proposals will make sure that is exactly what happens.

Chapter 12 MANDATORY MINIMUM PRISON SENTENCES FOR BURGLARS

12.1 The Government proposes that the court should be required to impose a **mandatory** minimum prison sentence of 3 years on offenders aged 18 or over who are convicted of domestic burglary and have two or more previous convictions for similar offences, unless there are genuinely exceptional circumstances. The courts would, of course, retain the **discretion** to impose higher sentences in appropriate cases.

12.2 Any burglary is disruptive and frequently costly. But domestic burglary is particularly distressing for victims. It involves the loss of property, sometimes of great sentimental value; considerable expense and inconvenience in sorting out the consequences; and perhaps most of all it leaves victims with the sense that the sanctity of their home has been violated. For old people, in particular, the fear of burglary and the distress it causes can have a devastating effect on their lives. Burglary is a **pernicious** and **predatory** crime, and sadly one of the most common offences.

[The White Paper here contains a graph showing recorded burglaries of dwellings in England and Wales between 1983 and 1994. The graph demonstrates a steep rise between 1989 and 1993 from just under 450,000 to about 700,000.]

12.3 Severe penalties are available for burglary. The maximum sentence is 14 years for burglary of a dwelling, and 10 years in other cases. In cases of aggravated burglary – where the offender has a weapon – the maximum penalty is life imprisonment. But in a substantial proportion of cases, the courts do not impose a custodial sentence on convicted burglars even if they have numerous previous convictions (see Fig. 11 . . .). The average sentence length imposed on a sample of offenders convicted for the first time of domestic burglary in 1993 and 1994 and given a custodial sentence was only 16.2 months in the Crown Court and 3.7 months in magistrates' courts. Even after 3 or more convictions, the average sentence imposed on conviction in the Crown Court was only 18.9 months; and after 7 or more convictions, 19.4 months. And 28% of offenders convicted in the Crown Court with 7 or more convictions for domestic burglary were not sent to prison at all. At magistrates' courts, 61% of offenders with 7 or more domestic burglary convictions were given a non-custodial sentence in 1993 and 1994.

12.4 Research shows that most burglars are highly persistent offenders: around 70% of burglars released in 1992 were reconvicted within two years. This demonstrates that the police are achieving good results in targeting persistent burglars (see paragraph 12.5–12.6 below). But it also shows that the penalties imposed on those convicted of burglary, even if they have numerous previous convictions, are not a sufficient deterrent. Too many burglars can hope to escape a prison sentence altogether, or to serve a short sentence before resuming their criminal career. In too many cases, a short spell in prison has become an acceptable risk.

12.5 It is sometimes argued that the likelihood of detection is a more effective deterrent than the severity of punishment. But improving detection rates and imposing stiff sentences are not alternatives: it is necessary to do both. The Metropolitan Police launched Operation Bumblebee in June 1991 – a coordinated and continuing campaign against burglary. The key element of this strategy is the targeting of persistent offenders, using sophisticated techniques developed to combat major crime. In the first phase of Bumblebee in north London, over 8,000 burglaries were solved and 5,000 suspects arrested. Since the **initiative** went force-wide in June 1993, there have been 8 London-wide operations resulting in 5,145 premises being searched and 3,836 people arrested. On 5 December 1995, 12,000 officers from 40 forces carried out Operation Christmas Cracker, which resulted in 3,772 premises being searched. In all 3,327 suspects were arrested and stolen property to the value of £1.8m was recovered.

12.6 There is evidence that the high priority the police are giving to burglary, and the targeting of persistent offenders, are achieving results. But persuading burglars there is a high likelihood that they will be caught is only half the battle. They also need to know they can expect a stiff prison sentence. That is what the new proposals for mandatory minimum sentences are all about.

12.7 The key elements of the Government's proposal are as follows:

- it will apply to offences of burglary or aggravated burglary of a dwelling;
- any previous convictions for relevant offences committed after commencement (but not before commencement) will count as qualifying convictions, including convictions as a young offender and convictions which are 'spent' under the Rehabilitation of Offenders Act 1974;
- the mandatory minimum sentence must be imposed where the three qualifying convictions all relate to offences committed after the new legislation has come into force. Previous convictions imposed before the legislation comes into force will not therefore 'count' as qualifying convictions. The offender must also have been at least 18 years old when he or she committed the final qualifying offence (although not necessarily the first two);
- the three qualifying convictions must relate to separate court appearances. Each of the qualifying convictions must relate to an offence committed after the previous conviction. This means that if an offender with no previous convictions was convicted of three offences of burglary at one court appearance, or two offences at one appearance and a third on a separate occasion, that would not trigger a mandatory minimum sentence;
- where an offender is liable to a mandatory sentence, the court will be required to impose a sentence of at least 3 years. However, the mandatory minimum sentence is just that: a minimum. The court will retain the discretion to impose a higher sentence in appropriate cases;
- the court will also have discretion not to pass the mandatory minimum sentence in genuinely exceptional cases. This is intended to allow for occasional quite unforeseeable circumstances where it would plainly be unjust and unnecessary to impose the mandatory sentence. But it should be emphasised that this provision will be designed to cover only genuinely exceptional cases – it will certainly not be open to the courts to set aside the mandatory sentence merely because it is higher than the sentence they would otherwise have been minded to impose. The court will be required to explain what were the exceptional circumstances which justified setting aside the mandatory sentence; and if an offender

who has already received a mandatory sentence is convicted of a fourth or subsequent offence, which was committed after the mandatory sentence was imposed, he or she will receive a further mandatory sentence. In such cases it may be appropriate for the court to consider imposing a higher sentence than the mandatory minimum.

12.8 The police will continue to give high priority to targeting known burglars – and nearly 38,000 burglars were convicted in 1994. Coordinated, large scale operations such as Bumblebee and Christmas Cracker will continue. Professional burglars already know there is a strong likelihood that sooner or later they will be caught – the high proportion of such offenders who have previous convictions for similar offences is proof of that. In future they will not be able to hope for a lenient sentence which allows them to walk free after a few months. They will know that if they continue their criminal activities the result will be a stiff prison sentence.
12.9 This White Paper, and the legislation the Government will be introducing to give effect to our proposals, puts burglars on notice. The Government believes these proposals will strongly reinforce the successful efforts the police are making to target some of the most callous and persistent professional criminals in this country. Mandatory minimum sentences for burglary will act as a powerful deterrent. Those who persist regardless will be taken out of circulation for a long time, thus protecting the public from their evil activities. The public is entitled to expect no less.

The proposals set out in the White Paper became law in the Crime (Sentences) Act 1997.

Crime (Sentences) Act 1997

1997 CHAPTER 43

An Act to make further provision with respect to the treatment of offenders; and for connected purposes. [21st March 1997]
BE IT ENACTED by the Queen's most Excellent Majesty, by and with the advice and consent of the Lords Spiritual and Temporal, and Commons, in this present Parliament assembled, and by the authority of the same, as follows:—

PART I

MANDATORY AND MINIMUM CUSTODIAL SENTENCES

1.—(1) This section has effect for the purposes of setting out the basis on which the court shall carry out its sentencing functions under this Part.
(2) Under section 2 below, when determining whether it would be appropriate not to impose a life sentence the court shall have regard to the circumstances relating to either of the offences or to the offender.

(3) Under sections 3 and 4 below, when determining whether it would be appropriate not to impose a custodial sentence of at least seven years under section 3(2) or, as the case may be, of at least three years under section 4(2) the court shall have regard to the specific circumstances which—

(a) relate to any of the offences or to the offender; and
(b) would make the prescribed custodial sentence unjust in all the circumstances.

2.—(1) This section applies where—

(a) a person is convicted of a serious offence committed after the commencement of this section; and
(b) at the time when that offence was committed, he was 18 or over and had been convicted in any part of the United Kingdom of another serious offence.

(2) The court shall impose a life sentence, that is to say—

(a) where the person is 21 or over, a sentence of imprisonment for life;
(b) where he is under 21, a sentence of custody for life under section 8(2) of the Criminal Justice Act 1982 ('the 1982 Act'),

unless the court is of the opinion that there are exceptional circumstances relating to either of the offences or to the offender which justify its not doing so.
(3) Where the court does not impose a life sentence, it shall state in open court that it is of that opinion and what the exceptional circumstances are.
(4) An offence the sentence for which is imposed under subsection (2) above shall not be regarded as an offence the sentence for which is fixed by law.
(5) An offence committed in England and Wales is a serious offence for the purposes of this section if it is any of the following, namely—

(a) an attempt to commit murder, a conspiracy to commit murder or an incitement to murder;
(b) an offence under section 4 of the Offences Against the Person Act 1861 (soliciting murder);
(c) manslaughter;
(d) an offence under section 18 of the Offences Against the Person Act 1861 (wounding, or causing grievous bodily harm, with intent);
(e) rape or an attempt to commit rape;
(f) an offence under section 5 of the Sexual Offences Act 1956 (intercourse with a girl under 13);
(g) an offence under section 16 (possession of a firearm with intent to injure), section 17 (use of a firearm to resist arrest) or section 18 (carrying a firearm with criminal intent) of the Firearms Act 1968; and

(h) robbery where, at some time during the commission of the offence, the offender had in his possession a firearm or imitation firearm within the meaning of that Act.

[Subsections 6 and 7 relate to equivalent offences in Scotland and Northern Ireland.]

3.—(1) This section applies where—

(a) a person is convicted of a class A drug trafficking offence committed after the commencement of this section;
(b) at the time when that offence was committed, he was 18 or over and had been convicted in any part of the United Kingdom of two other class A drug trafficking offences; and
(c) one of those other offences was committed after he had been convicted of the other.

(2) The court shall impose a custodial sentence for a term of at least seven years except where the court is of the opinion that there are specific circumstances which—

(a) relate to any of the offences or to the offender; and
(b) would make the prescribed custodial sentence unjust in all the circumstances.

(3) Where the court does not impose such a sentence, it shall state in open court that it is of that opinion and what the specific circumstances are.

(4) Where—

(a) a person is charged with a class A drug trafficking offence (which, apart from this subsection, would be triable either way); and
(b) the circumstances are such that, if he were convicted of the offence, he could be sentenced for it under subsection (2) above, the offence shall be triable only on indictment.

(5) In this section 'class A drug trafficking offence' means a drug trafficking offence committed in respect of a class A drug; and for this purpose—

'class A drug' has the same meaning as in the Misuse of Drugs Act 1971; 'drug trafficking offence' means a drug trafficking offence within the meaning of the Drug Trafficking Act 1994, the Proceeds of Crime (Scotland) Act 1995 or the Proceeds of Crime (Northern Ireland) Order 1996.

(6) In this section and section 4 below 'custodial sentence' means—

(a) in relation to a person who is 21 or over, a sentence of imprisonment;
(b) in relation to a person who is under 21, a sentence of detention in a young offender institution.

4.—(1) This section applies where—

(a) a person is convicted of a domestic burglary committed after the commencement of this section;
(b) at the time when that burglary was committed, he was 18 or over and had been convicted in England and Wales of two other domestic burglaries; and
(c) one of those other burglaries was committed after he had been convicted of the other, and both of them were committed after the commencement of this section.

(2) The court shall impose a custodial sentence for a term of at least three years except where the court is of the opinion that there are specific circumstances which—

(a) relate to any of the offences or to the offender; and
(b) would make the prescribed custodial sentence unjust in all the circumstances.

(3) Where the court does not impose such a sentence, it shall state in open court that it is of that opinion and what the specific circumstances are.
(4) Where—

(a) a person is charged with a domestic burglary which, apart from this subsection, would be triable either way; and
(b) the circumstances are such that, if he were convicted of the burglary, he could be sentenced for it under subsection (2) above,

the burglary shall be triable only on indictment.
(5) In this section 'domestic burglary' means a burglary committed in respect of a building or part of a building which is a dwelling.

Check your understanding

1 Can you explain the meaning of the words and phrases in **bold** type?

2 What do the expressions 'triable either way' and 'triable only on indictment' mean?

3 Can you explain the difference between 'policy issues' and 'practice issues' in sentencing?

Things to do

1 Part of the raw material for research into sentencing comes from government statistics, published at regular intervals and available in reference libraries. Have a look at *Criminal Statistics in England and Wales*, published annually by the Home Office. Try making statements about

particular offences or types of offender and supporting that statement with something from the statistics.

2 Imagine you are a judge who will be trying defendants to whom the Crime (Sentences) Act 1997 might apply. Construct yourself a flowchart to guide you through the Act's provisions. It might be simpler to deal with the relevant offences separately.

Discuss

1 Assuming that it is a good thing to make less use of imprisonment, devise policies that would result in fewer people being imprisoned and justify those policies.

2 Having regard to your arguments in 1, devise arguments to defend the proposals in the White Paper.

Write

1 Make a list of all the non-custodial sentences available to a court.

2 Summarise Professor Ashworth's arguments.

3 The excerpt from Professor Ashworth's book is academic writing of a very high standard. Notice how the arguments are balanced and how he cites authority for his statements of fact. Choose any topic you like and write a short piece imitating this style. Citation of authority is particularly important when you are writing about the substantive law – *why* is the law what you say it is? Always cite relevant cases and/or statutes in support of your arguments. When you are writing about the legal system, cite any relevant research of which you are aware, reports from the Law Commission, White Papers and opinions you have read in textbooks or newspaper articles.

Connections

1 Look at the excerpt from the Parliamentary debate beginning at p. 17. Hold your own debate on the proposed clause 14, using what you have learned about sentencing policy to construct sound arguments on each side.

2 Sentencing companies presents a different set of problems. Look at p. 151 for some suggested sentences.

3 Which words and phrases in the Crime (Sentences) Act do you consider are likely to give rise to problems of interpretation? What approaches might a court adopt?

PART TWO

Introduction to Part Two

This part of the book consists largely of excerpts from judgments in cases involving three areas of law that form a key part of any law course: crime, tort and contract. The particular excerpts have been chosen because they demonstrate how judges make decisions and their reasons for choosing one solution rather than another.

I am sure you will find the whole of Part Two useful and interesting, even if you are not studying all three of the substantive areas of law at the moment, because the skills you will practise are common to all areas of law. You will find the material more useful if you first look at the relevant area of law in a textbook, to give a basic understanding of the issues and some familiarity with the leading cases. When you have read an excerpt it is a very good idea to begin your work on it by making a note of the facts of the case, the decision, the reason for the decision and the reason for any dissenting judgment. This helps you to direct your mind to the relevant issues and will make subsequent work, whether discussion or written, much easier.

4 Crime

4.1 THE SCOPE OF CRIMINAL LAW

The criminal law is concerned with the relationship between the state and individuals. The state creates criminal offences, usually by **statute**, which forbid certain conduct. What sort of conduct can the state legitimately forbid?

It seems to be agreed that the state can forbid people to kill each other or steal from each other – although this gives rise to problems at the fringes, such as whether an unborn child can be murdered or whether certain things are protected by the law against theft – but there is a continuing difficulty about the extent to which the law should forbid some kinds of conduct. The problem arose in the case of *R v Brown & Others* [1993] 2 All ER 75. The defendants were charged with assault but claimed the defence of consent because the assaults were committed in the course of sado-masochistic practices in which all the defendants were willing participants.

Assaults are generally charged under one of three sections of the Offences Against the Person Act 1861:

s 18 provides that it is an offence 'unlawfully and maliciously by any means whatsoever to wound or cause any grievous bodily harm to any person' either with intent to cause grievous bodily harm to any person or with intent to 'resist or prevent the lawful apprehension or detainer of any person'.

s 20 makes it an offence to 'unlawfully and maliciously wound or inflict any grievous bodily harm upon any other person, either with or without any weapon or instrument'.

s 47 contains the offence of an assault occasioning actual bodily harm.

The question in *Brown* was whether it was possible to plead consent as a defence to such charges. In the House of Lords, Lord Templeman said:

> My Lords, the authorities dealing with the intentional infliction of bodily harm do not establish that consent is a defence to a charge under the 1861

Act [the Offences Against the Person Act 1861]. They establish that the courts have accepted that consent is a defence to the infliction of bodily harm in the course of some lawful activities. The question is whether the defence should be extended to the infliction of bodily harm in the course of sado-masochistic encounters. The **Wolfenden Committee** did not make any recommendations about sado-masochism and Parliament did not deal with violence in 1967 [when homosexual acts between consenting adults were legalised]. The 1967 Act is of no assistance for present purposes because the present problem was not under consideration.

The question whether the defence of consent should be extended to the consequences of sado-masochistic encounters can only be decided by consideration of policy and public interest. Parliament can call on the advice of doctors, psychiatrists, criminologists, sociologists and other experts and can also sound and take into account public opinion. But the question must at this stage be decided by this House in its judicial capacity in order to determine whether the convictions of the appellants should be upheld or quashed.

Counsel for some of the appellants argued that the defence of consent should be extended to the offence of occasioning actual bodily harm under s 47 of the 1861 Act but should not be available to charges of serious wounding and the infliction of serious bodily harm under s 20. I do not consider that this solution is practicable. Sado-masochistic participants have no way of foretelling the degree of bodily harm which will result from their encounters. The differences between actual bodily harm and serious bodily harm cannot be satisfactorily applied by a jury in order to determine acquittal or conviction.

Counsel for the appellants argued that consent should provide a defence to charges under both ss 20 and 47 because, it was said, every person has a right to deal with his body as he pleases. I do not consider that this slogan provides a sufficient guide to the policy decision which must now be made. It is an offence for a person to abuse his own body and mind by taking drugs. Although the law is often broken, the criminal law restrains a practice which is regarded as dangerous and injurious to individuals and which if allowed and extended is harmful to society generally. In any event the appellants in this case did not mutilate their own bodies. They inflicted bodily harm on willing victims. Suicide is no longer an offence but a person who assists another to commit suicide is guilty of murder or manslaughter.

The assertion was made on behalf of the appellants that the sexual appetites of sadists and masochists can only be satisfied by the infliction of bodily harm and that the law should not punish the **consensual** achievement of sexual satisfaction. There was no evidence to support the assertion that sado-masochist activities are essential to the happiness of the appellants or any other participants but the argument would be acceptable if

> sado-masochism were only concerned with sex, as the appellants contend. In my opinion sado-masochism is not only concerned with sex. Sado-masochism is also concerned with violence. The evidence discloses that the practices of the appellants were unpredictably dangerous and degrading to body and mind and were developed with increasing barbarity and taught to persons whose consents were dubious or worthless.

The House of Lords upheld the convictions by a majority of three to two. Lord Mustill gave one of the two **dissenting** judgments. He carefully analysed the law and came to the conclusion that the defendants had not breached the criminal law:

> The purpose of this long discussion has been to suggest that the decks are clear for the House to tackle completely anew the question whether the public interest requires s 47 of the 1861 Act to be interpreted as penalising an infliction of harm which is at the level of actual bodily harm, but not grievous bodily harm; which is inflicted in private (by which I mean that it is exposed to the view only of those who have chosen to view it); which takes place not only with the consent of the recipient but with his willing and glad co-operation; which is inflicted for the gratification of sexual desire, and not in a spirit of animosity or rage; and which is not engaged in for profit.
>
> My Lords, I have stated the issue in these terms to stress two considerations of cardinal importance. Lawyers will need no reminding of the first, but since this prosecution has been widely noticed it must be emphasised that the issue before the House is not whether the appellants' conduct is morally right, but whether it is properly charged under the 1861 Act. When proposing that the conduct is not rightly so charged I do not invite your Lordships' House to indorse it as morally acceptable. Nor do I pronounce in favour of a **libertarian** doctrine specifically related to sexual matters. Nor in the least do I suggest that ethical pronouncements are meaningless, that there is no difference between right and wrong, that sadism is praiseworthy, or that new opinions on sexual morality are necessarily superior to the old, or anything else of the same kind. What I do say is that these are questions of private morality; that the standards by which they fall to be judged are not those of the criminal law; and that if these standards are to be upheld the individual must enforce them upon himself according to his own moral standards, or have them enforced against him by moral pressures exerted by whatever religious or other community to whose ethical ideals he responds. The point from which I invite your Lordships to depart is simply this, that the state should interfere with the rights of an individual to live his or her life as he or she may choose no more than is necessary to ensure a proper balance between the special interests of the individual and the general interests of the individuals who together comprise the populace

at large. Thus, whilst acknowledging that very many people, if asked whether the appellants' conduct was wrong, would reply 'Yes, repulsively wrong', I would at the same time assert that this does not in itself mean that the prosecution of the appellants under ss 20 and 47 of the Offences Against the Person Act 1861 is well founded.

This point leads directly to the second. As I have ventured to formulate the crucial question, it asks whether there is good reason to impress upon s 47 an interpretation which **penalises** the relevant level of harm irrespective of consent: ie to recognise sado-masochistic activities as falling into a special category of acts, such as duelling and prize-fighting, which 'the law says shall not be done'. This is very important, for if the question were differently stated it might well yield a different answer. In particular, if it were to be held that as a matter of law all infliction of bodily harm above the level of common assault is incapable of being legitimated by consent, except in special circumstances, then we would have to consider whether the public interest required the recognition of private sexual activities as being in a specially exempt category. This would be an altogether more difficult question and one which I would not be prepared to answer in favour of the appellants, not because I do not have my own opinions upon it but because I regard the task as one which the courts are not suited to perform, and which should be carried out, if at all, by Parliament after a thorough review of all the medical, social, moral and political issues, such as was performed by the Wolfenden Committee . . .

. . . in the answer which I propose I do not advocate the decriminalisation of conduct which has hitherto been a crime; nor do I rebut a submission that a new crime should be created, penalising this conduct . . . The only question is whether these consensual private acts are offences against the existing law of violence. To this question I return a negative response.

Accordingly I would allow these appeals and quash such of the convictions as are now before the House.

Check your understanding

1 Can you explain the meaning of the words and phrases in **bold** type? Are there any other words you need to look up in a dictionary?

2 Look at ss 20 and 47 of the Offences Against the Person Act 1861. Make sure you understand the difference between them. Why would a s 18 charge be inappropriate in this case?

3 Note that the House of Lords has two functions: it is a legislative body and a judicial body. The judicial function is carried out by a group of about twelve senior judges, sitting as a Committee.

Discuss

1 What does Lord Templeman mean by the words 'policy and public interest' (p. 90)? Is he referring to two concepts or one?

2 Note Lord Templeman's use of the word 'slogan' (p. 90). Why do you think he uses this word?

3 Lord Mustill draws a clear distinction between what is morally right and what is a criminal offence. Discuss where the line should be drawn, having regard to as wide a range of activities as possible: in other words, bear in mind that this distinction goes beyond issues such as sex and drugs.

4 Organise a debate: 'This House urges Parliament to legislate forthwith to make sado-masochistic activities, conducted in private and with consent, legal.'

Write

1 Summarise the reasons Lord Templeman and Lord Mustill give for their decisions.

2 Essay: 'Discuss the proposition that the prevention of harm to others is the only proper objective of the criminal law.'

Connections

1 Lord Templeman considers he is making a policy decision and Lord Mustill that he is avoiding doing so. Consider their stances as examples of what Simon Lee is discussing at p. 40ff.

2 Look at the comments about value-laden language at p. 67. Read these judgments again, taking particular note of the language each judge uses. Can you identify any value-laden language? Try rewriting the material without the use of such language.

3 Lord Templeman refers to 'persons whose consents were dubious or worthless'. The issue of what amounts to valid consent arises in connection with the law of contract (see p. 249) and the law of tort (see p. 205). In the context of any of these areas of law, when might consent be regarded as 'dubious or worthless'?

4 Note that Lord Mustill's judgment is *obiter* because it is a dissenting judgment. What other *obiter* material can you find in excerpts from judgments in this book?

4.2 ELEMENTS OF A CRIME

In his judgment in *R v Brown & Others* (p. 91), Lord Mustill draws a distinction between conduct that is morally wrong and conduct that is criminal. He came to the conclusion in that case that what the defendants had done was not covered by the Offences Against the Person Act 1861 and was therefore not criminal.

Actus reus and mens rea

Lawyers make decisions about whether particular conduct falls within the wording of a statute by analysing the content of the offence. The offence is broken down into its constituent parts, which are grouped according to whether they are part of the physical manifestation of the offence or concerned with the defendant's mental processes. These two groups are labelled *actus reus* and *mens rea.* In the case of *Miller* [1983] 1 All ER 978 Lord Diplock explained these phrases, making the point that the actus reus may consist of something a defendant failed to do. The judgment is given in its entirety because it is a reasonably short one and a good example of the structure of judgments generally:

> My Lords, the facts which give rise to this appeal are sufficiently narrated in the written statement made to the police by the appellant Miller. That statement, subject to two minor **orthographical** corrections, reads:
>
> > 'Last night I went out for a few drinks and at closing time I went back to the house where I have been kipping for a couple of weeks. I went upstairs into the back bedroom where I've been sleeping. I lay on my mattress and lit a cigarette. I must have fell to sleep because I woke up to find the mattress on fire. I just got up and went into the next room and went back to sleep. Then the next thing I remember was the police and fire people arriving. I hadn't got anything to put the fire out with so I just left it.'
>
> He was charged on indictment with the offence of 'arson contrary to section 1(1) and (3) of the Criminal Damage Act, 1971'; the particulars of the offence were that he—
>
> > 'on a date unknown between the 13th and 16th days of August 1980, without lawful excuse damaged by fire a house known as No. 9 Grantham Road, Sparkbrook, intending to do damage to such property or recklessly as to whether such property would be damaged.'
>
> He was tried in the Crown Court at Leicester before a recorder and a jury. He did not give evidence, and the facts as set out in his statement

were not disputed. He was found guilty and sentenced to six months' imprisonment.

From his conviction he appealed to the Court of Appeal on the ground, which is one of law alone, that the undisputed facts did not disclose any offence under s 1 of the Criminal Damage Act 1971. This appeal was dismissed . . . but leave to appeal to your Lordships' House was granted by the Court of Appeal, which certified that the following question of law of general public importance was involved:

> 'Whether the actus reus of the offence of arson is present when a Defendant accidentally starts a fire and thereafter, intending to destroy or damage property belonging to another or being reckless as to whether any such property would be destroyed or damaged, fails to take any steps to extinguish the fire or prevent damage to such property by that fire?'

The question speaks of 'actus reus'. This expression is derived from Coke's **brocard** (3 Co Inst ch 1, fo 10), 'Actus non facit reum, nisi mens sit rea,' by converting incorrectly into an adjective the word reus which was there used correctly in the accusative case as a noun. As long ago as 1889 in *R v Tolson* 23 QBD 168 at 185–187, [1886–90] All ER Rep 26 at 36–37 Stephen J when dealing with a statutory offence, as are your Lordships in the instant case, condemned the phrase as likely to mislead, though his criticism in that case was primarily directed to the use of the expression 'mens rea'. In the instant case, as the argument before this House has in my view demonstrated, it is the use of the expression 'actus reus' that is liable to mislead, since it suggests that some positive act on the part of the accused is needed to make him guilty of a crime and that a failure or omission to act is insufficient to give rise to criminal liability unless some express provision in the statute that creates the offence so provides.

My Lords, it would I think be conducive to clarity of analysis of the ingredients of a crime that is created by statute, as are the great majority of criminal offences today, if we were to avoid bad Latin and instead to think and speak (as did Stephen J in those parts of his judgment in *R v Tolson* to which I referred at greater length in *Sweet v Parsley* [1969] 1 All ER 347 at 361, [1970] AC 132 at 162–163) about the conduct of the accused and his state of mind at the time of that conduct, instead of speaking of actus reus and mens rea.

Tolson concerned a woman charged with bigamy. She was found not guilty because she had reasonable grounds to believe and did honestly believe that her first husband was dead at the time of her second marriage. *Sweet v Parsley* concerned a woman who let a house. She was convicted of being concerned in the management of premises used for smoking cannabis but the House of Lords decided she was not guilty as the offence required mens rea and she did not know that cannabis was being smoked in the house.

The question before your Lordships in this appeal is one that is confined to the true construction of the words used in particular provisions in a particular statute, viz s 1(1) and (3) of the Criminal Damage Act 1971. Those particular provisions will fall to be construed in the light of general principles of English criminal law so well established that it is the practice of parliamentary draftsmen to leave them unexpressed in criminal statutes, on the confident assumption that a court of law will treat those principles as intended by Parliament to be applicable to the particular offence unless expressly modified or excluded. But this does not mean that your Lordships are doing any more than construing the particular statutory provisions. These I now set out:

> '(1) A person who without lawful excuse destroys or damages any property belonging to another intending to destroy or damage any such property or being reckless as to whether any such property would be destroyed or damaged shall be guilty of an offence . . .
> (3) An offence committed under this section by destroying or damaging property by fire shall be charged as arson.'

This definition of arson makes it a 'result-crime' in the classification adopted by Professor Gordon in his work *The Criminal Law of Scotland* (2nd edn, 1978). The crime is not complete unless and until the conduct of the accused has caused property belonging to another to be destroyed or damaged.

In the instant case property belonging to another, the house, was damaged; it was not destroyed. So in the interest of **brevity** it will be convenient to refer to damage to property and omit reference to destruction. I should also mention, in **parenthesis**, that in this appeal your Lordships are concerned only with the completed crime of arson, not with related **inchoate offences** such as attempt or conspiracy to destroy or damage property belonging to another, to which somewhat different considerations will apply. Nor does this appeal raise any question of 'lawful excuse'. None was suggested.

The first question to be answered where a completed crime of arson is charged is: did a physical act of the accused start the fire which spread and damaged property belonging to another (or did his act cause an existing fire, which he had not started but which would otherwise have burned itself out harmlessly, to spread and damage property belonging to another)? I have added the words in brackets for completeness. They do not arise in the instant case; in cases where they do, the accused, for the purposes of the analysis which follows, may be regarded as having started a fresh fire.

The first question is a pure question of **causation**; it is one of fact to be decided by the jury in a trial on indictment. It should be answered No if, in relation to the fire during the period starting immediately before its ignition and ending with its extinction, the role of the accused was at no time more than that of a passive bystander. In such a case the subsequent questions to which I shall be turning would not arise. The conduct of the **parabolical** priest and Levite on the road to Jericho may have been indeed deplorable, but English law has not so far developed to the stage of treating it as criminal; and if it ever were to do so there would be difficulties in defining what should be the limits of the offence.

If, on the other hand, the question which I now confine to: 'Did a physical act of the accused start the fire which spread and damaged property belonging to another' is answered 'Yes', as it was by the jury in the instant case, then for the purpose of the further questions the answers to which are determinative of his guilt of the offence of arson, the conduct of the accused, throughout the period from immediately before the moment of ignition to the completion of the damage to the property by the fire, is relevant; so is his state of mind throughout that period.

Since arson is a result-crime the period may be considerable, and during it the conduct of the accused that is causative of the result may consist not only of his doing physical acts which cause the fire to start or spread but also of his failing to take measures that lie within his power to counteract the danger that he has himself created. And if his conduct, active or passive, varies in the course of the period, so may his state of mind at the time of each piece of conduct. If, at the time of any particular piece of conduct by the accused that is causative of the result, the state of mind that actuates his conduct falls within the description of one or other of the states of mind that are made a necessary ingredient of the offence of arson by s 1(1) of the Criminal Damage Act 1971 (ie intending to damage property belonging to another or being reckless whether such property would be damaged), I know of no principle of English criminal law that would prevent his being guilty of the offence created by that subsection. Likewise I see no rational ground for excluding from conduct capable of giving rise to criminal liability conduct which consists of failing to take measures that lie within one's power to counteract a danger that one had oneself created, if at the time of such conduct one's state of mind is such as constitutes a necessary ingredient of the offence. I venture to think that the habit of lawyers to talk of 'actus reus', suggestive as it is of action rather than inaction, is responsible for any erroneous notion that failure to act cannot give rise to criminal liability in English law.

No one has been bold enough to suggest that if, in the instant case, the accused had been aware at the time that he dropped the cigarette that it would probably set fire to his mattress and yet had taken no steps to extinguish it he would not have been guilty of the offence of arson, since he would have damaged property of another being reckless whether any such property would be damaged.

I cannot see any good reason why, so far as liability under criminal law is concerned, it should matter at what point of time before the resultant damage is complete a person becomes aware that he has done a physical act which, whether or not he appreciated that it would at the time when he did it, does in fact create a risk that property of another will be damaged, provided that, at the moment of awareness, it lies within his power to take steps, either himself or by calling for the assistance of the fire brigade if this be necessary, to prevent or minimise the damage to the property at risk.

Let me take first the case of the person who has thrown away a lighted cigarette expecting it to go out harmlessly, but later becomes aware that, although he did not intend it to do so, it has, in the event, caused some inflammable material to smoulder and that unless the smouldering is extinguished promptly, an act that the person who dropped the cigarette could perform without danger to himself or difficulty, the inflammable material will be likely to burst into flames and damage some other person's property. The person who dropped the cigarette deliberately refrains from doing anything to extinguish the smouldering. His reason for so refraining is that he intends that the risk which his own act had originally created, though it was only subsequently that he became aware of this, should **fructify** in actual damage to that other person's property; and what he so intends in fact occurs. There can be no sensible reason why he should not be guilty of arson. If he would be guilty of arson, having appreciated the risk of damage at the very moment of dropping the lighted cigarette, it would be quite irrational that he should *not* be guilty if he first appreciated the risk at some later point in time but when it was still possible for him to take steps to prevent or minimise the damage.

In that example the state of mind involved was that described in the definition of the statutory offence as 'intending' to damage property belonging to another. This state of mind necessarily connotes an appreciation by the accused that the situation that he has by his own act created involves the risk that property belonging to another will be damaged. This is not necessarily so with the other state of mind, described in the definition of the statutory offence as 'being reckless as to whether any such property would be damaged'. To this other state of mind I now turn; it is the state of mind which is directly involved in the instant case. Where the state of mind relied on by the prosecution is that of 'intending', the risk of damage to property belonging to another created by the physical act of the accused need not be such as would be obvious to anyone who took the trouble to give his mind to it; but the accused himself cannot form the intention that it would fructify in actual damage unless *he himself* recognises the existence of some risk of this happening. In contrast to this, where the state of mind relied on is 'being reckless', the risk created by the physical act of the accused that property belonging to another would be damaged must be one that would be obvious to anyone who had given his mind to it at whatever is the relevant time for determining whether the state of mind of the accused fitted the description 'being reckless whether such property would be damaged': see *R v Caldwell* [1981] 1 All ER 961 at

965, [1982] AC 341 at 352; see also *R v Lawrence* [1981] 1 All ER 974 at 982, [1982] AC 510 at 526 for a similar requirement in the mental element in the statutory offence of reckless driving.

In *R v Caldwell* this House was concerned with what was treated throughout as being a single act of the accused, viz starting a fire in the ground floor room of a residential hotel which caused some damage to it; although, if closer analysis of his conduct, distinct from his state of mind, had been relevant, what he did must have been recognised as consisting of a series of successive acts. Throughout that sequence of acts, however, the state of mind of Caldwell remained unchanged, his acknowledged intention was to damage the hotel and to revenge himself on its owner, and he pleaded guilty to an offence under s 1(1) of the 1971 Act; the question at issue in the appeal was whether in carrying out this avowed intention he was reckless whether the life of another would be thereby endangered, so as to make him guilty also of the more serious offence under s 1(2). This House did not have to consider the case of an accused who, although he becomes aware that, as the result of an initial act of his own, events have occurred that present an obvious risk that property belonging to another will be damaged, only becomes aware of this at some time after he has done the initial act. So the precise language suggested in *R v Caldwell* as appropriate in summing up to a jury in the ordinary run of cases under s 1(1) of the 1971 Act requires some slight adaptation to make it applicable to the particular and unusual facts of the instant case.

My Lords, just as in the first example that I took the fact that the accused's intent to damage the property of another was not formed until, as a result of his initial act in dropping the cigarette, events had occurred which presented a risk that another person's property would be damaged ought not under any sensible system of law to **absolve** him from criminal liability, so too in a case where the relevant state of mind is not intent but recklessness I see no reason in common sense and justice why **mutatis mutandis** a similar principle should not apply to impose criminal liability on him. If in the former case he is criminally liable because he refrains from taking steps that are open to him to try to prevent or minimise the damage caused by the risk he has himself created and he so refrains because he intends such damage to occur, so in the latter case, when as a result of his own initial act in dropping the cigarette events have occurred which would have made it obvious to anyone who troubled to give his mind to them that they presented a risk that another person's property would be damaged, he should likewise be criminally liable if he refrains from taking steps that lie within his power to try and prevent the damage caused by the risk that he himself has created, and so refrains either because he has not given any thought to the possibility of there being any such risk or because, although he has recognised that there was some risk involved, he has none the less decided to take that risk.

My Lords, in the instant case the prosecution did not rely on the state of mind of the accused as being reckless during that part of his conduct that consisted of his lighting and smoking a cigarette while lying on his mattress and falling asleep without extinguishing it. So the jury were not invited to make any finding as to this. What the prosecution did rely on as being reckless was his state of mind during that part of his conduct after he awoke to find that he had set his mattress on fire and that it was smouldering, but did not then take any steps either to try to extinguish it himself or to send for the fire brigade, but simply went into the other room to resume his slumbers, leaving the fire from the already smouldering mattress to spread and to damage that part of the house in which the mattress was.

The recorder, in his **lucid** summing up to the jury (they took 22 minutes only to reach their verdict), told them that the accused, having by his own act started a fire in the mattress which, when he became aware of its existence, presented an obvious risk of damaging the house, became under a duty to take some action to put it out. The Court of Appeal upheld the conviction, but its ratio decidendi appears to be somewhat different from that of the recorder. As I understand the judgment, in effect it treats the whole course of conduct of the accused, from the moment at which he fell asleep and dropped the cigarette onto the mattress until the time the damage to the house by fire was complete, as a continuous act of the accused, and holds that it is sufficient to constitute the statutory offence of arson if at any stage in that course of conduct the state of mind of the accused, when he fails to try to prevent or minimise the damage which will result from his initial act, although it lies within his power to do so, is that of being reckless whether property belonging to another would be damaged.

My Lords, these alternative ways of analysing the legal theory that justifies a decision which has received nothing but commendation for its accord with common sense and justice have, since the publication of the judgment of the Court of Appeal in the instant case, provoked academic controversy. Each theory has distinguished support. Professor J C Smith espouses the 'duty theory' (see [1982] Crim LR 526 at 528); Professor Glanville Williams, who, after the decision of the Divisional Court in *Fagan v Metropolitan Police Comr* [1968] 3 All ER 442, [1969] 1 QB 439 appears to have been attracted by the duty theory, now prefers that of the continuous act (see [1982] Crim LR 773).

In *Fagan v Metropolitan Police* (1968), the defendant accidentally drove his car onto a policeman's foot. This constituted the actus reus of an assault but there was no mens rea. The policeman asked him to remove the car and he failed to do so. Since assault cannot be committed by omission, it was argued that there was no offence – as there was at that point mens rea but no actus reus. The conviction was upheld on the basis that the actus reus was a single continuous act of driving onto the foot and remaining there.

When applied to cases where a person has unknowingly done an act which sets in train events that, when he becomes aware of them, present an obvious risk that property belonging to another will be damaged, both theories lead to an identical result; and since what your Lordships are concerned with is to give guidance to trial judges in their task of summing up to juries, I would for this purpose adopt the duty theory as being the easier to explain to a jury; though I would commend the use of the word 'responsibility', rather than 'duty' which is more appropriate to civil than to criminal law since it suggests an obligation owed to another person, ie the person to whom the endangered property belongs, whereas a criminal statute defines combinations of conduct and state of mind which render a person liable to punishment by the state itself.

While, in the general run of cases of destruction or damage to property belonging to another by fire (or other means) where the prosecution relies on the recklessness of the accused, the direction recommended by this House in *R v Caldwell* is appropriate, in the exceptional case (which is most likely to be one of arson and of which the instant appeal affords a striking example), where the accused is initially unaware that he has done an act that in fact sets in train events which, by the time the accused becomes aware of them, would make it obvious to anyone who troubled to give his mind to them that they present a risk that property belonging to another would be damaged, a suitable direction to the jury would be that the accused is guilty of the offence under s 1(1) of the 1971 Act if, when he does become aware that the events in question have happened as a result of his own act, he does not try to prevent or reduce the risk of damage by his own efforts or if necessary by sending for help from the fire brigade and the reason why he does not is either because he has not given any thought to the possibility of there being any such risk or because having recognised that there was some risk involved he has decided not to try to prevent or reduce it.

So, while deprecating the use of the expression 'actus reus' in the certified question, I would answer that question Yes and would dismiss the appeal.

States of mind

Lord Diplock discusses two different states of mind in this judgment: intent and *Caldwell* recklessness. The state of mind required is laid down by Parliament or, if the offence is a common law offence, by the courts. There are, in fact, five possible states of mind: intent, *Cunningham* recklessness, *Caldwell* recklessness, gross negligence and negligence. The following excerpts explain each of the first four. Negligence is very rarely the basis of a criminal offence.

The issue of exactly what is meant by 'intent' arose in several cases in the mid-1980s:

Nedrick (1986) The defendant had poured petrol through a letter box and set fire to it, killing occupants of the house. The issue was what a jury should be told in order to decide whether the defendant had the intent to kill or cause serious harm.
Moloney (1985) The defendant shot and killed a man during a friendly shotgun loading competition. He pulled the trigger when the loaded gun was pointing at the victim, although he had not specifically aimed the gun at him.
Hancock & Shankland (1986) Two striking miners threw a lump of concrete from a bridge into the path of vehicles taking miners to work. A taxi driver was killed. The defendants claimed they had no intention to kill or cause serious harm: their objective was to frighten working miners.

In *Nedrick* [1986] 3 All ER 1, Lord Lane CJ explained what lawyers mean by 'intent'.

> . . . What then do a jury have to decide so far as the mental element in murder is concerned? They simply have to decide whether the defendant intended to kill or do serious bodily harm. In order to reach that decision the jury must pay regard to all the relevant circumstances, including what the defendant himself said and did.
>
> In the great majority of cases a direction to that effect will be enough, particularly where the defendant's actions amounted to a direct attack on his victim, because in such cases the evidence relating to the defendant's desire or motive will be clear and his intent will have been the same as his desire or motive. But in some cases, of which this is one, the defendant does an act which is manifestly dangerous and as a result someone dies. The primary desire or motive of the defendant may not have been to harm that person, or indeed anyone. In that situation what further directions should a jury be given as to the mental state which they must find to exist in the defendant if murder is to be proved?
>
> We have endeavoured to crystallise the effect of their Lordships' speeches in *R v Moloney* and *R v Hancock* in a way which we hope may be helpful to judges who have to handle this type of case.
>
> It may be advisable first of all to explain to the jury that a man may intend to achieve a certain result whilst at the same time not desiring it to come about. In *R v Moloney* [1985] 1 All ER 1025 at 1037, [1985] AC 905 at 926 Lord Bridge gave an illustration of the distinction:
>
>> 'A man who, at London Airport, boards a plane which he knows to be bound for Manchester, clearly intends to travel to Manchester, even though Manchester is the last place he wants to be and his motive for boarding the plane is simply to escape pursuit.'
>
> The man who knowingly boards the Manchester aircraft wants to go there in the sense that boarding is a voluntary act. His desire to leave London

predominates over his desire not to go to Manchester. When he decides to board the aircraft, if not before, he forms the intention to travel to Manchester.

In *R v Hancock* the House decided that the *R v Moloney* guidelines require a reference to probability. Lord Scarman said ([1986] 1 All ER 641 at 651, [1986] AC 455 at 4730):

> 'They also require an explanation that the greater the probability of a consequence the more likely it is that the consequence was foreseen and that if that consequence was foreseen the greater the probability is that that consequence was also intended.'

When determining whether the defendant had the necessary intent, it may therefore be helpful for a jury to ask themselves two questions. (1) How probable was the consequence which resulted from the defendant's voluntary act? (2) Did he foresee that consequence?

If he did not appreciate that death or serious harm was likely to result from his act, he cannot have intended to bring it about. If he did, but thought that the risk to which he was exposing the person killed was only slight, then it may be easy for the jury to conclude that he did not intend to bring about that result. On the other hand, if the jury are satisfied that at the material time the defendant recognised that death or serious harm would be virtually certain (barring some unforeseen intervention) to result from his voluntary act, then that is a fact from which they may find it easy to infer that he intended to kill or do serious bodily harm, even though he may not have had any desire to achieve that result.

As Lord Bridge said in *R v Moloney* [1985] 1 All ER 1025 at 1036, [1985] AC 905 at 925:

> '. . . the probability of the consequence taken to have been foreseen must be little short of overwhelming before it will suffice to establish the necessary intent.'

Later he uses the expression 'moral certainty' . . . and says, 'will lead to a certain consequence unless something unexpected supervenes to prevent it' . . .

Where the charge is murder and in the rare cases where the simple direction is not enough, the jury should be directed that they are not entitled to **infer** the necessary intention unless they feel sure that death or serious bodily harm was a virtual certainty (barring some unforeseen intervention) as a result of the defendant's actions and that the defendant appreciated that such was the case.

Where a man realises that it is for all practical purposes inevitable that his actions will result in death or serious harm, the **inference** may be irresistible that he intended that result, however little he may have desired or wished it to happen. The decision is one for the jury to be reached on a consideration of all the evidence.'

Until the decision in *Caldwell*, it was believed that the word 'recklessness' had one meaning: that given to it in the case of *Cunningham* [1957] 2 All ER 412. The defendant had pulled a gas meter off a wall in order to steal the money contained in the meter. He had not turned off the gas supply and gas therefore leaked into the adjoining house, endangering the life of a woman who was asleep there. The Court of Appeal's judgment was given by Byrne J, who said:

> Before this court, counsel for the appellant has taken three points, all dependent on the construction of [s 23 of the Offences Against the Person Act 1861, which] provides as follows:
>
>> 'Whosoever shall unlawfully and maliciously administer to or cause to be administered to or taken by any other person any poison or other destructive or noxious thing, so as thereby to endanger the life of such person, or so as thereby to inflict upon such person any grievous bodily harm, shall be guilty of **felony** . . .'
>
> Counsel argued first that mens rea of some kind is necessary. Secondly, that the nature of the mens rea required is that the appellant must intend to do the particular kind of harm that was done, or alternatively that he must foresee that harm may occur, yet nevertheless continue recklessly to do the act. Thirdly, that the learned judge misdirected the jury as to the meaning of the word 'maliciously'. He cited the following cases: *R v Pembliton* (1874) . . . ; *R v Latimer* (1886) . . . ; and *R v Faulkner* (1877) . . . In reply, counsel on behalf of the Crown cited *R v Martin* (1881).
>
> We have considered those cases, and we have also considered, in the light of those cases, the following principle which was propounded by the late Professor C S Kenney in the first edition of his *Outlines of Criminal Law* published in 1902, and repeated in the sixteenth edition, edited by Mr J W Cecil Turner and published in 1952 (**ibid**., at p. 186):
>
>> '. . . in any statutory definition of a crime "malice" must be taken not in the old vague sense of "wickedness" in general, but as requiring either (i) an actual intention to do the particular *kind* of harm that in fact was done, or (ii) recklessness as to whether such harm should occur or not (ie the accused has foreseen that the particular kind of harm might be done, and yet has gone on to take the risk of it). It is neither limited to, nor does it indeed require, any ill-will towards the person injured.'
>
> The same principle is repeated by Mr Turner in his tenth edition of *Russell on Crime*. We think that this is an accurate statement of the law. It derives some support from the judgments of Lord Coleridge CJ and Blackburn J in *R v Pembliton*. In our opinion, the word 'maliciously' in a statutory crime **postulates** foresight of consequence . . .

> . . . In our view, it should have been left to the jury to decide whether, even if the appellant did not intend the injury to Mrs Wade, he foresaw that the removal of the gas meter might cause injury to someone but nevertheless removed it. We are unable to say that a reasonable jury, properly directed as to the meaning of the word 'maliciously' in the context of s 23, would, without doubt, have convicted.
>
> In these circumstances, this court has no alternative but to allow the appeal and quash the conviction.

In summary, therefore, 'maliciously' means 'intentionally or recklessly' and 'recklessly' means realising there was a risk and going on to run that risk.

In 1981 the House of Lords had to consider the meaning of the word 'reckless' in a statute. Caldwell had started a fire at a hotel intentionally. He pleaded guilty to that offence but was further charged with being reckless as to whether life would be endangered. He had been drunk at the time he started the fire and, as well as deciding what the word 'reckless' meant, the House had also to decide whether intoxication was a defence to the charge of recklessly endangering life. All five Law Lords agreed that Caldwell's appeal should be dismissed. Lord Diplock gave the judgment of four of the judges. Whilst he agreed that the appeal should be dismissed, Lord Edmund-Davies disagreed with the reasoning.

Lord Diplock considered that in using the word 'reckless', Parliament had not meant to convey the same meaning as had been ascribed to 'malicious' in *Cunningham*:

> My Lords, I see no warrant for making any such assumption in an Act whose declared purpose is to revise the then existing law as to offences of damage to property, not to **perpetuate** it. 'Reckless' as used in the new statutory definition of the mens rea of these offences is an ordinary English word. It had not by 1971 become a term of legal art with some more limited **esoteric** meaning than that which it bore in ordinary speech, a meaning which surely includes not only deciding to ignore a risk of harmful consequences resulting from one's acts that one has recognised as existing, but also failing to give any thought to whether or not there is any such risk in circumstances where, if any thought were given to the matter, it would be obvious that there was.
>
> If one is attaching labels, the latter state of mind is neither more nor less 'subjective' than the first. But the label solves nothing. It is a statement of the obvious; mens rea is, by definition, a state of mind of the accused himself at the time he did the physical act that constitutes the actus reus of the offence; it cannot be the mental state of some non-existent, hypothetical person.
>
> Nevertheless, to decide whether someone has been 'reckless' whether harmful consequences of a particular kind will result from his act, as

> distinguished from his actually intending such harmful consequences to follow, does call for some consideration of how the mind of the ordinary prudent individual would have reacted to a similar situation. If there were nothing in the circumstances that ought to have drawn the attention of an ordinary prudent individual to the possibility of that kind of harmful consequence, the accused would not be described as 'reckless' in the natural meaning of that word for failing to address his mind to the possibility; nor, if the risk of the harmful consequences was so slight that the ordinary prudent individual on due consideration of the risk would not be deterred from treating it as negligible, could the accused be described as 'reckless' in its ordinary sense if, having considered the risk, he decided to ignore it. (In this connection the gravity of the possible harmful consequences would be an important factor. To endanger life must be one of the most grave.) So to this extent, even if one ascribes to 'reckless' only the restricted meaning, adopted by the Court of Appeal in *Stephenson* and *Briggs*, of foreseeing that a particular kind of harm might happen and yet going on to take the risk of it, it involves a test that would be described in part as 'objective' in current legal jargon. Questions of criminal liability are seldom solved by simply asking whether the test is subjective or objective.
>
> In my opinion, a person charged with an offence under s 1(1) of the 1971 Act is 'reckless as to whether or not any property would be destroyed or damaged' if (1) he does an act which in fact creates an obvious risk that property will be destroyed or damaged and (2) when he does the act he either has not given any thought to the possibility of there being any such risk or has recognised that there was some risk involved and has none the less gone on to do it. That would be a proper direction to the jury; cases in the Court of Appeal which held otherwise should be regarded as overruled.

Lord Edmund-Davies delivered what would have been a dissenting judgment, were it not for the fact that all five judges concurred in dismissing the appeal as the outcome was irrelevant to the defendant since he was simply convicted under a different provision of the same statute. He did not agree with this view of the meaning of 'reckless':

> The words 'intention' and 'recklessness' have increasingly displaced in statutory crimes the word 'maliciously', which has frequently given rise to difficulty in interpretation. In *R v Cunningham* . . . Byrne J in the Court of Criminal Appeal cited with approval the following passage which has appeared in Kenny's *Outline of Criminal Law* from its first edition in 1902 onwards [see the passage cited in the excerpt from *Cunningham* above].
>
> Byrne J's comment was **laconic** and **unqualified**: 'We think that this is an accurate statement of the law . . . In our opinion, the word "maliciously" in a statutory crime postulates foresight of consequence.' My Lords, my noble and learned friend Lord Diplock somewhat dismissively described

Professor Kenny as having been 'engaged in defining for the benefit of students the meaning of "malice" as a term of art in criminal law', adding:

> 'To do so he used ordinary English words in their *popular* meaning. Among the words he used was "recklessness", the noun derived from the adjective "reckless", of which the popular or dictionary meaning is "careless, regardless, or heedless of the possible harmful consequences of one's acts". It presupposes that, if thought were given to the matter by the doer before the act was done, *it would have been apparent to him* that there was a real risk of its having the relevant harmful consequences . . . This **parenthetical** restriction on the natural meaning of recklessness was necessary to an explanation of the meaning of the adverb "maliciously" when used as a term of art in the description of an offence under the Malicious Damage Act 1861 (which was the matter in point in *R v Cunningham*) (sic); but it was not directed to and consequently has no bearing on the meaning of the adjective "reckless" in s 1 of the Criminal Damage Act 1971.' (Emphasis added.)

[A bit of confusion here! The Malicious Damage Act was replaced by the Criminal Damage Act 1971; as you will be aware, the statute actually considered in *Cunningham* was the Offences Against the Person Act 1861. What actually matters is that both statutes used the word 'maliciously' so, at least at first sight, that word should bear the same meaning in each statute.]

> I have to say that I am in respectful, but profound, disagreement. The law in action compiles its own dictionary. In time, what was originally the common coinage of speech acquires a different value in the pocket of the lawyer than when in the layman's purse. Professor Kenny used lawyers' words in a lawyers' sense to express his distillation of an important part of the established law relating to mens rea, and he did so in a manner accurate not only in respect of the law as it stood in 1902 but also as it has been applied in countless cases ever since, both in the United Kingdom and in other countries where the common law prevails: see, for example, in Western Australia, *Lederer v Hitchins* (1961) . . . and, in the United States of America, Jethro Brown's *General Principles of Criminal Law* . . . And it is well known that the 1971 Act was in the main the work of the Law Commission, who defined recklessness by saying:
>
>> 'A person is reckless if, (a) knowing that there is a risk that an event may result from his conduct or that a circumstance may exist, he takes that risk, and (b) it is unreasonable for him to take it, having regard to the degree and nature of the risk which he knows to be present.'

> (See Working Paper no 31, Codification of the Criminal Law: General Principles: The Mental Element in Crime (16th June 1970).)
>
> It was surely with this **contemporaneous** definition and the much respected decision of *R v Cunningham* in mind that the draftsman proceeded to his task of drafting the 1971 Act.
>
> It has therefore to be said that, unlike negligence, which has to be judged objectively, recklessness involves foresight of consequences, combined with an objective judgment of the reasonableness of the risk taken. And recklessness **in vacuo** is an incomprehensible notion. It *must* relate to foresight of risk of the particular kind relevant to the charge preferred, which, for the purpose of s 1(2), is the risk of endangering life and nothing other than that.
>
> So, if a defendant says of a particular risk, 'It never crossed my mind', a jury could not on those words alone properly convict him of recklessness simply because they considered that the risk *ought* to have crossed his mind, though his words might well lead to a finding of negligence. But a defendant's admission that he 'closed his mind' to a particular risk could prove fatal, for 'A person cannot, in any intelligible meaning of the words, close his mind to a risk unless he first realises that there is a risk; and if he realises that there is a risk, that is the end of the matter' (see Glanville Williams, *Textbook of Criminal Law* . . .).
>
> In the absence of **exculpatory factors**, the defendant's state of mind is therefore all-important where recklessness is an element in the offence charged . . .

Finally, it is necessary to consider gross negligence as a state of mind. It had almost disappeared until the case of *Adamako* [1994] 3 All ER 79. Following *Caldwell*, the House of Lords decided in *Seymour* in 1983 that the mens rea of involuntary manslaughter was *Caldwell* recklessness; that is, that a defendant would be guilty of involuntary manslaughter if he caused a death in circumstances in which the reasonable person would have foreseen that there was a risk of serious harm. In *Adamako* the House of Lords overruled its decision in *Seymour*, reverting to the previous position and holding that the mens rea for involuntary manslaughter is gross negligence.

The defendant was an anaesthetist during an operation. A tube providing the patient with oxygen became disconnected and the defendant failed to notice or to act appropriately when he finally realised what had happened. The patient died. Lord Mackay:

> In opening his very **cogent** argument for the appellant before your Lordships, counsel submitted that the law in this area should have the characteristics of clarity, certainty, intellectual **coherence** and general applicability and acceptability. For these reasons he said the law applying to involuntary manslaughter generally should involve a universal test and that test should be the test already applied in this House to motor manslaughter. He criticised

> the concept of gross negligence which was the basis of the judgment of the Court of Appeal submitting that its formulation involved **circularity**, the jury being told in effect to convict of a crime if they thought a crime had been committed and that accordingly using gross negligence as the conceptual basis for the crime of involuntary manslaughter was unsatisfactory and the court should apply the law laid down in *R v Seymour* (1983) . . . generally to all cases of involuntary manslaughter or at least use this as the basis for providing general applicability and acceptability.

Lord Mackay then looked at the decisions in *Bateman* (1925) and *Andrews* (1937) and continued:

> In my opinion the law as stated in these two authorities is satisfactory as providing a proper basis for describing the crime of involuntary manslaughter. Since the decision in *Andrews* . . . was a decision of your Lordships' House, it remains the most authoritative statement of the present law which I have been able to find and although its relationship to *R v Seymour* . . . is a matter to which I shall have to return, it is a decision which has not been departed from. On this basis in my opinion the ordinary principles of the law of negligence apply to ascertain whether or not the defendant has been in breach of duty of care towards the victim who has died. If such breach of duty is established the next question is whether that breach of duty caused the death of the victim. If so, the jury must go on to consider whether that breach of duty should be characterised as gross negligence and therefore as a crime. This will depend on the seriousness of the breach of duty committed by the defendant in all the circumstances in which the defendant was placed when it occurred. The jury will have to consider whether the extent to which the defendant's conduct departed from the proper standard of care incumbent upon him, involving as it must have done a risk of death to the patient, was such that it should be judged criminal.
>
> It is true that to a certain extent this involves an element of circularity, but in this branch of the law I do not believe that is fatal to its being correct as a test of how far conduct must depart from accepted standards to be characterised as criminal. This is necessarily a question of degree and an attempt to specify that degree more closely is I think likely to achieve only a **spurious** precision. The essence of the matter, which is supremely a jury question, is whether, having regard to the risk of death involved, the conduct of the defendant was so bad in all the circumstances as to amount in their judgment to a criminal act or omission . . .
>
> I consider it perfectly appropriate that the word 'reckless' should be used in cases of involuntary manslaughter, but as Lord Atkin put it 'in the ordinary connotation of that word'. Examples in which this was done, to my mind, with complete accuracy are *R v Stone, R v Dobinson* (1977) . . . and *R v West London Coroner, ex p Gray* (1987) . . .

Stone and Dobinson had taken on the responsibility of caring for a relative. She died from neglect and they were convicted of gross negligence manslaughter.

All the elements

When a defendant has done something which goes against the spirit of the law, so that he intentionally harms another person or another person's interests, it must be tempting for judges to uphold convictions on the basis that the jury was satisfied as to the defendant's guilt. This leads, however, to uncertainty about what the law is, and is viewed by lawyers as the first step to a police state. The issue is usually one of statutory interpretation and may be very technical, as is demonstrated by the case of *Preddy* [1996] 3 All ER 481. Section 15(1) of the Theft Act 1968 provides:

> A person who by any deception dishonestly obtains property belonging to another, with the intention of permanently depriving the other of it, shall on conviction on indictment be liable to imprisonment for a term not exceeding ten years.

So the elements of the actus reus are deception and obtaining property belonging to another; the mens rea is dishonesty and intention to permanently deprive.

Preddy and others dishonestly induced building societies to lend them money. They were undoubtedly intending to keep the money and it is tempting to say that they were therefore guilty of the offence under s 15. The argument put on their behalf was that there had been no obtaining of property belonging to another – that is, that one element of the actus reus of the offence was missing. If *any* element of an offence is missing, the defendant has not committed the offence and is not guilty.

Lord Goff explained the problem thus:

> Let it be assumed that the lending institution's bank account is **in credit**, and that there is therefore no difficulty in identifying a credit balance standing in the account as representing property, ie a **chose in action**, belonging to the lending institution. The question remains, however, whether the debiting of the lending institution's bank, and the corresponding crediting of the bank account of the defendant or his solicitor, constitutes obtaining of that property. The difficulty in the way of that conclusion is simply that, when the bank account of the defendant (or his solicitor) is credited, he does not obtain the lending institution's chose in action. On the contrary, that chose in action is extinguished or reduced **pro tanto**, and a chose in action is brought into existence representing a debt in an equivalent sum owed by a different bank to the defendant or his solicitor. In these

circumstances, it is difficult to see how the defendant thereby obtained *property belonging to another*, ie to the lending institution.

Professor Sir John Smith, in his commentary on the decision of the Court of Appeal in the present case, has suggested that:

> 'Effectively, the victim's property has been changed into another form and now belongs to the defendant. There is the gain and equivalent loss which is characteristic of, and perhaps the substance of, obtaining.' (See [1995] Crim LR 564 at 565–566.)

But even if this were right, I do not for myself see how this can properly be described as obtaining property belonging to another. In truth, the property which the defendant has obtained is the new chose in action constituted by the debt now owed to him by his bank, and represented by the credit entry in his own bank account. This did not come into existence until the debt so created was owed to him by his bank, and so never belonged to anyone else. True, it corresponded to the debit entered in the lending institution's bank account; but it does not follow that the property which the defendant acquired can be identified with the property which the lending institution lost when its account was debited. In truth, s 15(1) is here being invoked for a purpose for which it was never designed, and for which it does not legislate.

Parliament's response to this House of Lords' decision was to pass the Theft (Amendment) Act 1996, which inserted a new s 15A into the Theft Act 1968:

> (1) A person is guilty of an offence if by any deception he dishonestly obtains a money transfer for himself or another.
> (2) A money transfer occurs when—
>
> (a) a debit is made to one account,
> (b) a credit is made to another, and
> (c) the credit results from the debit or the debit results from the credit. . . .

Parliament thus filled the gap revealed by the House of Lords' decision. Interestingly, Lord Goff examined the legislative history of the Theft Act in the course of his judgment and discovered that the gap arose as a result of amendments made to the Bill by the House of Lords acting in its legislative capacity. The Bill had been appended to a report from the Criminal Law Revision Committee but the House of Lords objected to the offence as drafted on the basis that it was too wide, although the clause was a compromise between members of the Committee:

> As I have said, therefore, the clause combined two specific offences with a general offence of deception. It was this compromise which exposed the

> clause to severe criticism when it came before your Lordships' House acting in its legislative capacity. On 12 March 1968 Viscount Dilhorne moved successfully (though by a small majority) that cl 12(3) be deleted from the Bill (see 290 HL Official Report (5th series) Cols 157ff). He relied in particular upon the overlap, and some inconsistency, between the particular offences in sub-cll (1) and (2), and the general offence in sub-cl (3). Lord Wilberforce, whose speech merits careful study, observed that nothing in sub-cll (1) or (2), or anywhere else in the Bill, dealt with services, the whole Bill being concentrated on property; though he recognised (cols 165–166) that 'the case of loans' also had to be addressed. In the result, sub-cl (2) – the improved version of obtaining credit by fraud – was jettisoned together with sub-cl (3); and a new clause (which became s 16 of the 1968 Act) concerned with 'obtaining pecuniary advantage by deception' was, as Professor Griew has put it in *The Theft Acts 1968 and 1978* (6th edn, 1990) p. 127, para 6-02 '. . . hurriedly devised to cover obtaining credit by deception together with so much of the rejected general offence as was felt to be acceptable'.
>
> Thus was the baby thrown out with the bathwater . . .

Lord Goff goes on to explain that s 16 was a disaster and was replaced by the Theft Act 1978 but that the circumstances of this particular case are simply not covered by either of the Acts.

Check your understanding

1 Can you explain the meaning of the words and phrases in **bold** type? Are there any other words you need to look up in a dictionary?

2 If you are not familiar with it, read the parable of the Good Samaritan in St Luke's Gospel, Ch 10, vv 30–37.

Things to do

1 Imagine you have broken a window. Vary the circumstances slightly to demonstrate doing so intentionally, *Cunningham* recklessly, *Caldwell* recklessly and through gross negligence.

2 Using a criminal law text (or original statutes if you have access to them), choose a number of different offences. Analyse each into its actus reus and mens rea. Bear in mind that there may be several different elements to the actus reus: conduct, circumstances, consequences and that you have to relate the mens rea to the actus reus: intent as to what? recklessness as to what?

Discuss

1 Miller was under a duty to act because he started the fire. There are several other situations in which a person has a duty to act and will be guilty of an offence if he or she does not. What are they?

2 Why would it not be possible to convict Miller simply on the basis that he *started* the fire? Why is it necessary to consider his conduct on *discovering* the fire?

3 Lord Diplock refers to consequences being 'obvious to anyone who troubled to give his mind to them'. Consider the case of *Elliott v C* (1983) in which the defendant was convicted of arson on the basis of *Caldwell* recklessness. She was not mentally capable of appreciating the risk she ran by setting fire to material in a garden shed. Could she be said to have failed to take the trouble to put her mind to what she was doing?

4 What is the '*Caldwell* gap'? Try applying it to the facts of *Miller*: if Miller had . . . he would not have been found guilty.

5 Do you agree that the 'duty approach' in *Miller* is preferable to the 'continuous act' approach? Would your answer be the same in respect of crimes involving commission of an act, as opposed to omission?

6 In *Miller* there is something of a sleight of hand at the point where Lord Diplock distinguishes between intention and recklessness for the purposes of the 1971 Act. What state of mind does he miss out?

7 Consider the arguments of Lord Diplock and Lord Edmund-Davies in *Caldwell*. Which do you prefer and why?

8 Is it appropriate to find people guilty of criminal offences on the basis of:

(a) *Caldwell* recklessness?
(b) gross negligence?

Write

Lord Diplock loves long sentences. However, they are not conducive to easy understanding. Try rewriting two or three paragraphs, retaining the meaning and most of the original wording but changing the punctuation so that the argument is easier to follow. Remember this exercise when you are writing essays: short sentences are easier to construct accurately and easier to understand.

Connections

1 The Good Samaritan crops up again, in the law of negligence, see p. 153 and note that the civil law concept of duty of care is used in gross negligence.

2 Find and make a note of references in judgments to: books and articles by academics, Hansard, the work of the Criminal Law Revision Committee and the Law Commission and cases from other jurisdictions.

3 *Caldwell* is an example of the House of Lords overruling Court of Appeal decisions. *Adamako* is an example of the use of the Practice Statement by the House of Lords to overrule a previous decision of its own.

4 Look for lovely use of language by judges. Lord Edmund-Davies' '. . . what was originally the common coinage of speech acquires a different value in the pocket of the lawyer than when in the layman's purse' is lyrical and very expressive. Be very careful about trying this yourself: it is irritating if over-used and students are best advised to admire such turns of phrase when they occur and be grateful for the help they give in understanding and remembering a point.

4.3 DEFENCES

If a person has committed the actus reus and the mens rea of an offence, are there circumstances in which they should, nevertheless, be found not guilty? Some statutes provide for such circumstances by incorporating specific defences within the statute. In addition, there are general defences which may be raised by defendants charged with any criminal offence. In deciding what the boundaries of these defences should be, the judges often engage in interesting and very informative discussion as to the nature of criminal law.

Intoxication

A seven-judge House of Lords discussed the defence of intoxication in the case of *DPP v Majewski* [1976] 2 All ER 142. Majewski had taken a combination of non-prescribed drugs and alcohol. He assaulted people in a pub brawl and while being arrested but claimed to have no memory of his actions. He was convicted. The Court of Appeal upheld his conviction but granted leave to appeal to the House of Lords on a point of law of general public importance:

> Whether a defendant may properly be convicted of assault notwithstanding that, by reason of his self-induced intoxication, he did not intend to do the act alleged to constitute the assault.

The judges all took the view that the law on intoxication was well settled but agreed that, as this kind of offence is very common, it was necessary to review the law and examine the justifications for it.

Lord Salmon gave a clear explanation of the history of the law on intoxication:

> It has long been established that except for special cases in which crimes of **absolute liability** are created by statute, no one can be convicted of any crime unless he has a guilty mind. The elements constituting a guilty mind naturally differ widely from crime to crime just as the elements constituting different crimes themselves necessarily differ widely. In cases such as assault and assault occasioning actual bodily harm, the accused is not guilty unless it is proved beyond reasonable doubt that he intended to do what he did, ie commit the assault, or was recklessly indifferent whether or not what he did might amount to an assault. It is not necessary to prove that he intended to cause the bodily harm which resulted from the assault. In other crimes such as causing grievous bodily harm with intent to cause grievous bodily harm, the accused cannot be convicted of the offence charged unless it is proved beyond reasonable doubt that he intended to do grievous bodily harm. If this latter element is not proved, the accused must be acquitted of the offence charged but may nevertheless be convicted of the lesser offence of unlawful wounding. Similarly, if the accused is charged with murder, he cannot be convicted unless it is proved beyond reasonable doubt that he killed with intent to murder or to cause grievous bodily harm. If neither of these latter elements is established, the accused must be acquitted of murder but may be convicted of the lesser offence of manslaughter.
>
> Prior to the 19th century, for a prisoner to have committed a crime, having voluntarily made himself drunk, was never regarded as any excuse or mitigation but rather as an aggravation of his offence: see Hawkins's Pleas of the Crown, Coke on Littleton, Blackstone's Commentaries. This attitude, however, began to change under the more humane influences of the 19th century. The penalty for murder or for causing grievous bodily harm with intent to cause grievous bodily harm was death or deportation. It was felt that sentencing a man to be hanged or deported who had done either of these things when so drunk that he had had no intention of doing what he in fact did was unnecessarily harsh. Accordingly, if a man killed or committed grievous bodily harm whilst he was drunk, this factor was taken into account with all the other evidence in deciding whether he had intended to kill or to commit grievous bodily harm. If this question were decided in the accused's favour, he would be found not guilty of murder or causing grievous bodily harm with intent to commit grievous bodily harm, but guilty of manslaughter or unlawful wounding and sentenced accordingly . . . This does not mean that drunkenness, of itself, is ever a defence. It is merely some evidence which may throw a doubt on whether the accused had formed the special intent which was an essential element of the crime with which he was charged.

So, the approach of English law is to regard intoxication as irrelevant except in some serious cases in which it is felt that it is not just to hold the defendant fully responsible. Lord Elwyn-Jones LC examined the rationale for this approach:

> There are, however, decisions of eminent judges in a number of Commonwealth cases in Australia and New Zealand (but generally not in Canada nor in the United States), as well as impressive academic comment in this country, to which we have been referred, supporting the view that it is illogical and inconsistent with legal principle to treat a person who of his own choice and volition has taken drugs and drink, even though he thereby creates a state in which he is not conscious of what he is doing, any differently from a person suffering from the various medical conditions like epilepsy or diabetic coma and who is regarded by the law as free from fault. However, our courts have for a very long time regarded in quite another light the state of self-induced intoxication. The authority which for the last half century has been relied on in this context has been the speech of Lord Birkenhead LC in *Director of Public Prosecutions v Beard*:
>
>> 'Under the law of England as it prevailed until early in the nineteenth century voluntary drunkenness was never an excuse for criminal misconduct; and indeed the classic authorities broadly assert that voluntary drunkenness must be considered rather an aggravation than a defence. This view was in terms based upon the principle that a man who by his own voluntary act debauches and destroys his will power shall be no better situated in regard to criminal acts than a sober man.'
>
> Lord Birkenhead LC made an historical survey of the way the common law from the 16th century on dealt with the effect of self-induced intoxication on criminal responsibility. This indicates how, from 1819 on, the judges began to **mitigate** the severity of the attitude of the common law in such cases as murder and serious violent crime when the penalties of death or transportation applied or where there was likely to be sympathy for the accused, as in attempted suicide. Lord Birkenhead LC concluded that (except in cases where insanity was pleaded) the decisions he cited—
>
>> 'establish that where a specific intent is an essential element in the offence, evidence of a state of drunkenness rendering the accused incapable of forming such an intent should be taken into consideration in order to determine whether he had in fact formed the intent necessary to constitute the particular crime. If he was so drunk that he was incapable of forming the intent required he could not be convicted of a crime which was committed only if the intent was proved. . . . In a charge of murder based upon intention to kill or to do grievous bodily harm, if the jury are satisfied that the accused

was, by reason of his drunken condition, incapable of forming the intent to kill or to do grievous bodily harm . . . he cannot be convicted of murder. But nevertheless unlawful homicide has been committed by the accused, and consequently he is guilty of unlawful homicide without malice aforethought, and that is manslaughter . . . the law is plain beyond all question that in cases falling short of insanity a condition of drunkenness at the time of committing an offence causing death can only, when it is available at all, have the effect of reducing the crime from murder to manslaughter.'

From this it seemed clear – and this is the interpretation which the judges have placed on the decision during the ensuing half-century – that it is only in the limited class of cases requiring proof of specific intent that drunkenness can **exculpate**. Otherwise in no case can it exempt completely from criminal liability. . . .

I do not for my part regard that general principle as either unethical or contrary to the principles of natural justice. If a man of his own **volition** takes a substance which causes him to cast off the restraints of reason and conscience, no wrong is done to him by holding him answerable criminally for any injury he may do while in that condition. His course of conduct in reducing himself by drugs and drink to that condition in my view supplies the evidence of mens rea, of guilty mind certainly sufficient for crimes of basic intent. . . .

This approach is in line with the American Model Code:

'When recklessness establishes an element of the offence, if the actor, due to self-induced intoxication, is unaware of a risk of which he would have been aware had he been sober, such unawareness is immaterial.'

. . . My noble and learned friends and I think it may be helpful if we give the following indication of the general lines on which in our view the jury should be directed as to the effect on the criminal responsibility of the accused of drink or drugs or both, whenever death or physical injury to another person results from something done by the accused for which there is no legal justification and the offence with which the accused is charged is manslaughter or assault at common law or the statutory offence of unlawful wounding under s 20, or of assault occasioning actual bodily harm under s 47 of the Offences against the Person Act 1861.

In the case of these offences it is no excuse in law that, because of drink or drugs which the accused himself had taken knowingly and willingly, he had deprived himself of the ability to exercise self-control, to realise the possible consequences of what he was doing or even to be conscious that he was doing it. As in the instant case, the jury may be properly instructed that they 'can ignore the subject of drink or drugs as being in any way a defence to charges of this character'.

The distinction between offences of basic intent and offences of specific intent is a difficult one to formulate. Perhaps the most helpful explanation was that given by Lord Simon of Glaisdale:

> . . . a crime of specific intent requires something more than contemplation of the prohibited act and foresight of its probable consequences. The mens rea in a crime of specific intent requires proof of a purposive element.

Lord Edmund-Davies addressed the criticisms that it is illogical and immoral to convict a person who has no mens rea:

> If logic is to be the sole guide, it follows that a man can never be regarded as committing an assault unless he is conscious of what he is doing. Whatever be the reason for its absence, if he in fact lacks such consciousness he cannot be said to act either intentionally or recklessly. It is submitted on the appellant's behalf that he was at all material times in a condition of 'non-insane automatism resulting from pathological intoxication'. In *Bratty v Attorney-General for Northern Ireland* Lord Kilmuir LC acceptably defined 'automatism' as—
>
>> 'the state of a person who, though capable of action, "is not conscious of what he is doing . . . It means unconscious involuntary action, and it is a defence because the mind does not go with what is being done."'
>
> In strict logic it may be that a physical action performed in such a state ought never to be punished as a criminal assault, no matter how grievous the injury thereby inflicted on the person attacked.
>
> Then is it the case that a man is always to be absolved by the criminal law from the consequences of acts performed when in a state of automatism, *regardless* of how that state was brought about? . . .
>
> Are the claims of logic, then, so compelling that a man behaving as the Crown witnesses testified the appellant did must be cleared of criminal responsibility? As to this, Lawton LJ [giving judgment in this case in the Court of Appeal] rightly said:
>
>> 'Although there was much reforming zeal and activity in the 19th century, Parliament never once considered whether self-induced intoxication should be a defence *generally* to a criminal charge. It would have been a strange result if the merciful relaxation of a strict rule of law has ended, without any Parliamentary intervention, by whittling it away to such an extent that the more drunk a man became, provided he stopped short of making himself insane, the better chance he had of an acquittal.'
>
> If such be the inescapable result of the strict application of logic in this branch of the law, it is indeed not surprising that illogicality has long reigned, and the prospect of its dethronement must be regarded as alarming. . . .

Illogical though the present law may be, it represents a compromise between the imposition of liability on **inebriates** in complete disregard of their condition (on the alleged ground that it was brought on voluntarily), and the total **exculpation** required by the defendant's actual state of mind at the time he committed the harm in issue. It is at this point **pertinent** to pause to consider why legal systems exist. The universal object of a system of law is obvious – the establishment and maintenance of order. . . .

Lord Edmund-Davies quoted from Smith & Hogan's *Criminal Law*:

> 'While a policy of not allowing a man to escape the consequence of his voluntary drunkenness is understandable, it is submitted that the principle that a man should not be held liable for an act over which he has no control is more important and should prevail.'

They add that this is not to say that such a man should in all cases escape criminal liability but that, if he is to be held liable, it should be for the voluntary act of taking the drink or drug. Such a suggestion is far from new. Thus, it appears from Hale's *Pleas of the Crown* that some lawyers of his day thought that the formal cause of punishment ought to be the drink and not the crime committed under its influence. Edwards (writing in *Criminal Law Quarterly*) expressed concern in 1965 over the possible existence of this gateway to exemption from criminal responsibility and stressed the need for urgent attention to the provision of new statutory powers under which the courts may place such offenders on probation or commit them, as the case may require, to a hospital capable of treating them for the underlying cause of their propensity to automatism. Glanville Williams anticipated in 1961 the Butler Report on Mentally Abnormal Offenders (1975) by recommending the creation of an offence of being drunk and dangerous and the committee itself proposed that a new offence of 'dangerous intoxication' be punishable on indictment for one year for a first offence or for three years on a second or subsequent offence.

The case of *Caldwell* (p. 105) was further complicated by the fact that the defendant had been drinking. Lord Diplock dealt with the issue thus:

If the only mental state capable of constituting the necessary mens rea for an offence under s 1(2) were that expressed in the words 'intending by the destruction or damage to endanger the life of another', it would have been necessary to consider whether the offence was to be classified as one of 'specific' intent for the purposes of the rule of law which this House affirmed and applied in *Director of Public Prosecutions v Majewski* . . . and this it plainly is. But this is not, in my view, a relevant inquiry where 'being reckless as to whether the life of another would be thereby endangered' is an alternative mental state that is capable of constituting the necessary mens rea of the offence with which he is charged.

The speech of Lord Elwyn-Jones LC in *Majewski*, with which Lord Simon, Lord Kilbrandon and I agreed, is authority that self-induced intoxication is

> no defence to a crime in which recklessness is enough to constitute the necessary mens rea . . . The charge in *Majewski* was of assault occasioning actual bodily harm and it was held by the majority of the House, approving *R v Venna* . . . that recklessness in the use of force was sufficient to satisfy the mental element in the offence of assault. Reducing oneself by drink or drugs to a condition in which the restraints of reason and conscience are cast off was held to be a reckless course of conduct and an integral part of the crime. . . .
>
> So, in the instant case, the fact that the respondent was unaware of the risk of endangering the lives of residents in the hotel owing to his self-induced intoxication would be no defence if that risk would have been obvious to him had he been sober.

Lord Edmund-Davies, continuing to disagree with the majority in *Caldwell* as he had on the mens rea issue, said:

> Something more must be said about [the issue of intoxication] having regard to the view expressed by my noble and learned friend Lord Diplock that the speech of Lord Elwyn-Jones LC in *Majewski* 'is authority that self-induced intoxication is no defence to a crime in which recklessness is enough to constitute the necessary mens rea'. It is a view which, with respect, I do not share. In common with all the Law Lords hearing that appeal, Lord Elwyn-Jones LC adopted the well-established (though not universally favoured) distinction between basic and specific intents. *Majewski* related solely to charges of assault, undoubtedly an offence of basic intent, and Lord Elwyn-Jones LC made it clear that his observations were confined to offences of that nature . . . My respectful view is that *Majewski* accordingly supplies no support for the proposition that, in relation to crimes of specific intent (such as that in s 1(2)(b) of the 1971 Act), incapacity to appreciate the degree and nature of the risk created by his action which is attributable to the defendant's self-intoxication is an irrelevance. Lord Elwyn-Jones LC was dealing simply with crimes of basic intent, and in my judgment it was strictly within that framework that he adopted the view expressed in the American Penal Code . . . and recklessness as an element in crimes of specific intent was, I am convinced, never within his contemplation. . . .
>
> It follows, therefore, that I agree with learned counsel for the respondent that the certified point of law should be answered in the following manner: 'Yes, evidence of self-induced intoxication can be relevant both to (a) whether the defendant *intended* to endanger the life of another, and to (b) whether the defendant was *reckless* whether the life of another would be endangered, within the meaning of s 1(2)(b) of the Criminal Damage Act 1971.'
>
> . . . with the progressive displacement of 'maliciously' by 'intentionally or recklessly' in statutory crimes, that [that such crimes will be crimes of

basic intent] will surely be the effect of the majority decision in this appeal. That I regret, for the consequence is that, however grave the crime charged, if recklessness can constitute its mens rea the fact that it was committed in drink can afford no defence. It is a very long time since we had so harsh a law in this country. Having revealed in *Majewski* my personal conviction that, on grounds of public policy, a plea of drunkenness cannot exculpate crimes of basic intent and so exercise unlimited sway in the criminal law . . . I am nevertheless unable to concur that your Lordships' decision should now become the law of the land. For, as Eveleigh LJ said in *R v Orpin* . . .

> '. . . there is nothing inconsistent in treating intoxication as irrelevant when considering the liability of a person who has willed himself to do that which the law forbids (for example, to do something which wounds another), and yet to make it relevant when a further mental state is postulated as an aggravating circumstance making the offence even more serious.'

By way of a postscript I would add that the majority view demonstrates yet again the folly of totally ignoring the recommendations of the Butler Committee (Report on Mentally Abnormal Offenders . . .).

It seems at this point that the judges are agreed that there is an illogical but socially necessary rule that a person who makes the decision to take drink and/or drugs will be responsible for the consequences of their action, although if they cannot form the necessary mens rea for an offence of specific intent (whatever that might mean) they will be convicted of some lesser offence. The case of *Kingston* introduced a new element.

Kingston was convicted of committing an indecent assault upon a fifteen-year-old boy. He had been photographed doing so, by a person who had drugged the boy and who intended to use the photographs and an audio tape to blackmail Kingston. Kingston's defence was that he too had been given some kind of drug and was thus not responsible for his actions because he was involuntarily intoxicated at the time the offence was committed. The offence is one of basic intent, so had his intoxication been voluntary it would have been irrelevant, but if you look at the judgments in *Majewski*, they all refer to *voluntary* intoxication. What, then, should the courts do about a person whose intoxication is in no sense their own fault?

In the Court of Appeal [1993] 4 All ER 373, Lord Taylor, the Lord Chief Justice, began by looking at the authorities. He found that they were few and far between. Hale, in *Pleas of the Crown*, drew a distinction between those who are responsible for their conduct and those who are not. He regarded those who were not responsible because they were drunk as being fully responsible for their actions, but:

> . . . if a person by the unskilfulness of his physician, or by the contrivance of his enemies, eat or drink such a thing as causeth such a temporary or permanent phrenzy . . . this puts him into the same condition, in reference to crimes, as any other phrenzy, and equally excuseth him.

There was also a reference to the issue in *Pearson's Case* (1835) in which Park J said:

> Voluntary drunkenness is no excuse for crime. If a party be made drunk by stratagem, or the fraud of another, he is not responsible.

This came from a very brief report of a case heard long before reports were reliable. Lord Taylor also noted that the Law Commission, in their consultation paper *Intoxication and Criminal Liability* (1993), rather assumed that involuntary intoxication is a good defence:

> Involuntary intoxication is always taken into account in determining the existence of subjective mens rea

without citing any authority.

Finally, Lord Taylor came to the conclusion that there is nothing explicit in *Majewski* on the issue of involuntary intoxication. In the absence of precedent, he looked at principle (see Professor Simon Lee on this at p. 40):

> In our judgment, the question can be answered by turning to first principles. The importance of ensuring, under a system of law, that members of the community are safeguarded in their persons and property is obvious and was firmly stated in *DPP v Majewski* . . . However, the purpose of the criminal law is to inhibit, by **proscription** and by penal sanction, antisocial acts which individuals may otherwise commit. Its unspoken **premise** is that people may have tendencies and impulses to do those things which are considered sufficiently objectionable to be forbidden. Having paedophiliac inclinations and desires is not proscribed; putting them into practice is. If the sole reason why the threshold between the two has been crossed is or may have been that the **inhibition** which the law requires has been removed by the **clandestine** act of a third party, the purposes of the criminal law are not served by nevertheless holding that the person performing the act is guilty of an offence. A man is not responsible for a condition produced by 'stratagem, or the fraud of another'. If therefore drink or a drug, surreptitiously administered, causes a person to lose his self-control and for that reason to form an intent which he would not otherwise have formed, it is consistent with the principle that the law should exculpate him because the operative fault is not his. The law permits a finding that the intent formed was not a criminal intent or, in other words, that the involuntary

> intoxication negatives the mens rea. As was pointed out in argument, there is some analogy to be found here in the rationale underlying the defence of duress. While it is not necessary for the decision of this case, it appears to us that, if the principle applies where the offence is one of basic intent, it should apply also where the offence is one of specific intent.

The Court of Appeal allowed the appeal but certified a point of law of general public importance:

> whether, if it is proved that the necessary intent was present when the necessary act was done by him, a defendant has open to him a defence of involuntary intoxication.

In the House of Lords [1994] 3 All ER 353, Lord Mustill considered the facts of the case and the decision of the Court of Appeal and said:

> On these facts there are three grounds on which the **respondent** might be held free from criminal responsibility. First, that his immunity flows from general principles of the criminal law. Secondly, that this immunity is already established by a solid line of authority. Finally, that the court should, when faced with a new problem, acknowledge the justice of the case and boldly create a new common law defence.
>
> It is clear from the passage already quoted that the Court of Appeal adopted the first approach. The decision was explicitly founded on general principle. There can be no doubt what principle the court relied upon, for at the outset the court recorded the submission of counsel for the respondent that 'the law recognises that, exceptionally, an accused person may be entitled to be acquitted if there is a possibility that, although his act was intentional, the intent itself arose out of circumstances for which he bears no blame . . .' The same proposition is implicit in the assumption by the court that if blame is absent the necessary mens rea must also be absent.
>
> My Lords, with every respect I must suggest that no such principle exists or, until the present case, had ever in modern times been thought to exist. Each offence consists of a prohibited act or omission coupled with whatever state of mind is called for by the statute or rule of the common law which creates the offence. In those offences which are not absolute the state of mind which the prosecution must prove to have underlain the act or omission – the 'mental element' – will in the majority of cases be such as to attract disapproval. The mental element will then be the mark of what may properly be called a 'guilty mind'. The professional burglar is guilty in a moral as well as a legal sense; he intends to break into the house to steal, and most would confidently assert that this is wrong. But this will not always be so. In respect of some offences the mind of the defendant, and still less his moral judgment, may not be engaged at all. In others, although a mental activity must be the motive power for the prohibited act or

omission the activity may be of such a kind or degree that society at large would not criticise the defendant's conduct severely or even criticise it at all. Such cases are not uncommon. Yet to assume that contemporary moral judgments affect the criminality of the act, as distinct from the punishment appropriate to the crime once proved, is to be misled by the expression 'mens rea', the ambiguity of which has been the subject of complaint for more than a century . . .

As I understand the position it is still the law that in the exceptional case where intoxication causes insanity the M'Naughten rules apply . . . Short of this, it is no answer for the defendant to say that he would not have done what he did had he been sober, provided always that whatever element of intent is required by the offence is proved to have been present. As was said in *R v Sheehan, R v Moore* (1975) 'a drunken intent is still an intent'. As to proof of intent, it appears that at least in some instances self-induced intoxication can be taken into account as part of the evidence from which the jury draws its conclusions; but that in others it cannot. I express the matter in this guarded way because it has not yet been decisively established whether for this purpose there is a line to be drawn between offences of 'specific' and of 'basic' intent. That in at least some cases a defendant cannot say that he was so drunk that he could not form the required intent is however clear enough. Why is this so? The answer must, I believe, be the same as that given in other common law jurisdictions: namely that such evidence is excluded as a matter of policy. As Mason J put the matter in *R v O'Connor* (1979) . . .

> 'the view is taken that the act charged is voluntary notwithstanding that it might not be ordinarily considered so by reason of the condition of the perpetrator, because his condition proceeds from a voluntary choice made by him. These cases therefore constitute an exception to the general rule of criminal responsibility.'

There remains the question by what reasoning the House put this policy into effect. As I understand it two different rationalisations were adopted. First that the absence of the necessary consent is cured by treating the intentional drunkenness (or more accurately, since it is only in the minority of cases that the drinker sets out to make himself drunk, the intentional taking of drink without regard to its possible effects) as a substitute for the mental element ordinarily required by the offence. The intent is transferred from the taking of drink to the commission of the prohibited act. The second rationalisation is that the defendant cannot be heard to rely on the absence of the mental element when it is absent because of his own voluntary acts. Borrowing an expression from a far distant field it may be said that the defendant is **estopped** from relying on his self-induced incapacity.

Your Lordships are not required to decide how these two explanations stand up to attack, for they are not attacked here. The task is only to place them in the context of an intoxication which is not voluntary. Taking first

> the concept of transferred intent, if the intoxication was not the result of an act done with an informed will there is no intent which can be transferred to the prohibited act, so as to fill the gap in the offence. As regards the 'estoppel' there is no reason why the law should preclude the defendant from relying on a mental condition which he had not deliberately brought about. Thus, once the involuntary nature of the intoxication is added the two theories of *Majewski* fall away, and the position reverts to what it would have been if *Majewski* had not been decided, namely that the offence is not made out if the defendant was so intoxicated that he could not form an intent. Thus, where the intoxication is involuntary *Majewski* does not *subtract* the defence of absence of intent; but there is nothing in *Majewski* to suggest that where intent is proved involuntary intoxication *adds* a further defence.

Lord Mustill went on to review the law in other jurisdictions, then said:

> To recognise a new defence of this type would be a bold step. The common law defences of duress and necessity (if it exists) and the limited common law defence of provocation are all very old. Since counsel for the appellant was not disposed to emphasise this aspect of the appeal the subject was not explored in argument, but I suspect that the recognition of a new general defence at common law has not happened in modern times. Nevertheless, the criminal law must not stand still, and if it is both practical and just to take this step, and if judicial decision rather than legislation is the proper medium, then the courts should not be deterred simply by the novelty of it. So one must turn to consider just what defence is now to be created. The judgment under appeal implies five characteristics.
>
> (1) The defence applies to all offences, except perhaps to absolute offences. It therefore differs from other defences such as provocation and diminished responsibility.
>
> (2) The defence is a complete answer to a criminal charge. If not rebutted it leads to an outright acquittal, and unlike provocation and diminished responsibility leaves no room for conviction and punishment for a lesser offence. The underlying assumption must be that the defendant is entirely free from **culpability**.
>
> (3) It may be that the defence applies only where the intoxication is due to the wrongful act of another and therefore affords no excuse when, in circumstances of no greater culpability, the defendant has intoxicated himself by mistake (such as by short-sightedly taking the wrong drug). I say that this may be so, because it is not clear whether, since the doctrine was founded in part on the dictum of Park J, the 'fraud or stratagem of another' is an essential element, or whether this was taken as an example of a wider principle.
>
> (4) The burden of disproving the defence is on the prosecution.

(5) The defence is subjective in nature. Whereas provocation and self-defence are judged by the reactions of the reasonable person in the situation of the defendant, here the only question is whether this particular defendant's inhibitions were overcome by the effect of the drug. The more susceptible the defendant to the kind of temptation presented, the easier the defence is to establish. . . .

On the practical side there are serious problems. Before the jury could form an opinion on whether the drug might have turned the scale witnesses would have to give a picture of the defendant's personality and susceptibilities, for without it the crucial effect of the drug could not be assessed; pharmacologists would be required to describe the potentially disinhibiting effect of a range of drugs whose identity would, if the present case is anything to go by, be unknown; psychologists and psychiatrists would express opinions, not on the matters of psychopathology familiar to those working within the framework of the Mental Health Acts but on altogether more elusive concepts. No doubt as time passed those concerned could work out techniques to deal with these questions. Much more significant would be the opportunities for a spurious defence. Even in the field of road traffic the 'spiked' drink as a special reason for not disqualifying from driving is a regular feature. Transferring this to the entire range of criminal offences is a disturbing prospect. The defendant would only have to assert, and support by the evidence of well-wishers, that he was not the sort of person to have done this kind of thing, and to suggest an occasion when by some means a drug might have been administered to him for the jury to be sent straight to the question of a possible disinhibition. The judge would direct the jurors that if they felt any legitimate doubt on the matter – and by its nature the defence would be one which the prosecution would often have no means to rebut – they must acquit outright, all questions of intent, mental capacity and the like being at this stage irrelevant.

My Lords, the fact that a new doctrine may require adjustment of existing principles to accommodate it, and may require those involved in criminal trials to learn new techniques, is not of course a ground for refusing to adopt it, if that is what the interests of justice require. Here, however, justice makes no such demands, for the interplay between the wrong done to the victim, the individual characteristics and frailties of the defendant, and the pharmacological effects of whatever drug may be potentially involved can be far better recognised by a tailored choice from the continuum of sentences available to the judge than by the application of a single yea-or-nay jury decision. To this, there is one exception. The mandatory life sentence for murder, at least at present administered, leaves no room for the trial judge to put into practice an informed and sympathetic assessment of the kind just described. It is for this reason alone that I have felt any hesitation about rejecting the argument for the respondent. In the end however I have concluded that this is not a sufficient reason to force on the theory and practice of the criminal law an exception which

> would otherwise be unjustified. For many years mandatory sentences have impelled juries to return merciful but false verdicts, and have stimulated the creation of partial defences such as provocation and diminished responsibility whose lack of a proper foundation has made them hard to apply in practice. I do not think it right that the law should be further distorted simply because of this **anomalous** relic of the history of the criminal law.
>
> All this being said, I suggest to your Lordships that the existing work of the Law Commission in the field of intoxication could usefully be enlarged to comprise questions of the type raised by this appeal, and to see whether by statute a merciful, realistic and intellectually sustainable statutory solution could be newly created. For the present, however, I consider that no such regime now exists, and that the common law is not a suitable vehicle for creating one.

As there were outstanding grounds for appeal from the original Crown Court decision, the case was remitted to the Court of Appeal for those to be dealt with.

Mistake

If a defendant makes a mistake about a situation, he or she is judged on the basis that the facts were as he or she believed them to be. This was established in the cases of *DPP v Morgan* (1975) and *Williams* (1983).

Morgan was a bizarre case in which men accused of rape defended themselves by saying that the victim's husband had invited them to have sex with his wife and told them her protests were not genuine – and that they believed the husband and so were mistaken as to the absence of the woman's consent. The House of Lords' decision that it was sufficient that the defendants' belief was honest, it did not have to be reasonable, was widely criticised. It should, however, be remembered that the defendants in *Morgan* were not acquitted, the House of Lords deciding that a properly directed jury would still have convicted. Plainly, no jury would decide that their mistake was reasonable. If the jury had been invited to consider whether the belief was honest, they might well have decided it was not. The Sexual Offences (Amendment) Act 1976 made it clear that a jury should consider whether the grounds for mistaken belief as to consent were reasonable in the course of deciding whether they were honest.

Williams was also a case with interesting facts. The defendant believed he was arresting a mugger, when he was actually assaulting a person who was attempting to arrest a mugger. He was honestly mistaken as to the facts of the situation.

In *Kimber* [1983] 3 All ER 316, it was confirmed that the test is a subjective one. Lawton LJ:

> The appeal raises these points. First, can a defendant charged with an indecent assault on a woman raise the defence that he believed she had consented to what he did? The trial judge, Mr Recorder Smyth QC, rules that he could not. Second, if he could, did the jury have to consider merely whether his belief was honestly held or, if it was, did they have to go on to consider whether it was based on reasonable grounds? . . .
>
> Before us counsel for the Crown submitted that the jury should have been directed that the appellant had a defence if he had believed that (the woman) was consenting and he had had reasonable grounds for thinking so. On the facts the appellant could not have had any such grounds with the result that, despite the recorder's misdirection, there had been no miscarriage of justice. We agree that on the evidence the appellant had no reasonable grounds for thinking that (the woman) was consenting and no jury other than a perverse one could have thought he had. Counsel for the appellant argued, relying on the decision in *DPP v Morgan*, that the sole issue was whether the appellant had honestly believed that Betty was consenting. Unless the jury were sure that he had not so believed, he was entitled to be acquitted. The grounds for his belief were irrelevant save in so far as they might have assisted the jury to decide whether he did believe what he said he did. . . .

Lawton LJ reviewed the law and concluded:

> The consequence is that the prosecution has to prove that the defendant intended to lay hands on his victim without her consent. If he did not intend to do this, he is entitled to be found not guilty; and if he did not so intend because he believed she was consenting, the prosecution will have failed to prove the charge. It is the defendant's belief, not the grounds on which it was based, which goes to negative the intent. . . .

What if the honest belief is formed when the defendant has been drinking? The Court of Appeal considered this in the case of *O'Grady* [1987] 3 All ER 420. The decision has been criticised on the basis that it could have been reached by applying the rule in *Majewski*: intoxication was no defence to manslaughter; but the Court of Appeal considered the case from the angle of the defendant having made a mistake whilst he was very drunk. He had killed a friend during a fight, in the belief that he was using reasonable force to defend himself. Lord Lane CJ said:

> How should the jury be invited to approach the problem? One starts with the decision of this court in *R v Williams* [1983] 3 All ER 411, namely that where the defendant might have been labouring under a mistake as to the facts he must be judged according to that mistaken view, whether the mistake was reasonable or not. It is then for the jury to decide whether the defendant's reaction to the threat (real or imaginary) was a reasonable one.

> The court was not in that case considering what the situation might be where the mistake was due to voluntary intoxication by alcohol or some other drug.
>
> We have come to the conclusion that, where the jury are satisfied that the defendant was mistaken in his belief that any force or the force which he in fact used was necessary to defend himself and are further satisfied that the mistake was caused by voluntarily induced intoxication, the defence must fail. We do not consider that any distinction should be drawn on this aspect of the matter between offences involving what is called specific intent, such as murder, and offences of so called basic intent, such as manslaughter. Quite apart from the problem of directing a jury in a case such as the present where manslaughter is an alternative verdict to murder, the question of mistake can and ought to be considered separately from the question of intent. A sober man who mistakenly believes he is in danger of immediate death at the hands of an attacker is entitled to be acquitted of both murder and manslaughter if his reaction in killing his supposed assailant was a reasonable one. What his intent may have been seems to us to be irrelevant to the problem of self-defence or no. . . .
>
> This brings us to the question of public order. There are two competing interests. On the one hand the interest of the defendant who has only acted according to what he believed to be necessary to protect himself, and on the other hand that of the public in general and the victim in particular who, probably through no fault of his own, has been injured or perhaps killed because of the defendant's drunken mistake. Reason recoils from the conclusion that in such circumstances a defendant is entitled to leave the court without a stain on his character. . . .

Lord Lane considered *Majewski* and then the case of *Lipman* (1969), in which the defendant claimed he was unable to form the intent necessary for a murder conviction because at the time he killed his girlfriend he was intoxicated by LSD and believed he was fighting off serpents. The House of Lords had decided that intoxication was a good defence to crimes of specific intent.

> The defence in that case was put on the grounds that the defendant, because of the a hallucinatory drug which had been taken, had not formed the necessary intent to found a conviction for murder, thus resulting in his conviction for manslaughter. If the appellant's contentions here are correct, Lipman could successfully have escaped conviction altogether by raising the issue that he believed he was defending himself legitimately from an attack by serpents. It is significant that no one seems to have considered that possibility. . . .
>
> We have therefore come to the conclusion that a defendant is not entitled to rely, so far as self-defence is concerned, on a mistake of fact which has been induced by voluntary intoxication.

Duress

A defendant may commit a crime because he has been threatened. The law on duress was explained by Lord Lane CJ in *R v Graham* [1982]. He said:

> As a matter of public policy, it seems to us essential to limit the defence of duress by means of an objective criterion formulated in terms of reasonableness. Consistency of approach in defences to criminal liability is obviously desirable. Provocation and duress are **analogous**. In provocation the words or actions of one person break the self-control of another. In duress the words or actions of one person break the will of another. The law requires a defendant to have the self-control reasonably to be expected of the ordinary citizen in his situation. It should likewise require him to have the steadfastness reasonably to be expected of the ordinary citizen in his situation. So too with self-defence, in which the law permits the use of no more force than is reasonable in the circumstances. And, in general, if a mistake is to excuse what would otherwise be criminal, the mistake must be a reasonable one . . . the correct approach on the facts of this case would have been as follows: (1) was the defendant, or may he have been, impelled to act as he did because, as a result of what he reasonably believed King had said or done, he had good cause to fear that if he did not so act King would kill him or (if this is to be added) cause him serious physical injury? (2) if so, have the prosecution made the jury sure that a sober person of reasonable firmness, sharing the characteristics of the defendant, would not have responded to whatever he reasonably believed King said or did by taking part in the killing? The fact that a defendant's will to resist has been eroded by the voluntary consumption of drink or drugs or both is not relevant to this test.

Lord Lane drew an analogy between the defence of duress and the defence of provocation in terms that they both consisted of outside pressures that cause a defendant to do something he would not otherwise have done. Each defence has an objective element – would the reasonable person subjected to this pressure have acted in this way? – and the question arises in each case, therefore, what is meant by the 'reasonable person'. In *Bowen* [1996] 4 All ER 837, Stuart-Smith LJ considered this point and came to this conclusion:

> (1) The mere fact that the accused is more pliable, vulnerable, timid or susceptible to threats than a normal person are not characteristics with which it is legitimate to invest the reasonable/ordinary person for the purpose of considering the objective test.
>
> (2) The defendant may be in a category of person who the jury may think less able to resist pressure than people not within that category.

Obvious examples are age, where a young person may well not be so robust as a mature one, possibly sex, though many women would doubtless consider they had as much moral courage to resist pressure as men; pregnancy, where there is added fear for the unborn child; serious physical disability, which may inhibit self-protection; recognised mental illness or psychiatric condition, such as post-traumatic stress disorder leading to **learned helplessness**.

(3) Characteristics which may be relevant in considering provocation, because they relate to the nature of the provocation itself, will not necessarily be relevant in cases of duress. Thus homosexuality may be relevant to provocation if the provocative words or conduct are related to this characteristic; it cannot be relevant in duress, since there is no reason to think that homosexuals are less robust in resisting threats of the kind that are relevant in duress cases.

(4) Characteristics due to self-induced abuse, such as alcohol, drugs or glue sniffing, cannot be relevant.

(5) Psychiatric evidence may be admissible to show that the accused is suffering from some mental illness, mental impairment or a recognised psychiatric condition, provided persons generally suffering from such a condition may be more susceptible to pressure and threats, and thus to assist the jury in deciding whether a reasonable person suffering from such a condition might have been impelled to act as the defendant did. It is not admissible simply to show that in the doctor's opinion an accused, who is not suffering from such illness or condition, is especially timid, suggestible or vulnerable to pressure and threats. Nor is medical opinion admissible to bolster or support the credibility of the accused.

Bowen had an IQ of 68, which is well below average, but the Court of Appeal held that this was not a relevant characteristic. He had bought goods worth about £20,000 in total under a number of different credit arrangements and then failed to pay for them. He claimed that he did so because two men threatened to petrol-bomb the house where he and his family lived if he did not obtain the goods for them.

The standard set for the 'reasonable man' is very high in cases of murder: he is expected to allow himself to be killed rather than to kill another person in order to protect himself from threats. In *Howe* [1987] 1 All ER 771, Lord Hailsham LC considered whether duress could be a defence to murder:

This brings me back to the question of principle. I begin by affirming that, while there can never be a direct correspondence between law and morality, an attempt to divorce the two entirely is and has always proved to be doomed to failure, and, in the present case, the overriding objects of the criminal law must be to protect innocent lives and to set a standard of conduct which ordinary men and women are expected to observe if they are to avoid criminal responsibility.

No one who has read *R v Dudley and Stephens*, whether in the law reports or in the more popular and **discursive** volume published by Professor Simpson *Cannibalism in the Common Law* (1984), can fail to be moved by the **poignant** and anguished situation to which the two shipwrecked mariners with Brooks (who was not guilty) and the innocent boy of 17, who was the victim, were exposed and which led the Home Secretary of the day to **commute** a death sentence for murder to one of six months' imprisonment. [The defendants were adrift in an open boat and agreed that the only way to save their lives was to kill and eat the cabin boy, who was the weakest among those in the boat.] Nevertheless, when one comes to examine the case as one of legal principle it is, I believe, the case that the conclusion reached by the judges of the Queen's Bench Division and voiced by Lord Coleridge CJ, not with **manifest** compassion, has met with very wide acceptance. He said . . .

> 'Now it is admitted that the deliberate killing of this unoffending and unresisting boy was clearly murder, unless the killing can be justified by some well-recognised excuse admitted by the law. It is further admitted that there was in this case no such excuse, unless the killing was justified by what has been called "necessity". But the temptation to the act which existed here was not what the law has ever called necessity. Nor is this to be regretted. Though law and morality are not the same, and many things may be immoral which are not necessarily illegal, yet the absolute divorce of law from morality would be of fatal consequence; and such divorce would follow if the temptation to murder in this case were to be held by law an absolute defence of it. It is not so. To preserve one's life is generally speaking a duty, but it may be the plainest and the highest duty to sacrifice it. War is full of instances in which it is a man's duty not to live, but to die. The duty, in case of shipwreck, of a captain to his crew, of the crew to the passengers, of soldiers to women and children, as in the noble case of the *Birkenhead*; these duties impose on men the moral necessity, not of the preservation, but of the sacrifice of their lives for others, from which in no country, least of all, it is to be hoped, in England, will men ever shrink, as indeed, they have not shrunk . . . It is not needful to point out the awful danger of admitting the principle which has been contended for. Who is to be the judge of this sort of necessity? By what measure is the comparative value of lives to be measured? Is it to be strength, or intellect, or what? It is plain that the principle leaves to him who is to profit by it to determine the necessity which will justify him in deliberately taking another's life to save his own. In this case the weakest, the youngest, the most unresisting, was chosen. Was it

> more necessary to kill him than one of the grown men? The answer must be "No" . . .'
>
> It was pointed out in a footnote in this case (attributed to Grove J) that, if the principle were once admitted and the castaways not rescued, in the meantime it would have been lawful for the strongest of the four men to eat his way through the whole crew of the drifting boat in order to be rescued himself . . .
>
> In general, I must say that I do not at all accept in relation to the defence of duress that it is either good morals, good policy or good law to suggest, as did the majority in *Lynch's* case and the minority in *Abbott v R*, that the ordinary man of reasonable fortitude is not to be supposed to be capable of heroism if he is asked to take an innocent life rather than sacrifice his own. Doubtless in actual practice many will succumb to temptation, as they did in *R v Dudley and Stephens*. But many will not, and I do not believe that as a 'concession to human frailty' (see Smith and Hogan *Criminal Law* (5th edn, 1983) p 215) the former should be exempt from liability to criminal sanctions if they do. I have known in my own lifetime of too many acts of heroism by ordinary human beings of no more than ordinary fortitude to regard a law as either 'just or humane' which withdraws the protection of the criminal law from the innocent victim and casts the cloak of its protection on the coward and the **poltroon** in the name of a 'concession to human frailty'.

The defence of necessity, the very existence of which seemed to be in doubt, appears now to have been replaced by a defence of duress of circumstances: a person who commits a criminal offence in order to avoid a dangerous situation may be found not guilty.

Statutory defences

The defences so far have all been common law defences, developed over the years through decisions of the courts. Parliament often provides a defence as an integral part of a statute: see, for example, the Theft Act 1968 and the Criminal Damage Act 1971. The Homicide Act 1957, passed at a time when people were still hanged for murder, introduced several defences which reduced murder to manslaughter. Two of these are diminished responsibility and provocation:

> s 2 Where a person kills or is party to the killing of another, he shall not be convicted of murder if he was suffering from such abnormality of mind (whether arising from a condition of arrested or retarded development of mind or any inherent causes or induced by disease or injury) as substantially impaired his mental responsibility for his acts and omissions in doing or being party to the killing.

> s 3 Where on a charge of murder there is evidence on which the jury can find that the person charged was provoked (whether by things done or by things said or by both together) to lose his self-control, the question whether the provocation was enough to make a reasonable man do as he did shall be left to be determined by the jury; and in determining that question the jury shall take into account everything both done and said according to the effect which, in their opinion, it would have on a reasonable man.

The interpretation of these sections has exercised the courts on many occasions. In particular, the question arises: 'Who is the reasonable man for the purposes of s 3?' In lawyers' terms: 'What characteristics of the defendant is it fair to attribute to the reasonable man when making the comparison between what the defendant did and what the reasonable man might have done in the same situation'? Age and gender are appropriate and, though the reasonable man is always sober, physical characteristics and failings such as being an alcoholic or a glue sniffer are relevant. There is a string of cases on 'battered wives', ending with *Thornton (No 2)* [1996] 2 All ER 1023 in which the Court of Appeal held that mental characteristics should be taken into account.

Thornton had killed her husband with a knife which she had sharpened before using it – so it could not be said that she acted 'in hot blood'. Her defence was that she was suffering from 'battered wife syndrome' and the Court of Appeal accepted that this was a material characteristic – so she would be not guilty if the 'reasonable battered wife' would have been provoked to do as she did.

Three months after that decision, the Privy Council considered the matter in *Luc Thiet Thuan v R* [1996] 2 All ER 1033. The defendant had killed a former girlfriend. He pleaded provocation, claiming that brain damage made it difficult for him to exercise self-control and that 'the reasonable man' with whom he should be compared was 'the reasonable man with brain damage'.

Lord Goff considered the Hong Kong equivalent of the Homicide Act 1957, noting that it was identical, and therefore he looked at the interpretation of the 1957 Act. He considered the leading case on provocation after the 1957 Act, *Camplin* (1978). In that case, the defendant was a 15-year-old boy and the point at issue was whether the 'reasonable man' against whose standard the defendant should be judged was an adult or a 15-year-old. The House of Lords decided that age was a relevant characteristic, so the 'reasonable man' would be a 15-year-old. Lord Goff began by considering words of Lord Diplock in *Camplin*:

> '. . . for the purposes of the law of provocation the "reasonable man" has never been confined to the adult male. It means an ordinary person of either sex, not exceptionally excitable or pugnacious, but possessed of such powers of self-control as everyone is entitled to

> expect that his fellow citizens will exercise in society as it is today. A crucial factor in the defence of provocation from earliest times has been the relationship between the gravity of provocation and the way in which the accused retaliated, both being judged by the social standards of the day... But now that the law has been changed so as to permit of words being treated as provocation, even though unaccompanied by any other acts, the gravity of verbal provocation may well depend on the particular characteristics or circumstances of the person to whom a taunt or insult is addressed. To taunt a person because of his race, his physical infirmities or some shameful incident in his past may well be considered by the jury to be more offensive to the person addressed, however **equable** his temperament, if the facts on which the taunt is founded are true than it would be if they were not . . .
>
> The judge should state what the question is, using the very terms of the section. He should then explain to [the jury] that the reasonable man referred to in the question is a person having the power of self-control to be expected of an ordinary person of the sex and age of the accused, but in other respects sharing such of the accused's characteristics as they think would affect the gravity of the provocation to him, and that the question is not merely whether such a person would in like circumstances be provoked to lose his self-control but also would react to the provocation as the accused did.'

It is of some interest to refer at this stage to Professor AJ Ashworth's article 'The Doctrine of Provocation' [1976] CLJ 292, to which their Lordships wish to express their indebtedness. In his article Professor Ashworth observed of the common law that 'the Law's paramount concern is to ascertain whether the accused showed a reasonable amount of self-restraint' (see [1976] CLJ 292 at 299). He went on to observe that provocation can rarely be described as 'grave' **per se**; in general, this can only be so in relation to persons of a particular class. From this he concluded (at 300):

> 'The proper distinction . . . is that individual peculiarities which bear on the gravity of the provocation should be taken into account, whereas individual peculiarities bearing on the accused's level of self-control should not.'

This conclusion, of course, also involved the rejection of the decision of the House of Lords in *Bedder v DPP* (1954) . . .

Professor Ashworth's article was published in 1976, and *Camplin* was decided by the House of Lords only two years later. The similarity between the approach recommended by Professor Ashworth, and that adopted by the House of Lords in *Camplin*, is so great that it is difficult to believe that his article did not, at least indirectly, influence the reasoning and the conclusion in that case.

> Their Lordships wish to add that the recent decision of the House of Lords in *R v Morhall* (1995) is in no way inconsistent with the reasoning in *Camplin*. That case was concerned with the question whether a defendant who was taunted with his addiction to glue sniffing, or solvent abuse, was precluded from saying that that characteristic could be taken into account when considering the objective test, because such a characteristic was inconsistent with the concept of the reasonable man. The House of Lords rejected that approach, holding that a characteristic such as this should not be excluded merely because it was discreditable. In so holding, the House invoked Lord Diplock's statement that the 'reasonable man' in the section should be understood to be a person with the *ordinary* person's power of self-control, but in other respects sharing such of the defendant's characteristics as the jury might think would affect the gravity of the provocation to him.

Lord Goff then expressed the view that English law on the subject had gone astray because judges had considered New Zealand cases, even though they related to 'a different statute in another jurisdiction'. The decisions in *Ahluwalia* (1992), that being a 'battered wife' was a relevant characteristic, and *Humphries* (1995), that permanent personality defects were relevant characteristics, were, therefore, wrong.

> In these circumstances, their Lordships return to the interpretation placed on the English statute in *Camplin* for guidance in answering the question posed for their consideration in the present case. Their conclusion is that, on the principles there stated, there is no basis upon which mental infirmity on the part of the defendant which has the effect of reducing his powers of self-control below that to be expected of an ordinary person can, as such, be attributed to the ordinary person for the purposes of the objective test in provocation.
>
> . . . It is, of course, consistent with Lord Diplock's analysis in *Camplin*, and indeed with the decision of the House of Lords in *Morhall*, that mental infirmity of the defendant, if itself the subject of taunts by the deceased, may be taken into account as going to the gravity of the provocation as applied to the defendant. Such a conclusion was also consistent with the opinion expressed obiter by North J in *McGregor*. But this is a far cry from the appellant's submission that the mental infirmity of the defendant, impairing his power of self-control, should as such be attributed to the reasonable man for the purposes of the objective test.
>
> . . . the recognition by the legislature of the defence of diminished responsibility gives a defendant suffering from abnormality of mind the opportunity to establish a defence upon which a very wide interpretation has been placed by the courts and which, if proved, has, like provocation, the effect of reducing to manslaughter what would otherwise be murder. For the courts, in interpreting s 2 of the Act, have given to the words 'abnormality of mind' a very broad meaning, wide enough to embrace not

only cases of 'irresistible impulse', but also those cases in which the difficulty of the defendant in controlling (or rather failing to control) his behaviour was 'substantially greater than would be experienced in like circumstances by an ordinary man, not suffering from mental abnormality' (see Smith and Hogan *Criminal Law* (7th edn, 1992) . . .

Their Lordships wish to add, as a footnote, that it may be open to a defendant to establish provocation in circumstances in which the act of the deceased, though relatively unprovocative if taken in isolation, was the last of a series of acts which finally provoked the loss of self-control by the defendant and so precipitated his extreme reaction which led to the death of the deceased . . . Whether such a principle could be successfully invoked in cases such as, for example, the 'battered wife syndrome' is a matter upon which their Lordships can in the present case express no opinion, having heard no argument upon it, but must await a case in which the point arises for decision.

. . . There is . . . one point in the reasoning of the Court of Appeal [of Hong Kong] to which [their Lordships] wish to refer, viz that it is necessary for the provocation to have been *directed at* the relevant characteristic of the defendant. Their Lordships accept that in the great majority of cases in which a characteristic of the defendant is relevant to the gravity of the provocation to him, the provocation will in fact have been directed at that characteristic, as where it is the subject of taunts by the deceased. But they wish to observe that this need not always be so, for there may be cases in which, for example, previous events mislead the defendant into believing that an innocent remark by the deceased was so directed when in fact it was not.

Check your understanding

1 Can you explain the meaning of the words and phrases in **bold** type? Are there any other words you need to look up in a dictionary?

2 Do you have a firm understanding of the expressions 'objective' and 'subjective'?

3 In *Kingston*, Lord Mustill says a defendant will be guilty 'provided always that whatever element of intent is required by the offence is proved to have been present'. Assume he meant 'mens rea', rather than 'intent' and beware yourself of writing or saying 'intent' when you mean 'mens rea'.

Discuss

1 Why is a defence of intoxication allowed for some offences but not for others?

2 Do the justifications for limiting the availability of the defence of intoxication as given in earlier House of Lords' decisions apply to the circumstances of *Kingston*?

3 Do you prefer the Court of Appeal or the House of Lords' decision in *Kingston*? What are your reasons for your preference?

4 On what grounds did Lord Edmund-Davies disagree with the majority decision on intoxication in *Caldwell*? Do you agree with him, or with Lord Diplock?

5 Do you think the facts of *Kingston* may have influenced the House of Lords in the view they took as to the law? Do you think the same might have been true of the majority in *Brown* (p. 89)?

6 The judges are concerned to balance the interests of victims, defendants and society at large. Using evidence from the judgments, consider whether they get this balance right.

7 Why does a mistaken belief generally have only to be honest, whereas in duress and provocation there is also an objective element?

8 Stuart-Smith LJ's fourth rule about characteristics and duress (p. 131) refers to 'self-induced' intoxication. Would a person who had been drugged by the 'stratagem or fraud of another' be able to plead duress on the basis that he was more susceptible to pressure whilst intoxicated?

9 Hold a balloon debate. Lord Coleridge, quoted by Lord Hailsham in *Howe*, asked how one can determine the relative value of lives: here's your chance! Imagine there are four eminent judges in a hot air balloon – choose your four from among those with whose judgments you are familiar. The balloon is going down and it is necessary to throw three judges out to save one. Each participant becomes one of the judges and puts arguments as to why he should stay in the balloon. Other members of the group can ask questions and will, at the end of the debate, decide who stays in and who goes.

   This is a very good pre-exam exercise, as it will sharpen your knowledge of what was said in particular judgments. You could fill your balloon with a magistrate, a juror, a barrister and a mediator, who would argue about their relative contributions to the legal system. You could put in four defendants: for example, Brown, Kingston, Majewski and O'Grady, who might argue the merits of their cases or the contributions of their cases to the criminal law.

Write

1 Lord Hailsham's final sentence in *Howe* (p. 133) is rather colourful. Redraft it in the kind of language you would normally expect of a judge.

2 Find and make a note of the advice given in the judgments for directing juries.

3 From the judgments in *Majewski* and *Caldwell*, make a note of the justifications given for finding a person who is too drunk to know what he is doing guilty of offences of basic intent.

4 Summarise the judgments of the Court of Appeal and House of Lords in *Kingston*.

5 Consider what Professor Simon Lee says at p. 43 about decisions based on precedent, principle and future consequences. Write an essay: 'The decisions in *Kingston* illustrate the alternative approaches a judge must choose between when making a decision. The House of Lords made the correct decision.' Discuss.

6 Defences of self-defence, automatism, insanity, necessity and duress of circumstance are mentioned in passing in the judgments. Make notes on each by gathering what information you can from the judgments, then using other sources, such as your textbook, to complete your notes.

Connections

1 Note that in *R v Graham* Lord Lane refers to mistakes generally having to be reasonable. There is a similar statement by him in *O'Grady*. Look at the dates of the cases and consider when the law moved from an objective to a subjective approach and whether the move was clear-cut or piecemeal.

2 The House of Lords comments in *Kingston* on the difficulties that arise if the courts create a new defence. Why is creation of law by Parliament preferable? In what circumstances is it appropriate for the courts to make new law?

3 Stuart-Smith LJ's comment in *Bowen* that 'many women would doubtless consider they had as much moral courage to resist pressure as men' speaks volumes about his underlying premise as to the inherent characteristics of men and women. Think about this comment in connection with the material on the selection of judges (p. 38). Do you think a woman would have made the point in this way? Can you devise a more neutral wording to explain the relevance of gender as a characteristic in the defence of duress?

Reading

You will have noticed that judges make reference to Smith & Hogan, *Criminal Law*, though they do not always agree with it. It is an excellent book to dip in and out of when you need a particular point explained in depth and with great precision. As with all law books, make sure you are using the most up-to-date edition.

4.4 STRICT LIABILITY

The criminal law aims to protect the person and property of individuals. The easiest way to do this is to convict anyone who damages either, but criminal law is also concerned to do justice. These conflicting aims can be seen in the general necessity for a voluntary act or omission accompanied by some form of mens rea. The conflict also arises when considering what defences to allow, and we have seen in cases such as *Howe*, *Kingston* and *O'Grady* that when in doubt over the right decision judges tend to lean in favour of the interests of the victim.

There is a range of offences created by Parliament in which it is deemed more important to deter offenders and protect victims than to be concerned with doing justice to the defendant. They are known as strict liability offences and are committed by a defendant who commits the actus reus, regardless of that defendant's state of mind at the time. The statute that creates the offence often provides for a defence or defences but the overall effect of strict liability offences seems harsh when one compares them with normal criminal offences.

It is an exercise in statutory interpretation to determine whether an offence is one of strict liability or whether it requires mens rea. In *Sweet v Parsley* [1969] 1 All ER 347 a teacher who let a house to students and did not herself live there was convicted of being concerned in the management of premises used for smoking cannabis. She appealed to the House of Lords and Lord Reid explained how the statute should be approached:

> Our first duty is to consider the words of the Act; if they show a clear intention to create an absolute offence, that is an end of the matter. But such cases are very rare. Sometimes the words of the section which creates a particular offence make it clear that mens rea is required in one form or another. Such cases are quite frequent. But in a very large number of cases there is no clear indication either way. In such cases there has for centuries been a **presumption** that Parliament did not intend to make criminals of persons who were in no way blameworthy in what they did. That means that, whenever a section is silent as to mens rea, there is a presumption that, in order to give effect to the will of Parliament, we must read in words appropriate to require mens rea.
>
> Where it is contended that an absolute offence has been created, the words of Alderson B in *A G v Lockwood* have often been quoted:
>
>> 'The rule of law, I take it, upon the construction of all statutes, and therefore applicable to the construction of this, is, whether they be

> **penal** or **remedial**, to construe them according to the plain literal and grammatical meaning of the words in which they are expressed unless that construction leads to a plain and clear contradiction of the apparent purpose of the act or to some **palpable** and evident absurdity.'

That is perfectly right as a general rule and where there is no legal presumption. But what about the multitude of criminal enactments where the words of the Act simply make it an offence to do certain things but where everyone agrees that there cannot be a conviction without proof of mens rea in some form? This passage, if applied to the present problem, would mean that there is no need to prove mens rea unless it would be 'a plain and clear contradiction of the apparent purpose of the Act' to convict without proof of mens rea. But that would be putting the presumption the wrong way round; for it is firmly established by a host of authorities that mens rea is an essential ingredient of every offence unless some reason can be found for holding that that is not necessary. It is also firmly established that the fact that other sections of the Act expressly require mens rea, for example because they contain the word 'knowingly', is not in itself sufficient to justify a decision that a section which is silent as to mens rea creates an absolute offence. In the absence of a clear indication in the Act that an offence is intended to be an absolute offence, it is necessary to go outside the Act and examine all relevant circumstances in order to establish that this must have been the intention of Parliament. I say 'must have been', because it is a universal principle that if a penal provision is reasonably capable of two interpretations, that interpretation which is most favourable to the accused must be adopted.

What, then, are the circumstances which it is proper to take into account? In the well-known case of *Sherras v De Rutzen*, Wright J only mentioned the subject-matter with which the Act deals. But he was there dealing with something which was one of a class of acts which 'are not criminal in any real sense, but are acts which in the public interest are prohibited under a penalty'. It does not in the least follow that, when one is dealing with a truly criminal act, it is sufficient merely to have regard to the subject-matter of the enactment. [In *Sherras v De Rutzen* (1895) a licensee had been convicted by magistrates of serving alcohol to a police officer on duty. His conviction was quashed by the Divisional Court, who held that this was not a strict liability offence and that the defendant had reasonable grounds for believing that the constable was off duty. Wright J said: '. . . if guilty knowledge is not necessary, no care on the part of the publican could save him from conviction . . .'] One must put oneself in the position of a legislator. It has long been the practice to recognise absolute offences in this class of **quasi**-criminal acts, and one can safely assume that, when Parliament is passing new legislation dealing with this class of offences, its silence as to mens rea means that the old practice is to apply. But when one comes to acts of a truly criminal character, it appears to me that there are at least two other factors which any reasonable legislator would have in mind. In the first place, a stigma still attaches to any person convicted of a truly criminal offence, and the more serious or more disgraceful the offence the greater the stigma. So he would have to consider whether, in a case of this gravity, the public interest really requires that an innocent person should be prevented from proving his innocence in order that fewer guilty men may escape. And equally important is the fact that, fortunately, the press in this country are vigilant to expose injustice, and every manifestly unjust conviction made known to the public tends to injure the body politic by undermining public confidence in the justice of the law and of its administration. But I regret to observe that, in some recent cases where serious offences have been held to be absolute offences, the court has taken into account no more than the wording of the Act and the character and seriousness of the mischief which constitutes the offence.

Lord Morris of Borth-y-Gest, in the same case, said:

. . . as Parliament is supreme, it is open to Parliament to legislate in such a way that an offence may be created of which someone may be found guilty though mens rea is lacking. There may be cases in which, as Channell J said in *Pearks, Gunston & Tee Ltd v Ward, Hennen v Southern Counties Dairies Co Ltd*:

> '. . . the Legislature has thought it so important to prevent the particular act from being committed that it absolutely forbids it to be done; and if it is done the offender is liable to a penalty whether he had any mens rea or not and whether or not he intended to commit a breach of the law'.

Thus in diverse situations and circumstances and for any one of a variety of reasons Parliament may see fit to create offences and make people responsible before criminal courts although there is an absence of mens rea . . .

. . . in considering whether Parliament has decided to displace what is a general and somewhat fundamental rule, it would not be reasonable lightly to **impute** to Parliament an intention to create an offence in such a way that someone could be convicted of it who by all reasonable and sensible standards is without fault . . .

The question must always be – what has Parliament enacted? That is the question in the present case and to that I now turn. The wording of s 5 of the Dangerous Drugs Act 1965 is as follows:

> 'If a person—(a) being the occupier of any premises, permits those premises to be used for the purpose of smoking cannabis or cannabis resin or of dealing in cannabis and cannabis resin (whether by sale or otherwise); or (b) is concerned in the management of any

premises used for any such purpose as aforesaid; he shall be guilty of an offence against this Act.'

The words are nearly the same as and presumably were devised from words in s 5 of the Dangerous Drugs Act 1920, concerning opium. In the present case, the appellant was charged with being concerned in the management of certain premises situate in Fries Farm which were used for the purpose of smoking cannabis or cannabis resin. I need not recite the facts which are set out in the **Case Stated**. It was for the prosecution to prove the guilt of the appellant. It was found by the magistrates that the appellant had no knowledge whatsoever that cannabis had been smoked in the house. The prosecution contended that guilt can be established, of the offence created by s 5(b), if a person is concerned in the management of premises in which cannabis is in fact smoked. The consequence was acknowledged and, indeed, asserted that, if some persons managed a hostel containing say 50 to 100 rooms, and if on one day, in one room, an occupant smoked one cannabis cigarette, without the knowledge of the persons managing, they would have no defence to a charge under s 5(b). If Parliament has so enacted, then the law must be enforced. But I am sure that that is not what Parliament has decreed. . . .

. . . I consider that, on a fair reading of the phrase 'concerned in the management of any premises used for any such purpose', a link is denoted between management and user for a purpose. To say that someone is concerned in the management of premises used for the purpose of smoking cannabis involves, in my view, that his management is with knowledge that the premises are so used.

Lord Pearce said:

. . . Before the court will dispense with the necessity for mens rea it has to be satisfied that Parliament so intended. The mere absence of the word 'knowingly' is not enough. But the nature of the crime, the punishment, the absence of social **obloquy**, the particular mischief and the field of activity in which it occurs, and the working of the particular section and its context, may show that Parliament intended that the act should be prevented by punishment regardless of intent or knowledge.

Viewing the matter on these principles, it is not possible to accept the respondent's contention. Even granted that this were in the public health class of case, such as, for instance, are offences created to ensure that food shall be clean, it would be unreasonable. It is one thing to make a man absolutely responsible for all his own acts and even vicariously liable for his servants if he engages in a certain type of activity. But it is quite another matter to make him liable for persons over whom he has no control. The innocent hotel-keeper, the lady who keeps lodgings or takes paying guests, the manager of a cinema, the warden of a hostel, the matron of a hospital, the housemaster and matron of a boarding school, all these, it is conceded, are on the respondent's argument liable to conviction the moment that irresponsible occupants smoke cannabis cigarettes. And for what purpose is this harsh imposition laid on their backs? No vigilance by night or day can make them safe. The most that vigilance can attain is advance knowledge of their own guilt. If a smell of cannabis comes from a sitting-room, they know that they have committed the offence. Should they then go at once to the police and confess their guilt in the hope that they will not be prosecuted? They may think it easier to conceal the matter in the hope that it may never be found out. For if, though morally innocent, they are prosecuted, they may lose their livelihood, since thereafter, even though not punished, they are objects of suspicion. I see no real, useful object achieved by such hardship to the innocent. And so wide a possibility of injustice to the innocent should not be justified by any benefit achieved in the determent and punishment of the guilty.

. . . Parliament might, of course, have taken what was conceded in argument to be a fair and sensible course. It could have said, in appropriate words, that a person is to be liable unless he proves that he had no knowledge or guilty mind. Admittedly, if the prosecution have to prove a defendant's knowledge beyond reasonable doubt, it may be easy for the guilty to escape. But it would be very much harder for the guilty to escape if the burden of disproving *mens rea* or knowledge is thrown on the defendant. And if that were done, innocent people could satisfy a jury of their innocence on a balance of probabilities. It has been said that a jury might be confused by the different nature of the onus of satisfying 'beyond reasonable doubt' which the prosecution have to discharge and the onus 'on a balance of probabilities' which lies on a defendant in proving that he had no knowledge or guilt. I do not believe that this would be so in this kind of case. Most people can easily understand rules that express in greater detail that which their own hearts and minds already feel to be fair and sensible. What they find hard to understand is rules that go 'against the grain' of their own common sense.

Check your understanding

1 Can you explain the meaning of the words and phrases in **bold** type? Are there any other words you need to look up in a dictionary?

2 The expression 'absolute offence' is used by the judges here as if it were interchangeable with 'strict liability offence'. More recently, 'absolute liability' is used to mean offences for which the actus reus does not have to be voluntary, such as *Larsonneur* (1933), leaving 'strict liability' to mean offences for which the defendant's state of mind is irrelevant. Larsonneur was convicted of 'being found in the UK' illegally, even though she was

under arrest at the time she was brought into the UK and therefore had no control over whether she entered the UK.

Discuss

1 Compare what Lord Morris says about the 'general and somewhat fundamental rule' that a person should not be convicted unless they are at fault with Lord Mustill's contention in *Kingston* (p. 123) that there is no principle that if blame is absent, mens rea must be absent. Are they talking about the same thing?

2 It has been suggested that all offences should be offences of strict liability. Matters relating to mens rea would then be relevant to mitigation but not to guilt. Do you agree?

Write

1 From all the excerpts from speeches in *Sweet v Parsley*, make a list of the factors a judge should consider when deciding whether an offence is one of strict liability.

2 Various presumptions made by courts when interpreting statutes are mentioned in *Sweet v Parsley*. List them and, using a textbook, find out what other presumptions a court may make.

Connections

See the explanation of literal and purposive construction in *Jones v Tower Boot Co* (1997) at p. 30.

4.5 COMPANIES AS DEFENDANTS

The defendant in a criminal case is usually an individual but the development of, and increase in, business has meant that forbidden acts and omissions may be committed by companies. How should the law deal with this?

The perceived problems are that it is very difficult to speak of an artificial being having a 'state of mind'. If this problem is overcome and a company is convicted of a criminal offence, how can you sentence a company?

As the House of Lords made clear in *Sweet v Parsley*, it is considered appropriate for offences which are 'not truly criminal in nature' and which exist to protect the public to be strict liability offences. As these require no state of mind, companies can be convicted of them. The case of *R v Gateway Foodmarkets Ltd* [1997] 3 All ER 78 demonstrates how such offences can have very serious consequences. The supermarket had problems at one of its branches with a lift. The staff were constantly having to call out the lift contractors because the lift was jamming. The contractors showed the manager how to free the faulty contact that was causing the problem. It then became the practice for the duty manager to do so whenever the lift jammed. Routine maintenance work was done on the lift and, the next day, it jammed. The duty manager went into the control room to free it and fell through a trap door that had been left open by the lift contractors. He died from his injuries.

The company that owned the supermarket was prosecuted under s 2(1) of the Health and Safety at Work Act 1974, which provides:

> It shall be the duty of every employer to ensure, so far as is reasonably practicable, the health, safety and welfare at work of all his employees.

In the Court of Appeal, Evans LJ delivered the judgment of the Court:

> The House of Lords held in *R v Associated Octel Co Ltd* [1996] 4 All ER 846 . . . that s 3(1) of the 1974 Act does impose strict liability on the employer. In our judgment, the significance of Lord Hoffmann's speech in *Associated Octel*, for present purposes, is that it emphasises, in relation to s 3(1), the need to avoid 'confusion between two quite different concepts: an employer's vicarious liability for the tortious act of another and a duty imposed upon the employer himself'. The former depends generally on the contractual relationship between the employer and the other person, the latter does not. The duty under s 3 is imposed on the employer himself, 'by reference to a certain kind of activity, namely, the conduct by the employer of his undertaking'. The question, therefore (the statutory defence apart), was simply 'whether the activity in question can be described as part of the employer's undertaking' . . .
>
> I would respectfully adopt the same approach to s 2(1). The structure of the two subsections is the same. The duty is imposed on the employer. It is a duty to 'ensure . . . the health, safety and welfare at work of all his employees'. If the duty is broken, the employer is guilty of an offence . . .
>
> There is no reference in s 2(1) to the conduct of the undertaking, which is the basis for liability under s 3(1), and so it is manifest that the content of the duty under s 2(1) is different from that under s 3(1). But, in our judgment, it is the same kind of duty: the company, as employer, is liable when the necessary conditions for liability are fulfilled. Having regard to the statutory qualification 'so far as is reasonably practicable', the interpretation of s 2(1) in this way seems to us to be entirely consistent with the principle identified by Lord Reid in *Tesco Supermarkets Ltd v Nattrass*. [in

which the company was held not to be responsible for the conduct of a store manager, being able to claim under the particular statute a defence of 'due diligence'] . . . Parliament can be assumed to have balanced the need for regulation, achieved by making the employer liable, against the injustice of convicting a person who is blameless, hence the statutory defence. . . .

We agree that it is a somewhat extreme contention that the employer should be held criminally liable even for an isolated act of negligence by a junior employee, affecting the health, safety or welfare either of a fellow employee (s 2(1)), or of some other person (s 3(1)). The question is, whether that extreme consequence is one which results from the proper construction of the two subsections.

We would hold not, but we hasten to add that a conclusion on this issue is not necessary for the purposes of the present appeal.

The answer lies, we suggest, in the application of the qualification or **caveat** contained in the statute itself. The duty under each section is broken if the specified consequences occur, but only if 'so far as is reasonably practicable' they have not been guarded against. So the company is in breach of the duty unless all reasonable precautions have been taken, and we would interpret this as meaning 'taken by the company or on its behalf'. In other words, the breach of duty and liability under the section do not depend upon any failure by the company itself, meaning those persons who embody the company, to take all reasonable precautions. Rather, the company is liable in the event that there is a failure to ensure the safety etc of any employee, unless all reasonable precautions have been taken – as we would add, by the company or on its behalf.

If this is correct, then it follows that the qualification places upon the company the **onus** of proving that all reasonable precautions were taken both by it and by its servants and agents on its behalf. The concept of the 'directing mind' of the company has no application here.

The Court of Appeal then dealt with the issue of sentencing. The Crown Court had fined the company £15,000 and awarded £5,000 compensation to the family of the deceased.

The judge recognised that there are statutory limits to the amount of compensation payable to the estate of a deceased person who was unmarried. 'The way [the] law operates on civil compensation, neither his estate nor his relatives are entitled to receive even the statutory level of bereavement damages because he was over 18 and unmarried'. He continued, however, 'I believe I should consider carefully whether it is right for me to award a sum to his estate which could in some small but meaningful way help to compensate for his sad loss'. The appellants had already paid £5,000 **ex gratia**. He ordered them to pay a further £5,000, and this part of his order they appeal.

> Section 35 of the Powers of Criminal Courts Act 1973 empowers the court to make a compensation order and the question which arises is whether the amount is entirely at large, or is restricted to sums which could be awarded by way of damages in civil proceedings. Section 35(3D) limits the amount of compensation 'in respect of bereavement' to the amount specified in s 1A(3) of the Fatal Accidents Act 1976. We would be prepared to hold that the amount of compensation which can be ordered to be paid under s 35 (as amended) is limited to the court's assessment of the amount which might be recovered by action in the civil courts, but we need not go so far. In the present case, notwithstanding our sympathy for the family of Mr Finn, we do not consider that there were grounds on which the court could hold that the amount should be greater than £5,000 already paid ex gratia to his estate. We, therefore, conclude that the compensation order should be set aside.

The company in this case might be viewed as relatively free of moral blame. No one at head office knew of the practice that had been developed to deal with the faulty lift. If a company's conduct is regarded as blameworthy, the CPS may decide to charge a more serious offence, requiring mens rea. The Law Commission looked at this problem in its 1996 report, Legislating the Criminal Code: Involuntary Manslaughter:

> **Corporate Manslaughter**
>
> 1.10 In this report we have decided to devote special attention to corporate liability for manslaughter, for three reasons. First, as we will show, a number of recent cases have evoked demands for the use of the law of manslaughter following public disasters, and there appears to be a widespread feeling among the public that in such cases it would be wrong if the criminal law placed all the blame on junior employees who may be held individually responsible, and did not also fix responsibility in appropriate cases on their employers, who are operating, and profiting from, the service they provide to the public, and may be at least as culpable. Second, we are conscious of the large number of people who die in factory and building site accidents and disasters each year: many of those deaths could and should have been prevented. Third, there appear to have been only four prosecutions of a corporation for manslaughter in the history of English law, and only the last of these cases resulted in a conviction; significantly, this was a 'one man company'. It has been suggested that there are a number of outside factors which contribute to the low level of prosecutions brought against corporations for criminal offences generally.
>
> 1.11 To highlight the problems with the present law, it is helpful to refer to a series of recent disasters followed by inquiries which found corporate bodies at fault and meriting very serious criticisms. Perhaps surprisingly, no successful prosecution for manslaughter has been brought against any of the criticised parties.

1.12 On 18 November 1987 a fire of catastrophic proportions occurred in the King's Cross underground station, claiming the lives of 31 people. In his report on the fire, Mr Desmond Fennell QC (as he then was) was critical of London Underground for not guarding against the unpredictability of the fire, and also because no one person was charged with overall responsibility.

1.13 In July 1988, the Piper Alpha oil platform disaster in the North Sea caused 167 deaths. In a public inquiry, conducted by Lord Cullen, which also served in effect as an inquest, serious criticism was directed at the platform operator, holding it responsible for the deaths.

1.14 On 12 December 1988, the Clapham rail crash caused 35 deaths and nearly 500 injuries when three rush-hour trains collided after a signal breakdown. In his report, Mr Anthony Hidden QC (as he then was) was very critical of British Rail, whose 'concern for safety was permitted to co-exist with working practices which . . . were positively dangerous . . . the evidence showed the reality of [their] failure to carry that concern through into action'. Further, 'the errors go much wider and higher in the organisation than merely to remain at the hands of those who were working that day', and the report lists 16 serious relevant errors.

1.15 The reason for the absence of any conviction is probably the difficulty of mounting a manslaughter prosecution against a large-scale corporate defendant. This is illustrated by the prosecution following the tragedy which occurred on 6 March 1987, when the *Herald of Free Enterprise*, a roll-on roll-off car ferry, departed from Zeebrugge for Dover and shortly afterwards foundered with substantial loss of life. A judicial inquiry severely criticised P & O European Ferries (formerly Townsend Car Ferries Ltd). The jury at the inquest returned verdicts of unlawful killing in 187 cases, and eventually in June 1989 the DPP launched prosecutions against the company and seven individuals. But the trial collapsed after Turner J directed the jury to acquit the company and the five most senior individual defendants.

1.16 The outcome of this case provoked much criticism. The principal ground for the decision in relation to the case against the company was that, in order to convict the company of manslaughter, individual defendants who could be 'identified' with the company would have themselves to be guilty of manslaughter; since there was on the facts insufficient evidence to convict any such individual defendant, the case against the company also had to fail. This decision highlighted the major difficulty that has to be overcome before a company can be successfully prosecuted, namely that the relevant acts have to be committed by those 'identified as the embodiment of the company itself'. This principle is usually called the identification doctrine.

1.17 The great difficulty arises in identifying the people who are the embodiment of the company. As one commentator has pointed out, one effect of the identification doctrine is that the more diffuse the company structure, and the more devolved the powers that are given to semi-autonomous managers, the easier it will be to avoid liability. Other critics have said that this point is of particular importance given the increasing tendency of many organisations to decentralise safety services in particular; they point out that it is in the interest of shrewd and unscrupulous management to do so. They also quote from a study which shows that companies sought to **abrogate** responsibility for the quality of their safety research by using contract laboratories, where the effects of fierce competition over price on the standard of safety checks could be said to be the responsibility of the laboratory itself. Another problem which was identified in the Zeebrugge inquiry was that no single individual had responsibility for safety matters. If responsibility for the development of safety monitoring is not vested in a particular group or individual, it becomes almost impossible to identify the 'directing mind' for whose shortcomings the company can be liable.

1.18 The problems that confront a prosecution for corporate manslaughter explain why there has only been one successful prosecution in England and Wales, and in that case against a small company. We have welcomed the opportunity to reconsider the principles of corporate liability in the light of the great obstacles now confronting those wishing to bring a prosecution; but we are also conscious of the need to ensure that companies are not unjustly convicted merely because they are in charge of an operation or a vessel on which there has been a disaster.

1.19 In our Consultation Paper we suggested that there was no justification for applying to corporations a different law of manslaughter from that which would apply to natural persons. We accordingly provisionally proposed that a special regime should apply to corporate liability for manslaughter. Under this regime the direct question would be whether the corporation's conduct fell within the criteria for liability of the offence, namely that

(1) the accused ought reasonably to have been aware of a significant risk that his conduct could result in death or serious injury; and
(2) his conduct fell seriously and significantly below that which could reasonably have been demanded of him in preventing that risk from occurring or in preventing the risk, once in being, from resulting in the prohibited harm.

1.20 In Part VI, we set out our understanding of the way in which the present law on corporate liability has developed. In Part VII, we reconsider the proposal we made in Consultation Paper No 135 and the responses on consultation, which showed that most respondents thought that corporations should be held liable for manslaughter and were broadly in favour of the form of offence we had proposed. After considering one more recent case, we look at the options for extending corporate liability before concluding that we should seek to apply to corporations the elements of the 'individual' offence of killing by gross carelessness, in a form that is adapted to a corporate context but does not involve the principle of identification. In reaching this conclusion we have been greatly assisted by our consultant

Mr R C Nolan, Fellow and Director of Studies in Law, St John's College, Cambridge.
1.21 In Part VIII we set out the details of our new offence of corporate killing. Our main recommendations are as follows:

(1) There should be a special offence of corporate killing, broadly corresponding to the individual offence of killing by gross carelessness.
(2) Like the individual offence, the corporate offence should be committed only where the defendant's conduct in causing the death falls far below what could reasonably be expected.
(3) Unlike the individual offence, the corporate offence should *not* require that the risk be obvious, or that the defendant be capable of appreciating the risk.
(4) For the purposes of the corporate offence, a death should be regarded as having been caused by the conduct of a corporation if it is caused by a failure, in the way in which the corporation's activities are managed or organised, to ensure the health and safety of persons employed in or affected by those activities.
(5) For the purposes of the corporate offence, it should be possible for a management failure on the part of a corporation to be a cause of a person's death even if the immediate cause is the act or omission of an individual. . . .

The Court's Powers on Conviction
. . . we recommend that
(1) a court before which a corporation is convicted of corporate killing should have power to order the corporation to take such steps, within such time, as the order specifies for remedying the failure in question and any matter which appears to the court to have resulted from the failure and been the cause or one of the causes of the death;
(2) the power to make such an order should arise only on an application by the prosecution (or the Health and Safety Executive or any other body or person designated for this purpose by the Secretary of State, either generally or in relation to the case in question) specifying the terms of the proposed order; and
(3) any such order should be on such terms (whether those proposed or others) as the court considers appropriate having regard to any representation made, and any evidence **adduced**, by the prosecution (or any other body or person applying for such an order) or on behalf of the corporation.

Check your understanding

1 Can you explain the meaning of the words and phrases in **bold** type? Are there any other words you need to look up in a dictionary?

2 What is the concept of the 'directing mind' of the company, referred to by Evans LJ?

Discuss

1 Compare the defence of taking reasonable precautions with the proposal in *Sweet v Parsley* (p. 144) that a defendant might prove he had no mens rea. Which do you regard as the better solution?

2 If the Law Commission's proposals for a corporate offence of manslaughter were enacted, would a company be convicted of that offence if a situation similar to that in *R v Gateway* occurred again?

3 Do you consider that the Law Commission's proposal deals appropriately with the problem of sentencing a company? Can you make any other suggestions for sentences to suit corporate defendants?

Write

Imagine you are safety officer of Gateway Foodstores Ltd. The practice of staff 'mending' the lift has come to your attention: no accident has yet occurred. Draft a memo to the manager of the store, explaining the legal consequences of this practice and suggesting the correct procedure to be followed to deal with the problem of the jamming lift.

Connections

This material is about *primary* liability of companies. They may also be *vicariously* liable, particularly in civil matters.

5 Torts

Torts are civil wrongs. They developed during the Middle Ages through different forms of action and, therefore, each tort is distinct: there are not the general principles running through all torts that one finds running through all crimes. The purpose of suing in tort is usually to gain compensation.

5.1 NEGLIGENCE: THE DUTY OF CARE

The starting point for most courses in tort law is the tort of negligence, which is the most important tort now in the sense that many actions in negligence are brought each year. It protects people using roads, people at work, people making use of the specialist services of others, and so on. It has become so wide that the major concern over the past twenty years or so has been determining the scope of the tort.

Negligence as a distinct tort began with the case of *Donoghue v Stevenson*, decided by the House of Lords in 1932. That case was decided on the basis of earlier authorities, but it drew them together to make a significant new principle. The plaintiff had drunk ginger beer from a bottle that contained a dead snail; she sued the manufacturer of the ginger beer. The House of Lords decided that a manufacturer owes a duty of care to the ultimate consumer of a product who suffers physical harm through a defect in the product. Lord Atkin explained the circumstances in which one person would be liable for injury to or damage suffered by another by narrowing down the responsibility for our fellow man described by Jesus in the parable of the Good Samaritan. He said:

> The rule that you are to love your neighbour becomes in law that you must not injure your neighbour; and the lawyer's question, Who is my neighbour? receives a restricted reply. You must take reasonable care to avoid acts or omissions which you can reasonably foresee would be likely to injure your neighbour. Who then is my neighbour? The answer seems to be – persons who are so directly affected by my act that I ought reasonably to

> have them in contemplation as being so affected when I am directing my mind to the acts or omissions which are called in question.

The problem the courts have found over the years with this approach to the duty of care is that it tends to give rise to liability on a very wide scale. It has been narrowed by subsequent decisions, though the precise scope of the law of negligence can be likened to a tide coming and going on a beach: sometimes a lot of activities are held to be within the tort, sometimes it is restricted to fewer activities. It is certainly arguable that the courts have developed different standards according to the kind of damage suffered.

Economic loss

The first distinction to note is that drawn between a loss arising from physical injury or damage to property and 'pure economic loss', that is, monetary loss without any kind of injury to a person or damage to property. Not all judges agree with the logic of this distinction but it was explained in the House of Lords' decision in *Murphy v Brentwood District Council* [1990] 2 All ER 908. The case concerned a house which was worth far less than it should have been because there were defects in the foundations. The argument was that the local authority had a statutory duty to check the foundations and that their failure to do so gave a right of action in negligence to a subsequent owner of the property who lost money because the defect came to light and adversely affected the value of the house. This was not the first time the problem had been considered. In *Dutton v Bognor Regis United Building Co* (1972) the Court of Appeal had decided that such a right of action existed and the House of Lords agreed in *Anns v Merton London Borough* (1977). Both these cases had very similar facts to *Murphy*. Giving judgment in *Murphy*, Lord Keith said:

> My Lords, this appeal raises directly the question whether *Anns v Merton London Borough* [1977] 2 All ER 492 . . . was in all respects correctly decided.
>
> The leading speech was that of Lord Wilberforce. His examination of law started with the formulation of the two-stage test of liability in negligence which, though it has since become very familiar, I venture to quote again . . .
>
>> 'Through the trilogy of cases in this House, *Donoghue v Stevenson* (1932) . . . , *Hedley Byrne & Co Ltd v Heller & Partners Ltd* (1963) . . . and *Home Office v Dorset Yacht Co Ltd* (1970) . . . , the position has now been reached that in order to establish that a duty of care arises in a particular situation, it is not necessary to bring the facts of that situation within those of previous situations in which a

> duty of care has been held to exist. Rather the question has to be approached in two stages. First one has to ask whether, as between the alleged wrongdoer and the person who has suffered damage, there is a sufficient relationship of proximity or neighbourhood such that, in the reasonable contemplation of the former, carelessness on his part may be likely to cause damage to the latter, in which case a prima facie duty of care arises. Secondly, if the first question is answered affirmatively, it is necessary to consider whether there are any considerations which ought to negative, or to reduce or limit the scope of, the duty or the class of person to whom it is owed or the damages to which a breach of it may give rise . . .'

I observe at this point that the two-stage test has not been accepted as stating a universally applicable principle.

Lord Keith then referred to several occasions on which the decision in *Anns* had been criticised in the House of Lords and elsewhere and distinguished between defects in buildings which cause injury and defects which cause economic loss:

. . . It is the latency of the defect which constitutes the mischief. There may be room for disputation whether the likelihood of intermediate examination and consequent actual discovery of the defect has the effect of negativing a duty of care or of breaking the chain of causation . . . But there can be no doubt that, whatever the **rationale**, a person who is injured through consuming or using a product of the defective nature of which he is well aware has no remedy against the manufacturer. In the case of a building, it is right to accept that a careless builder is liable, on the principle of *Donoghue v Stevenson*, where a latent defect results in physical injury to anyone, whether owner, occupier, visitor or passer-by, or to the property of any such person. But that principle is not apt to bring home liability towards an occupier who knows the full extent of the defect yet continues to occupy the building. . . .

Consideration of the nature of the loss suffered in this category of cases is closely tied up with the question of when the cause of action arises. Lord Wilberforce in *Anns* . . . regarded it as arising when the state of the building is such that there is present an **imminent** danger to the health or safety of persons occupying it. That state of affairs may exist when there is no actual physical damage to the building itself, though Lord Wilberforce had earlier referred to the relevant damage being material physical damage. So his meaning may have been that there must be a **concurrence** of material physical damage and also present or imminent danger to the health or safety of occupants. On that view there would be no cause of action where the building had suffered no damage (or possibly, having regard to the word 'material', only very slight damage) but a structural survey had revealed an underlying defect, presenting imminent danger. Such a discovery would inevitably cause a fall in the value of the building, resulting in economic loss to the owner. . . .

In my opinion it must now be recognised that, although the damage in *Anns* was characterised as physical damage by Lord Wilberforce, it was purely economic loss. . . .

On analysis, the nature of the duty held by *Anns* to be **incumbent** on the local authority went very much further than a duty to take reasonable care to prevent injury to safety or health. The duty held to exist may be formulated as one to take reasonable care to avoid putting a future inhabitant owner of a house in a position in which he is threatened, by reason of a defect in the house, with avoidable physical injury to person or health and is obliged, in order to continue to occupy the house without suffering such injury, to expend money for the purpose of rectifying the defect.

The existence of a duty of that nature should not, in my opinion, be affirmed without a careful examination of the implications of such affirmation. To start with, if such a duty is incumbent on the local authority, a similar duty must necessarily be incumbent also on the builder of the house. If the builder of the house is to be so subject, there can be no grounds in logic or in principle for not extending liability on like grounds to the manufacturer of a **chattel**. That would open an exceedingly wide field of claims, involving the introduction of something in the nature of a transmissible **warranty** of quality. The purchaser of an article who discovered that it suffered from a dangerous defect before that defect had caused any damage would be entitled to recover from the manufacturer the cost of rectifying the defect, and, presumably, if the article was not capable of economic repair, the amount of loss sustained through discarding it. Then it would be open to question whether there should not also be a right to recovery where the defect renders the article not dangerous but merely useless. The economic loss in either case would be the same. There would also be a problem where the defect causes the destruction of the article itself, without causing any personal injury or damage to other property. . . .

In my opinion there can be no doubt that *Anns* has for long been widely regarded as an unsatisfactory decision. In relation to the scope of the duty owed by a local authority it proceeded on what must, with due respect to its source, be regarded as a somewhat superficial examination of principle and there has been extreme difficulty, highlighted most recently by the speeches in the *D & F Estates* case, in ascertaining on exactly what basis of principle it did proceed. I think it must now be recognised that it did not proceed on any basis of principle at all, but constituted a remarkable example of judicial legislation. It has **engendered** a vast spate of litigation, and each of the cases in the field which have reached this House has been distinguished. Others have been distinguished in the Court of Appeal. The result has been to keep the effect of the decision within reasonable bounds, but that has been achieved only by applying strictly the words of Lord Wilberforce and by refusing to accept the logical implications of the decision itself. These logical implications show that the case properly considered has potentiality for collision with long-established principles regarding liability in the tort of negligence for economic loss. There can be no doubt that to depart from the decision would re-establish a degree of certainty in this field of law which it has done a remarkable amount to upset. . . .

It must, of course, be kept in mind that the decision has stood for some 13 years. On the other hand, it is not a decision of the type that is to a significant extent taken into account by citizens or indeed local authorities in ordering their affairs. No doubt its existence results in local authorities having to pay increased insurance premiums, but to be relieved of that necessity would be to their advantage, not to their **detriment**. To overrule it is unlikely to result in significantly increased insurance premiums for householders. It is perhaps of some significance that most litigation involving the decisions consists in contests between insurance companies, as is largely the position in the present case. The decision is capable of being regarded as affording a measure of justice, but as against that the impossibility of finding any coherent and logically based doctrine behind it is calculated to put the law of negligence into a state of confusion defying rational analysis. It is also material that *Anns* has the effect of imposing on builders generally a liability going far beyond that which Parliament thought fair to impose on house builders alone by the Defective Premises Act 1972, a statute very material to the policy of the decision but not **adverted** to in it. There is much to be said for the view that in what is essentially a consumer protection field, as was observed by Lord Bridge in *D & F Estates Ltd v Church Comrs for England* (1988) . . . , the precise extent and limits of the liabilities which in the public interest should be imposed on builders and local authorities are best left to the legislature.

My Lords, I would hold that *Anns* was wrongly decided as regards the scope of any private law duty of care resting on local authorities in relation to their function of taking steps to secure compliance with buildings byelaws or regulations and should be departed from. It follows that *Dutton v Bognor Regis United Building Co Ltd* (1972) . . . should be overruled, as should all cases subsequent to *Anns* which were decided in reliance on it.

Lord Bridge, in *Murphy*, gave a useful explanation of the difference between dangerous defects and defects of quality:

If a manufacturer negligently puts into circulation a chattel containing a latent defect which renders it dangerous to persons or property, the manufacturer, on the well-known principles established by *Donoghue v Stevenson* . . . will be liable in tort for injury to persons or damage to property which the chattel causes. But if a manufacturer produces and sells a chattel which is merely defective in quality, even to the extent that it is valueless for the

> purpose for which it is intended, the manufacturer's liability at common law arises only under and by reference to the terms of any contract to which he is a party in relation to the chattel; the common law does not impose on him any liability in tort to persons to whom he owes no duty in contract but who, having acquired the chattel, suffer economic loss because the chattel is defective in quality. If a dangerous defect in a chattel is discovered before it causes any personal injury or damage to property, because the danger is now known and the chattel cannot be safely used unless the defect is repaired, the defect becomes merely a defect in quality. The chattel is either capable of repair at economic cost or it is worthless and must be scrapped. In either case the loss sustained by the owner or hirer of the chattel is purely economic. It is recoverable against any party who owes the loser a relevant contractual duty. But it is not recoverable in tort in the absence of a special relationship of **proximity** imposing on the tortfeasor a duty of care to safeguard the plaintiff from economic loss. There is no such special relationship between the manufacturer of a chattel and a remote owner or hirer.

He also commented on the policy implications of the distinction being made:

> In *Dutton* Lord Denning MR said:
>
> '. . . Mrs Dutton has suffered a grievous loss. The house fell down without any fault of hers. She is in no position herself to bear the loss. Who ought in justice to bear it? I should think those who were responsible. Who are they? In the first place, the builder was responsible. It was he who laid the foundations so badly that the house fell down. In the second place, the council's inspector was responsible. It was his job to examine the foundations to see if they would take the load of the house. He failed to do it properly. In the third place, the council should answer for his failure. They were entrusted by Parliament with the task of seeing that houses were properly built. They received public funds for the purpose. The very object was to protect purchasers and occupiers of houses. Yet, they failed to protect them. Their shoulders are broad enough to bear the loss.'
>
> These may be cogent reasons of social policy for imposing liability on the authority. But the shoulders of a public authority are only 'broad enough to bear the loss' because they are financed by the public at large. It is pre-eminently for the legislature to decide whether these policy reasons should be accepted as sufficient for imposing on the public the burden of providing compensation for private financial losses. If they do so decide, it is not difficult for them to say so.

Negligent statements

So, economic loss arising from a defect in a building or a chattel is not recoverable; but economic loss caused by a negligent statement may be recoverable. The major authority for this is the case of *Hedley Byrne v Heller & Partners* [1963] 2 All ER 575. An advertising agency had asked a bank for a reference about the financial stability of one of the bank's customers. The reference was good and, in reliance on it, the advertising agency did work on credit for the customer. The customer was unable to pay the agency's bill and the agency sued the bank, claiming that the reference was negligent. The result of the case was that the bank did not have to pay anything to the agency because the bank had put a clause in the reference excluding themselves from any liability. The importance of the case, however, lies in the establishment of a principle that there can be liability for negligent statements.

Lord Reid:

> Before coming to the main question of law it may be well to dispose of an argument that there was no sufficiently close relationship between these parties to give rise to any duty. It is said that the respondents did not know the precise purpose of the inquiries and did not even know whether National Provincial Bank Ltd wanted the information for its own use or for the use of a customer: they knew nothing of the appellants. I would reject that argument. They knew that the inquiry was in connexion with an advertising contract, and that it was at least probable that the information was wanted by the advertising contractors. It seems to me quite immaterial that they did not know who these contractors were: there is no suggestion of any speciality which could have influenced them in deciding whether to give information or in what form to give it. I shall therefore treat this as if it were a case where a negligent misrepresentation is made directly to the person seeking information, opinion or advice, and I shall not attempt to decide what kind or degree of proximity is necessary before there can be a duty owed by the defendant to the plaintiff.
>
> The **appellants**' first argument was based on *Donoghue v Stevenson*. That is a very important decision, but I do not think that it has any direct bearing on this case. That decision may encourage us to develop existing lines of authority, but it cannot entitle us to disregard them. Apart altogether from authority I would think that the law must treat negligent words differently from negligent acts. The law ought so far as possible to reflect the standards of the reasonable man, and that is what *Donoghue v Stevenson* sets out to do. The most obvious difference between negligent words and negligent acts is this. Quite careful people often express definite opinions on social or informal occasions, even when they see that others are likely to be influenced by them; and they often do that without taking that care which they would take if asked for their opinion professionally, or

in a business connexion. The appellants agree that there can be no duty of care on such occasions, and we were referred to American and South African authorities where that is recognised although their law appears to have gone much further than ours has yet done. But it is at least unusual casually to put into circulation negligently made articles which are dangerous. A man might give a friend a negligently prepared bottle of home-made wine and his friend's guest might drink it with dire results; but it is by no means clear that those guests would have no action against the negligent manufacturer. Another obvious difference is that a negligently-made article will only cause one accident, and so it is not very difficult to find the necessary degree of proximity or neighbourhood between the negligent manufacturer and the person injured. But words can be broadcast with or without the consent or the foresight of the speaker or writer. It would be one thing to say that the speaker owes a duty to a limited class, but it would be going very far to say that he owes a duty to every ultimate 'consumer' who acts on those words to his detriment. It would be no use to say that a speaker or writer owes a duty, but can disclaim liability if he wants to. He, like the manufacturer, could make it part of a contract that he is not to be liable for his negligence: but that contract would not protect him in a question with a third party at least if the third party was unaware of it.

So it seems to me that there is good sense behind our present law that in general an innocent but negligent misrepresentation gives no cause of action. There must be something more than the mere misstatement. I therefore turn to the authorities to see what more is required. The most natural requirement would be that expressly or by implication from the circumstances the speaker or writer has undertaken some responsibility, and that appears to me not to conflict with any authority which is binding on this House.

Lord Reid then made a careful analysis of the cases of *Derry v Peek* (1889), *Nocton v Lord Ashburton* (1914), *Candler v Crane, Christmas & Co* (1951), *Le Lievre v Gould* (1893) and *Robinson v National Bank of Scotland* (1916) and in the course of doing so he observed:

A reasonable man, knowing that he was being trusted or that his skill and judgment were being relied on, would, I think, have three courses open to him. He could keep silent or decline to give the information or advice sought: or he could give an answer with a clear qualification that he accepted no responsibility for it or that it was given without that reflection or inquiry which a careful answer would require: or he could simply answer without any qualification. If he chooses to adopt the last course he must, I think, be held to have accepted some responsibility for his answer being given carefully, or to have accepted a relationship with the inquirer which requires him to exercise such care as the circumstances require.

Lord Devlin agreed that there is liability for negligent statements, but on a different basis:

> Counsel for the respondents has given your lordships three reasons why the appellants should not recover. The first is founded on a general statement of the law which, if true, is of immense effect. Its hypothesis is that there is no general duty not to make careless statements. No one challenges that hypothesis. There is no duty to be careful in speech, as there is a duty to be honest in speech. Nor indeed is there any general duty to be careful in action. The duty is limited to those who can establish some relationship of proximity such as was found to exist in *Donoghue v Stevenson*. A plaintiff cannot therefore recover for financial loss caused by a careless statement unless he can show that the maker of the statement was under a special duty to him to be careful. Counsel submits that this special duty must be brought under one of three categories. It must be contractual; or it must be **fiduciary**; or it must arise from the relationship of proximity, and the financial loss must flow from physical damage done to the person or the property of the plaintiff. The law is now settled, counsel submits, and these three categories are **exhaustive**. . . .
>
> Counsel for the appellants agrees that outside contractual and fiduciary duty there must be a relationship of proximity – that is, *Donoghue v Stevenson* – but he disputes that recovery is then limited to loss flowing from physical damage. He has not been able to cite a single case in which a defendant has been held liable for a careless statement leading, otherwise than through the channel of physical damage, to financial loss; but he submits that in principle such loss ought to be recoverable and that there is no authority which prevents your lordships from acting on that principle. Unless counsel for the appellants can persuade your lordships of this, his case fails at the outset. . . .
>
> Originally it was thought that the tort of negligence must be confined entirely to deeds and could not extend to words. That was supposed to have been decided by *Derry v Peek*. I cannot imagine that anyone would now dispute that, if this were the law, the law would be gravely defective. The practical proof of this is that the supposed deficiency was, in relation to the facts in *Derry v Peek*, immediately made good by Act of Parliament. Today it is unthinkable that the law could permit directors to be as careless as they liked in the statements that they made in a **prospectus**.
>
> A simple distinction between negligence in word and negligence in deed might leave the law defective but at least it would be **intelligible**. This is not, however, the distinction that is drawn in counsel for the respondents' argument and it is one which would be unworkable. A defendant who is given a car to overhaul and repair if necessary is liable to the injured driver (a) if he overhauls it and repairs it negligently and tells the driver that it is safe when it is not; (b) if he overhauls it and negligently finds it not to be in need of repair and tells the driver that it is safe when

it is not; and (c) if he negligently omits to overhaul it at all and tells the driver that it is safe when it is not. It would be absurd in any of these cases to argue that the proximate cause of the driver's injury was not what the defendant did or failed to do but his negligent statement on the faith of which the driver drove the car and for which he could not recover. In this type of case where if there were a contract there would undoubtedly be a duty of service, it is not practicable to distinguish between the inspection or examination, the acts done or omitted to be done, and the advice or information given. So neither in this case nor in *Candler v Crane, Christmas & Co* (Denning LJ noted the point when he gave the example of the analyst who negligently certifies food to be harmless) has counsel for the respondents argued that the distinction lies there.

This is why the distinction is now said to depend on whether financial loss is caused through physical injury or whether it is caused directly. The interposition of the physical injury is said to make a difference of principle. I can find neither logic nor commonsense in this. If irrespective of contract, a doctor negligently advises a patient that he can safely pursue his occupation and he cannot and the patient's health suffers and he loses his livelihood, the patient has a remedy. But if the doctor negligently advises him that he cannot safely pursue his occupation when in fact he can and he loses his livelihood, there is said to be no remedy. Unless, of course, the patient was a private patient and the doctor accepted half a guinea for his trouble: then the patient can recover all. I am bound to say, my lords, that I think this to be nonsense. It is not the sort of nonsense that can arise even in the best system of law out of the need to draw nice distinctions between borderline cases. It arises, if it is the law, simply out of a refusal to make sense. The line is not drawn on any intelligible principle. It just happens to be the line which those who have been driven from the extreme assertion that negligent statements in the absence of contractual or fiduciary duty give no cause of action have in the course of their retreat so far reached.

Lord Devlin then turned to the authorities considered by Lord Reid and continued:

Now it is not in my opinion a sensible application of what Lord Atkin was saying [in *Donoghue v Stevenson*] for a judge to be invited on the facts of any particular case to say whether or not there was 'proximity' between the plaintiff and the defendant. That would be a misuse of a general conception and it is not the way in which English law develops. What Lord Atkin did was to use his general conception to open up a category of cases giving rise to a special duty. It was already clear that the law recognised the existence of such duty in the category of articles that were dangerous in themselves. What *Donoghue v Stevenson* did may be described either as the widening of an old category or as the creation of a new and similar one. The general conception can be used to produce other categories in the same way. An existing category grows as instances of its application multiply, until the time comes when the cell divides. . . .

The real value of *Donoghue v Stevenson* to the argument in this case is that it shows how the law can be developed to solve particular problems. Is the relationship between the parties in this case such that it can be brought within a category giving rise to a special duty? As always in English law the first step in such an inquiry is to see how far the authorities have gone, for new categories in the law do not spring into existence overnight.

It would be surprising if the sort of problem that is created by the facts of this case had never until recently arisen in English law. As a problem it is a byproduct of the doctrine of **consideration**. If the respondents had made a nominal charge for the reference, the problem would not exist. If it were possible in English law to construct a contract without consideration, the problem would move at once out of the first and general phase into the particular; and the question would be, not whether on the facts of the case there was a special relationship, but whether on the facts of the case there was a contract.

The respondents in this case cannot deny that they were performing a service. Their sheet anchor is that they were performing it **gratuitously** and therefore no liability for its performance can arise. My lords, in my opinion this is not the law. A promise given without consideration to perform a service cannot be enforced as a contract by the **promisee**; but if the service is in fact performed and done negligently, the promisee can recover in an action in tort.

. . . I think, therefore, that there is ample authority to justify your lordships in saying now that the categories of special relationships, which may give rise to a duty to take care in word as well as in deed, are not limited to contractual relationships or to relationships of fiduciary duty, but include also relationships which in the words of Lord Shaw in *Nocton v Lord Ashburton* are 'equivalent to contract' that is, where there is an assumption of responsibility in circumstances in which, but for the absence of consideration, there would be a contract. . . . Where there is no consideration, it will be necessary to exercise greater care in distinguishing between social and professional relationships and between those which are of a contractual character and those which are not. It may often be material to consider whether the adviser is acting purely out or good nature or whether he is getting his reward in some indirect form. The service that a bank performs in giving a reference is not done simply out of a desire to assist commerce. It would discourage the customers of the bank if their deals fell through because the bank had refused to testify to their credit when it was good. . . .

I shall therefore content myself with the proposition that wherever there is a relationship equivalent to contract there is a duty of care. . . .

I regard this proposition as an application of the general conception of proximity. Cases may arise in the future in which a new and wider proposition, quite independent of any notion of contract, will be needed. There

> may, for example, be cases in which a statement is not supplied for the use of any particular person, any more than in *Donoghue v Stevenson* the ginger beer was supplied for consumption by any particular person; and it will then be necessary to return to the general conception of proximity and to see whether there can be evolved from it, as was done in *Donoghue v Stevenson,* a specific proposition to fit the case. When that has been done, the speeches of your lordships today as well as the judgment of Denning LJ [his dissenting judgment in *Candler v Crane, Christmas & Co*], to which I have referred . . . will afford good guidance as to what ought to be said. I prefer to see what shape such cases take before committing myself to any formulation, for I bear in mind Lord Atkin's warning, which I have quoted, against placing unnecessary restrictions on the adaptability of English law. I have, I hope, made it clear that I take quite literally the **dictum** of Lord Macmillan, so often quoted from the same case, that 'the categories of negligence are never closed'. English law is wide enough to embrace any new category or proposition that **exemplifies** the principle of proximity.

Over twenty-five years after this decision, the lines of authority coming from *Hedley Byrne v Heller* and leading to *Murphy v Brentwood* were considered together in the case of *Caparo v Dickman* [1990] 1 All ER 568. The plaintiffs had bought shares in a company which had been the clients of the defendant accountants. The accountants had audited their client company's accounts but the audit had been negligent, so the accounts were inaccurate. Audited accounts have to be lodged at Companies House and become public documents. The plaintiffs relied on information in the audited accounts when deciding to buy the company. The plaintiffs had thus lost money because the company they had purchased was worth much less than they had believed. They sued the accountants in negligence.

Lord Bridge referred to the cases since *Anns* and said:

> What emerges is that, in addition to the foreseeability of damage, necessary ingredients in any situation giving rise to a duty of care are that there should exist between the party owing the duty and the party to whom it is owed a relationship characterised by the law as one of 'proximity' or 'neighbourhood' and that the situation should be one in which the court considers it fair, just and reasonable that the law should impose a duty of a given scope on the one party for the benefit of the other. But it is **implicit** in these passages referred to that the concepts of proximity and fairness embodied in these additional ingredients are not **susceptible** of any such precise definition as would be necessary to give them **utility** as practical tests, but amount in effect to little more than convenient labels to attach to the features of different specific situations which, on a detailed examination of all the circumstances, the law recognises **pragmatically** as giving rise to a duty of care of a given scope. Whilst recognising, of course, the importance of the underlying general principles common to the whole field

of negligence, I think the law has now moved in the direction of attaching greater significance to the more traditional categorisation of distinct and recognisable situations as guides to the existence, the scope and the limits of the varied duties of care which the law imposes.

Turning to the specific area of liability for negligent statements, he said:

The damage which may be caused by the negligently spoken or written word will normally be confined to economic loss sustained by those who rely on the accuracy of the information or advice they receive as a basis for action. The question what, if any, duty is owed by the maker of a statement to exercise due care to ensure its accuracy arises typically in relation to statements made by a person in the exercise of his calling or profession. In advising the client who employs him the professional man owes a duty to exercise that standard of skill and care appropriate to his professional status and will be liable both in contract and in tort for all losses which his client may suffer by reason of any breach of that duty. But the possibility of any duty of care being owed to third parties with whom the professional man was in no contractual relationship was for long denied because of the wrong turning taken by the law in *Le Lievre v Gould* (1893) in overruling *Cann v Willson* (1888). In *Candler v Crane Christmas & Co* (1951) Denning LJ, in his dissenting judgment, made a valiant attempt to correct the error. But it was not until the decision of this House in *Hedley Byrne & Co Ltd v Heller Partners Ltd* (1963) that the law was once more set on the right path.

Consistently with the traditional approach it is to these authorities and to subsequent decisions directly relevant to this relatively narrow corner of the field that we should look to determine the essential characteristics of a situation giving rise, independently of any contractual or fiduciary relationship, to a duty of care owed by one party to another to ensure that [*sic*] the accuracy of any statement which the one party makes and on which the other party may foreseeably rely to his economic detriment. . . .

The **salient** feature of all these cases is that the defendant giving advice or information was fully aware of the nature of the transaction which the plaintiff had in contemplation, knew that the advice or information would be communicated to him directly or indirectly and knew that it was very likely that the plaintiff would rely on that advice or information in deciding whether or not to engage in the transaction in contemplation. In these circumstances the defendant could clearly be expected, subject always to the effect of any disclaimer of responsibility, specifically to anticipate that the plaintiff would rely on the advice or information given by the defendant for the very purpose for which he did in the event rely on it. So also the plaintiff, subject again to the effect of any disclaimer, would in that situation reasonably suppose that he was entitled to rely on the advice or

> information communicated to him for the very purpose for which he required it. The situation is entirely different where a statement is put into more or less general circulation and may foreseeably be relied on by strangers to the maker of the statement for any one of a variety of different purposes which the maker of the statement has no specific reason to anticipate. To hold the maker of the statement to be under a duty of care in respect of the accuracy of the statement to all and sundry for any purpose for which they may choose to rely on it is not only to subject him, in the classic words of Cardozo CJ, to 'liability in an **indeterminate** amount for an indeterminate time to an indeterminate class' (see *Ultramares Corp v Touche* (1931)), it is also to confer on the world at large a quite unwarranted entitlement to appropriate for their own purposes the benefit of the expert knowledge or professional expertise attributed to the maker of the statement. Hence, looking only at the circumstances of these decided cases where a duty of care in respect of negligent statements has been held to exist, I should expect to find that the 'limit or control mechanism . . . imposed on the liability of a wrongdoer towards those who have suffered economic damage in consequence of his negligence' (see the *Candlewood* case) rested on the necessity to prove, in this category of the tort of negligence, as an essential ingredient of the 'proximity' between the plaintiff and the defendant, that the defendant knew that his statement would be communicated to the plaintiff, either as an individual or as a member of an identifiable class, specifically in connection with a particular transaction or transactions of a particular kind (eg in a prospectus inviting investment) and that the plaintiff would be very likely to rely on it for the purpose of deciding whether or not to enter on that transaction or on a transaction of that kind.

The *Caparo* approach has since been used in a variety of cases. In *Spring v Guardian Assurance* [1994] 3 All ER 129 it was applied to decide that an ex-employee could bring an action in respect of a negligent reference. In the insurance industry it is a requirement that a company asked for a reference by another company in the insurance industry *must* 'make full and frank disclosure of all relevant matters which are believed to be true'. In other words, whereas in any other situation it is open to a person or a company to refuse to give a reference, this is not an option in the insurance industry. Guardian Assurance gave a bad reference about the plaintiff, which was untrue and had been negligently prepared. Lord Woolf considered whether there could be a claim in negligence:

> The claim here is in respect of economic loss. Before there can be a duty owed in respect of economic loss, it is now clearly established that it is important to be able to show foreseeability of that loss, coupled with the necessary degree of proximity between the parties. It is also necessary to establish that in all the circumstances it is fair, just and reasonable for a duty to be imposed in respect of the economic loss.

He then looked at the guidance given in *Hedley Byrne v Heller* and said:

> Applying that guidance to the different situation of the relationship between the person giving and the person who is the subject of the reference, it is immediately clear that a distinction can be drawn between cases where the subject of the reference is an employee . . . or an ex-employee and where the relationship is social and has never been contractual. . . . Here the relationship is of a different order because there is or has been a contract of employment or services. Of course the period which elapses between the end of the engagement and the giving of the reference is capable of reducing the degree of proximity.
>
> In addition, the relationship is one where the employer should, as I have already indicated, appreciate that the terms of any reference which he gives could materially affect the ability of the subject of the reference to find alternative employment. Furthermore, in a contemporary employment context it is appropriate to regard the employer as obtaining an indirect benefit from giving a reference. Employers in industry, commerce and the professions are all dependent on the reciprocity which exists among employers as to the giving of references on prospective recruits. Without that **reciprocity** recruitment of staff would be more difficult. It would also directly affect an employer's ability to recruit staff if it became known that he was not prepared to assist those he has previously engaged by giving them references. Employees are unlikely to regard as attractive employment at the end of which they would find themselves without a reference.

The principle of *Hedley Byrne v Heller* has probably been stretched to its outer limit by the House of Lords' decision in *White v Jones* [1995] 1 All ER 691. The House found that a solicitor who negligently failed to prepare a new will for a client, having been instructed to do so, owed a duty of care to the intended beneficiaries under the new will, who received nothing on the death of the testator because of the solicitor's negligence.

Lord Goff explained that the decision in *Ross v Caunters* (1979), in which testators had been able to recover from a firm of solicitors in respect of a will that had not been properly witnessed and was therefore invalid, had stood for some years but that it raised conceptual problems that should be dealt with by the House:

> It is right however that I should immediately summarise these **conceptual** difficulties. They are as follows:
>
> (1) First, the general rule is well established that a solicitor acting on behalf of a client owes a duty of care only to his client. The relationship between a solicitor and his client is nearly always contractual, and the scope of the solicitor's duties will be set by the terms of his retainer: but a duty of care owed by a solicitor to his client will arise concurrently in

> contract and in tort (see *Midland Bank Trust Co Ltd v Hett, Stubbs & Kemp (a firm)* [1978] 3 All ER 571 . . . recently approved by your Lordships' House in *Henderson v Merrett Syndicates Ltd* [1994] 3 All ER 506 . . .). But, when a solicitor is performing his duties to his client, he will generally owe no duty of care to third parties. . . .
>
> In these circumstances, it is said, there can be no liability of the solicitor to a beneficiary under a will who has been disappointed by reason of negligent failure by the solicitor to give effect to the testator's intention. There can be no liability in contract, because there is no contract between the solicitor and the disappointed beneficiary; if any contractual claim was to be recognised, it could only be by way of a **ius quaesitum tertio**, and no such claim is recognised in English law. Nor could there be liability in tort, because in the performance of his duties to his client a solicitor owes no duty of care in tort to a third party such as a disappointed beneficiary under his client's will.
>
> (2) . . . the plaintiff's claim is one for purely financial loss; and as a general rule, apart from cases of assumption of responsibility arising under the principle in *Hedley Byrne & Co v Heller & Partners Ltd* (1963), no action will lie in respect of such loss in the tort of negligence. Furthermore, in particular, no claim will lie in tort for damages in respect of a mere loss of an expectation, as opposed to damages in respect of damage to an existing right or interest of the plaintiff. . . .
>
> (3) A third, and distinct, objection is that, if liability in tort was recognised in cases such as *Ross v Caunters*, it would be impossible to place any sensible bounds to cases in which such recovery was allowed. In particular, the same liability should logically be imposed in cases where an **inter vivos** transaction was ineffective, and the defect was not discovered until the donor was no longer able to repair it. Furthermore, liability could not logically be restricted to cases where a specific named beneficiary was disappointed, but would inevitably have to be extended to cases in which wide, even indeterminate, classes of persons could be said to have been adversely affected. . . .
>
> (5) There is however another objection of a conceptual nature, which was not **adumbrated** in argument before the Appellate Committee. In the present case, unlike *Ross v Caunters* itself, there was no act of the defendant solicitor which could be characterised as negligent. All that happened was that the solicitor did nothing at all for a period of time, with the result that the testator died before his new testamentary intentions could be implemented in place of the old. As a general rule, however, there is no liability in tortious negligence for an omission, unless the defendant is under some pre-existing duty. Once again, therefore, the question arises how liability can arise in the present case in the absence of a contract. . . .

Lord Goff considered the policy reasons for finding a duty owed to beneficiaries. He noted that:

> if such a duty is not recognised, the only persons who might have a valid claim (ie the testator and his estate) have suffered no loss, and the only person who has suffered a loss (ie the disappointed beneficiary) has no claim,

that legacies are important to those who receive them, more so if they are of modest means, and that if a solicitor has been negligent it is just that he should be liable to pay damages. Coming back to the conceptual problems, he continued:

> . . . It is however my opinion that, these conceptual arguments having been squarely raised in argument in the present case, they cannot lightly be dismissed. They have to be faced; and it is immediately apparent that they raise the question whether the claim properly falls within the law of contract or the law of tort. This is because, although the plaintiff's claim has been advanced, and indeed held by the Court of Appeal to lie, in the tort of negligence, nevertheless the response of the appellants has been that the claim, if properly analysed, must necessarily have contractual features which cannot ordinarily exist in the case of an ordinary tortious claim. Here I refer not only to the fact that the claim is one for damages for pure economic loss, but also to the need for the defendant solicitor to be entitled to invoke as against the disappointed beneficiary any terms of the contract with his client which may limit or exclude his liability; to the fact that the damages claimed are for the loss of an expectation; and also to the fact (not adverted to below) that the claim in the present case can be said to arise from a pure omission, and as such will not (apart from special circumstances) give rise to a claim in tortious negligence.

Lord Goff considered at some length various approaches to the problem through the law of contract and concluded that the answer must lie in the law of tort.

> For the reasons I have already given, an ordinary action in tortious negligence on the lines proposed by Megarry V-C in *Ross v Caunters* (1979) . . . must, with the greatest respect, be regarded as inappropriate because it does not meet any of the conceptual problems which have been raised. Furthermore, for the reasons I have previously given, the *Hedley Byrne* principle cannot, in the absence of special circumstances, give rise on ordinary principles to an assumption of responsibility by the testator's solicitor towards an intended beneficiary. Even so, it seems to me that it is open to your Lordships' House, as in *Linden Gardens Trust Ltd v Lenesta Sludge Disposals Ltd* (1993) . . . , to fashion a remedy to fill a lacuna in the law and so prevent the injustice which would otherwise occur on the facts of cases such as the present. In the *Lenesta Sludge* case, as I have said, the House made available a remedy as a matter of law to solve the problem of

transferred loss in the case before them. The present case is, if anything, **a fortiori**, since the nature of the transaction was such that, if the solicitors were negligent and their negligence did not come to light until after the death of the testator, there would be no remedy for the ensuing loss unless the intended beneficiary could claim. In my opinion, therefore, your Lordships' House should in cases such as these extend to the intended beneficiary a remedy under the *Hedley Byrne* principle by holding that the assumption of responsibility by the solicitor towards his client should be held in law to extend to the intended beneficiary who (as the solicitor can reasonably foresee) may, as a result of the solicitor's negligence, be deprived of his intended legacy in circumstances in which neither the testator nor his estate will have a remedy against the solicitor. Such liability will not of course arise in cases in which the defect in the will comes to light before the death of the testator, and the testator either leaves the will as it is or otherwise continues to exclude the previously intended beneficiary from the relevant benefit. I only wish to add that, with the benefit of experience during the 15 years in which *Ross v Caunters* has been regularly applied, we can say with some confidence that a direct remedy by the intended beneficiary against the solicitor appears to create no problems in practice. That is therefore the solution which I would recommend to your Lordships.

As I see it, not only does this conclusion produce practical justice as far as all parties are concerned, but it also has the following beneficial consequences.

(1) There is no unacceptable **circumvention** of established principles of the law of contract.

(2) No problem arises by reason of the loss being of a purely economic character.

(3) Such assumption of responsibility will of course be subject to any term of the contract between the solicitor and the testator which may exclude or restrict the solicitor's liability to the testator under the principle in *Hedley Byrne*. It is true that such a term would be most unlikely to exist in practice; but as a matter of principle it is right that this largely theoretical question should be addressed.

(4) Since the *Hedley Byrne* principle is founded upon an assumption of responsibility, the solicitor may be liable for negligent omissions as well as negligent acts or commission: see *Midland Bank Trust Co Ltd v Hett, Stubbs & Kemp* (1978) . . . per Oliver J, and my own speech in *Henderson v Merrett Syndicates Ltd* (1994) . . .

(5) I do not consider that damages for loss of an expectation are excluded in cases of negligence arising under the principle in *Hedley Byrne*, simply because the cause of action is classified as tortious. Such damages may in principle be recoverable in cases of contractual negligence; and I cannot see that, for present purposes, any relevant distinction can be drawn between the two forms of action. In particular, an expectation loss may well occur in

cases where a professional man, such as a solicitor, has assumed responsibility for the affairs of another; and I for my part can see no reason in principle why the professional man should not, in an appropriate case, be liable for such loss under the *Hedley Byrne* principle. . . .

I come finally to the objection that, if liability is recognised in a case such as the present, it will be impossible to place any sensible limits to cases in which recovery is allowed. Before your Lordships, as before the Court of Appeal, Mr Matheson conjured up the spectre of solicitors being liable to an indeterminate class, including persons unborn at the date of the testator's death. . . . We are concerned here with a liability which is imposed by law to do practical justice in a particular type of case. There must be boundaries to the availability of a remedy in such cases; but these will have to be worked out in the future, as practical problems come before the courts. . . . If by any chance a more complicated case should arise to test the precise boundaries of the principle in cases of this kind, that problem can await solution when such a case comes forward for decision.

Lord Browne-Wilkinson agreed with Lord Goff's conclusion, saying:

In my view, although the present case is not directly covered by the decided cases, it is legitimate to extend the law to the limited extent proposed using the incremental approach by way of analogy advocated in *Caparo Industries plc v Dickman* (1990).

Lord Keith, however, did not agree:

To admit the plaintiffs' claim in the present case would in substance, in my opinion, be to give them the benefit of a contract to which they were not parties.

Further, there is, in my opinion, no decided case the grounds of decision in which are capable of being extended incrementally and by way of analogy so as to admit of a remedy in tort being made available to the plaintiffs. In [*Hedley Byrne v Heller*] there was a direct relationship between the parties creating such proximity as to give rise to a duty of care. Here there was no relationship between the plaintiffs and [the solicitor], nor did [the solicitor] do or say anything upon which the plaintiffs acted to their prejudice. No damage was done by [the solicitor] to any existing financial or other interest of the plaintiffs.

Physical damage and injury

Following the decision in *Caparo v Dickman*, the courts tend to reason by analogy in deciding to extend or restrict liability. The principles applied to physical injury or damage to property are generally well settled but there are occasionally interesting cases on the issue of what is 'fair, just and reasonable'. *Mulcahy v Ministry of Defence* [1996] 2 All ER 758 concerned an action by a soldier whose hearing had been damaged during the Gulf War. His gun commander had ordered that a howitzer be fired when the plaintiff was in an unsafe position. He argued that the gun commander had been negligent and that the Ministry of Defence were in breach of their duty to maintain a safe system of work. The Court of Appeal decided that no duty of care was owed in battle conditions. Neill LJ said:

> In *Marc Rich & Co AG v Bishop Rock Marine Co Ltd, The Nicholas H* [1995] 3 All ER 307 . . . Lord Steyn drew attention to the fact that since the decision in *Home Office v Dorset Yacht Co Ltd* (1970) '. . . it has been settled law that the elements of foreseeability and proximity as well as considerations of fairness, justice and reasonableness are relevant to all cases of alleged negligence whatever the nature of the harm sustained by the plaintiff.'
>
> In the present case it is accepted on behalf of the defendants that two of these components of a duty of care, proximity and foreseeability of damage, are present. The issue to be determined is whether it is fair, just and reasonable that a duty of care should be imposed on one soldier in his conduct towards another when engaging the enemy during hostilities. In the light of the recent amendment to the plaintiff's **pleading** the same question has to be asked in relation to the alleged duty to maintain a safe system of work.
>
> It is plain from the decision of the House of Lords in the *Marc Rich* case that in order to decide whether it is fair, just and reasonable to impose a duty of care one must consider all the circumstances including the position and role of the alleged tortfeasor and any relevant policy consideration. In this context one should bear in mind the dictum of Lord Pearce in *Hedley Byrne & Co Ltd v Heller & Partners Ltd* (1963):
>
>> 'How wide the sphere of the duty of care in negligence is to be laid depends ultimately upon the courts' assessment of the demands of society for protection from the carelessness of others.'
>
> This dictum was cited by Lord Diplock in the *Dorset Yacht* case (1970) . . . In the absence of legislative guidance the question of policy has to be resolved by the courts.
>
> I am satisfied that in a hypothetical case a court would require proof that the injury was sustained in battle conditions. But here, as it seems to me, the plaintiff's pleaded case makes the position clear. The question then becomes: 'Is a duty of care to be imposed in such conditions so as to make one serviceman liable for his negligent act towards another?' In my opinion, despite the careful arguments addressed to us on behalf of the plaintiff,

> there is no basis for extending the scope of the duty of care so far. . . . I reach the same conclusion on the plaintiff's alternative claim. In my opinion there was no duty on the defendants in these battle conditions to maintain a safe system of work.

In *John Munroe (Acrylics) Ltd v London Fire and Civil Defence Authority and others* [1996] 4 All ER 318 the High Court had to decide whether the fire brigade owes a duty to the owners of property which is on fire. The judgment is interesting because it draws on similar cases with regard to the liability of the police and prison service. It was given by Rougier J, who referred to the practice of developing the law incrementally and by analogy and continued:

> Following, I hope, this line of approach, it seems to me necessary to consider what are the services or organisations and their operations which are sufficiently comparable in kind, so that the incremental approach referred to can enable one to say that a duty of common law should or should not be implied to the fire brigade. In doing so, I regard as an essential feature of true comparability that the duty postulated should be a duty to protect or assist the plaintiff from the harm done or threatened by third parties, or from some peril not brought about by any act or omission of the fire brigade itself.
>
> This leads me straight to the principal case on the subject, namely the decision of the House of Lords in *Hill v Chief Constable of West Yorkshire* [1988] 2 All ER 238 . . . , where the mother of one of the victims of the so-called Yorkshire Ripper attempted to sue the police for their alleged negligence in failing to identify and apprehend the killer in good and sufficient time. The House held that there was no general duty of care owed by police officers, either to identify or apprehend an unknown criminal; nor did they owe a duty of care to individual members of the public who might suffer injury through the criminal's activities, except in situations where their failure to apprehend him had created an exceptional added risk beyond that to which all, or at any rate, a large section of the public were subject. Their Lordships further held that the fact that the plaintiff's daughter had been young and female, in line with the killer's other victims, did not of itself place her at special risk, and that there were no other additional characteristics capable of establishing sufficient proximity to cast upon the police a common law duty of care.
>
> [Lord Keith] further considered *Home Office v Dorset Yacht Co Ltd* [1970] 2 All ER 294 . . . , on which Mrs Hill and the present plaintiffs placed reliance, and illustrated the essential distinction between that case and *Hill's* case as follows:
>
> > 'The *Dorset Yacht* case dealt with a situation where some Borstal boys, who having records of previous escapes, were encamped

> on Brownsea Island under the supervision of prison officers and escaped in the night while their guardians slept, boarded a yacht moored nearby in order to make their way to the mainland and manoeuvred it so as to damage the plaintiff's yacht. One of the features of the case was that the damage sustained by the plaintiffs was the direct consequence of a tortious act done with **conscious volition** by a third party responsible for his own acts, which was interposed between the allegedly negligent conduct of the prison officers and the damage suffered. The actual decision, which was on a preliminary point of law, was that a special relationship existed on the one hand between the prison officers and the Borstal boys who were in their custody, and on the other hand between the prison officers and the owners of yachts moored near the encampment. That the boys might seek to make use of a yacht in order to get away to the mainland and might damage it in the process was the very thing which the prison officers ought reasonably to have foreseen. The prison officers had brought the boys, of whose **propensity** to attempt escape they were aware, into the locality where the yachts were moored and so had created a potential situation of danger for the owners of those yachts. Accordingly liability was capable of being established on the facts.'

In other words, the *Dorset Yacht* case is explicable on the basis that, by their actions in bringing the youths, known to be criminal, into close physical proximity with the yachts moored nearby, and leaving them unsupervised, the prison officers had effectively created an additional risk and brought themselves into legal proximity with the owners of the boats.

In considering whether it would be 'fair, just and reasonable' to impose liability on the fire brigade, the judge referred to a passage from *Clerk and Lindsell on Torts* (17th edn, 1995) and continued:

I think that as regards the fire brigade, many of these considerations are applicable and militate on grounds of public policy against the imposition of any common law duty. In particular, I would single out the following; (1) I do not think that any extra standard of care would be achieved. (2) Rather the reverse; if a common law duty of care can lead to defensive policing, by the same token it can lead to defensive fire-fighting. Fearful of being accused of leaving the scene too early, the officer in charge might well commit his resources when they would have been better employed elsewhere. He would be open to criticism every time there was a balance to be struck or that sort of operational choice to be made. (3) If the efficiency of the emergency services is to be tested, it should be done not in private litigation but by an inquiry instituted by national or local authorities who are responsible to the electorate. This follows the reasoning of Lord

> Templeman in *Hill's* case. (4) The case of *Marc Rich & Co AG v Bishop Rock Marine Co Ltd, The Nicholas H* (1995) . . . suggests that the fact that a defendant in the position of the fire brigade acts for the collective welfare is one that should be taken into account. (5) Last, and to my mind by far the most important consideration, is what is sometimes referred to as the **'floodgates' argument**.
>
> . . . There seems to be a growing belief that every misfortune must, in pecuniary terms at any rate, be laid at someone else's door, and after every mishap, every tragedy, the cupped palms are outstretched for the solace of monetary compensation. Claims which would have been unheard of 30 years ago are now being seriously entertained, and public money provided for pursuing them. When performing their primary function, namely fighting fires, the fire brigade are very often reacting to a situation created either by the hand of God or that of a lunatic or of a criminal. Pecuniary compensation is notoriously difficult to obtain from such persons, particularly the first named. The consequence of this is that the party suffering damage will be eager to fix his cannon against a defendant who may be in a position to meet the claim. Just as with the police, as part of any action brought against the fire brigade it may be necessary to institute an elaborate investigation into the facts so that one can decide whether or not any decision or exercise of discretion was one which the courts would allow to be called in question. This is in relation to decisions which are almost always made in dangerous and rapidly developing situations. One can envisage protracted arguments between various experts in this field. In relation to such claims as may succeed, the money to meet those claims will, whether by straight award or increased premium, ultimately have to be subscribed by the general public.

In *Capital and Counties plc v Hampshire County Council and others* [1996] 4 All ER 336, another High Court judge decided a similar case only a few weeks later. In this case, the fire brigade were called to a fire and the officer in charge negligently gave instructions for the sprinkler system in the building to be turned off. This led to the damage being much greater than would have been the case had the system been left on. Judge Havery QC came to the conclusion that, in this case, the fire brigade *did* owe a duty of care to the owner of the building:

> . . . where the fire brigade are fighting a fire, they should be under a duty to exercise reasonable care in doing so. However, it is unnecessary for me to decide that general proposition, and I do not do so. What I do decide is that it is fair, just and reasonable that the defendants should have owed a duty of care, and that they did owe a duty of care, to the plaintiffs in relation to the shutting down of the sprinkler system, and that there is no immunity on grounds of public policy from liability in relation to the decision to shut it down. Here there was a positive act: shutting down the sprinkler.

> If the sprinklers had not been automatic, but operated manually, and the complaint had been of negligent failure to turn them on, the position might be different.

He distinguished the *Munroe* case and a similar case decided the same way as *Munroe*, saying:

> In both of the other cases the matters complained of were entirely or substantially negative in character: in the one case failure properly to maintain the hydrants; in the other failure to discover on site that a fire was still smouldering. The existence of liability in those cases must depend on the existence of a duty, whether absolute or a duty of care, to maintain the hydrants or to fight the fire. My decision in the instant case does not depend on the existence of such a duty. I have found that the fire brigade have committed a positive act of negligence for which anyone else would be liable; and that neither on grounds of fairness, justice and reasonableness nor on considerations of public policy (which overlap with those grounds) should the fire brigade not be liable.
>
> The reasoning which appears in both judgments in relation to those overlapping matters appears to me to apply with far greater force to the exercise of administrative discretion than it does to operational matters. Of course, there can be an overlap between the two. For example, there is the possibility that a fire brigade on the site of a fire might have other urgent calls on its hands justifying its removal from the site before fully investigating whether the fire was still smouldering. I derive that example from what Rougier J said in the context of defensive fire-fighting. But it seems to me a strong thing to say that, because of possibilities of that kind, the brigade should have a blanket immunity so that no remedy would be available to an injured plaintiff even in the case of the most glaring negligence.
>
> The floodgates argument has been persuasive. It does not persuade me. The courts are not **astute** to find professional persons who make a mistake guilty of negligence. I have considered the law on this aspect of the matter in my earlier judgment. In the case of the fire brigade there are often, as there were here, the added elements of danger and urgency. Unmeritorious actions against fire brigades will not be successful. I do not think it likely that there would be a flood of such actions in the absence of blanket immunity. Certainly, I do not consider that the possible risk of that is a reason for denying an otherwise just claim.

These cases were both the subject of appeals and both decisions were **affirmed** by the Court of Appeal, so the law is that a fire brigade owes a duty of care only in respect of acts (such as turning the sprinkler system off), not omissions (failing to check adjoining premises). Stuart-Smith LJ said:

> In our judgment, a fire brigade does not enter into a sufficiently proximate relationship with the owner or occupier of premises to come under a duty of care merely by attending at the fire ground and fighting the fire; this is so, even though the senior officer actually assumes control of the fire-fighting operation.

This did not mean, however, that there is a blanket immunity for firefighters. Having decided that there was insufficient proximity when there is an omission to act, it was not necessary to look at whether it was 'just, fair and reasonable' to impose a duty of care but the Court of Appeal believed that the three elements of the *Caparo* test are so closely interrelated that it would be appropriate to consider the policy issues. They concluded that there was 'no general immunity for professionals or others carrying out difficult tasks in stressful circumstances' but the dividing line between liability and non-liability was whether the damage was caused by an act or an omission. The Court of Appeal was critical of Rougier J's policy arguments in the *Munroe* case.

Psychiatric harm

We have seen that the courts are very cautious about economic loss. They are similarly wary about granting damages to a plaintiff who has suffered psychiatric, rather than physical, injury. The Court of Appeal explained the kind of psychiatric injury for which damages would be awarded in *Vernon v Bosley (No 1)* [1997] 1 All ER 577. The plaintiff had been called to a river where his young children were trapped underwater in a car. He claimed to have suffered psychiatric harm as a result of this experience. Stuart-Smith LJ explained that the shock must be a 'sudden appreciation by sight or sound of a horrifying event, which violently agitates the mind', as required in *Alcock v Chief Constable of South Yorkshire Police* [1991] 4 All ER 907, and that the plaintiff must suffer from a recognised psychiatric illness. He identified this illness as post-traumatic stress disorder and laid out the definition of it given in a leading text used by psychiatrists. He then distinguished between the plaintiff who is suffering from PTSD, who may recover damages, and the plaintiff who is suffering 'the pangs of grief and bereavement', who will not be awarded damages, even if that grief is serious enough to give rise to the illness of pathological grief disorder. He said:

> There are in fact two separate illnesses, PTSD and PGD; their symptoms may in some respects be similar, ie include depression and anxiety, but their **aetiology** is different. The plaintiff in this case can recover if he can show that his present condition is PTSD, that is to say was caused or substantially contributed to by the shock of witnessing the event. He cannot do so if his

condition is due to a grief reaction or other causes such as reaction to business stress.

A leading case on damages for psychiatric harm is the House of Lords' decision in *Alcock*. The case arose from the Hillsborough Disaster, when 95 people were killed in a crush in a stand at a football ground caused by the negligence of the police in crowd management. The question was whether relatives of the deceased could recover damages in respect of their psychiatric illness caused by shock. Lord Keith explained how the principle of *Donoghue v Stevenson* is applied in such cases:

> The concept of a person being closely and directly affected has been conveniently labelled 'proximity', and this concept has been applied in certain categories of cases, particularly those concerned with pure economic loss, to limit and control the consequences as regards liability which would follow if reasonable foreseeability were the sole criterion.
>
> As regards the class of person to whom a duty may be owed to take reasonable care to avoid inflicting psychiatric illness through nervous shock sustained by reason of physical injury or peril to another, I think it sufficient that reasonable foreseeability should be the guide. I would not seek to limit the class by reference to particular relationships such as husband and wife or parent and child. The kinds of relationship which may involve close ties of love and affection are numerous, and it is the existence of such ties which leads to mental disturbance when the loved one suffers a catastrophe. They may be present in family relationships or those of close friendship, and may be stronger in the case of engaged couples than in that of persons who have been married to each other for many years. It is common knowledge that such ties exist, and reasonably foreseeable that those bound by them may in certain circumstances be at real risk of psychiatric illness if the loved one is injured or put in peril. The closeness of the tie would, however, require to be proved by a plaintiff, though no doubt being presumed in appropriate cases. The case of a bystander unconnected with the victims of an accident is difficult. Psychiatric injury to him would not ordinarily, in my view, be within the range of reasonable foreseeability, but could not perhaps be entirely excluded from it if the circumstances of a catastrophe occurring very close to him were particularly horrific.

Lord Ackner said:

> A recital of the cases over the last century shows that the extent of the liability for shock-induced psychiatric illness has been greatly expanded. This has largely been due to a better understanding of mental illness and its relation to shock. The extension of the scope of this cause of action sought in these appeals is not on any such ground but, so it is contended, by the application of established legal principles. . . .

> Even though the risk of psychiatric illness is reasonably foreseeable, the law gives no damages if the psychiatric injury was not induced by shock. Psychiatric illnesses caused in other ways, such as from the experience of having to cope with the deprivation consequent upon the death of a loved one, attracts no damages.

What emerged from the *Alcock* case was that damages could be recovered only by people who had a close tie of love and affection with the victim and had seen or heard the incident or its immediate aftermath.

In *Page v Smith* [1995] 2 All ER 736 the House of Lords held that these strict requirements applied only to *secondary victims.* The plaintiff had been involved in a car accident caused by the defendant's negligence. He was not injured but the accident caused a recurrence of a pre-existing condition of chronic fatigue syndrome.

Lord Lloyd considered the earlier cases of *Bourhill v Young* (1942), in which a woman had suffered shock on looking at the scene of a motorbike crash, *McLoughlin v O'Brian* (1982), in which a mother had suffered psychiatric harm after seeing her family in hospital immediately after a bad road accident, and *Alcock v Chief Constable of the South Yorkshire Police* (1991):

> In all these cases the plaintiff was the secondary victim of the defendant's negligence. He or she was in the position of a spectator or bystander. In the present case, by contrast, the plaintiff was a participant. He was himself directly involved in the accident, and well within the range of foreseeable physical injury. He was the primary victim. This is thus the first occasion on which your Lordships have had to decide whether, in such a case, the foreseeability of physical injury is enough to enable the plaintiff to recover damages for nervous shock. . . .
>
> Although the plaintiff was, as I have said, the primary victim, the peculiarity of the present case is that, by good fortune, he suffered no broken bones and no bruising; indeed he had no external physical injury of any kind. But as a direct result of the accident he suffered a **recrudescence** of an illness or condition known variously as ME, CFS, or PVFS, from which he had previously suffered in a mild form on sporadic occasions, but which, since the accident, has become an illness of 'chronic intensity and permanency'. . . .
>
> Why should it make any difference that the physical illness that the plaintiff undoubtedly suffered as a result of the accident operated through the medium of the mind, or of the nervous system, without physical injury? If he had suffered a heart attack, it cannot be doubted that he would have recovered damages for pain and suffering, even though he suffered no broken bones. It would have been no answer that he had a weak heart.
>
> . . . Foreseeability of psychiatric injury remains a crucial ingredient when the plaintiff is the secondary victim, for the very reason that the secondary victim is almost always outside the area of physical injury. But where the

plaintiff is the primary victim of the defendant's negligence, the nervous shock cases, by which I mean the cases following on from *Bourhill v Young*, are not in point. Since the defendant was admittedly under a duty of care not to cause the plaintiff foreseeable physical injury, it was unnecessary to ask whether he was under a separate duty of care not to cause foreseeable psychiatric injury.

Lord Lloyd then looked at the 'floodgates argument':

. . . this is a very important consideration in claims by secondary victims. It is for this reason that the courts have, as a matter of policy, rightly insisted on a number of control mechanisms. Otherwise, a negligent defendant might find himself being made liable to all the world. Thus in the case of secondary victims, foreseeability of injury by shock is not enough. The law also requires a degree of proximity: see *Alcock* . . . and the illuminating judgment of Stuart-Smith LJ in *McFarlane v EE Caledonia Ltd* [1994] 2 All ER 1. This means not only proximity to the event in time and space, but also proximity of relationship between the primary victim and the secondary victim. A further control mechanism is that the secondary victim will only recover damages for nervous shock if the defendant should have foreseen injury by shock to a person of normal fortitude or '**ordinary phlegm**'.

None of these mechanisms are required in the case of a primary victim. Since liability depends on foreseeability of physical injury, there could be no question of the defendant finding himself liable to all the world. Proximity of relationship cannot arise, and proximity in time and space goes without saying.

Nor in the case of a primary victim is it appropriate to ask whether he is a person of 'ordinary phlegm'. In the case of physical injury there is no such requirement. The negligent defendant, or more usually his insurer, takes his victim as he finds him. The same should apply in the case of psychiatric injury. There is no difference in principle . . . between an eggshell skull and an eggshell personality. Since the number of potential claimants is limited by the nature of the case, there is no need to impose any further limit by reference to a person of ordinary phlegm. Nor can I see any justification for doing so. . . .

. . . it was enough to ask whether the defendant should have reasonably foreseen that the plaintiff might suffer physical injury as a result of the defendant's negligence, so as to bring him within the range of the defendant's duty of care. It was unnecessary to ask, as a separate question, whether the defendant should reasonably have foreseen injury by shock; and it is irrelevant that the plaintiff did not, in fact, suffer any external physical injury. . . .

In conclusion, the following propositions can be supported.

(1) In cases involving nervous shock, it is essential to distinguish between the primary victim and secondary victims.

(2) In claims by secondary victims the law insists on certain control mechanisms, in order as a matter of policy to limit the number of potential claimants. Thus, the defendant will not be liable unless psychiatric injury is foreseeable in a person of normal fortitude. These control mechanisms have no place where the plaintiff is the primary victim.

(3) In claims by secondary victims, it may be legitimate to use hindsight in order to be able to apply the test of reasonable foreseeability at all. Hindsight, however, has no part to play where the plaintiff is the primary victim.

(4) Subject to the above qualifications, the approach in all cases should be the same, namely, whether the defendant can reasonably foresee that his conduct will expose the plaintiff to the risk of personal injury, whether physical or psychiatric. If the answer is yes, then the duty of care is established, even though physical injury does not, in fact, occur. There is no justification for regarding physical and psychiatric injury as different 'kinds of damage'.

(5) A defendant who is under a duty of care to the plaintiff, whether as primary or secondary victim, is not liable for damages for nervous shock unless the shock results in some recognised psychiatric illness. It is no answer that the plaintiff was predisposed to psychiatric illness. Nor is it relevant that the illness takes a rare form or is of unusual severity. The defendant must take his victim as he finds him.

In *Frost v Chief Constable of South Yorkshire Police* [1997] 1 All ER 540 the Hillsborough Disaster was again considered. This time, the actions had been brought by police officers who had suffered psychiatric illness as a result of their experiences whilst on duty at the time of the incident. As they were not primary victims, in that they were not themselves in immediate physical danger, and as they did not have close ties of love and affection with the victims, it would appear that their actions would fail. The Court of Appeal decided that they should receive damages. This is from Henry LJ's explanation of why:

. . . it is not the fact that the police officers were exposed to events which foreseeably caused them psychiatric injury that founds their claim. Exposure to injury is a fact of police life. The essential ingredient of their cause of action is that they were so exposed because of the negligence of their employer, who was (subject to questions of neighbourhood and proximity) in breach of his duty to take reasonable care not to expose them to injuries from nervous shock. It is the *negligent* exposure to nervous shock that founds the liability, so it is nothing to the point to observe (correctly) that the chief constable owes no insurer's duty 'not to expose a police officer to injury by nervous shock', nor that there is here no allegation 'that there was any breach of duty in deploying the police officers at the scene'. . . .

My emphasis has been on the police officers as direct victims because of the employer/employee relationship. While that duty of care to them is a factor in a case such as this where their employer was negligent, I would expect a duty to be owed to them by any defendant who caused such a disaster as this. Deterrence is part of the public policy behind tort law. Prevention is better than cure, and potential defendants should face up to their safety responsibilities before rather than after an accident. I see no case for any relaxation of the rejection of the **fireman's rule** in *Ogwo v Taylor* [1987] 3 All ER 961 . . .

I believe that where a plaintiff is a direct victim because of the duty that either his employer or the tortfeasor owes to him, that that should be the first head of recovery to be considered, because it might be wider and will not (so far as I can foresee) be narrower than any entitlement as a rescuer.

Dealing with the entitlement of a rescuer, it seems to me that public policy favours a wide rather than a narrow definition, to ensure that those brave and unselfish enough to go to the help of their fellow men will be properly compensated if they suffer damage as a result. . . .

Finally, I am aware that many people regard it as fundamentally unjust that the police should recover damages for post-traumatic stress disorder sustained on that terrible day while the relatives claiming in *Alcock*'s case failed. While respecting their feelings of disappointment that the relatives failed, in this court we can only consider whether these plaintiffs should recover on the different principles of law applicable to them. In my judgment they should, and that conclusion cannot properly be affected by my sympathy for the relatives.

Judge LJ dissented, saying:

. . . in principle, an employee who establishes that his employer's breach of duty has caused him psychiatric illness is not automatically to be categorised as a primary victim of his employer's negligence. As with rescuers, depending on their involvement in the incident, some will be primary victims and others will be secondary victims, subject to the relevant control mechanisms. The same principle applies to claims by police officers against their chief constables.

Check your understanding

1 Can you explain the meaning of the words and phrases in **bold** type? Are there any other words you need to look up in a dictionary?

2 Define *primary victim* and *secondary victim* in your own words.

3 Explain the *Anns* two-stage test in your own words.

4 What does Lord Lloyd mean in *Page v Smith* (p. 181) when he speaks of using hindsight to apply the test of reasonable foreseeability?

5 The complexities of duty of care cry out for a diagram. Using a mind map (spider diagram), summarise duty of care by listing what a plaintiff would have to prove to establish that he or she is owed a duty of care in cases involving different kinds of loss.

Discuss

1 In *Murphy*, Lord Keith says that a reason for not allowing actions for pure economic loss is that it would logically extend to liability for faulty goods. This is, perhaps, a 'floodgates' argument. Compare it with other floodgates arguments; see especially Rougier J in *Munroe* (p. 175) and look out for the rare judicial joke in that passage; then compare what Judge Havery QC says at p. 176 in *Capital and Counties v Hampshire*. Are judges consistent in their use of the floodgates argument?

2 Can you reconcile Lord Devlin's remarks in *Hedley Byrne v Heller* that a distinction between loss caused by physical injury and loss caused by negligent advice has 'neither logic nor commonsense' with the distinctions drawn in *Murphy v Brentwood* between loss through injury or damage to property and pure economic loss?

3 In *White v Jones* Lord Browne-Wilkinson regarded the majority decision as an expansion of the law by an incremental approach. Lord Keith did not agree. Who do you think was right?

4 Were the police officers in the Hillsborough Disaster primary or secondary victims? Was that distinction considered relevant by the judges in *Frost*?

5 In *Murphy v Brentwood* Lord Keith is about as close as judges get to being rude about another judge in his comment on Lord Wilberforce's judgment in *Anns*. He says it 'did not proceed on any basis of principle at all, but constituted a remarkable example of judicial legislation'. He dissented in *White v Jones*. Explain how this is evidence of consistency of approach on his part. Do you think he reached the right conclusion, for the right reasons, in both cases?

6 Do you consider the Court of Appeal decision in the appeals on the fire brigade cases to be satisfactory?

Write

1 Write a note on *Hedley Byrne v Heller*, making clear the bases on which Lord Reid and Lord Devlin believed liability to arise. Which basis was adopted by the House of Lords in *Caparo*?

2 Essay: 'What factors do and should courts consider in deciding what is "fair, just and reasonable"?'

Connections

1 In *Hedley Byrne v Heller*, at p. 160, Lord Reid says: 'it is by no means clear that those guests would have no action against the negligent manufacturer'. This is a horrible double negative, making the statement difficult to understand on the first reading. Compare this with Lord Denning in *Dutton* at p. 158: whilst the content of Lord Denning's judgments was often controversial, his writing was always a model of clarity.

2 In *White v Jones*, the House of Lords essentially ignored the doctrine of privity. See the materials on contract for an understanding of this doctrine and the problems it causes.

5.2 NEGLIGENCE: BREACH AND LOSS

Once it has been established that the defendant owed the plaintiff a duty of care, there are two other elements that the plaintiff must prove: that there was a breach of duty and that the breach caused foreseeable loss.

All one needs to know about breach was said a long time ago by Baron Alderson in *Blyth v Birmingham Waterworks Co* (1856): 'Negligence is the omission to do something which a reasonable man guided upon those considerations which ordinarily regulate the conduct of human affairs would do, or doing something which a prudent and reasonable man would not do.' This is applied to the particular circumstances of each case. The court conducts a balancing exercise, considering how serious a risk was being run, what the consequences of a lapse might have been, the importance of the work being done at the time and the cost of taking precautions.

The general rule is that an expert is expected to reach the standard of the reasonable expert and an amateur the standard of the reasonable amateur. The standard is judged in the light of what is known at the time of the incident – so a factory owner is expected to reach the standard of the reasonable factory owner with the state of knowledge of risks inherent in the process concerned that the reasonable factory owner would have at the time. This was the issue in *Paris v Stepney Borough Council* [1951] 1 All ER 42. A man who had lost his sight in one eye was blinded when his good eye was injured in an accident at work. The evidence was that men engaged in this job did not usually wear goggles as the risk to eyesight was believed to be small. The House of Lords held that the standard of care was to be judged with regard to each individual employee and that a higher standard was owed to a person with only one eye who stood to lose his sight altogether if there was an accident. Lord Normand said:

> The test is what precautions would the ordinary, reasonable and prudent man take? The relevant considerations include all those facts which could affect the conduct of a reasonable and prudent man and his decision on the precautions to be taken. Would a reasonable and prudent man be influenced, not only by the greater or less probability of an accident occurring but also by the gravity of the consequences if an accident does occur?

and Lord MacDermott added:

> For workman and employer alike such expressions as 'risk', 'danger' and 'safety' would lose much of their everyday meaning if divorced from the results to life and limb. In this sphere they must surely, in the very nature of things, connote consequences as well as causes. If a bricklayer says that the risk is greater at the top of a building, he means that a slip there is more likely to bring him death or injury, and if he says that a particular form of scaffolding is dangerous or not safe, he means not merely that it may fall, but that those who use it may get hurt. What may happen to those engaged is no less important than how it may happen. It is the consequences that necessitate the precautions in this field. The habitual association of cause and effect in workshop and factory is, perhaps, nowhere more clearly recognised than in the nature of some of the safeguards in common use. Suitable goggles, for example, must be worn by those employed at grinding machines. The particles that fly upwards may strike the cheeks as readily as the eyes, but the eyes are protected and the cheeks are not because the eyes are delicate organs and the consequences of their being struck are likely to be serious. Again, special precautions to prevent electric leakage are the usual practice in places like wash-houses where those working are well 'earthed' and a shock might prove fatal. Instances of this sort could be multiplied, but I think it is enough to say that the employer's duty to take reasonable care for the safety of his workmen . . . must be related to both the risk and the degree of the injury. If that is so, and if, as was very properly conceded, the duty is that owed to the individual and not to a class, it seems to me to follow that the known circumstance that a particular workman is likely to suffer a graver injury than his fellows from the happening of a given event is one which must be taken into consideration in assessing the nature of the employer's obligation to that workman.

An exception to the rule that one is judged by the standard of expertise one professes occurred in the case of *Nettleship v Weston* [1971] 3 All ER 581. Lord Denning MR explained:

Mrs Weston is a married woman. She wanted to learn to drive. Her husband was quite ready for her to learn on his car. She asked a friend of hers, Mr Nettleship, if he would give her some lessons. Mr Nettleship said he would do so, but, in case there was an accident, he wanted to check up on the insurance. Mr and Mrs Weston assured him that they had a fully comprehensive insurance which covered him as a passenger in the event of an accident. This was correct. They showed him the policy and certificate of insurance. Mr Weston was insured under an ordinary Lloyd's policy. By it the **underwriters** agreed to **indemnify** Mr Weston and 'any person driving the car with his permission' against liability at law for damages in respect of bodily injury to any person 'including any passenger'. On being so assured, Mr Nettleship said that he would give her some lessons.

On 25th October 1967 Mrs Weston took out a provisional driving licence. Mr Nettleship went with her in the car on Sunday, 28th October, and Sunday, 5th November, and gave her driving lessons. He found her very receptive to instruction and a very good learner-driver. On Sunday, 12th November, he went with her on her third lesson. She sat in the driving seat. He sat beside her. She held the steering wheel and controlled the pedals for the clutch and foot brake and accelerator. He assisted her by moving the gear lever; and applying the hand brake. Very occasionally he assisted in the steering.

They came to a road junction where there was a halt sign. They had to turn left. She stopped the car. He moved the gear lever into neutral and applied the hand brake. The road was clear. He said to her: 'Move off, slowly, round the corner.' He took off the hand brake. She let in the clutch. He put the gear lever into first gear. The car made a smooth start. She turned the steering wheel to the left and the car moved round the corner at walking pace. He said to her: 'Now straighten out.' But she did not do so. She panicked. She held the steering wheel, as he said, 'in a vice-like grip'; or, as she said, 'my hands seemed to freeze on the wheel'. He at once took hold of the hand brake with his right hand and tried to get hold of the steering wheel with his left hand to straighten it out. As bad luck would have it, there was a lamp standard just by the kerb at that point. The nearside struck the lamp standard. Mr Nettleship was injured. His left knee-cap was broken.

On 25th January 1968 Mrs Weston was convicted by the Sheffield magistrates of driving without due care and attention. She was fined £10 and her driving licence was endorsed. Mr Nettleship now claims damages for negligence against Mrs Weston. She denies negligence, alleges contributory negligence, and also pleads that he impliedly consented to run the risk of injury. The judge dismissed the claim. He said that the only duty owed by Mrs Weston to Mr Nettleship was that she should do her best, and that she did not fail in that duty.

Mrs Weston was rightly convicted of driving without due care and attention. In the criminal law it is no defence for a driver to say: 'I was a learner-driver under instruction. I was doing my best and could not help it.' Such a plea may go to **mitigation** of sentence, but it does not go in exculpation of guilt. The criminal law insists that every person driving a car must attain an objective standard measured by the standard of a skilled, experienced and careful driver. That is shown by *McCrone v Riding* (1938) . . . So the criminal law is clear. No one would dream of throwing any doubt on it. Mrs Weston was convicted in accordance with it. The conviction is admissible in civil proceedings as **prima facie** evidence of negligence . . .

Mrs Weston is clearly liable for the damage to the lamp-post. In the civil law if a driver goes off the road on to the pavement and injures a pedestrian, or damages property, he is prima facie liable. Likewise if he goes on to the wrong side of the road. It is no answer for him to say: 'I was a learner-driver under instruction. I was doing my best and could not help it.' The civil law permits no such excuse. It requires of him the same standard of care as any other driver. 'It eliminates the personal equation and is independent of the **idiosyncrasies** of the particular person whose conduct is in question': see *Glasgow Corpn v Muir* (1943) per Lord Macmillan. The learner-driver may be doing his best, but his incompetent best is not good enough. He must drive in as good a manner as a driver of skill, experience and care, who is sound in wind and limb, who makes no errors of judgment, has good eyesight and hearing and is free from any infirmity: see *Richley v Faull* (1965) and *Watson v Thomas S Whitney & Co Ltd* (1966).

The high standard thus imposed by the judges is, I believe, largely the result of the policy of the Road Traffic Acts. Parliament requires every driver to be insured against third-party risks. The reason is so that a person injured by a motor-car should not be left to bear the loss on his own, but should be compensated out of the insurance fund. The fund is better able to bear it than he can. But the injured person is only able to recover if the driver is liable in law. So the judges see to it that he is liable . . . Thus we are, in this branch of the law, moving away from the concept: 'No liability without fault'. We are beginning to apply the test: 'On whom should the risk fall?' Morally the learner-driver is not at fault; but legally she is liable to be because she is insured and the risk should fall on her.

. . . I do not say that the professional instructor – who agrees to teach for reward – can likewise sue. There may well be implied in the contract an agreement by him to waive any claim for injury. He ought to insure himself, and may do so, for aught I know. But the instructor who is just a friend helping to teach never does insure himself. He should, therefore, be allowed to sue.

The standard of care owed varies according to the circumstances, as was pointed out by Milmo J in the case of *Marshall v Osmand* [1982] 2 All ER 610. The plaintiff had been a passenger in a stolen car and was injured when he was in collision with a police car containing officers who were attempting to arrest him and others from the stolen car. Clearly, the police officer owed him a duty of care because all drivers owe all road users a duty of care: but what was the *standard* of that duty?

> In my judgment a police officer driving a motor car in hot pursuit of a person or persons whom he rightly suspects of having committed an arrestable offence does not owe that person the same duty of care which he owes to a lawful and innocent user of the highway going about his lawful occasions. He must not deliberately injure such a person unless it is reasonably necessary to do so in order to arrest him, and his actions must not be judged by standards which would be applicable if the situation were such that the officer had time to consider all possible alternative courses of action that he could have taken to discharge his duty successfully.
>
> I make the following findings of fact: (1) at all material times the plaintiff was willingly being carried in the Cortina motor car knowing that it had been taken and driven away without the consent of the owner; (2) at the time when he sustained his injury the plaintiff was fully aware of the fact that the police were in hot pursuit of the Cortina and were seeking to stop, question and inevitably arrest its occupants; (3) the other occupants of the Cortina had already made their getaway into the bushes and it was the plaintiff's intention to do so himself as quickly as possible; (4) the whole incident between the high-speed chase from the first lay-by until the Cortina stopped by the second lay-by took a very short time and the events thereafter occurred in a matter of seconds; (5) when he was endeavouring to make his escape and avoid arrest, the plaintiff sustained the injuries in respect of which he now claims damages by reason of being struck by some part of the police vehicle or by some part of the Cortina after it had been struck by the police vehicle; and (6) the defendant did not intend to injure the plaintiff or any of the occupants of the car and was not guilty of any want of reasonable care in all the circumstances of the case.
>
> I therefore find that the claim in negligence fails . . .

Moving on to the third element of negligence, assuming the defendant owes the plaintiff a duty of care and has fallen below the standard to be expected in the circumstances and that the plaintiff has been injured or his property has been damaged or he has suffered some kind of economic loss: how much money can the plaintiff claim from the defendant? Can he claim all the loss he has suffered? The question was considered by the Privy Council in *Wagon Mound (No 1)* [1961] 1 All ER 404. The plaintiffs were ship repairers. Their wharf was damaged by a fire caused by sparks from welding work igniting furnace oil negligently discharged into the harbour by the defendants. The evidence was that it was not foreseeable that furnace oil floating on water would cause fire, though it was foreseeable that it would cause pollution. Viscount Simonds considered the law:

There can be no doubt that the decision of the Court of Appeal in *Polemis* (1921) plainly asserts that, if the defendant is guilty of negligence, he is responsible for all the consequences, whether reasonably foreseeable or not. The generality of the proposition is, perhaps, qualified by the fact that each of the lords justices refers to the outbreak of fire as the direct result of the negligent act. There is thus introduced the conception that the negligent actor is not responsible for consequences which are not 'direct', whatever that may mean. It has to be asked, then, why this conclusion should have been reached. The answer appears to be that it was reached on a consideration of certain authorities, comparatively few in number, that were cited to the court. Of these, three are generally regarded as having influenced the decision. The earliest in point of date was *Smith v London & South Western Ry. Co.* (1870). In that case, it was said that '. . . when it has been once determined that there is evidence of negligence, the person guilty of it is equally liable for its consequences, whether he could have foreseen them or not', see per Channell, B. Similar observations were made by other members of the court. Three things may be noted about this case: the first, that, for the sweeping proposition laid down, no authority was cited; the second, that the point to which the court directed its mind was not unforeseeable damage of a different kind from that which was foreseen, but more extensive damage of the same kind; and the third, that so little was the mind of the court directed to the problem which has now to be solved that no one of the seven judges who took part in the decision thought it necessary to qualify in any way the consequences for which the defendants were to be held responsible. It would, perhaps, not be improper to say that the law of negligence as an independent tort was then of recent growth and that its implications had not been fully examined. . . .

Next, one of many cases may be cited which show how shadowy is the line between so-called culpability and compensation. In *Sharp v Powell* (1872), the defendant's servant, in breach of the Metropolitan Police Act, 1839, washed a van in a public street and allowed the waste water to run down the gutter towards a grating leading to the sewer, about twenty-five yards off. In consequence of the extreme severity of the weather, the grating was obstructed by ice, and the water flowed over a portion of the causeway and froze. There was no evidence that the defendant knew of the grating being obstructed. The plaintiff's horse, while being led past the spot, slipped on the ice and broke its leg. The defendant was held not to be liable. The judgment of Bovill, CJ, is particularly valuable and interesting. He said:

> 'No doubt one who commits a wrongful act is responsible for the ordinary consequences which are likely to result therefrom; but, generally speaking, he is not liable for damage which is not the natural or ordinary consequence of such an act, unless it be shown that he knows, or has reasonable means of knowing, that consequences not

usually resulting from the act are, by reason of some existing cause, likely to intervene so as to occasion damage to a third person. Where there is no reason to expect it, and no knowledge in the person doing the wrongful act that such a state of things exists as to render the damage probable, if injury does result to a third person it is generally considered that the wrongful act is not the proximate cause of the injury, so as to render the wrongdoer liable to an action.'

. . . The impression that may well be left on the reader of the scores of cases in which liability for negligence has been discussed is that the courts were feeling their way to a **coherent** body of doctrine, and were at times in grave danger of being led astray by scholastic theories of causation and their ugly and barely intelligible jargon.

. . . Instances might be multiplied of deviation from the rule in *Polemis*, but their Lordships think it sufficient to refer to certain later cases in the House of Lords and then to attempt to state what they conceive to be the true principle. . . .

In *Hay (or Bourhill) v Young* (1942) . . . Lord Russell of Killowen said:

'In considering whether a person owes to another a duty a breach of which will render him liable to that other in damages for negligence, it is material to consider what the defendant ought to have contemplated as a reasonable man. This consideration may play a double role. It is relevant in cases of admitted negligence (where the duty and breach are admitted) to the question of remoteness of damages, ie, to the question of compensation not to culpability; but it is also relevant in testing the existence of a duty as the foundation of the alleged negligence, ie to the question of culpability not to that of compensation.'

. . . Enough has been said to show that the authority of *Polemis* has been severely shaken, though lip-service has from time to time been paid to it. In their Lordships' opinion, it should no longer be regarded as good law. It is not probable that many cases will for that reason have a different result, though it is hoped that the law will be thereby simplified, and that, in some cases at least, palpable injustice will be avoided. For it does not seem consonant with current ideas of justice or morality that, for an act of negligence, however slight or venial, which results in some trivial foreseeable damage, the actor should be liable for all consequences, however unforeseeable and however grave, so long as they can be said to be 'direct'. It is a principle of civil liability, subject only to qualifications which have no present relevance, that a man must be considered to be responsible for the probable consequences of his act. To demand more of him is too harsh a rule, to demand less is to ignore that civilised order requires the observance of a minimum standard of behaviour. This concept, applied to the slowly developing law of negligence, has led to a great variety of expressions which can, as it appears to their Lordships, be harmonised with little difficulty with the single exception of the so-called rule in *Polemis*. For, if it is asked why a man should be responsible for the natural or necessary or probable consequences of his act (or any other similar description of them), the answer is that it is not because they are natural or necessary or probable, but because, since they have this quality, it is judged, by the standard of the reasonable man, that he ought to have foreseen them. . . .

It is proper to add that their Lordships have not found it necessary to consider the so-called rule of 'strict liability' exemplified in *Rylands v Fletcher* (1868) and the cases that have followed or distinguished it. Nothing that they have said is intended to reflect on that rule.

Check your understanding

Can you explain the meaning of the words and phrases in **bold** type? Are there any other words you need to look up in a dictionary?

Discuss

1 In *Nettleship v Weston* the Court of Appeal applied an objective standard on all drivers. Why? Do you agree that this is a just approach? What standard would you expect the law to apply to a medical student treating a patient?

2 Lord Denning says in *Nettleship v Weston* 'we are . . . moving away from the concept "No liability without fault" '. Is the fault principle a suitable ground on which to decide who should be compensated and who should not? You may like to consider this question with respect to the plaintiffs in *Alcock v Chief Constable of South Yorkshire Police* (1991) and *Frost v Chief Constable of South Yorkshire Police* (1997).

3 Lord Russell, quoted by Viscount Simonds at p. 190, neatly makes the point that foresight is relevant both to whether there is a duty of care and whether damages are recoverable for the loss sustained. Why, then, do we consider twice over what the reasonable person could have foreseen?

Connections

1 The cost of precautions, relevant to the issue of whether there has been a breach of duty in negligence, is also relevant in the tort of nuisance; see p. 197, *Leakey v National Trust*.

2 Note Lord Denning's great ability to 'tell the story'. All judges begin a judgment by giving the facts but Lord Denning always managed a graphic account. What features of his written style do you like? What do you dislike?

3 Note the explanation in *Nettleship v Weston* of the policy reasons behind the decision, as well as the citation of precedent. This is a good example of the process Professor Simon Lee discusses at p. 43.

4 Being a law student would be easier if judges were perfect. In *Marshall v Osmand* Milmo J speaks of 'duty of care' when he presumably means 'standard of care'. One either owes a duty or one does not, but the *standard* may vary with the circumstances, as we have seen in *Paris v Stepney Borough Council*. Look out for judges using words and phrases differently: for example, the term 'specific intent' in criminal law (see p. 118) seems to have no settled meaning.

5.3 OTHER TORTS

It is important not to form the impression that negligence is the only tort. Lack of space prohibits discussion of all torts but material on two more is given below. Do not forget that there are some important statutes in this area, such as the Occupiers' Liability Acts of 1957 and 1984, the Consumer Protection Act 1987 and the Animals Act 1971, each of which has given rise to little litigation, suggesting that they are well drafted, clear in their scope and working well in practice.

Nuisance

The tort of private nuisance protects the owner of land from the unreasonable behaviour of his neighbour. It may be defined as 'unreasonable interference with the use or enjoyment of land'. In *Hunter v Canary Wharf Ltd* [1997] 2 All ER 426 Lord Hope looked at the similarities and the differences between negligence and nuisance:

> The tort of nuisance is an invasion of the plaintiff's interest in the possession and enjoyment of land. It is closely linked to the law of property and is often regarded as part of the law of neighbourhood. . . . The function of the tort, in the context of private nuisance, is to control the activities of the owner or occupier of property within the boundaries of his own land which may harm the interests of the owner or occupier of other land.
>
> The tort of negligence is also, in a very real sense, concerned with the relationship between neighbours. But, as can be seen clearly since the development of this branch of the law in *Donoghue v Stevenson* . . .

> the answer to the question, 'Who in law is my neighbour?' is a different one from that which would be given in the context of property law. A duty of care is owed to all those who are so closely and directly affected by my act that I ought reasonably to have them in contemplation. These persons may include the owners or occupiers of property which lies beside the property of which I am the owner or occupier. But the duty of care is not restricted to those who are in law the owners or occupiers. It extends to anyone who may happen to be present on that property whom my acts or omissions may affect. Of course, it extends to many other situations also which have nothing to do with the ownership or occupation of property. In the present case, however, it is helpful to see how the two torts may overlap in relation to each other. In some cases they may provide **concurrent** remedies, although the tort of nuisance is a tort of strict liability in the sense that it is no defence to say that the defendant took all reasonable care to prevent it. . . . Where it is available it will be unnecessary to rely also on the tort of negligence. In other cases it may be necessary to rely on the tort of negligence, because the person who is affected by the act or omission on the neighbouring property has no interest in the land where he or she happens to be at the time.
>
> . . . where it is the tort of nuisance which is being relied on to provide the remedy . . . the plaintiff must show that he has an interest in the land that has been affected by the nuisance of which he complains. Mere presence on the land will not do. . . . It may then be said that there is an unlawful interference with his use or enjoyment of the land or of his right over or in connection with it.

One of the issues in *Hunter* was whether a person who has no legal interest in the land which is affected by a nuisance can sue in respect of it. The nuisance complained of was caused by the building of Canary Wharf and some of the plaintiffs were not owners or tenants of property near Canary Wharf but occupied it as members of the family of owners or occupiers. One of their complaints was that the building interfered with reception of television signals. The House of Lords decided that this was not an actionable nuisance. Lord Goff said:

> As a general rule, a man is entitled to build on his own land, though nowadays this right is inevitably subject to our system of planning controls. Moreover, as a general rule, a man's right to build on his land is not restricted by the fact that the presence of the building may of itself interfere with his neighbour's enjoyment of his land. The building may spoil his neighbour's view . . . in the absence of an **easement**, it may restrict the flow of air onto his neighbour's land . . . and, again in the absence of an easement, it may take away light from his neighbour's windows: nevertheless his neighbour generally cannot complain of the presence of the building, though this may seriously detract from the enjoyment of his land. . . .

From this it follows that, in the absence of an easement, more is required than the mere presence of a neighbouring building to give rise to an actionable private nuisance. Indeed, for an action in private nuisance to lie in respect of interference with the plaintiff's enjoyment of his land, it will generally arise from something emanating from the defendant's land. Such an emanation may take many forms – noise, dirt, fumes, a noxious smell, vibrations, and such like.

With reference to the question of the status of the plaintiff in a nuisance action, Lord Goff continued:

. . . it has for many years been regarded as settled law that a person who has no right in the land cannot sue in private nuisance. For this proposition, it is usual to cite the decision of the Court of Appeal in *Malone v Laskey* (1907). . . .

Recently, however, the Court of Appeal departed from this line of authority in *Khorasandjian v Bush* [1993] 3 All ER 669, . . . a case which I must examine with some care.

The plaintiff, a young girl who at the time of the appeal was 18, had formed a friendship with the defendant, then a man of 28. After a time the friendship broke down and the plaintiff decided that she would have no more to do with the defendant, but the defendant found this impossible to accept. There followed a catalogue of complaints against the defendant, including assaults, threats of violence, and pestering the plaintiff at her parents' home where she lived. As a result of the defendant's threats and abusive behaviour he spent some time in prison. An injunction was granted restraining the defendant from various forms of activity directed at the plaintiff, and this included an order restraining him from 'harassing, pestering or communicating with' the plaintiff. The question before the Court of Appeal was whether the judge had jurisdiction to grant such an injunction, in relation to telephone calls made to the plaintiff at her parents' home. The home was the property of the plaintiff's mother, and it was recognised that her mother could complain of persistent and unwanted telephone calls made to her; but it was submitted that the plaintiff, as a mere **licensee** in her mother's house, could not invoke the tort of private nuisance to complain of unwanted and harassing telephone calls made to her in her mother's home.

The Court of Appeal held in *Khorasandjian v Bush* that the daughter could bring an action in nuisance. Lord Goff considered that they were wrong:

If a plaintiff, such as the daughter of the householder in *Khorasandjian v Bush*, is harassed by abusive telephone calls, the gravamen of the complaint lies in the harassment which is just as much an abuse, or indeed an invasion of her privacy, whether she is pestered in this way in her mother's or her husband's house, or she is staying with a friend, or is at her place of work, or even in her car with a mobile phone. In truth, what the Court of Appeal appears to have been doing was to exploit the law of private nuisance in order to create by the back door a tort of harassment which was only partially effective in that it was artificially limited to harassment which takes place in her home. I myself do not consider that this is a satisfactory manner in which to develop the law, especially when, as in the case in question, the step so taken was inconsistent with another decision of the Court of Appeal, viz *Malone v Laskey* (1907) . . . , by which the court was bound. [In *Malone v Laskey* a woman was held to be unable to recover damages in respect of an injury suffered when a toilet cistern fell on her head because she had no legal right in the property on which the incident occurred.] In any event, a tort of harassment has now received statutory recognition (see the Protection from Harassment Act 1997). We are therefore no longer troubled with the question whether the common law should be developed to provide such a remedy. For these reasons, I do not consider that any assistance can be derived from *Khorasandjian v Bush* by the plaintiffs in the present appeals.

It follows that, on the authorities as they stand, an action in private nuisance will only lie at the suit of a person who has a right to the land affected. . . .

At the heart of this question lies a more fundamental question, which relates to the scope of the law of private nuisance. Here, I wish to draw attention to the fact that although, in the past, damages for personal injury have been recovered at least in actions of public nuisance, there is now developing a school of thought that the appropriate remedy for such claims as these should lie in our now fully developed law of negligence, and that personal injury claims should be altogether excluded from the domain of nuisance. . . .

Since preparing this opinion, I have had the opportunity of reading in draft the speech of my noble and learned friend Lord Cooke of Thorndon, and I have noticed his citation of academic authority which supports the view that the right to sue in private nuisance in respect of interference with amenities should no longer be restricted to those who have an interest in the affected land. I would not wish it to be thought that I myself have not consulted the relevant academic writings. I have, of course, done so, as is my usual practice; and it is my practice to refer to those which I have found to be of assistance, but not to refer, critically or otherwise, to those which are not. In the present circumstances, however, I feel driven to say that I found in the academic works which I consulted little more than an assertion of the desirability of extending the right of recovery in the manner favoured by the Court of Appeal in the present case. I have to say (though I say it in no spirit of criticism, because I know full well the limits within

> which writers of textbooks on major subjects must work) that I have found no analysis of the problem; and, in circumstances such as this, a crumb of analysis is worth a loaf of opinion. Some writers have uncritically commended the decision of the Court of Appeal in *Khorasandjian v Bush* . . . without reference to the misunderstanding in *Motherwell v Motherwell* . . . on which the Court of Appeal relied, or consideration of the undesirability of making a fundamental change to the tort of private nuisance to provide a partial remedy in cases of individual harassment. For these and other reasons, I did not, with all respect, find the stream of academic authority referred to by my noble and learned friend to be of assistance in the present case.

Lord Cooke gave a dissenting judgment. He began by acknowledging the legal logic of the majority view of the law but he believed the approach in *Khorasandjian v Bush* was preferable:

> In logic more than one answer can be given. Logically it is possible to say that the right to sue for interference with the amenities of a home should be confined to those with proprietary interests and licensees with exclusive possession. No less logically, the right can be accorded to all who live in the home. Which test should be adopted, that is to say which should be the governing principle, is a question of the policy of the law. It is a question not capable of being answered by analysis alone. All that analysis can do is expose the alternatives. Decisions such as *Malone*'s case do not attempt that kind of analysis, and in refraining from recognising that value judgments are involved they compare less than favourably with the approach of the present-day Court of Appeal in *Khorasandjian*'s case and this case. The reason why I prefer the alternative . . . is that it gives better effect to widespread conceptions concerning the home and family.

We are all free to a certain extent to do what we wish on our own property but if the noise, smells or other *indirect* interference with our neighbour's property becomes unreasonable, then the tort of nuisance is being committed. A certain degree of tolerance is expected, so an action in nuisance will not usually be appropriate if there has been only one incident. In *British Celanese v Hunt* [1969] 2 All ER 1252 the High Court considered a situation that had occurred twice in three and a half years. Metal foil strips stored on the defendant's property had been blown by the wind onto an electricity sub-station and had caused a power cut at the plaintiffs' factory. The plaintiffs brought their action in negligence, public nuisance, private nuisance and *Rylands v Fletcher*. With reference to the action in nuisance, Lawton J said:

> As to private nuisance [the plaintiffs] say that the defendants' alleged method of storing metal foil resulted, as the defendants knew it would, in an interference with the beneficial enjoyment of their own premises whereby they suffered damage; and as to public nuisance their case is that the

nuisance was one which affected a class of person, namely, those members of the public supplied with electricity from the sub-station, and that as members of that class they suffered special damage.

The defendants made three answers to these contentions: first, that an isolated happening such as the plaintiffs relied on was not enough to found an action in nuisance since this tort can only arise out of a continuing condition; secondly, that if there was a nuisance on the defendants' premises, it did not affect the plaintiffs' premises directly; and thirdly, that the re-amended statement of claim did not disclose enough facts to justify a ruling that a class of the public had been injuriously affected by the alleged nuisance.

In my judgment, all three answers are misconceived. Most nuisances do arise from a long continuing condition; and many isolated happenings do not constitute a nuisance. It is, however, clear from the authorities that an isolated happening by itself can create an actionable nuisance. Such an authority is *Midwood & Co Ltd v Manchester Corpn.* (1905) . . .

The second of the defendants' answers is a repetition of the argument which was addressed to me on remoteness of damage. I accept that those who are only indirectly affected by a nuisance cannot sue for any damage which they may suffer; but for the reasons I have already given I adjudge that the plaintiffs were directly and foreseeably affected. . . .

Finally [as to public nuisance, the question is whether the plaintiffs were members of a class]. Whether this class was big enough to attract the description 'public' to the nuisance must await the evidence at the trial. In *AG v PYA Quarries Ltd* (1957) Romer LJ, after a learned examination of the authorities, summarised the law as follows:

> '. . . any nuisance is "public" which materially affects the reasonable comfort and convenience of life of a class of Her Majesty's subjects. The sphere of the nuisance may be described generally as "the neighbourhood"; but the question whether the local community within that sphere comprises a sufficient number of persons to constitute a class of the public is a question of fact in every case.'

It was held that the plaintiffs had a right to damages in private nuisance, possibly in public nuisance and also in negligence on the basis that 'those who do work on or near electric power cables owe a duty of care to those whom they should reasonably foresee are likely to be injuriously affected by what they do'.

It had long been thought that if a nuisance arose from something that was not the neighbour's fault and, thus, not a matter of his being unreasonable, there could be no nuisance. The Court of Appeal took a look at this idea in *Leakey v National Trust* [1980] 1 All ER 17. The National Trust owned a piece of land called Burrow Mump which was slipping onto adjoining land. As this was caused by the forces of nature, the National

Trust denied that it was liable for damage to adjoining property and, whilst it was happy to allow the adjoining landowners access to its land to do work necessary to prevent the slippage, it was not prepared to pay for such work itself. Megaw LJ considered the law:

> If, as a result of the working of the forces of nature, there is, poised above my land, or above my house, a boulder or a rotten tree, which is liable to fall at any moment of the day or night, perhaps destroying my house, and perhaps killing or injuring me or members of my family, am I without remedy? (Of course the standard of care required may be much higher when there is risk to life or limb as contrasted with mere risk to property, but can it be said that the duty exists in the one case and not in the other?) Must I, in such a case, if my protests to my neighbour go unheeded, sit and wait and hope that the worst will not befall? If it is said that I have in such circumstances a remedy of going on my neighbour's land to **abate** the nuisance, that would, or might, be an unsatisfactory remedy. But in any event, if there were such a right of **abatement**, it would, as counsel for the plaintiffs rightly contended, be because my neighbour owed me a duty. There is, I think, ample authority that, if I have a right to abatement, I have also a remedy in damages if the nuisance remains unabated and causes me damage or personal injury. . . .
>
> This leads on to the question of the scope of the duty. This is discussed, and the nature and extent of the duty is explained, in the judgment in *Goldman v Hargrave* (1966). The duty is a duty to do that which is reasonable in all the circumstances, and no more than what, if anything, is reasonable, to prevent or minimise the known risk of damage or injury to one's neighbour or to his property. The considerations with which the law is familiar are all to be taken into account in deciding whether there has been a breach of duty, and, if so, what that breach is, and whether it is causative of the damage in respect of which the claim is made. Thus, there will fall to be considered the extent of the risk. What, so far as reasonably can be foreseen, are the chances that anything untoward will happen or that any damage will be caused? What is to be foreseen as to the possible extent of the damage if the risk becomes a reality? Is it practicable, how simple or how difficult are the measures which could be taken, how much and how lengthy work do they involve, and what is the probable cost of such works? Was there sufficient time for preventive action to have been taken, by persons acting reasonably in relation to the known risk, between the time when it became known to, or should have been realised by, the defendant, and the time when the damage occurred? Factors such as these, so far as they apply in a particular case, fall to be weighed in deciding whether the defendant's duty of care requires, or required, him to do anything, and, if so, what. . . .
>
> The defendant's duty is to do that which is reasonable for him to do. The criteria of reasonableness include, in respect of a duty of this nature,

> the factor of what the particular man, not the average man, can be expected to do, having regard, amongst other things, where a serious expenditure of money is required to eliminate or reduce the danger, to his means. Just as, where physical effort is required to avert an immediate danger, the defendant's age and physical condition may be relevant in deciding what is reasonable, so also logic and good sense require that, where the expenditure of money is required, the defendant's capacity to find the money is relevant. But this can only be in the way of a broad, and not detailed, assessment; and, in arriving at a judgment on reasonableness, a similar broad assessment may be relevant in some cases as to the neighbour's capacity to protect himself from damage, whether by way of some form of barrier on his own land or by way of providing funds for expenditure on agreed works on the land of the defendant.

On this basis, the National Trust were held to be responsible for making their land safe so that it no longer caused a nuisance to the owners of adjoining land.

Rylands v Fletcher

The damage and potential future damage in the case of *Leakey v National Trust* was caused by the forces of nature. It was argued in that case that this meant there could be no liability because liability would arise not in nuisance, but in the tort of Rylands v Fletcher, which governed the escape from land of substances *not* naturally occurring. The tort is derived from the case of *Rylands v Fletcher* (1866). A landowner had a reservoir constructed on his land. Unknown to him there were mine workings underneath the reservoir. Water leaked into the mine owned by the adjoining landowner. It was held that, even though there had been no negligence, the landowner was liable for the damage. Blackburn J said:

> We think that the true rule of law is, that the person who for his own purposes brings on his land and collects and keeps there anything likely to do mischief if it escapes, must keep it in at his peril, and, if he does not do so, is prima facie answerable for all the damage which is the natural consequence of its escape. He can excuse himself by showing that the escape was owing to the plaintiff's default; or perhaps that the escape was the consequence of **vis major**, or the act of God; but as nothing of this sort exists here, it is unnecessary to inquire what excuse would be sufficient. The general rule, as above stated, seems on principle just. The person whose grass or corn is eaten down by the escaping cattle of his neighbour, or whose mine is flooded by the water from his neighbour's reservoir, or whose cellar is invaded by the filth of his neighbour's privy, or whose habitation is made unhealthy by the fumes and noisome vapours of his

> neighbour's alkali works, is **damnified** without any fault of his own; and it seems but reasonable and just that the neighbour, who has brought something on his own property which was not naturally there, harmless to others so long as it is confined to his own property, but which he knows to be mischievous if it gets on his neighbour's, should be obliged to make good the damage which **ensues** if he does not succeed in confining it to his own property. But for his act in bringing it there no mischief could have accrued, and it seems but just that he should at his peril keep it there so that no mischief may accrue, or answer for the natural and anticipated consequences. And upon authority, this we think is established to be the law whether the things so brought be beasts, or water, or filth, or stenches.

This principle was limited by the judgment of the House of Lords in *Read v Lyons* [1946] 2 All ER 471. The plaintiff was injured in an explosion in a munitions factory. The House of Lords held that she could not recover damages because there had been no 'escape' but they doubted whether Rylands v Fletcher could be used to claim damages for personal injury. Their Lordships were not in agreement over whether the use of land for a munitions factory was a natural or unnatural user. Lord Macmillan said:

> The doctrine of Rylands v Fletcher as I understand it, derives from a conception of the mutual duties of adjoining or neighbouring landowners and its **congeners** are trespass and nuisance. If its foundation is to be found in the injunction *sic utere tuo ut alienum non laedas* [so use your own property as not to injure your neighbour's property], then it is manifest that it has nothing to do with personal injuries. The duty is to refrain from injuring not *alium* but *alienum* [not *others* but *the property of others*]. The two **prerequisites** of the doctrine are that there must be the escape of something from one man's close to another man's close and that that which escapes must have been brought on the land from which it escapes in consequence of some non-natural use of that land whatever precisely that may mean. Neither of these features exists in the present case . . .

In *British Celanese v Hunt* it was held that storing metal foil on an industrial estate was a natural use of land and therefore the defendants were not liable in *Rylands v Fletcher.*

A further limitation on the use of *Rylands v Fletcher* was created by the House of Lords in *Cambridge Water v Eastern Counties Leather* [1994] 1 All ER 53. The defendant company had used land over a long period for tanning leather. Chemicals used for the process had leaked into the soil and into the water supply. They had long ceased using the chemical concerned and at the time the chemical was used it was not known that its use was harmful to the water supply. Lord Goff considered the relationship between nuisance and *Rylands v Fletcher*:

> Of course, although liability for nuisance has generally been regarded as strict, at least in the case of a defendant who has been responsible for the creation of a nuisance, even so that liability has been kept under control by the principle of reasonable user – the principle of give and take as between neighbouring occupiers of land, under which 'those acts necessary for the common and ordinary use and occupation of land and houses may be done, if conveniently done, without subjecting those who do them to an action': see *Bamford v Turnley* (1862) . . . per Bramwell B. The effect is that, if the user is reasonable, the defendant will not be liable for consequent harm to his neighbour's enjoyment of his land; but if the user is not reasonable, the defendant will be liable, even though he may have exercised reasonable care and skill to avoid it. Strikingly, a comparable principle has developed which limits liability under the rule in Rylands v Fletcher. This is the principle of natural use of the land. . . . The effect of this principle is that, where it applies, there will be no liability under the rule in Rylands v Fletcher; but that where it does not apply, ie where there is a non-natural use, the defendant will be liable for harm caused to the plaintiff by the escape, notwithstanding that he has exercised all reasonable care and skill to prevent the escape from occurring.

Lord Goff then looked at the position with regard to foresight in the law of nuisance. He concluded that since *The Wagon Mound (No 2)* (1967), a further case arising from the situation that gave rise to *Wagon Mound* (1961) (see p. 188), the law has been that there is liability in nuisance only for consequences that are foreseeable, so that the law in negligence and nuisance is identical in this respect. He then looked at the passage from the judgment of Blackburn J in *Rylands v Fletcher* which is given above (p. 199) and said:

> In that passage Blackburn J spoke of 'anything *likely* to do mischief if it escapes'; and later he spoke of something 'which he *knows* to be mischievous if it gets on to his neighbour's [property]', and the liability to 'answer for the natural *and anticipated* consequences'. Furthermore, time and again he spoke of the strict liability imposed upon the defendant as being that he must keep the thing in at his peril; and, when referring to liability in actions for damage occasioned by animals, he referred to the established principle 'that it is quite immaterial whether the escape is by negligence or not'. The general tenor of his statement of principle is therefore that knowledge, or at least foreseeability of the risk, is a prerequisite of the recovery of damages under the principle; but that the principle is one of strict liability in the sense that the defendant may be held liable notwithstanding that he has exercised all due care to prevent escape from occurring. . . .
>
> The point is one on which academic opinion appears to be divided: **cf** *Salmond and Heuston on Torts* (20th edn, 1992) pp. 324–325, which favours the prerequisite of foreseeability, and *Clerk and Lindsell on Torts*

(16th edn, 1989) para 25.09, which takes a different view. However, quite apart from the indications to be derived from the judgment of Blackburn J . . . itself, to which I have already referred, the historical connection with the law of nuisance must now be regarded as pointing towards the conclusion that foreseeability of damage is a prerequisite of the recovery of damages under the rule. I have already referred to the fact that Blackburn J himself did not regard his statement of principle as having broken new ground; furthermore, Professor Newark has convincingly shown that the rule in *Rylands v Fletcher* was essentially concerned with an extension of the law of nuisance to cases of isolated escape. Accordingly since, following the observations of Lord Reid when delivering the advice of the Privy Council in *The Wagon Mound (No 2)* . . . , the recovery of damages in private nuisance depends on foreseeability by the defendant of the relevant type of damage, it would appear logical to extend the same requirement to liability under the rule in Rylands v Fletcher.

Even so, the question cannot be considered solely as a matter of history. It can be argued that the rule in Rylands v Fletcher should not be regarded simply as an extension of the law of nuisance, but should rather be treated as a developing principle of strict liability from which can be derived a general rule of strict liability for damage caused by ultra-hazardous operations, on the basis of which persons conducting such operations may properly be held strictly liable for the extraordinary risk to others involved in such operations. As is pointed out in *Fleming on Torts* (8th edn, 1992) pp. 327–328, this would lead to the practical result that the cost of damage resulting from such operations would have to be absorbed as part of the overheads of the relevant business rather than be borne (where there is no negligence) by the injured person or his insurers, or even by the community at large.

Lord Goff referred to the Law Commission's Report *Civil Liability for Dangerous Things and Activities* (Law Com no 32) 1970:

In paras 14–16 of the report the Law Commission expressed serious misgivings about the adoption of any test for the application of strict liability involving a general concept of 'especially dangerous' or 'ultra-hazardous' activity, having regard to the uncertainties and practical difficulties of its application. If the Law Commission is unwilling to consider statutory reform on this basis, it must follow that judges should if anything be even more reluctant to proceed down that path.

Like the judge in the present case, I incline to the opinion that, as a general rule, it is more appropriate for strict liability in respect of operations of high risk to be imposed by Parliament, than by the courts. If such liability is imposed by statute, the relevant activities can be identified, and those concerned can know where they stand. Furthermore, statute can

> where appropriate lay down precise criteria establishing the **incidence** and scope of such liability.
>
> It is of particular relevance that the present case is concerned with environmental pollution. The protection and preservation of the environment is now perceived as being of crucial importance to the future of mankind; and public bodies, both national and international, are taking significant steps towards the establishment of legislation which will promote the protection of the environment, and make the polluter pay for damage to the environment for which he is responsible – as can be seen from the WHO, EEC and national regulations to which I have previously referred. But it does not follow from these developments that a common law principle, such as the rule in Rylands v Fletcher, should be developed or rendered more strict to provide for liability in respect of such pollution. On the contrary, given that so much well-informed and carefully structured legislation is now being put in place for this purpose, there is less need for the courts to develop a common law principle to achieve the same end, and indeed it may well be undesirable that they should do so.
>
> Having regard to these considerations, and in particular to the step which this House has already taken in *Read v Lyons* to contain the scope of liability under the rule in Rylands v Fletcher, it appears to me to be appropriate now to take the view that foreseeability of damage of the relevant type should be regarded as a prerequisite of liability in damages under the rule.

Eastern Counties Leather were thus held not liable in respect of the pollution because it was not foreseeable at the time the chemicals 'escaped'. On the issue of natural use, however, Lord Goff said: 'I feel bound to say that the storage of substantial quantities of chemicals on industrial premises should be regarded as an almost classic case of non-natural use; and I find it very difficult to think that it should be thought objectionable to impose strict liability for damage caused in the event of their escape.'

Check your understanding

Can you explain the meaning of the words and phrases in **bold** type? Are there any other words you need to look up in a dictionary?

Discuss

1 Was the Court of Appeal decision in *Khorasandjian v Bush* appropriate at the time it was made?

2 Why did Lord Cooke dissent in *Hunter v Canary Wharf*? Do you prefer his view or that of Lord Goff: in other words, is the Court of Appeal decision in *Khorasandjian v Bush* appropriate *now*?

3 What does Lord Goff mean at p. 196 when he says: 'a crumb of analysis is worth a loaf of opinion'?

4 In deciding whether there is an actionable nuisance in *Leakey v National Trust* Megaw LJ (at p. 198) identifies some objective elements and some subjective elements. What are they?

5 At p. 203 Lord Goff is referring to the principle that 'the polluter should pay'. He says this policy decision is a matter for Parliament. Is he right? Should the House of Lords be bolder in such cases and implement a policy its members believe to be right, on the basis that Parliament can change the law if it does not approve?

Write

1 Outline the main features of the torts of private nuisance and *Rylands v Fletcher* and distinguish between the two torts.

2 Using Lawton J's judgment in *British Celanese v Hunt*, outline the tort of public nuisance and distinguish it from private nuisance.

Connections

1 The decision in *Leakey v National Trust* is based on the decision in *Goldman v Hargrave* (1966), which is a Privy Council decision. Look at the material on precedent (p. 34) to see the significance of this.

2 At p. 198 Megaw LJ considers the factors to be taken into account when deciding whether there will be liability in nuisance. Note how similar these are to those used to decide whether there has been a breach of duty in negligence.

5.4 DEFENCES

If a defendant is prima facie liable in tort, it may be that that liability can be eliminated or reduced by successfully pleading a defence. The most common defence is probably one based on the claim that the events were in some part the fault of the plaintiff. This can take two forms: the complete defence of *volenti non fit injuria* or the partial defence of contributory negligence.

Volenti non fit injuria

Volenti is a rare defence now but it was successfully pleaded in the case of *Morris v Murray* [1990] 3 All ER 801. The plaintiff had been the passenger in a light aircraft piloted by Murray. Murray had, to the plaintiff's knowledge, drunk a considerable amount of alcohol: he was, in fact, three times over the permitted limit for driving a car. The plane crashed, Murray was killed (the action was brought against his **estate**) and Morris was badly injured. Fox LJ looked at the authorities on *volenti non fit injuria, Dann v Hamilton* [1939] 1 All ER 59, a 'drunk driver' case, and *Nettleship v Weston*, see p. 185, in which Lord Denning said:

> The special factor in this case is that Mr Nettleship was not a mere passenger in the car. He was an instructor teaching Mrs Weston to drive. Seeing that the law lays down, for all drivers of motor cars, a standard of care to which all must conform, I think that even a learner-driver, so long as he is the sole driver, must attain the same standard towards all passengers in the car, including an instructor. But the instructor may be debarred from claiming for a reason peculiar to himself. He may be debarred because he has voluntarily agreed to waive any claim for any injury that may befall him. Otherwise he is not debarred. He may, of course, be guilty of contributory negligence and have his damages reduced on that account. He may, for instance, have let the learner take control too soon, he may not have been quick enough to correct his errors, or he may have participated in the negligent act himself . . . But, apart from contributory negligence, he is not excluded unless it be that he had voluntarily agreed to incur the risk.
>
> This brings me to the defence of volenti non fit injuria. Does it apply to the instructor? In former times this defence was used almost as an alternative defence to contributory negligence. Either defence defeated the action. Now that contributory negligence is not a complete defence, but only a ground for reducing the damages, the defence of volenti non fit injuria has been closely considered, and, in consequence, it has been severely limited. Knowledge of the risk of injury is not enough. Nor is a willingness to take the risk of injury. Nothing will suffice short of an agreement to waive any claim for negligence. The plaintiff must agree, expressly or impliedly, to waive any claim for any injury that may befall him due to the lack of reasonable care by the defendant: or more accurately, due to the failure of the defendant to measure up to the standard of care that the law requires of him. That is shown in England by *Dann v Hamilton* (1939) . . . The doctrine has been so severely curtailed that in the view of Diplock LJ: '. . . the maxim, in the absence of express contract, has no application to negligence simpliciter where the duty of care is based solely on proximity or "neighbourship" in the Atkinian sense': see *Wooldridge v Sumner* (1962).

> Applying the doctrine in this case, it is clear that Mr Nettleship did not agree to waive any claim for injury that might befall him. Quite the contrary. He enquired about the insurance policy so as to make sure that he was covered. If and insofar as Mrs Weston fell short of the standard of care which the law required of her, he has a cause of action.

Fox LJ also referred to *ICI v Shatwell* [1964] 2 All ER 999, in which Lord Pearce said:

> So far as concerns common law negligence, the defence of volenti non fit injuria is clearly applicable if there was a genuine full agreement, free from any kind of pressure, to assume the risk of loss.

In that case a workman who was injured through the negligence of his fellow worker, who happened also to be his brother, was held to have fully understood and agreed to the risk that was being taken with some detonators. The employer was thus able to plead *volenti non fit injuria* and the injured plaintiff received no damages.

Finally, Fox LJ quoted Lord Herschell in *Smith v Baker & Sons* (1891):

> The maxim is founded on good sense and justice. One who has invited or assented to an act being done towards him cannot, when he suffers from it, complain of it as a wrong.

Smith v Baker & Sons concerned a quarry worker who was struck by a falling stone. It was held he was not *volenti*: he knew of the risk but could not be said to have consented to it. This is very important in employment cases, where the employee has, in reality, little choice about the risks inherent in the working environment.

Fox LJ then considered the facts of the case before him:

> If the plaintiff had himself been sober on the afternoon of the flight it seems to me that, by agreeing to be flown by Mr Murray, he must be taken to have accepted fully the risk of serious injury. The danger was both obvious and great. He could not possibly have supposed that Mr Murray, who had been drinking all the afternoon, was capable of discharging a normal duty of care.
>
> But as he himself had been drinking, can it be assumed that he was capable of appreciating the risks? The matter was not very deeply examined at the trial, but he was certainly not 'blind drunk'. . . .
>
> In my opinion, on the evidence the plaintiff knew that he was going on a flight, he knew that he was going to be piloted by Mr Murray and he knew that Mr Murray had been drinking heavily that afternoon. The plaintiff's actions that afternoon, from leaving the Blue Boar to the take-off, suggest that he was capable of understanding what he was doing. There is no clear evidence to the contrary. I think that he knew what he was doing

and was capable of appreciating the risks. I do not overlook that the plaintiff's evidence was that, if he had been sober, he would not have gone on the flight. That is no doubt so but it does not establish that he was in fact incapable of understanding what he was doing that afternoon.

If he was capable of understanding what he was doing, then the fact is that he knowingly and willingly embarked on a flight with a drunken pilot. The flight served no useful purpose at all; there was no need or compulsion to join it. It was just entertainment. The plaintiff co-operated fully in the joint activity and did what he could to assist it. He agreed in evidence that he was anxious to start the engine and to fly. A clearer source of great danger could hardly be imagined. The sort of errors of judgment which an intoxicated pilot may make are likely to have a disastrous result. The high probability was that Mr Murray was simply not fit to fly an aircraft. Nothing that happened on the flight itself suggests otherwise, from the take-off downwind to the violence of the manoeuvres of the plane in flight. . . .

I think that in embarking on the flight the plaintiff had implicitly waived his rights in the event of injury consequent on Mr Murray's failure to fly with reasonable care.

The facts go far beyond *Dann v Hamilton*, *Nettleship v Weston* and *Slater v Clay Cross Co Ltd*. It is much nearer to the dangerous experimenting with the detonators in *Imperial Chemical Industries Ltd v Shatwell* . . . I would conclude, therefore, that the plaintiff accepted the risks and implicitly discharged Mr Murray from liability from injury in relation to the flying of the plane.

The result, in my view, is that the maxim volenti non fit injuria does apply in this case. . . .

Considerations of policy do not lead me to any different conclusion. Volenti as a defence has, perhaps, been in retreat during this century, certainly in relation to master and servant cases. It might be said that the merits could be adequately dealt with by the application of the contributory negligence rules. . . . It seems to me, however, that the wild irresponsibility of the venture is such that the law should not intervene to award damages and should leave the loss where it falls. Flying is intrinsically dangerous and flying with a drunken pilot is great folly. The situation is very different from what has arisen in motoring cases.

I should mention that the defence of volenti has been abrogated in relation to passengers in motor vehicles covered by comprehensive insurance (see s 148 of the Road Traffic Act 1972). It is not suggested, however, that there is any similar enactment relating to aircraft and applicable to this case.

Contributory negligence

Far more common than *volenti* is the defence of contributory negligence, by which the damages awarded are reduced by a percentage equal to what the court considers to be the amount the plaintiff was to blame for the consequences of the defendant's negligence. In *Nettleship v Weston*, Lord Denning went on to consider contributory negligence once he had decided that *volenti* did not apply:

> ... But his claim may be reduced insofar as he was at fault himself – as in letting her take control too soon or in not being quick enough to correct her error....
>
> In my opinion when a learner-driver is being taught to drive a car under the instruction of an experienced driver, then if the car runs off the road and there is an accident in which one or other, or both of them are injured, it should be regarded as the fault of one or other or both of them. In the absence of any evidence enabling the court to draw a distinction between them, they should be regarded as equally to blame, with the result that the injured one gets damages from the other, but they are reduced by one-half owing to his own contributory negligence. The only alternative is to hold that the accident is the fault of neither, so that the injured person gets no compensation from anyone. To my mind, that is not an acceptable solution, at any rate in these days of compulsory insurance.

A favourite case with generations of students is *Sayers v Harlow UDC* [1958] 2 All ER 342. It would be nice to think that its popularity rested on a particularly learned exposition of the law, but one suspects it has something to do with the facts. The unfortunate plaintiff was locked in a public lavatory operated by the defendants and, having tried and failed to draw attention to herself by shouting and banging on the door, she decided to see whether she could climb out. She fell and was injured. Lord Evershed MR explained the effect her actions had on the damages awarded to her:

> ... it would not be right to say that the plaintiff was herself free from blame. I think that, in getting to the position where she could see, and did see, that escape via the top of the door was impossible, she acted without carelessness; but it is true to say – though, no doubt, it is being wise after the event – that, in getting back to terra firma again, she should have appreciated that she could not and ought not to allow her balance to depend on anything so unstable as a toilet roll and a fixture of a somewhat slender kind. It was not a grave error, and I think that the consequences were unduly unfortunate in the circumstances; but it is impossible to acquit the plaintiff altogether from some carelessness. In these matters the apportionment must be largely a question of, I will not say hazard, but at any rate of doing the best one can in fractions; and applying myself to it in that way, and not desiring to do more than indicate that the plaintiff was, as I think, in some degree careless and in some degree, therefore, blameworthy, I would apportion the matter as to three-fourths liability to the

> defendants, and one-fourth to her. In other words, I think that the plaintiff ought to recover from the defendants seventy-five per cent . . . of whatever be the appropriate measure of damage suffered.

In *Revill v Newbery* [1996] 1 All ER 291 contributory negligence was used when deciding what damages would be payable. This is an unusual case because the plaintiff had trespassed on the defendant's property with the intention of stealing from him. The defendant shot the burglar with a shotgun and the burglar sued for damages. The Court of Appeal decided he was entitled to damages, but they would be reduced by two-thirds because of his contributory negligence. It is worth noting that the Court of Appeal upheld the trial judge's decision that the defendant 'used greater violence than was justified in lawful self-defence and was negligent even by reference to the standard of care to be expected from the reasonable man placed in the situation in which he found himself'.

Necessity

Just as in criminal law, the courts are very wary of any attempt to claim a defence of necessity in tort. In *Borough of Southwark v Williams* [1971] 2 All ER 175 Lord Denning considered the defence. The defendants were squatting in empty property that belonged to the plaintiffs:

> . . . So those families occupied empty houses which the council evidently had thought were not worthy of repair and were not fit to be occupied. The evidence shows that there are some hundreds of empty houses in Southwark – 400, we were told, at any rate – and there is some evidence that their actual conversion or development may not take place for some little time. The squatters, in their distress, felt that they were morally justified in entering into occupation. But have they any legal justification?

Lord Denning looked at the legislation governing a local authority's duty to provide accommodation but concluded:

> It cannot have been intended by Parliament that every person who was in need of temporary accommodation should be able to sue the local authority for it; or to take the law into his own hands for the purpose.
>
> I will next consider the defence of 'necessity'. There is authority for saying that in case of great and imminent danger, in order to preserve life, the law will permit of an encroachment on private property. That is shown by *Mouse's Case* (1608), where the ferryman at Gravesend took 47 passengers into his barge to carry them to London. A great tempest arose and all were in danger. Mr Mouse was one of the passengers. He threw a casket belonging to the plaintiff overboard so as to lighten the ship. Other

passengers threw other things. It was proved that, if they had not done so, the passengers would have been drowned. It was held by the whole court that 'in any case of necessity, for the safety of the lives of the passengers' it was lawful for Mr Mouse to cast the casket out of the barge. The court said it was like the pulling down of a house, in time of fire, to stop it spreading; which has always been held justified **pro bono publico**.

The doctrine so **enunciated** must, however, be carefully **circumscribed**. Else necessity would open the door to many an excuse. It was for this reason that it was not admitted in *R v Dudley and Stephens* (1884), where the three shipwrecked sailors, in extreme despair, killed the cabin-boy and ate him to save their own lives. They were held guilty of murder. The killing was not justified by necessity. Similarly, when a man who is starving enters a house and takes food in order to keep himself alive. Our English law does not admit the defence of necessity. It holds him guilty of larceny. Lord Hale said (in *Pleas of the Crown*) that 'if a person, being under necessity for want of victuals or clothes, shall upon that account clandestinely, and in *animus furandi*, steal another man's food, it is felony'. The reason is because, if hunger were once allowed to be an excuse for stealing, it would open a way through which all kinds of disorder and lawlessness would pass. So here. If homelessness were once admitted as a defence to trespass, no one's house could be safe. Necessity would open a door which no man could shut. It would not only be those in extreme need who would enter. There would be others who would imagine that they were in need, or would invent a need, so as to gain entry. Each man would say his need was greater than the next man's. The plea would be an excuse for all sorts of wrongdoing. So the courts must, for the sake of law and order, take a firm stand. They must refuse to admit the pleas of necessity to the hungry and the homeless; and trust that their distress will be relieved by the charitable and the good. Applying these principles, it seems to me in [*sic*] the circumstances of these squatters are not such as to afford any justification or excuse in law for their entry into these houses. We can sympathise with the plight in which they find themselves. We can recognise the orderly way in which they made their entry. But we can go no further.

Statutory defences

The defence of contributory negligence is statutory, having been created by the Law Reform (Contributory Negligence) Act 1945. If a statute governs a tort, it will often provide for defences to that tort. An example is the Occupiers' Liability Act 1957, which provides a defence of having warned the visitor of a danger. In *Roles v Nathan* [1963] 1 WLR 1117, Lord Denning explained how this defence applied to the death of two chimney sweeps who had died after being overcome by fumes caused by a blocked flue:

> I am quite clear that the warnings which were given to the sweeps were enough to enable them to be reasonably safe. The sweeps would have been quite safe if they had heeded these warnings. They should not have come back that evening and attempted to seal up the sweep-hole while the fire was still alight. They ought to have waited till next morning, and then they should have seen that the fire was out before they attempted to seal up the sweep-hole. In any case they should not have stayed too long in the sweep-hole. In short, it was entirely their own fault. The judge held that it was contributory negligence. I would go further and say that, under the Act, the occupier has, by the warnings, discharged his duty.

Check your understanding

1. Can you explain the meaning of the words and phrases in **bold** type? Are there any other words you need to look up in a dictionary?
2. Why is the defence of *volenti non fit injuria* not available to defendant drivers in road traffic cases?

Discuss

1. Distinguish between *volenti* and contributory negligence. Where do the judges draw the line? Would you draw it in the same place? Make sure you can justify your arguments by reference to the cases.
2. Is the justification for not allowing a defence of necessity in most cases a 'floodgates argument'? Compare with the arguments in respect of duty of care in negligence.

Write

Choose a statute that gives rise to liability in tort, for example, the Animals Act 1971 or the Consumer Protection Act 1987. Working either from a textbook or from the original statute, explain the defence(s) the statute provides.

Connections

The defendant in *Revill v Newbery* was using a self-help remedy of self-defence. Look at what was said about the self-help remedy of abatement in the material on nuisance at p. 198. These remedies are so dangerous that they are almost always best avoided.

5.5 DAMAGES

The most common remedy in tort is the award of damages. As we have seen (p. 188), they are usually awarded in respect of losses which were foreseeable. The Law Commission explained the law and the problems it gives rise to with regard to damages for personal injuries in *Structured Settlements and Interim and Provisional Damages* in 1994:

> 2.1 The principles governing the award of damages have in the main been worked out by the courts and are not based on statute. Damages in a tort action almost invariably take the form of a lump sum made up of special damages (for past pecuniary loss) and general damages (for future pecuniary loss including loss of earning capacity and the cost of future care, and non-pecuniary loss whenever occurring, such as pain and suffering and loss of amenity). The commonly espoused purpose of these damages is restitutio in integrum; that the plaintiff shall be restored, as far as is possible in money terms, to the position occupied prior to the accident. This is done by a 'lump sum', that is, a once-and-for-all assessment paid in the form of a single sum. The tendency to take it for granted that only a one-off lump sum constitutes acceptable compensation was noted but rejected by the Royal Commission on Civil Liability and Compensation for Personal Injury. Increasing acknowledgment of the deficiencies of the lump sum award and the growth in size of claims have combined to change the focus in a number of cases to alternative forms of payment of damages.
>
> 2.2 The most forceful criticism of the lump sum is that even where the loss to the plaintiff is capable of being expressed in pecuniary terms the award does not in fact accurately replace what has been lost. The tort system offers the full compensation implicit in restitutio in integrum. Apart from symbolically compensating pain and lost pleasures in money terms, this also means that lost earnings, out of pocket expenses, and possible ill-effects of the injury, such as medical complications and loss of marriage or employment prospects, will all be recoverable. Reasonable future medical and nursing expenses are also recoverable. The difficulty with a lump sum for general damages is that 'all future **contingencies** must be crudely translated into a present value' despite a general awareness that uncertainty as to the future may mean that the present value is seriously inaccurate. . . .
>
> 2.3 One dimension of the 'present value' problem is the need for the court in estimating pecuniary loss to make 'guesstimates' of both the future general financial situation and the plaintiff's future. The judicial approach to the quantification of loss entails, broadly speaking, an identification of the net annual loss (the multiplicand), and the number of years for which the loss will last (the multiplier). The multiplicand is adjusted for any prospect of increased earnings whilst the multiplier is scaled down to reflect the contingencies of life and the fact that the money will be available to the

> plaintiff sooner under a lump sum award than it would otherwise have been, thereby allowing the plaintiff to invest the money to produce a positive real return during the years of the loss. It is the choice of multiplier which is generally the more difficult part of the calculation. The court often has to make judgments about the likelihood of different contingencies occurring when it is deciding whether to downrate the multiplier. It also has to take a view on the size of the discount to be made because the lump sum is receivable in advance. An alternative approach . . . is an **actuarial** one, using combined annuity and life expectation tables.
>
> 2.4 A number of criticisms have been made of the way in which the multiplier system operates in practice. In some cases the multiplier is lowered to take account of the risk of early death even when this has already been fully discounted in the determination of the number of years the loss is expected to endure. The size of the discount made for contingencies may also be somewhat arbitrary at times. More importantly, the assumption which is implicit in the present approach of the courts in calculating multipliers is that the real rate of return on investment after tax is around 4 to 5%. For this reason courts will usually apply a discount of this amount to the multiplier.

The Law Commission went on to recommend a change to an actuarial approach to the calculation of damages. It then considered structured settlements:

> 3.1 The structured settlement provides an alternative form of damages to the lump sum award. Structured settlements have developed in the United Kingdom without legislative assistance as a result of their tax status. They usually consist of an initial lump sum part payment followed by a series of further instalments of the damages for which the defendant is liable. The initial lump sum tends to represent compensation for past pain and suffering and costs and expenses already incurred. The defendant or the defendant's insurer uses the balance of the sum due under the settlement to purchase an annuity or a series of annuities from a life insurance company. The payments made under the annuities are used to fund the periodic payments, which usually last for the life of the plaintiff or a specified term, whichever is the longer. At present, in the United Kingdom, structures are agreed voluntarily between the parties. . . .
>
> 3.10 One of the advantages of structuring is said to be that it benefits both parties, thereby encouraging early settlement with attendant savings in cost and time. Parties that are far apart on a lump sum figure, perhaps because of differences over life expectancy, may be able to take a different approach which will eventually lead to an acceptable compromise.
>
> 3.11 However, the main advantage cited for plaintiffs is certainty. This consists of a number of elements. The plaintiff is relieved of the burden of managing a large sum of money and is protected from possible dissipation

of the funds. There is the assurance of regular payments for life and of payments to dependants if the payments are guaranteed for a period longer than the plaintiff's life, together with the assurance that the payments will not decline in value if they are index-linked. These features make structured settlements particularly appropriate in cases where there are serious injuries and the conventional award would be large, and particularly where the plaintiff is a child and a long period of future care is envisaged. It is regarded as unlikely the state will ever have to step in to provide for the plaintiff where a settlement is structured.

3.12 Flexibility is seen as a further attractive feature of structuring for the plaintiff. The projected settlement can be tailored individually to the plaintiff's needs. Damages are linked to life expectancy without an absolute date having to be specified to provide a cut-off point. Cash flow is also based on projected future cash requirements. Provided these are considered carefully, the annuity package can be set up to provide at the appropriate time for education, changing nursing needs, asset accumulation, housing, marriage and children, and limited work or business prospects, if any. The damages will not be spent before these needs arise. The way to achieve these aims is to include the payment of periodic lump sums at key stages in the plaintiff's life. By this means structuring focuses on the plaintiff's needs, unlike the conventionally assessed lump sum, thereby in principle reducing the adversarial nature of the proceedings. . . .

3.14 From a policy point of view the favourable tax treatment given to structured settlements and the consequent incentive to make such agreements seem to be justified for several reasons. Firstly, structured settlements developed as a result of dissatisfaction with lump sums, which fail to replace like with like, substitute capital sums for continuing future losses, and may be insufficient to meet the plaintiff's long term needs, being based on considerable guesswork. The state has moved to meet this dissatisfaction by **facilitating** structuring through the tax structure. Structuring diversifies the range of remedies available to victims of personal injury. Secondly, the state has a significant interest in preventing recipients of damages from becoming unnecessarily dependent on welfare benefits. The public has in fact paid once to compensate the victim in the form of insurance premiums. If the victim later has to fall back on welfare benefits, the public is in effect being forced to pay twice over.

3.15 Thirdly, the victim's future needs may be better met by regular payments which are more likely to be spent upon the purposes for which damages are awarded. The result is an award of damages which is as close to real compensation as is possible. Finally, the victim has the real certainty of regular income. In fact, a victim will have more certainty than prior to the accident, in the sense that the risk of unemployment no longer forms part of the equation. The certainty of a future income stream is seen to be better than the prospect presented by the receipt of a lump sum which then has to be invested and managed by the victim. For the victim who has

> suffered particularly serious personal injuries, and who faces a life of dependency stretching into some unknown future, the certainty of regular income is a prime concern. . . .
>
> 3.17 Our qualitative survey revealed that although those who had received structured settlements were generally offered them by the other side as opposed to specifically requesting them, and although some felt pressured, for the same reasons as with lump sum offers (such as 'It's either this or they go to court', or a desire to return to normality and reduce stress), into accepting the structure, respondents generally held very positive views about the structured settlement they had received. Indeed, there was a general agreement from those who had actual experience of structures that this form of compensation was preferable to lump sum only payments. To them the structure was seen as providing lifelong security and peace of mind, allowing the individual to plan, financially, for the future, while the income is sorted out for the present and for the future and keeps in line with inflation through index-linking: moreover the individual does not carry the responsibility for investment, and this removes the temptation to 'blow the lot in one go', particularly when the recipient comes of age.

The Law Commission's recommendation was that structured settlements continue to be voluntary but that their use should be developed.

Whilst the main purpose of damages in tort is compensation, it is very occasionally possible for a court to register its disapproval of a defendant's conduct by awarding exemplary damages, designed to punish the defendant. The grounds on which these will be awarded were considered by a High Court judge, Wright J, in the case of *AB v South West Water Services Ltd* [1992] 4 All ER 574. The defendant water company had supplied water that had been negligently contaminated. Many people were made ill. The claim for exemplary damages arose because the water company, knowing that the water supply was dangerous, assured consumers that it was safe.

Wright J began by considering the precedents on exemplary damages, making particular reference to principles laid down by Lord Devlin in *Rookes v Barnard* [1964] 1 All ER 367. Lord Devlin said:

> Exemplary damages are essentially different from ordinary damages. The object of damages in the usual sense of the term is to compensate. The object of exemplary damages is to punish and deter. It may well be thought that this confuses the civil and criminal functions of the law; and indeed, so far as I know, the idea of exemplary damages is peculiar to English law. There is not any decision of this House approving an award of exemplary damages and your lordships therefore have to consider whether it is open to the House to remove an anomaly from the law of England.

He decided that:

> . . . your lordships could not without a complete disregard of precedent, and indeed of statute, now arrive at a determination that refused altogether to recognise the exemplary principle. Secondly, that there are certain categories of cases in which an award of exemplary damages can serve a useful purpose in **vindicating** the strength of the law, and thus affording a practical justification for admitting into the civil law a principle which ought logically to belong to the criminal.

Lord Devlin then laid down two categories of case in which exemplary damages might be awarded. Wright J explained what these categories are:

> . . . first, cases of oppressive, arbitrary or unconstitutional action by the servants of the government (and I should say in parentheses that it is here conceded for the purposes of the argument in the present hearing that the defendants' employees are servants of government within the meaning of this category) and, secondly, cases in which the defendant's conduct has been calculated by him to make a profit for himself which may well exceed the compensation payable to the plaintiff.

Wright J then considered cases after *Rookes v Barnard* and concluded:

> Accordingly, almost by definition, exemplary damages will never be recoverable in a case where the claim is based upon a straightforward allegation of negligence. The concept of an unintended and unlooked for outcome of a course of conduct which may be inadvertent, thoughtless or at worst reckless is obviously not one which could easily be fitted into either of Lord Devlin's two categories. . . . On the other hand, where the conduct complained of by the plaintiff consists of a deliberate, calculated and wilful attack upon the plaintiff's rights by a defendant whose status falls within Lord Devlin's first category, or whose motivation falls within the second, then I for my part can see no reason why such a defendant should not be laid open to the sanction of exemplary damages . . . I believe that this view of the law reconciles *Rookes v Barnard* itself with all the authorities that postdate it. . . .
>
> I will not conceal the fact that I have had very considerable hesitation in coming to the conclusion that I have set out. There can be no doubt, as Lord Devlin stressed in *Rookes v Barnard*, that the existence of this particular punitive sanction in English law is an **anomaly**, but, as he himself said, it is an anomaly which is too deeply rooted to be dug out by the court. In the circumstances I have come to the conclusion that the allegations pleaded, containing as they do allegations of nuisance based upon the allegedly deliberate acts of the defendants' employees in continuing to supply contaminated water to their customers' homes and premises in the full knowledge of and

intent to do what they were doing . . . are capable of supporting a claim for an award of exemplary damages. . . .

But it is, however, at this point that I feel it incumbent upon me to issue a general warning, in one sense speaking over the heads of the lawyers before me to the plaintiffs themselves. The fact that I have refused to strike out the claim for exemplary damages in the master statement of claim should not mislead any plaintiff into thinking that he or she is necessarily or even probably going to recover any such award. The precise nature of the conduct of the defendants and their employees and whether in the final analysis it will justify such an award must depend upon the evidence, and it may very well be that in the final analysis that conduct will not justify the language in which it has been described in the statement of claim. Furthermore, no consideration has been given to one major aspect of this case which is very relevant to the issue of exemplary damages, and I refer again to the fact that the defendants have already been prosecuted, convicted and punished for the contamination of the water supply for which they as the water authority are responsible. Mr Symons QC on behalf of the defendants, properly in my view, conceded in argument that the impact of that conviction upon any entitlement that the plaintiffs might have to exemplary damages must depend upon the evidence, and I merely point out that it must be at least possible that the effect of that conviction and punishment may easily be to disentitle the plaintiffs to any award under this head at all. I sound this warning so that any individual plaintiff who has received or receives hereafter an offer in settlement of his claim, which would in all other respects be acceptable and satisfactory, should consider very carefully what his position may be before he continues further in his litigation against the defendants merely in the hope or expectation of receiving a further award under the head of exemplary . . . damages. Notwithstanding my present ruling, I can well see that his entitlement to such remedy may still be the subject of very considerable argument.

Check your understanding

Can you explain the meaning of the words and phrases in **bold** type? Are there any other words you need to look up in a dictionary?

Discuss

1 With reference to the comment in para 3.14 of the Law Commission's paper, explain how the public has already paid compensation in the form of insurance premiums.

2 Our present system of awarding damages in personal injury cases rests on the plaintiff being able to find someone else to blame. Consider whether it

would be preferable to have a system of state benefits paid to all those in need, whatever the cause of their need.

3 Why can damages for pain and suffering and loss of amenity be only 'symbolic compensation'?

4 Many factory accidents occur because employers use profitable but unsafe systems of work. Do you consider it more effective to deal with such employers through prosecution under the Health and Safety at Work Act 1974, by the award of exemplary damages, or a combination of the two?

Write

List the advantages and disadvantages of lump sum payments and structured settlements for payment of damages in personal injury cases. Is it fair to criticise structured settlements as amounting to a paternalistic approach to plaintiffs?

Connections

1 Law Commission reports and consultative documents are extremely useful sources for students because they set out the existing law in fairly accessible language, explain the criticisms of the law and propose changes for which they also give advantages and disadvantages. Look at the other Law Commission material used in this book.

2 At para 3.17 the Law Commission refers to plaintiffs feeling under pressure to accept a structured settlement. Note that pressure on plaintiffs is a common feature of personal injury litigation in which the defendant is very often an insurance company with large resources. This is relevant to the issue of funding civil litigation, discussed at p. 64 *et seq*.

3 Note that Wright J was not trying the case in *AB v South West Water Services*; he was hearing a preliminary issue. This is quite a common process. Armed with a ruling on what the law is, the parties may well then reach a settlement, saving the considerable expense of a full trial.

6 Contract

When asked to advise about a dispute, a lawyer's first task is to decide which rules will apply to the situation. If the rules of contract law are to apply, there must be a contract between the parties to the dispute – so the first question is, 'Is there a contract?' Sometimes it will be better to bring an action in tort, even though there is a contract between the parties to the dispute. This is entirely possible, provided the plaintiff is not trying to avoid a term of the contract. In *Barclays Bank v Fairclough* (1995) a dispute between two contracting parties about the way in which an asbestos roof had been cleaned was held by the Court of Appeal to give rise to liability in tort. This made it possible for the defendants to plead contributory negligence by the plaintiffs. So the lawyer's duty also includes choosing whether to sue in contract or in tort if both are possible: one would probably begin by pleading both.

6.1 FORMATION

A contract has several recognisable and essential features: there must be an offer by one party, accepted by the other; they must intend to create legal relations and the party who wishes to sue must have provided consideration.

Was there an offer? In the case of *Fisher v Bell* [1960] 3 All ER 731 the Divisional Court of Queen's Bench considered an appeal from a magistrates' court. The police had prosecuted the respondent for offering a flick-knife for sale. Section 1(1) of the Restriction of Offensive Weapons Act 1959 reads:

> Any person who manufactures, sells or hires or offers for sale or hire, or lends or gives to any other person—(a) any knife which has a blade which opens automatically by hand pressure applied to a button, spring or other device in or attached to the handle of the knife, sometimes known as a 'flick knife' . . . shall be guilty of an offence . . .

The magistrates held that there had not been an offer for sale and the police appealed against that decision as being wrong in law. Lord Parker CJ:

> The sole question is whether the exhibition of that knife in the window with the ticket constituted an offer for sale within the statute. I think that most lay people would be inclined to the view (as, indeed, I was myself when I first read these papers), that if a knife were displayed in a window like that with a price attached to it, it was nonsense to say that that was not offering it for sale. The knife is there inviting people to buy it, and in ordinary language it is for sale; but any statute must be looked at in the light of the general law of the country, for Parliament must be taken to know the general law. It is clear that, according to the ordinary law of contract, the display of an article with a price on it in a shop window is merely an invitation to treat. It is in no sense an offer for sale the acceptance of which constitutes a contract. That is clearly the general law of the country. Not only is that so, but it is to be observed that, in many statutes and orders which prohibit selling and offering for sale of goods, it is very common, when it is so desired, to insert the words 'offering or exposing for sale', 'exposing for sale' being clearly words which would cover the display of goods in a shop window. Not only that, but it appears that under several statutes – we have been referred in particular to the Prices of Goods Act, 1939, and the Goods and Services (Price Control) Act, 1941 – Parliament, when it desires to enlarge the ordinary meaning of those words, has a definition section enlarging the ordinary meaning of 'offer for sale' to cover other matters including, be it observed, exposure of goods for sale with the price attached.
>
> In those circumstances I, for my part, though I confess reluctantly, am driven to the conclusion that no offence was here committed. At first sight it appears absurd that knives of this sort may not be manufactured, they may not be sold, they may not be hired, they may not be lent, they may not be given, but apparently they may be displayed in shop windows; but even if this is a **casus omissus** – and I am by no means saying that it is – it is not for this court to supply the omission. I am mindful of the strong words of Lord Simons in *Magor & St Mellons Rural District Council v Newport Corpn* (1951). In that case one of the lords justices in the Court of Appeal had, in effect, said that the court, having discovered the supposed intention of Parliament, must proceed to fill in the gaps – what the legislature has not written, the court must write – and in answer to that contention Lord Simons in his speech said:
>
>> 'It appears to me to be a naked usurpation of the legislative function under the thin disguise of interpretation . . .'.

The court looks at what has happened between the parties and decides, from an **objective** standpoint, whether there has been an offer and whether that offer has been accepted. The need for this kind of analysis arose in the case of *Gibson v Manchester City Council* [1979] 1 All ER 973. Mr Gibson was in the process of buying his council house from Manchester City Council when there was a local election and Manchester Council changed from being controlled by Conservatives to being controlled by Labour. The new council decided that no more council houses were to be sold. The trial judge had decided that there was a binding contract and made an order of specific performance in Mr Gibson's favour. The council appealed, first to the Court of Appeal and then to the House of Lords. In the House of Lords, Lord Diplock said:

> The council's appeal against this judgment was dismissed by a majority of the Court of Appeal (Lord Denning MR and Ormrod LJ); Geoffrey Lane LJ dissented. Lord Denning MR rejected what I have described as the conventional approach of looking to see whether on the true construction of the documents relied on there can be discerned an offer and acceptance. One ought, he said, to 'look at the correspondence as a whole and at the conduct of the parties and see therefrom whether the parties have come to an agreement on everything that was material'. This approach, which in referring to the conduct of the parties . . . appears to me to overlook the provisions of s 40 of the Law of Property Act 1925 [which provided that contracts for the sale of land had to be evidenced in writing] led him however to the conclusion that there should be imported into the agreement to be specifically performed additional conditions, against use except as a private dwelling-house and against advertising and a restriction not to sell or lease the property for five years. These are conditions which would not be implied by law in an open contract for the sale of land. The reason for so varying the county court judge's order was that clauses in these terms were included in the standard form of 'Agreement for Sale of a Council House' which, as appears from the earlier case of *Storer v Manchester City Council* (1974), was entered into by the council and council tenants whose applications to purchase the freehold of their council house reached the stage at which contracts were exchanged. There was, however, no reference to this standard form of agreement in any of the documents said to constitute the contract relied on in the instant case, nor was there any evidence that Mr Gibson had knowledge of its terms at or before the time that the alleged contract was concluded. . . .
>
> My Lords, there may be certain types of contract, though I think they are exceptional, which do not fit easily into the normal analysis of a contract as being constituted by offer and acceptance; but a contract alleged to have been made by an exchange of correspondence between the parties in which the successive communications other than the first are in reply to one another is not one of these. I can see no reason in the instant case for departing from the conventional approach of looking at the handful of documents relied on as constituting the contract sued on and seeing whether

> on their true construction there is to be found in them a contractual offer by the council to sell the house to Mr Gibson and an acceptance of that offer by Mr Gibson. I venture to think that it was by departing from this conventional approach that the majority of the Court of Appeal was led into error.

Lord Diplock then looked at a letter sent by the council to Mr Gibson and noted that it said, among other things, that the council '*may be prepared* to sell the house to you at the purchase price of £2,725 less 20%' and ended 'If you would like to make formal application to buy your Council house, please complete the enclosed application form and return it to me as soon as possible'. He took the view that these words made it quite impossible to regard this letter as an offer:

> The words 'may be prepared to sell' are fatal to this, so is the invitation, not, be it noted, to accept the offer, but 'to make formal application to buy' on the enclosed application form. It is, to quote Geoffrey Lane LJ, a letter setting out the financial terms on which it may be the council would be prepared to consider a sale and purchase in due course. . . .
>
> Mr Gibson did fill in the application form enclosed with this letter. It was in three sections: section A headed 'Application to buy a council house', section B 'Application for a loan to buy a council house', and section C 'Certificate to be completed by all applicants'. He left blank the space for the purchase price in section A and sent the form to the council on 5th March 1971 with a covering letter in which he requested the council either to undertake at their own expense to carry out repairs to the tarmac path forming part of the premises or to make a deduction from the purchase price to cover the cost of repairs. The letter also intimated that Mr Gibson would like to make a down payment of £500 towards the purchase price instead of borrowing the whole amount on mortgage. In reply to the request made in this letter the council, by letter of 12th March 1971, said that the condition of the property had been taken into consideration in fixing the purchase price and that repairs to the tarmac by the council could not be authorised at this stage. This letter was acknowledged by Mr Gibson by his letter to the council of 18th March 1971 in which he asked the council to 'carry on with the purchase as per my application already in your possession'.
>
> My Lords, the application form and letter of 18th March 1971 were relied on by Mr Gibson as an unconditional acceptance of the council's offer to sell the house; but this cannot be so unless there was a contractual offer by the council available for acceptance, and, for the reason already given, I am of opinion that there was none. It is unnecessary to consider whether the application form and Mr Gibson's letters of 5th and 18th March 1971 are capable of amounting to a contractual offer by him to purchase the freehold interest in the house at a price of £2,180 on the

> terms of an open contract, for there is no suggestion that, even if it were, it was ever accepted by the council. Nor would it ever have been even if there had been no change in the political control of the council, as the policy of the council before the change required the incorporation in all agreements for sale of council houses to tenants of the conditions referred to by Lord Denning MR in his judgment and other conditions inconsistent with an open contract.
>
> I therefore feel compelled to allow the appeal. One can sympathise with Mr Gibson's disappointment on finding that his expectations that he would be able to buy his council house at 20% below its market value in the autumn of 1970 cannot be realised. Whether one thinks this makes it a hard case perhaps depends on the political views that one holds about council housing policy. But hard cases offer strong temptation to let them have their proverbial consequences. It is a temptation that the judicial mind must be vigilant to resist.

In *Errington v Errington* [1952] 1 All ER 149 Denning LJ gave judgment in another case in which it had to be decided whether there was a contract:

> The facts are reasonably clear. In 1936 the father bought the house for his son and daughter-in-law to live in. The father put down £250 in cash and borrowed £500 from a building society on the security of the house, repayable with interest by instalments of 15*s* a week. He took the house in his own name and made himself responsible for the instalments. The father told the daughter-in-law that the £250 was a present for them, but he left them to pay the building society instalments of 15*s* a week themselves. He handed the building society book to the daughter-in-law and said to her: 'Don't part with this book. The house will be your property when the mortgage is paid.' He said that when he retired he would transfer it into their names. She has, in fact, paid the building society instalments regularly from that day to this with the result that much of the mortgage has been repaid, but there is a good deal yet to be paid. . . .
>
> Ample content is given to the whole arrangement by holding that the father promised that the house should belong to the couple as soon as they had paid off the mortgage. The parties did not discuss what was to happen if the couple failed to pay the instalments to the building society, but I should have thought it clear that, if they did fail to pay the instalments, the father would not be bound to transfer the house to them. The father's promise was a unilateral contract – a promise of the house in return for their act of paying the instalments. It could not be revoked by him once the couple entered on performance of the act, but it would cease to bind him if they left it incomplete and unperformed, which they have not done. If that was the position during the father's lifetime, so it must be after his death. If the daughter-in-law continues to pay all the building society instalments, the couple will be entitled to have the property transferred

> to them as soon as the mortgage is paid off, but if she does not do so, then the building society will claim the instalments from the father's estate and the estate will have to pay them. I cannot think that in those circumstances the estate would be bound to transfer the house to them any more than the father himself would have been.

Lord Denning then considered what the legal relationship between the parties to the arrangement had been: were the couple 'tenants at will', paying no rent; were they tenants paying a rent of 15*s* a week or were they licensees? He decided that they were licensees:

> . . . the couple were licensees, having a permissive occupation short of a tenancy, but with a contractual right, or, at any rate, an equitable right to remain so long as they paid the instalments, which would grow into a good equitable title to the house itself as soon as the mortgage was paid. . . . They had a mere personal privilege to remain there, with no right to assign or sub-let. They were, however, not bare licensees. They were licensees with a contractual right to remain. As such they have no right in law to remain, but only in equity, and equitable rights now prevail.

6.2 CONSIDERATION

The party who sues on the contract must show that he or she provided consideration. This means that something of value was given or promised. There are several interesting cases that revolve round the question of whether the 'something' was of value.

In *Chappell & Co v Nestle* [1959] 2 All ER 701 the argument was a very technical one about royalty payments for the use of a piece of music, but the argument came down to whether three chocolate wrappers could be described as being 'of value' and, thus, part of the consideration for a recording that was being supplied by the chocolate company to anyone who sent 1*s* 6*d* (7.5p) and three chocolate wrappers. The judges in the House of Lords did not agree on the issue. The majority thought the wrappers were part of the consideration. Lord Reid explains why:

> I can now turn to what appears to me to be the crucial question in this case: was the 1*s* 6*d* an 'ordinary retail selling price' within the meaning of s. 8 [of the Copyright Act 1956]? That involves two questions, what was the nature of the contract between the respondents Nestle and a person who sent 1*s* 6*d* plus three wrappers in acceptance of their offer, and what is meant by 'ordinary retail selling price' in this context. To determine the nature of the contract, one must find the intention of the parties as shown by what they said and did. The respondents Nestle's intention can hardly be in doubt. They were using these records to increase their sales of chocolate.

Their offer was addressed to everyone. It might be accepted by a person who was already a regular buyer of their chocolate; but, much more important to them, it might be accepted by people who might become regular buyers of their chocolate if they could be induced to try it and found they liked it. The inducement was something calculated to look like a bargain, a record at a very cheap price. It is in evidence that the ordinary price for a dance record is 6*s* 6*d*. It is true that the ordinary record gives much longer playing time than the Nestle records and it may have other advantages. But the reader of the respondents Nestle's offer was not in a position to know that. It seems to me clear that the main intention of the offer was to induce people interested in this kind of music to buy (or, perhaps, get others to buy) chocolate which otherwise would not have been bought. It is, of course, true that some wrappers might come from chocolate which had already been bought, or from chocolate which would have been bought without the offer, but that does not seem to me to alter the case. Where there is a large number of transactions – the notice mentions 30,000 records – I do not think we should simply consider an isolated case where it would be impossible to say whether there had been a direct benefit from the acquisition of the wrappers or not. The requirement that wrappers should be sent was of great importance to the respondents Nestle; there would have been no point in their simply offering records for 1*s* 6*d* each. It seems to me quite unrealistic to divorce the buying of the chocolate from the supplying of the records. It is a perfectly good contract if a person accepts an offer to supply goods if he (a) does something of value to the supplier and (b) pays money; the consideration is both (a) and (b). There may have been cases where the acquisition of the wrappers conferred no direct benefit on the respondents Nestle but there must have been many cases where it did. I do not see why the possibility that, in some cases, the acquisition of the wrappers did not directly benefit the respondents Nestle should require us to exclude from consideration the cases where it did; and even where there was no direct benefit from the acquisition of the wrappers there may have been an indirect benefit by way of advertisement.

I do not think that it matters greatly whether this kind of contract is called a sale or not. The appellants did not take the point that this transaction was not a sale. But I am bound to say that I have some doubts. If a contract under which a person is bound to do something as well as to pay money is a sale, then either the price includes the obligation as well as the money, or the consideration is the price plus the obligation. And I do not see why it should be different if he has to show that he has done something of value to the seller. It is, to my mind, illegitimate to argue – this is a sale, the consideration for a sale is the price, price can only include money or something which can readily be converted into an ascertainable sum of money, therefore anything like wrappers which have no money value when delivered cannot be part of the consideration. The respondents avoid this difficulty by submitting that acquiring and delivering the wrappers was merely a condition which gave a qualification to buy and was not part of the consideration for the sale. Of course, a person may limit his offer to a person qualified in a particular way, eg, members of a club. But where the qualification is the doing of something of value to the seller, and where the qualification only suffices for one sale and must be re-acquired before another sale, I find it hard to regard the repeated acquisitions of the qualification as anything other than parts of the consideration for the sales. The purchaser of records had to send three wrappers for each record, so he had first to acquire them. The acquisition of wrappers by him was, at least in many cases, of direct benefit to the respondents Nestle, and required expenditure by the acquirer which he might not otherwise have incurred. To my mind, the acquiring and delivering of the wrappers was certainly part of the consideration in these cases, and I see no good reason for drawing a distinction between these and other cases.

Viscount Simonds took the opposite view:

In my opinion, my Lords, the wrappers are not part of the selling price. They are, admittedly, themselves valueless and are thrown away, and it was for that reason, no doubt, that Upjohn J [the trial judge] was constrained to say that their value lay in the evidence they afforded of success in an advertising campaign. That is what they are. But what, after all, does that mean? Nothing more than that someone, by no means necessarily the purchaser of the record, has in the past bought not from the respondents Nestle but from a retail shop three bars of chocolate and that the purchaser has thus directly or indirectly acquired the wrappers. How often he acquires them for himself, how often through another, is pure speculation. The only thing that is certain is that, if he buys bars of chocolate from a retail shop or acquires the wrappers from another who has bought them, that purchase is not, or at the lowest is not necessarily, part of the same transaction as his subsequent purchase of a record from the manufacturers.

In *Williams v Roffey Brothers* [1990] 1 All ER 512 the Court of Appeal was faced with an argument that a person who makes a fresh promise to do something he is already contractually bound to do is not providing any consideration. The plaintiff had contracted to do some carpentry for the defendants. He then discovered that he had quoted too low a price for the work. The defendants wanted the job completed on time, so promised to pay the plaintiff more money for the same work he was already contracted to do. They later refused to pay him and he sued. Glidewell LJ:

Counsel for the defendants relies on the principle of law which, traditionally, is based on the decision in *Stilk v Myrick* (1809) 2 Camp 317, 170 ER 1168. That was a decision at first instance of Lord Ellenborough CJ. On a voyage to the Baltic, two seamen deserted. The captain agreed with the rest of the crew that if they worked the ship back to London without the two seamen being replaced, he would divide between them the pay which would have been due to the two deserters. On arrival at London this extra pay was refused, and the plaintiff's action to recover his extra pay was dismissed. Counsel for the defendant argued that such an agreement was contrary to public policy, but Lord Ellenborough CJ's judgment (as reported in Campbell's Reports) was based on lack of consideration. It reads . . .

> 'I think *Harris v Watson* . . . was rightly decided; but I doubt whether the ground of public policy, upon which Lord Kenyon is stated to have proceeded, be the true principle on which the decision is to be supported. Here, I say the agreement is void for want of consideration. There was no consideration for the ulterior pay promised to the mariners who remained with the ship. Before they sailed from London they had undertaken to do all they could under the emergencies of the voyage. They had sold all their services till the voyage should be completed. If they had been at liberty to quit the vessel at Cronstadt, the case would have been quite different; or if the captain had capriciously discharged the two men who were wanting, the others might not have been compellable to take the whole duty upon themselves, and their agreeing to do so might have been a sufficient consideration for the promise of an advance of wages. But the desertion of a part of the crew is to be considered an emergency of the voyage as much as their death; and those who remain are bound by the terms of their original contract to exert themselves to the utmost to bring the ship in safety to her destined port. Therefore, without looking to the policy of this agreement, I think it is void for want of consideration, and that the plaintiff can only recover at the rate of £5 a month.'

In *North Ocean Shipping Co Ltd v Hyundai Construction Co Ltd, The Atlantic Baron* [1978] 3 All ER 1170 . . . Mocatta J regarded the general principle of the decision in *Stilk v Myrick* as still being good law. He referred to two earlier decisions of this court, dealing with wholly different subjects, in which Denning LJ sought to escape from the confines of the rule, but was not accompanied in this attempt by the other members of the court.

In *Ward v Byham* [1956] 2 All ER 318 . . . the plaintiff and the defendant lived together unmarried for five years, during which time the plaintiff bore their child. After the parties ended their relationship, the defendant promised to pay the plaintiff £1 per week to maintain the child, provided that she was well looked after and happy. The defendant paid this sum for some months, but ceased to pay when the plaintiff married another man. On her suing for the amount due at £1 per week, he pleaded that there was no consideration for his agreement to pay for the plaintiff to maintain her child, since she was obliged by law to do so . . . The county court judge upheld the plaintiff mother's claim, and this court dismissed the defendant's appeal.

Denning LJ said . . . :

> 'I approach the case, therefore, on the footing that, in looking after the child, the mother is only doing what she is legally bound to do. Even so, I think that there was sufficient consideration to support the promise. I have always thought that the promise to perform an existing duty, or the performance of it, should be regarded as good consideration, because it is a benefit to the person to whom it is given. Take this very case. It is as much a benefit for the father to have the child looked after by the mother as by a neighbour. If he gets the benefit for which he stipulated, he ought to honour his promise, and he ought not to avoid it by saying that the mother was herself under a duty to maintain the child. I regard the father's promise in this case as what is sometimes called a unilateral contract, a promise in return for an act, a promise by the father to pay £1 a week in return for the mother's looking after the child. Once the mother embarked on the task of looking after the child, there was a binding contract. So long as she looked after the child, she would be entitled to £1 a week. . . .'

However, Morris LJ put it rather differently. He said . . . :

> 'Counsel for the father submits that there was a duty on the mother to support the child, that no affiliation proceedings were in prospect or were contemplated, and that the effect of the arrangement that followed the letter was that the father was merely agreeing to pay a bounty to the mother. It seems to me that the terms of the letter negative those submissions, for the father says: "providing you can prove that [the child] will be well looked after and happy and also that she is allowed to decide for herself whether or not she wishes to come and live with you". The father goes on to say that the child is then well and happy and looking much stronger than ever before. "If you decide what to do let me know as soon as possible." It seems to me, therefore, that the father was saying, in effect: Irrespective of what may be the strict legal position, what I am asking is that you shall prove that the child will be well looked after and happy, and also that you must agree that the child is to be allowed to decide for herself whether or not she wishes to come and live with you. If those conditions were fulfilled the father was agreeable to pay. On those terms, which in fact became operative, the father agreed to pay £1 a week. In my judgment, there was ample consideration there to be found for his promise, which I think was binding.'

> Parker LJ agreed. As I read the judgment of Morris LJ, he and Parker LJ held that, though in maintaining the child the plaintiff was doing no more than she was obliged to do by law, nevertheless her promise that the child would be well looked after and happy was a practical benefit to the father, which amounted to consideration for his promise. . . .
>
> There is, however, another legal concept of relatively recent development which is relevant, namely that of economic duress. Clearly, if a sub-contractor has agreed to undertake work at a fixed price, and before he has completed the work declines to continue with it unless the contractor agrees to pay an increased price, the sub-contractor may be held guilty of securing the contractor's promise by taking unfair advantage of the difficulties he will cause if he does not complete the work. In such a case an agreement to pay an increased price may well be voidable because it was entered into under duress.

Glidewell LJ then considered Lord Scarman's judgment in the Privy Council case of *Pao On v Lau Yiu* [1979] 3 All ER 65, during which Lord Scarman said:

> [The] question . . . is whether, in a case where duress is not established, public policy may nevertheless invalidate the consideration if there has been a threat to repudiate a pre-existing contractual obligation or an unfair use of a dominating bargaining position. Their Lordships' conclusion is that where businessmen are negotiating at arm's length it is unnecessary for the achievement of justice, and unhelpful in the development of the law, to invoke such a rule of public policy. It would also create unacceptable anomaly. It is unnecessary because justice requires that men, who have negotiated at arm's length, be held to their bargains unless it can be shown that their consent was vitiated by fraud, mistake or duress. If a promise is induced by coercion of a man's will, the doctrine of duress suffices to do justice. The party coerced, if he chooses and acts in time, can avoid the contract. If there is no coercion, there can be no reason for avoiding the contract where there is shown to be a real consideration which is otherwise legal. Such a rule of public policy as is now being considered would be unhelpful because it would render the law uncertain. It would become a question of fact and degree to determine in each case whether there had been, short of duress, an unfair use of a strong bargaining position. It would create anomaly because, if public policy invalidates the consideration, the effect is to make the contract void. But unless the facts are such as to support a plea of **non est factum**, which is not suggested in this case, duress does no more than confer on the victim the opportunity, if taken in time, to avoid the contract. It would be strange if conduct less than duress could render a contract **void**, whereas duress does no more than render a contract **voidable**. . . .

Glidewell LJ then continued:

> It is true that *Pao On v Lau Yiu* is a case of tripartite relationship, ie a promise by A to perform a pre-existing contractual obligation owed to B, in return for a promise of payment by C. But Lord Scarman's words seem to me to be of general application, equally applicable to a promise made by one of the original two parties to a contract.
>
> Accordingly, following the view of the majority in *Ward v Byham* . . . and that of the Privy Council in *Pao On v Lau Yiu* the present state of the law on this subject can be expressed in the following proposition: (i) If A has entered into a contract with B to do work for, or to supply goods or services to, B in return for payment by B and (ii) at some stage before A has completely performed his obligations under the contract B has reason to doubt whether A will, or will be able to, complete his side of the bargain and (iii) B thereupon promises A an additional payment in return for A's promise to perform his contractual obligations on time and (iv) as a result of giving his promise B obtains in practice a benefit, or **obviates** a disbenefit, and (v) B's promise is not given as a result of economic duress or fraud on the part of A, then (vi) the benefit to B is capable of being consideration for B's promise, so that the promise will be legally binding.
>
> As I have said, counsel for the defendants accepts that in the present case by promising to pay the extra £10,300 the defendants secured benefits. There is no finding, and no suggestion, that in this case the promise was given as a result of fraud or duress.
>
> If it be objected that the propositions above **contravene** the principle in *Stilk v Myrick*, I answer that in my view they do not: they refine and limit the application of that principle, but they leave the principle unscathed, eg where B secures no benefit by his promise. It is not in my view surprising that a principle enunciated in relation to the rigours of seafaring life during the Napoleonic wars should be subjected during the succeeding 180 years to a process of refinement and limitation in its application in the present day.
>
> It is therefore my opinion that on his findings of fact in the present case, the judge was entitled to hold, as he did, that the defendants' promise to pay the extra £10,300 was supported by valuable consideration, and thus constituted an enforceable agreement.

The Court of Appeal reconsidered the point in *Re Selectmove Ltd* [1995] 2 All ER 531. A company had proposed to pay the Inland Revenue arrears of tax and national insurance by monthly instalments. There was a dispute as to whether this proposal had been accepted by the Revenue and the Court of Appeal held that it had not. There was thus no contract and what followed on the question of consideration was therefore *obiter* – but given that the decision in *Williams v Roffey Brothers* was controversial, it is of interest. Peter Gibson LJ said:

The judge held that the case fell within the principle of *Foakes v Beer* (1884) . . . In that case a judgment debtor and creditor agreed that in consideration of the debtor paying part of the judgment debt and costs immediately and the remainder by instalments the creditor would not take any proceedings on the judgment. The House of Lords held that the agreement was nudum pactum, being without consideration, and did not prevent the creditor, after payment of the whole debt and costs, from proceeding to enforce payment of the interest on the judgment. Although their Lordships were unanimous in the result, that case is notable for the powerful speech of Lord Blackburn, who made plain his disagreement with the course the law had taken in and since *Pinnel's Case* (1602) . . . and which the House of Lords in *Foakes v Beer* decided should not be reversed. Lord Blackburn expressed his conviction that

> 'all men of business, whether merchants or tradesmen, do every day recognise and act on the ground that prompt payment of a part of their demand may be more beneficial to them than it would be to insist on their rights and enforce payment of the whole.'

Yet it is clear that the House of Lords decided that a practical benefit of that nature is not good consideration in law.

Foakes v Beer has been followed and applied in numerous cases subsequently, of which I shall mention two. In *Vanbergen v St Edmunds Properties Ltd* (1933) . . . Lord Hanworth MR said:

> 'It is a well established principle that a promise to pay a sum which the debtor is already bound by law to pay to the promisee does not afford any consideration to support the contract.'

More recently in *D & C Builders Ltd v Rees* [1965] 3 All ER 837 . . . this court also applied *Foakes v Beer*, Danckwerts LJ saying that the case:

> 'settled definitely the rule of law that payment of a lesser sum than the amount of a debt due cannot be a satisfaction of the debt, unless there is some benefit to the creditor added so that there is an accord and satisfaction.'

Mr Nugee [counsel for the company], however, submitted that an additional benefit to the Crown was conferred by the agreement in that the Crown stood to derive practical benefits therefrom: it was likely to recover more from not enforcing its debt against the company, which was known to be in financial difficulties, than from putting the company into liquidation. He pointed to the fact that the company did in fact pay its further PAYE and NIC liabilities and £7,000 of its arrears. He relied on the decision of this court in *Williams v Roffey Bros* . . . for the proposition that a promise to perform an existing obligation can amount to good consideration provided that there are practical benefits to the promisee.

Peter Gibson LJ then gave an account of *Williams v Roffey Brothers* and continued:

> Mr Nugee submitted that although Glidewell LJ in terms confined his remarks to a case where B is to do the work for or supply goods or services to A, the same principle must apply where B's obligation is to pay A, and he referred to an article by Adams and Brownsword 'Contract, Consideration and the Critical Path' (1990) 53 MLR 536 at 539–540 which suggests that *Foakes v Beer* might need reconsideration. I see the force of the argument, but the difficulty that I feel with it is that if the principle of *Williams'* case is to be extended to an obligation to make payment, it would in effect leave the principle in *Foakes v Beer* without any application. When a creditor and a debtor who are at arm's length reach agreement on the payment of the debt by instalments to accommodate the debtor, the creditor will no doubt always see a practical benefit to himself in so doing. In the absence of authority there would be much to be said for the enforceability of such a contract. But that was a matter expressly considered in *Foakes v Beer* yet held not to constitute good consideration in law. *Foakes v Beer* was not even referred to in *Williams'* case, and it is in my judgment impossible, consistently with the doctrine of precedent, for this court to extend the principle of *Williams'* case to any circumstances governed by the principle of *Foakes v Beer*. If that extension is to be made, it must be by the House of Lords or, perhaps even more appropriately, by Parliament after consideration by the Law Commission.
>
> In my judgment, the judge was right to hold that if there was an agreement between the company and the Crown it was unenforceable for want of consideration.

It might be argued that there is evidence in some of these cases of judges trying to do justice in the case before them, at the expense of stretching the rules. An alternative route is to find an equitable principle that allows the judge to put the common law to one side, on the basis that equity prevails when the common law and equity do not agree. In the *High Trees* case in 1947 Lord Denning (as Denning J) revived the doctrine of promissory estoppel. A defendant who had relied on a promise made by the plaintiff could defend the plaintiff's subsequent action for payment by saying that it would be inequitable to allow the plaintiff to go back on his promise. There is a body of cases on the doctrine, mainly decided by Lord Denning, but by the decision in *Brikom Investments Ltd v Carr* [1979] 2 All ER 753 the doctrine seems to have been pushed to its fullest possible extent.

The landlords of blocks of flats claimed the cost of repairing the roofs from the tenants, in accordance with the terms of their leases. The tenants claimed that before they had signed the leases the landlords had promised that they would repair the roofs at their own expense. The case was decided in favour of the tenants by all three members of the Court of Appeal, but their reasons differed. Lord Denning MR was happy to rely on the doctrine of promissory estoppel:

> Counsel for the landlords submitted that Mrs Dufton (now Mrs Carr) could not rely on the principle in the *High Trees* case, because it was essential that she should have *acted* on the representation; and here she had not acted on it. On her own admission, he said, she would have gone on and taken the lease even if she had not been told about the roof. In all the cases, said counsel for the landlords, the courts had said that the party must have *acted* on the promise or representation in the sense that he must have altered his position on the faith of it, meaning that he must have been led to act differently from what he would otherwise have done: see *Alan & Co v El Nasr Export & Import Co* [1972] 2 All ER 127. This argument gives, I think, too limited a scope to the principle. The principle extends to all cases where one party makes a promise or representation, intending that it should be binding, intending that the other should rely on it, and on which that other does in fact rely, by acting on it, by altering his position on the faith of it, by going ahead with a transaction then under discussion, or by any other way of reliance. It is no answer for the maker to say: 'You would have gone on with the transaction anyway.' That must be mere speculation. No one can be sure what he would, or would not, have done in a hypothetical state of affairs which never took place . . . Once it is shown that a representation was calculated to influence the judgment of a reasonable man, the presumption is that he was so influenced. The judge put it quite simply:
>
>> 'Mrs Dufton had an assurance from Mr Stacpoole, before she signed the contract on 19th January 1972, that the landlords would repair the roof, and she was aware of the assurance by Mr Jarvis before she signed the lease. The landlords should not be allowed to go back on these assurances.' . . .
>
> So it seems to me that the judge was quite right in the way he put the case. He held that in all these cases the landlords could not go back to the strict rights under the lease. They had given the tenants their promise or representation to repair the roofs at their own cost, and the tenants relied on it. That gives rise to an equity which makes it unjust and inequitable for the landlords to seek to charge the tenants for a contribution; and the benefit of this equity avails the **assignees** of the tenants also.
>
> But I may say there is another way in which the cases can be put which seems to me equally valid. Although this is called a 'promise' or 'representation', it seems to me that it might also qualify for what we call a 'collateral contract' or 'collateral warranty'. On the faith of it these tenants signed the leases. . . . This seems to me a roundabout way of reaching the same result as the *High Trees* principle. It is a technical way of overcoming technical

> difficulties. I prefer the simple way which is the way the judge put it. I would like to pay tribute to him for the careful way in which he analysed the evidence and for his statement of the law, which I think was correct.

Roskill LJ was happy with the result, but not the route by which Lord Denning had got to it:

> I have found this case more difficult than Lord Denning MR. While I agree this appeal should be dismissed, I wish, with respect, to make plain that my reasons differ from the first fact of those given in his judgment. I do not rest my decision on any question of promissory estoppel; and I do not think it necessary on the facts of this case to investigate the **jurisprudential** basis of that doctrine in order to arrive at what I conceive to be the right decision. It is necessary to do no more than to apply that which was said by the House of Lords and especially by Lord Cairns LC in *Hughes v Metropolitan Railway Co* (1877).

He then adopted an academic's criticism of Lord Denning's interpretation of *Hughes* in an earlier case. In the third edition of *Spencer Bower on Estoppel* (1977) it was said:

> . . . the estoppel which the Lord Chancellor held to arise in such cases was founded on: 'a course of negotiation which has the effect of leading *one of the parties* to suppose that the strict rights arising *under the contract* will not be enforced'. *Hughes v Metropolitan Railway Co* can certainly not be validly cited in support of any wider proposition than this. There appear to be serious dangers involved in any wider extension of the new estoppel, and those who place value on the doctrine of consideration may think that some degree of caution is clearly indicated.

Roskill LJ continued:

> I would respectfully add to that that it would be wrong to extend the doctrine of promissory estoppel, whatever its precise limits at the present day, to the extent of abolishing in this back-handed way the doctrine of consideration.
>
> I would also add to that passage a reference to what Lord Hailsham of St Marylebone LC said in *Woodhouse AC Israel Cocoa Ltd AS v Nigerian Produce Marketing Co Ltd*, cited by Sir Alexander Turner in Spencer Bower. Lord Hailsham LC said:
>
> > 'I desire to add that the time may soon come when the whole sequence of cases based on promissory estoppel since the war, beginning with *Central London Property Trust Ltd v High Trees House*

> *Ltd*, may need to be reviewed and reduced to a coherent body of doctrine by the courts. I do not mean to say that any are to be regarded with suspicion. But, as is common with an expanding doctrine, they do raise problems of coherent exposition which have never been systematically explored. However this may be, we are not in a position to carry out this exploration here and in the present proceedings.'

I would respectfully adopt that passage.

It seems to me in the present case that counsel for the tenants' argument (in so far as it rests on promissory estoppel) involves taking that doctrine a great deal further than it has hitherto been taken. With great respect, I would not go as far as Lord Denning MR in saying it is now the law that benefits and burdens arising from a promise made in circumstances such as those presently found by the judge, to quote the phrase he used a few moments ago, 'run down both sides'. It seems to me that the problem is far more complex. Accordingly, I do not rest my conclusion that this appeal should be dismissed on any question of promissory estoppel. . . .

But, whichever is the right way of putting it, ever since *Hughes v Metropolitan Railway Co*, through a long line of cases of which there are many examples in the books, one finds that where parties have made a contract which provides one thing and where, by a subsequent course of dealing, the parties have worked that contract out in such a way that one party leads the other to believe that the strict rights under that contract will not be adhered to, the courts will not allow that party who had led the other to think the strict rights will not be adhered to, suddenly to seek to enforce those strict rights against him. That seems to me to be precisely what the landlords are trying to do here.

Check your understanding

1 Can you explain the meaning of the words and phrases in **bold** type? Are there any other words you need to look up in a dictionary?

2 Make a brief note of each of the cases dealt with above. It should contain an account of the facts, the decision and the reason(s) for the decision.

3 Write a brief paragraph explaining what 'consideration' is in contract law.

Discuss

1 In *Gibson v Manchester City Council* Lord Diplock is sympathetic with Mr Gibson but decides in favour of the council. Why did he decide the case as he did? What would have been the consequences for the law of contract if he had upheld the Court of Appeal's decision?

2 It is said that English law takes an objective approach to determining whether there is a contract and what its terms are. What evidence is there in the cases to support this contention?

3 What is the rule regarding payment of a lesser sum in satisfaction of the whole debt owed in each of *Foakes v Beer*, *Pinnel's Case* and *Re Selectmove*? What might it now be if the Court of Appeal in *Re Selectmove* had followed *Williams v Roffey Brothers* instead of distinguishing it?

Write

1 From the judgments of Lord Reid and Viscount Simonds in *Chappell v Nestle*, and with reference to any relevant cases with which you are familiar, construct arguments for and against the chocolate wrappers being good consideration.

2 Essay: 'Consider the proposition that the doctrine of consideration serves no useful purpose.'

Connections

'. . . and equitable rights now prevail', said Lord Denning in *Errington v Errington*. What does this mean: what are equitable rights? why do they 'prevail'?

6.3 PRIVITY

It is the provision of consideration that gives a party to an agreement the right to enforce it as a contract. The doctrine of privity is that a person who is not a party to a contract cannot enforce it, even if it is for his benefit. This rule has been criticised as giving rise to injustice. In *Jackson v Horizon Holidays* [1975] 3 All ER 92 the Court of Appeal awarded damages to all the members of a family who had had a disappointing holiday, even though the contract was between only one member of the family and the holiday company. This decision was criticised by members of the House of Lords in *Woodar Investment v Wimpey Construction* [1980] 1 All ER 571. Lord Keith said of it:

> That case is capable of being regarded as rightly decided on a reasonable view of the measure of damages due to the plaintiff as the original contracting party, and not as laying down any rule of law regarding the recovery

> of damages for the benefit of third parties. There may be a certain class of cases where third parties stand to gain indirectly by virtue of a contract, and where their deprivation of that gain can properly be regarded as no more than a consequence of the loss suffered by one of the contracting parties. In that situation there may be no question of the third parties having any claim to damages in their own right, but yet it may be proper to take into account in assessing the damages recoverable by the contracting party an element in respect of expense incurred by him in replacing by other means benefits of which the third parties have been deprived or in mitigating the consequences of that deprivation. The decision in *Jackson v Horizon Holidays Ltd* is not, however, in my opinion, capable of being supported on the basis of the true ratio decidendi in *Lloyds v Harper*, which rested entirely on the principles of agency.

The facts of *Woodar Investment v Wimpey Construction* were a little complex, involving the revocation of a contract for the purchase of land, but what their Lordships had to say on an issue of privity was interesting, although strictly *obiter*.

Reference is made in the following judgment of Lord Scarman to two leading cases on privity. *Tweddle v Atkinson* concerned an agreement between two men to each pay a sum of money to the son of one who was marrying the daughter of the other. One paid the agreed sum and the other failed to pay and died. The court held that no action could be brought by the son-in-law because the promise to pay was made not to the son-in-law but to his father. In *Beswick v Beswick* the promise was made by a nephew to his uncle. When the uncle died, the nephew failed to pay his aunt the sums he had promised. It was held that she could not sue in her own capacity, as she was not a party to the contract; but she *could* sue as her husband's **administratrix**, enforcing an obligation to the estate.

Lord Scarman said:

> Woodar agreed to sell the land to Wimpey for £850,000. They also required Wimpey to pay £150,000 to a third party. The covenant for this payment was in the following terms: 'Upon completion of the purchase of the whole or any part of the land the purchaser shall pay to Transworld Trade Limited of 25 Jermyn Street, London, SW1 a sum of £150,000.' No relationship of **trust** or **agency** was proved to exist between Woodar and Transworld. No doubt, it suited Mr Cornwell [who originally owned the land in question] to split up the moneys payable under the contract between the two companies; but it is not known, let alone established by evidence (though an intelligent guess is possible) why he did so, or why Woodar desired this money to be paid to Transworld. It is simply a case of B agreeing with A to pay a sum of money to C.
>
> B, in breach of his contract with A, has failed to pay C. C, it is said, has no remedy, because the English law of contract recognises no 'jus quaesitum

tertio', see *Tweddle v Atkinson* (1861). No doubt, it was for this reason that Transworld is not a party to the suit. A, it is acknowledged, could in certain circumstances obtain specific performance of the promise to pay C: see *Beswick v Beswick* (1967). But, since the contract in the present case is admitted (for reasons which do not fall to be considered by the House) to be no longer in existence, specific performance is not available. A's remedy lies only in an award of damages to himself. It is submitted that, in the absence of any evidence that A has suffered loss by reason of B's failure to pay C, A is only entitled to nominal damages.

I wish to add nothing to what your Lordships have already said about the authorities which the Court of Appeal cited as leading to the conclusion that Woodar is entitled to substantial damages for Wimpey's failure to pay Transworld. I agree that they do not support the conclusion. But I regret that this House has not yet found the opportunity to reconsider the two rules which effectually prevent A or C recovering that which B, for value, has agreed to provide.

First, the jus quaesitum tertio. I respectfully agree with Lord Reid that the denial by English law of a jus quaesitum tertio calls for reconsideration. In *Beswick v Beswick* (1967), Lord Reid, after referring to the Law Revision Committee's recommendation that the third party should be able to enforce a contractual promise taken by another for his benefit, observed: 'If one had to contemplate a further long period of Parliamentary **procrastination**, this House might find it necessary to deal with this matter.' The committee reported in 1937; *Beswick v Beswick* was decided in 1967. It is now 1979; but nothing has been done. If the opportunity arises, I hope the House will reconsider *Tweddle v Atkinson* and the other cases which stand guard over this unjust rule.

Likewise, I believe it open to the House to declare that, in the absence of evidence to show that he has suffered no loss, A, who has contracted for a payment to be made to C, may rely on the fact that he required the payment to be made as prima facie evidence that the promise for which he contracted was a benefit to him and that the measure of his loss in the event of non-payment is the benefit which he intended to C but which has not been received. Whatever the reason, he must have desired the payment to be made to C and he must have been relying on B to make it. If B fails to make the payment, A must find the money from other funds if he is to confer the benefit which he sought by his contract to confer on C. Without expressing a final opinion on a question which is clearly difficult, I think the point is one which does require consideration by your Lordships' House.

Certainly the crude proposition for which Wimpey contends, namely that the state of English law is such that neither C for whom the benefit was intended nor A who contracted for it can recover it if the contract is terminated by B's refusal to perform, calls for review, and now, not 40 years on.

In *New Zealand Shipping Co v Satterthwaite* [1974] 1 All ER 1015 the Privy Council considered whether a company that was not a party to a written contract could claim the benefit of an exclusion clause within that contract on the basis that the contract itself provided that it should be able to do so. The clause in question read:

> It is hereby expressly agreed that no servant or agent of the Carrier (including every independent contractor from time to time employed by the Carrier) shall in any circumstances whatsoever be under any liability whatsoever to the Shipper, Consignee or Owner of the goods or to any holder of this Bill of Lading for any loss or damage or delay of whatsoever kind arising or resulting directly or indirectly from any act, neglect or default on his part while acting in the course of or in connection with his employment and, without prejudice to the generality of the foregoing provisions in this Clause, every exemption, limitation, condition and liberty herein contained and every right, exemption from liability, defence and immunity of whatsoever nature applicable to the Carrier or to which the Carrier is entitled hereunder shall also be available and shall extend to protect every such servant or agent of the Carrier acting as aforesaid and for the purpose of all the foregoing provisions of this Clause the Carrier is or shall be deemed to be acting as agent or trustee on behalf of and for the benefit of all persons who are or might be his servants or agents from time to time (including independent contractors as aforesaid) and all such persons shall to this extent be or be deemed to be parties to the contract in or evidenced by this Bill of Lading . . .

New Zealand Shipping were unloading a machine tool belonging to Satterthwaites from a ship when they damaged it. They were not parties to the contract, which was between the seller of the machine tool, the buyer and the shipper. The question was whether they could make themselves a party to the contract by providing consideration. Lord Wilberforce:

> If the choice, and the **antithesis**, is between a gratuitous promise, and a promise for consideration, as it must be, in the absence of a **tertium quid**, there can be little doubt which, in commercial reality, this is. The whole contract is of a commercial character, involving service on one side, rates of payment on the other, and qualifying stipulations as to both. The relations of all parties to each other are commercial relations entered into for business reasons of ultimate profit. To describe one set of promises, in this context, as gratuitous, or nudum pactum, seems **paradoxical** and is prima facie **implausible**. It is only the precise analysis of this complex of relations into the classical offer and acceptance, with identifiable consideration, that seems to present difficulty, but this same difficulty exists in many situations of daily life, eg sales at auction; supermarket purchases; boarding an omnibus; purchasing a train ticket; tenders for the supply of goods; offers of reward; acceptance by post; warranties of authority by agents; manufacturers'

guarantees; gratuitous bailments; bankers' commercial credits. These are all examples which show that English law, having committed itself to a rather technical and schematic doctrine of contract, in application takes a practical approach, often at the cost of forcing the facts to fit uneasily into the marked slots of offer, acceptance and consideration.

In their Lordships' opinion the present contract presents much less difficulty than many of those above referred to. It is one of carriage from Liverpool to Wellington. The carrier assumes an obligation to transport the goods and to discharge at the port of arrival. The goods are to be carried and discharged, so the transaction is inherently contractual. It is contemplated that a part of this contract, viz discharge, may be performed by independent contractors – viz the stevedore. By Cl 1 of the bill of lading the shipper agrees to exempt from liability the carrier, his servants and independent contractors in respect of the performance of this contract of carriage. Thus, if the carriage, including the discharge, is wholly carried out by the carrier, he is exempt. If part is carried out by him, and part by his servants, he and they are exempt. If part is carried out by him and part by an independent contractor, he and the independent contractor are exempt. The exemption is designed to cover the whole carriage from loading to discharge, by whomsoever it is performed: the performance attracts the exemption or immunity in favour of whoever the performer turns out to be. There is possibly more than one way of analysing this business transaction into the necessary components; that which their Lordships would accept is to say that the bill of lading brought into existence a bargain initially unilateral but capable of becoming mutual, between the shippers and the stevedore, made through the carrier as agent. This became a full contract when the stevedore performed services by discharging the goods. The performance of these services for the benefit of the shipper was the consideration for the agreement by the shipper that the stevedore should have the benefit of the exemptions and limitations contained in the bill of lading. The conception of a 'unilateral' contract of this kind was recognised in *Great Northern Railway Co v Witham* and is well established. . . .

In the opinion of their Lordships, to give the stevedore the benefit of the exemptions and limitations contained in the bill of lading is to give effect to the clear intentions of a commercial document, and can be given within existing principles. They see no reason to strain the law or the facts in order to defeat these intentions. It should not be overlooked that the effect of denying validity to the clause would be to encourage actions against servants, agents and independent contractors in order to get round exemptions (which are almost invariable and often compulsory) accepted by shippers against carriers, the existence, and presumed efficacy, of which is reflected in the rates of freight. They see no attraction in this consequence.

Their Lordships will humbly advise Her Majesty that the appeal be allowed and the judgment of Beattie J be restored. The consignee must pay the costs of the appeal and in the Court of Appeal.

The Law Commission, in its Report *Privity of Contract: Contracts for the Benefit of Third Parties*, published in July 1996, having given its usual comprehensive account of the law, considered the arguments for reform:

1. The Intentions of the Original Contracting Parties are Thwarted

3.1 A first argument in favour of reform, as stated in the Consultation Paper, is that the third party rule prevents effect being given to the intentions of the contracting parties. If the theoretical justification for the enforcement of contracts is seen as the realisation of the promises or the will or the bargain of the contracting parties, the failure of the law to afford a remedy to the third party where the contracting parties intended that it should have one frustrates their intentions, and undermines the general justifying theory of contract.

2. The Injustice to the Third Party

3.2 A second argument focuses on the injustice to the third party where a valid contract, albeit between two other parties, has engendered in the third party reasonable expectations of having the legal right to enforce the contract particularly where the third party has relied on that contract to regulate his or her affairs. In most circumstances this argument complements the above argument based on the intentions of the contracting parties. For in most circumstances the intentions of the contracting parties and the reasonable expectations of the third party are consistent with each other. However, one of the most difficult issues that we face is the extent to which the contracting parties can vary or discharge the contract. That issue can be presented as raising the conflict between these two fundamental arguments for reform. In other words, should the injustice to the third party trump the intentions of the parties *where those intentions change*? As will become clear, we believe that where the injustice to the third party is sufficiently 'strong' (that is, where the third party has not merely had expectations engendered by knowledge of the contract but has relied on the contract or has accepted it by communicating its assent to the promisor) it should trump the changed intentions of the contracting parties. That is, the original parties' right to change their minds and vary the contract should be overridden once the third party has relied on, or accepted, the contractual promise.

3. The Person Who Has Suffered the Loss Cannot Sue, While the Person Who Has Suffered No Loss Can Sue

3.3 In a standard situation, the third party rule produces the perverse, and unjust, result that the person who has suffered the loss (of the intended benefit) cannot sue, while the person who has suffered no loss can sue. This can be illustrated by reference to *Beswick v Beswick*. In that case, as we have seen, the House of Lords held that the widow could not enforce the promise in her personal capacity, since the contract was one to which she was not privy. However, as administratrix of her husband's estate, she was able to sue as **promisee**, albeit that she could only recover nominal damages because the uncle, and hence his estate, had suffered no loss from the nephew's breach. Hence we see that the widow in her personal capacity, who had suffered the loss of the intended benefit, had no right to sue, while the estate, represented by the widow in her capacity as administratrix, who had suffered no loss, had that right. As it was, a just result was achieved by their Lordships' decision that nominal damages were, in this three party situation, inadequate so that specific performance of the nephew's obligation to pay the annuity to the widow should be ordered in respect of the claim by the administratrix. But where specific performance is not available (for example, where the contract is not one supported by valuable consideration or where the contract is one for personal service) the standard result is both perverse and unjust.

4. Even if the Promisee Can Obtain a Satisfactory Remedy for the Third Party, the Promisee May Not be Able to, or Wish to, Sue

3.4 In *Beswick v Beswick*, the promisee, as represented by the widow as administratrix, clearly wanted to sue to enforce the contract made for her personal benefit. However, in many other situations in which contracts are made for the benefit of third parties, the promisee may not be able to, or wish to, sue, even if specific performance or substantial damages could be obtained. Clearly the stress and strain of litigation and its cost will deter many promisees who might fervently want their contract enforced for the benefit of third parties. Or the contracting party may be ill or outside the jurisdiction. And if the promisee has died, his or her personal representatives may reasonably take the view that it is not in the interests of the estate to seek to enforce a contract for the benefit of the third party.

5. The Development of Non-Comprehensive Exceptions

3.5 A number of statutory and common law exceptions to the third party rule exist. . . . Where an exception to the third party rule has been either recognised by case-law or created by statute, the rule may now not cause difficulty. Self-evidently, this is not the case where the situation is a novel one in which devices to overcome the third party rule have not yet been tested. We believe that the existence of exceptions to the third party rule is a strong justification for reform. This is for two reasons. First, the existence of so many legislative and common law exceptions to the rule demonstrates its basic injustice. Secondly, the fact that these exceptions continue to evolve and to be the subject of extensive litigation demonstrates that the existing exceptions have not resolved all the problems.

6. Complexity, Artificiality and Uncertainty

3.6 The existence of the rule, together with the exceptions to it, has given rise to a complex body of law and to the use of elaborate and often artificial stratagems and structures in order to give third parties enforceable rights. Reform would enable the artificiality and some of the complexity to be avoided. The technical hurdles which must be overcome if one is to circumvent the rule in individual cases also lead to uncertainty, since it will often be possible for a defendant to raise arguments that a technical requirement has not been fulfilled. Such uncertainty is commercially inconvenient.

7. Widespread Criticism Throughout the Common Law World

3.7 In Part II, we saw that there had been criticism of the third party rule and calls for its reform from academics, law reform bodies and the judiciary. We shall see in Part IV that the rule has been abrogated throughout much of the common law world, including the United States, New Zealand, and parts of Australia. The extent of the criticism and reform elsewhere is itself a strong indication that the privity doctrine is flawed.

8. The Legal Systems of Most Member States of the European Union Allow Third Parties to Enforce Contracts

3.8 A further factor in support of reforming the third party rule in English law is the fact that the legal systems of most of the member states of the European Union recognise and enforce the rights of third party beneficiaries under contracts. In France, for example, the general principle that contracts have effect only between the parties to them is qualified by Art 1121 of the *Code Civil*, which permits a stipulation for the benefit of a third party as a condition of a stipulation made for oneself or of a gift made to another. The French courts interpreted this as permitting the creation of an enforceable stipulation for a person in whose welfare the stipulator had a moral interest. In so doing, they widened the scope of the Article so as to permit virtually any stipulation for a third person to be enforced by him or her, where the agreement between the stipulator and the promisor was intended to confer a benefit on the third person. In Germany, contractual rights for third parties are created by Art 328 of the *Burgerliches Gesetzbuch* permitting stipulations in contracts for performances to third parties with the effect that the latter acquires the direct right to demand performance, although the precise scope of these rights depends on the terms and circumstances of the contract itself. Surveying the member states of the European Union, we are aware that the laws of France, Germany, Italy, Austria, Spain, Portugal, Netherlands, Belgium, Luxembourg, and Greece, recognise such rights (as does Scotland); whereas only the laws of England and Wales (and Northern Ireland) and the Republic of Ireland do not. With the growing recognition of the need for harmonisation of the commercial law of the states of the European Union – illustrated most importantly by the work being carried out by the Commission on European Contract Law under the chairmanship of Professor Ole Lando – it seems likely that there will be ever increasing pressure on the UK to bring its law on privity of contract into line with that predominantly adopted in Europe.

The Law Commission then gave examples of the difficulties the privity doctrine causes in commercial contracts. The Law Commission recommended that third parties should be able to enforce contracts. The Report contains an exhaustive examination of the implications of this recommendation and the associated changes necessary to the law and ends with a Draft Contracts (Rights of Third Parties) Bill.

Check your understanding

Can you explain the meaning of the words and phrases in **bold** type? Are there any other words you need to look up in a dictionary?

Discuss

1 In *Woodar v Wimpey* Lord Scarman was plainly losing patience with Parliament's failure to change 'this unjust rule'. Lord Reid had expressed similar frustration twelve years earlier in *Beswick v Beswick*. Why was the House of Lords (a) unable and, possibly, (b) unwilling to change the rule itself in *Woodar v Wimpey*?

2 Do you consider the privity rule serves any useful purpose?

3 What devices are used to avoid the privity rule?

Write

1 Lord Wilberforce, in *New Zealand Shipping Co v Satterthwaite*, gives examples of various kinds of contracts and says: 'These are all examples which show that English law, having committed itself to a rather technical and schematic doctrine of contract, in application takes a practical approach, often at the cost of forcing the facts to fit uneasily into the marked slots of offer, acceptance and consideration.' Choose three of the situations he lists and explain how the courts analyse each of those situations into 'marked slots'.

2 Summarise the Law Commission's arguments for abolition of the doctrine of privity.

Connections

1 Having regard to evidence drawn from the material on contract as a whole, to what extent do you think it is true to say, as the Law Commission does in

its para 3.1, that 'the theoretical justification for the enforcement of contracts is seen as the realisation of the . . . will . . . of the contracting parties'?

2 Consider how far the law of tort may be used to circumvent the privity rule. In particular, have a look at the case of *White v Jones* (p. 167).

6.4 INTENTION TO CREATE LEGAL RELATIONS

The courts will enforce only those agreements which the parties intended to be legally binding. Of course, when the parties are in dispute this is one of the issues they dispute about and, once again, the court has to take an objective look at the evidence. The court begins, however, from different standpoints, depending on whether the contract in question is a business agreement or a social arrangement. The law was explained in the case of *Merritt v Merritt* [1970] 2 All ER 760 by Widgery LJ:

> When a husband and wife are living together in amity it is natural enough to presume that their discussions about money matters are not intended to create legally binding contracts. As Atkin LJ said in *Balfour v Balfour* (1919):
>
> > 'The common law does not regulate the form of agreements between spouses. Their promises are not sealed with seals and sealing wax. The consideration that really obtains for them is that natural love and affection which counts for so little in these cold Courts.'
>
> But, of course, once that natural love and affection has gone, as it normally has when the marriage has broken up, there is no room at all for the application of such a presumption. Salmon LJ made this clear in *Jones v Padavatton*, . . . where he said:
>
> > '. . . as a rule when arrangements are made between close relations, for example, between husband and wife, parent and child or uncle and nephew in relation to an allowance, there is a presumption against an intention of creating any legal relationship. This is not a presumption of law, but of fact. It derives from experience of life and human nature which shows that in such circumstances men and women usually do not intend to create legal rights and obligations, but intend to rely solely on family ties of mutual trust and affection.'
>
> The experience of life and human nature which raises this presumption in the case of a husband and wife living together in amity does not support it when the affection which produces that relationship of confidence has gone.
>
> I find it unnecessary to go so far as to say that there is a presumption in favour of the creation of legal relationships when the marriage is breaking up, but certainly there is no presumption against the creation of such legal relations as there is when the parties are living happily together.

In *Merritt v Merritt* the agreement in question had been made after the breakdown of the marriage and was held to be binding. In *Balfour v Balfour* the agreement was made during the marriage and held not to be binding. The complex arrangement in *Jones v Padavatton* (1969) was between mother and daughter and was found to be a domestic arrangement, rather than a binding contract. It is important to note that, whilst the courts begin with the presumption that domestic and social arrangements are not intended to be legally binding, they always look at the surrounding circumstances and it is for the party alleging that the agreement was a contract to bring sufficient evidence to rebut the presumption.

In business arrangements, the courts begin with the presumption that there is an intention to be legally bound. The burden of proving otherwise lies with the person who claims that there was no intention to create legal relations.

In *Esso v Commissioners of Customs and Excise* [1976] 1 All ER 117 the House of Lords was considering a situation similar to that in *Chappell v Nestle* (see p. 224) in that Esso had offered coins to people who bought its petrol and the case was concerned with whether the coins had been 'sold', so becoming taxable. One of the issues considered was whether there was an intention to be contractually bound to supply the coins. Lord Simon gave a very useful review of the law on intention to contract:

> I am . . . not prepared to accept that the promotion material put out by Esso was not envisaged by them as creating legal relations between the garage proprietors who adopted it and the motorists who yielded to its blandishments. In the first place, Esso and the garage proprietors put the material out for their commercial advantage, and designed it to attract the custom of motorists. The whole transaction took place in a setting of business relations. In the second place, it seems to me in general undesirable to allow a commercial promoter to claim that what he has done is a mere puff, not intended to create legal relations (cf *Carlill v Carbolic Smoke Ball Co*). The coins may have been themselves of little intrinsic value; but all the evidence suggests that Esso contemplated that they would be attractive to motorists and that there would be a large commercial advantage to themselves from the scheme, an advantage in which the garage proprietors also would share. Thirdly, I think that authority supports the view that legal relations were envisaged. In *Rose and Frank Co v J R Crompton & Bros Ltd* [1924] All ER 245 Scrutton LJ said:
>
>> 'Now it is quite possible for parties to come to an agreement by accepting a proposal with the result that the agreement concluded does not give rise to legal relations. The reason of this is that the parties do not intend that their agreement shall give rise to legal relations. This intention may be implied from the subject matter of the agreement, but it may also be expressed by the parties. In social

> and family relations such an intention is readily implied, while in business matters the opposite result would ordinarily follow.'

In the same case Atkin LJ said:

> 'To create a contract there must be a common intention of the parties to enter into legal obligations, mutually communicated expressly or impliedly. Such an intention ordinarily will be inferred when parties enter into an agreement which in other respects conforms to the rules of law as to the formation of contracts. It may be negatived impliedly by the nature of the agreed promise or promises, as in the case of offer and acceptance of hospitality, or of some agreements made in the course of family life between members of a family as in *Balfour v Balfour* (1919).'

In *Edwards v Skyways Ltd* [1964] 1 All ER 494 Megaw J quoted these passages, and added:

> 'In the present case, the subject-matter of the agreement is business relations, not social or domestic matters . . . I accept the proposition . . . that in a case of this nature the onus is on the party who asserts that no legal effect was intended, and the onus is a heavy one.'

I respectfully agree. And I would venture to add that it begs the question to assert that no motorist who bought petrol in consequence of seeing the promotion material prominently displayed in the garage forecourt would be likely to bring an action in the county court if he were refused a coin. He might be a suburb Hampden who was not prepared to forego what he conceived to be his rights or to allow a tradesman to go back on his word.

Believing as I do that Esso envisaged a bargain of some sort between the garage proprietor and the motorist, I must try to analyse the transaction. The analysis that most appeals to me is one of the ways in which Lord Denning MR considered the case, namely a collateral contract of the sort described by Lord Moulton in *Heilbut, Symons & Co v Buckleton* (1913):

> '. . . there may be a contract the consideration for which is the making of some other contract. "If you will make such and such a contract I will give you one hundred pounds", is in every sense of the word a complete legal contract. It is collateral to the main contract . . .'

So here. The law happily matches the reality. The garage proprietor is saying, 'If you will buy four gallons of my petrol, I will give you one of these coins'. None of the reasons which have caused the law to consider advertising or display material as an invitation to treat, rather than an offer, applies here. What the garage proprietor says by his placards is in fact and in law an offer of consideration to the motorist to enter into a contract of sale of petrol. Of course, not every motorist will notice the placard, but nor will every potential offeree of many offers be necessarily conscious that they have been made. However, the motorist who does notice the placard, and in reliance thereon drives in and orders the petrol, is in law doing two things at the same time. First, he is accepting the offer of a coin if he buys four gallons of petrol. Secondly, he is himself offering to buy four gallons of petrol: this offer is accepted by the filling of his tank.

Check your understanding

1 Can you explain the meaning of the words and phrases in **bold** type? Are there any other words you need to look up in a dictionary?

2 Who was Hampden?

Discuss

1 Why does the court make a presumption in favour of an intention to create legal relations in some kinds of contract and a presumption against in others?

2 If you were a solicitor advising members of a family who wished to enter into a legally binding agreement, how would you ensure that they succeeded in making a contract that the courts would uphold?

3 Do you think the dates of the cases of *Balfour v Balfour* and *Merritt v Merritt* are of any relevance in explaining the different results reached in broadly similar circumstances?

Write

Explain what is meant by the expression 'collateral contract' and give at least two examples of how this device is used by judges.

6.5 VITIATING FACTORS

A vitiating factor is something that is wrong with a contract. It may make the contract void (of no effect), it may make it voidable (which means one of the parties has a choice as to whether the contract should continue or not) or it might make it unenforceable (which means the court will not assist the parties to the contract). It is not possible to look at all the vitiating factors in any detail in the space available, but what follows is a fairly detailed consideration of the doctrine of undue influence and then a flavour of other vitiating factors.

Undue influence

Undue influence is an equitable doctrine allowing a person who has made a contract because of pressure exerted by someone else to have the contract set aside. The House of Lords' decision in *Barclays Bank v O'Brien* [1993] 4 All ER 417 is very important, especially as it deals with the common problem of people using their homes as security for bank loans to businesses. If the business is unable to repay the loan, the house has to be sold to repay the bank.

Mrs O'Brien signed a second mortgage on the house she owned jointly with Mr O'Brien to secure a loan for £135,000 for three weeks and then £120,000 thereafter. Her husband had told her that the loan was £60,000 for three weeks. When Mr O'Brien was unable to repay the loan, the bank brought an action for possession of the house. Mrs O'Brien claimed that her husband had exercised undue influence over her and, acting as the bank's **agent**, had misrepresented the nature of the transaction. The House of Lords decided that the bank could not have possession of the house. Lord Browne-Wilkinson said:

> The large number of cases of this type coming before the courts in recent years reflects the rapid changes in social attitudes and the distribution of wealth which have recently occurred. Wealth is now more widely spread. Moreover a high proportion of privately owned wealth is invested in the matrimonial home. Because of the recognition by society of the equality of the sexes, the majority of matrimonial homes are now in the joint names of both spouses. Therefore in order to raise finance for the business enterprises of one or other of the spouses, the jointly owned home has become a main source of security. The provision of such security requires the consent of both spouses.
>
> In parallel with these financial developments, society's recognition of the equality of the sexes has led to a rejection of the concept that the wife is subservient to the husband in the management of the family's finances. A number of the authorities reflect an unwillingness in the court to perpetuate law based on this outmoded concept. Yet, as Scott LJ in the Court of Appeal rightly points out, although the concept of the ignorant wife leaving all financial decisions to the husband is outmoded, the practice does not yet coincide with the ideal . . . In a substantial proportion of marriages it is still the husband who has the business experience and the wife is willing to follow his advice without bringing a truly independent mind and will to bear on financial decisions. The number of recent cases in this field shows that in practice many wives are still subjected to, and yield to, undue influence by their husbands. Such wives can reasonably look to the law for some protection when their husbands have abused the trust and confidence reposed in them.

> On the other hand, it is important to keep a sense of balance in approaching these cases. It is easy to allow sympathy for the wife who is threatened with the loss of her home at the suit of a rich bank to obscure an important public interest, viz the need to ensure that the wealth currently tied up in the matrimonial home does not become economically sterile. If the rights secured to wives by the law renders vulnerable loans granted on the security of matrimonial homes, institutions will be unwilling to accept such security, thereby reducing the flow of loan capital to business enterprises. It is therefore essential that a law designed to protect the vulnerable does not render the matrimonial home unacceptable as security to financial institutions.
>
> With these policy considerations in mind I turn to consider the existing state of the law. . . .
>
> A person who has been induced to enter into a transaction by the undue influence of another (the wrongdoer) is entitled to set that transaction aside as against the wrongdoer. Such undue influence is either actual or presumed.

Lord Browne-Wilkinson considered the case of *Bank of Credit and Commerce International SA v Aboody* [1992] 4 All ER 955, in which the Court of Appeal classified undue influence as follows:

Class 1: actual undue influence – the plaintiff has to prove that there was undue influence.
Class 2: presumed undue influence – the plaintiff has to prove only that there was a relationship of trust and confidence between the plaintiff and the wrongdoer. It is then for the wrongdoer to prove that the plaintiff was not unduly influenced. Class 2 is split into 2A: relationships in which the law presumes undue influence exists, such as the relationship between solicitor and client; and 2B: relationships in which the plaintiff has to prove the existence of trust and confidence.

A wife who can show that she relies on her husband in financial matters comes within class 2B.

Lord Browne-Wilkinson continued:

> Up to this point I have been considering the right of a claimant wife to set aside a transaction as against the wrongdoing husband when the transaction has been procured by his undue influence. But in surety cases the decisive question is whether the claimant wife can set aside the transaction, not against the wrongdoing husband, but against the creditor bank. Of course, if the wrongdoing husband is acting as agent for the creditor bank in obtaining the surety from the wife, the creditor will be fixed with the wrongdoing of its own agent and the surety contract can be set aside as against the creditor. Apart from this, if the creditor bank has notice, actual

> or constructive, of the undue influence exercised by the husband (and consequentially of the wife's equity to set aside the transaction) the creditor will take subject to that equity and the wife can set aside the transaction against the creditor . . . Similarly, in cases such as the present where the wife has been induced to enter into the transaction by the husband's misrepresentation, her equity to set aside the transaction will be enforceable against the creditor if either the husband was acting as the creditor's agent or the creditor had actual or constructive notice. . . .
>
> The key to the problem is to identify the circumstances in which the creditor will be taken to have notice of the wife's equity to set aside the transaction.
>
> The doctrine of notice lies at the heart of equity. Given that there are two innocent parties, each enjoying rights, the earlier right prevails against the later right if the acquirer of the later right knows of the earlier right (actual notice) or would have discovered it had he taken proper steps (constructive notice). In particular, if the party asserting that he takes free of the earlier rights of another knows of certain facts which put him on inquiry as to the possible existence of the rights of that other and he fails to make such inquiry or take such other steps as are reasonable to verify whether such earlier right does or does not exist, he will have constructive notice of the earlier right and take subject to it. Therefore where a wife has agreed to stand surety for her husband's debts as a result of undue influence or misrepresentation, the creditor will take subject to the wife's equity to set aside the transaction if the circumstances are such as to put the creditor on inquiry as to the circumstances in which she agreed to stand surety.

Lord Browne-Wilkinson concluded that in this type of case it was necessary for the bank to ensure that the wife was advised to take independent legal advice. Exceptionally, if the bank knew that the wife was being unduly influenced, it would have to insist that the wife was separately advised.

He pointed out that these rules did not apply only to wives, but also to cohabitees, whether heterosexual or homosexual, and said:

> I can therefore summarise my views as follows. Where one cohabitee has entered into an obligation to stand as surety for the debts of the other cohabitee and the creditor is aware that they are cohabitees: (1) the surety obligation will be valid and enforceable by the creditor unless the suretyship was procured by the undue influence, misrepresentation or other legal wrong of the principal debtor; (2) if there has been undue influence, misrepresentation or other legal wrong by the principal debtor, unless the creditor has taken reasonable steps to satisfy himself that the surety entered into the obligation freely and in knowledge of the true facts, the creditor will be unable to enforce the surety obligation because he will be

> fixed with constructive notice of the surety's right to set aside the transaction; (3) unless there are special exceptional circumstances, a creditor will have taken such reasonable steps to avoid being fixed with constructive notice if the creditor warns the surety (at a meeting not attended by the principal debtor) of the amount of her potential liability and of the risks involved and advises the surety to take independent legal advice.

The decision was discussed and applied by the Court of Appeal in *Massey v Midland Bank plc* [1995] 1 All ER 929. Miss Massey had a long-standing relationship with Mr Potts, although they did not live together. Miss Massey agreed to a second **legal charge** on her house to secure business borrowing by Mr Potts. The business failed and Miss Massey became liable to pay £25,000 to Lloyds Bank, although they did not take legal proceedings against her. In 1989 Mr Potts began a new business and asked Miss Massey to again give a legal charge, this time to Midland Bank, to secure his business borrowings. He told her that the debt of £25,000 to Lloyds Bank would be paid. Midland Bank (through their Mr Dixon) insisted that Miss Massey should be independently advised by a solicitor and Mr Potts arranged an appointment with a reputable firm of solicitors, but Miss Massey saw the solicitor in the presence of Mr Potts. The second business failed and Midland Bank sued for possession of the house. Miss Massey defended the action, claiming that she had been induced to sign the charge by the misrepresentation and undue influence of Mr Potts.

Steyn LJ said:

> The judge's finding of fact that Mr Potts procured the execution of the legal charge by fraudulent misrepresentation is not challenged on appeal. The judge's finding of fact that Mr Potts was not the agent of the bank in obtaining the charge from Miss Massey is also not challenged. Instead the focus of the appeal has shifted to the application of the doctrine of notice. There was no evidence that the bank had actual knowledge of any misrepresentation or undue influence on the part of Mr Potts. It is therefore to the doctrine of constructive notice that we must turn. Due to the way in which the case was presented before him, the judge did not directly consider this aspect. However, his judgment is detailed and careful. And the bank realistically accepts that on this appeal the appellant is free to canvass the issue of constructive notice. . . .
>
> When speaking of wives Lord Browne-Wilkinson had in mind that in the given circumstances the capacity for self-management of wives is frequently impaired by the emotional ties between the spouses. He recognised, however, that the reality was the determinative factor cannot be a marriage certificate. He observed that the same approach applies equally to heterosexual and homosexual cohabitees. Miss Massey never cohabited with Mr Potts. But she had a stable sexual and emotional relationship with

him over many years, and they had two children. While it is an extension of the approach enunciated by Lord Browne-Wilkinson, I have no doubt that in terms of impairment of Miss Massey's judgmental capacity this case should be approached as if she was a wife or cohabitee of Mr Potts. . . . I would therefore hold that the bank was put on inquiry as to the possible existence of rights in Miss Massey to set aside the transaction.

That brings me to the question whether the bank took reasonable steps to assure itself that Miss Massey's agreement to grant the charge was properly obtained. If so, the bank will avoid being fixed with constructive notice. If not, the bank cannot avoid the setting aside of the charge. . . .

In the present case the bank required Miss Massey to be independently advised. The bank has been put in touch with a reputable firm of solicitors to whom it sent the charge. When the solicitors returned the duly executed charge to the bank they confirmed that they had explained the document to Miss Massey.

. . . it is generally sufficient for the bank to avoid a finding of constructive notice if the bank urged the proposed surety to take independent advice from a solicitor. How far a solicitor should go in probing the matter, and in giving advice, is a matter for the solicitor's professional judgment and a matter between him and his client. The bank is not generally involved in the nature and extent of the solicitor's advice. And in my judgment there is nothing in the circumstances of the present case which required the bank to do more than urge or insist on independent advice.

But counsel for Miss Massey emphasises what he described as undesirable features of this case. First, he says the crucial point is that Mr Dixon never saw Miss Massey alone. I have already dealt with this point. The short answer to this point is that the solicitors confirmed to the bank that they had given independent advice to Miss Massey. The objective of Lord Browne-Wilkinson's guidance had been achieved: the surety received independent advice.

Secondly, counsel for Miss Massey emphasises that Mr Potts selected the firm of solicitors, he gave the instructions to the solicitors, and he attended the interview with the solicitors. . . .

The bank did not know what happened between Mr Jones [the solicitor] and Miss Massey, or how the interview was conducted. And it was under no duty to inquire. But the bank had every reason to believe (as was the case on the judge's findings) that Miss Massey had received independent advice. . . .

I conclude that the bank took reasonable steps to ensure that Miss Massey's agreement to the charge was properly obtained. I would dismiss the appeal.

A little thought might bring one to the conclusion that if a couple have mortgaged their home and are then unable to keep up payments, it is in their interest to encourage a court to believe that the wife acted under the undue influence of the husband. If she did not, the bank gets the house. If she did, although they still owe a lot of money to the bank, the bank cannot get possession of the house, and it has been held in *Albany Home Loans v Massey* [1997] 2 All ER 609 that it would not be proper to grant possession as against the husband alone. So both husband and wife still have a roof over their heads.

It may be that this was in the minds of the High Court in the interesting case of *Dunbar Bank v Nadeem* [1997] 2 All ER 253. Mr Nadeem, a solicitor, had borrowed money to cover his business debts, using as security a new long lease on the property occupied by himself and his wife. Until the long lease was taken out, the property was in Mr Nadeem's name alone. Robert Englehart QC, sitting as a deputy High Court judge, said:

> It is a question to be decided on the precise facts of each individual case whether or not the circumstances were such as to put the creditor on enquiry that there might have been undue influence and, if so, whether or not the creditor took reasonable steps to satisfy himself that the wife's agreement had been properly obtained. The question of the reasonableness of any steps taken does not arise in the instant case, for it is not suggested that in relation to Mrs Nadeem herself the bank took any steps at all. . . .
>
> I therefore approach the present case from the standpoint of constructive notice (actual notice was not suggested) of undue influence and the question whether the circumstances were such as to put the bank on inquiry as to the possible existence of the undue influence. I consider that the following features are particularly relevant to this question on the present facts.
>
> (1) Mr Nadeem was very heavily indebted to the bank and in personal financial difficulties over meeting his interest obligations; he was presenting the transaction to the bank as one which would assist him with these difficulties.
>
> (2) . . . the transaction had all the appearance of a short term money raising operation; it was certainly not a typical long term loan on mortgage to fund the purchase of a matrimonial home.
>
> (3) On any showing some 20% of the joint loan was to be applied solely for Mr Nadeem's personal advantage.
>
> (4) The standard form of charge presented to Mrs Nadeem via Mr Nadeem for execution was obviously to her disadvantage in purporting to make her liable, and her interest in the lease security for, all Mr Nadeem's debts.
>
> (5) The bank had no communication at all with Mrs Nadeem other than through Mr Nadeem either at meetings in person or in communications sent to his business address.

(6) Mr Nadeem not only negotiated the transaction but also was acting as solicitor not only for himself but also, in the bank's perception, for his wife; as far as the bank was concerned, there was no possibility of any independent scrutiny of either the transaction in general or the terms of the charge in particular.

It would have been a simple matter for the bank to do as NatWest did and propose that Mrs Nadeem should receive independent advice. However, beyond requiring for its own protection that Mrs Nadeem sign the facility letter and charge, the bank dealt exclusively with Mr Nadeem. It never concerned itself with even the possibility that Mrs Nadeem's interests might not precisely coincide with those of her husband. I consider that the circumstances as a whole were such as to put the bank on inquiry and, it not having taken any let alone reasonable steps to ascertain whether Mrs Nadeem truly appreciated what she was doing, there was constructive notice of the undue influence. It follows that, but for the very important point with which I now deal, Mrs Nadeem would be entitled to set aside the charge against the bank.

If the charge were simply to be set aside as between Mrs Nadeem and the bank, there would on the present facts be a curious and on the face of it unjust consequence. Mrs Nadeem has acquired with the bank's money a joint interest in a relatively long lease over 152 Pavilion Road, but on her case she does not have to contribute to the cost of its acquisition. It would be very odd if the equitable remedy of setting aside were to lead to such a conclusion.

For Mrs Nadeem Mr Price submits that, undue influence and constructive notice having been established, she is entitled to have the charge set aside unconditionally . . . He says that the bank has to take the consequences of its own failure to take any steps to safeguard its position vis-à-vis Mrs Nadeem and points out that the bank still has rights as far as Mr Nadeem's interest in the joint lease is concerned. I have to say that I consider the latter aspect to be of most dubious practical worth to the bank so long as Mrs Nadeem retains her joint interest.

Mr Cherryman, on the other hand, relies on various well-known passages in the speech of Lord Blackburn in *Erlanger v New Sombrero Phosphate Co* (1878) . . . to the effect that a party seeking **rescission** must be in a position to make **restitutio in integrum**. He submits that there can be no setting aside here unless Mrs Nadeem accounts to the bank for the benefit she has received from the use of its money. She must refund to the bank either the whole £210,000 used to acquire the lease, or at any rate half that sum, with simple interest at an ordinary discretionary commercial rate.

Subject to the question whether it is all or half the £210,000, I consider that Mr Cherryman is in principle correct on the facts of the present case. . . . In my view Mrs Nadeem must make restitution if she is to be granted the equitable remedy of setting aside.

The judge made an order that the charge should be set aside as against Mrs Nadeem only if she paid £105,000 to the bank.

Check your understanding

1 Can you explain the meaning of the words and phrases in **bold** type? Are there any other words you need to look up in a dictionary?

2 What are 'actual notice' and 'constructive notice'?

Discuss

1 The trial judge in *Massey v Midland Bank* had said that Miss Massey was 'not unintelligent or lacking in business knowledge'? Why was that relevant?

2 In this kind of financial arrangement there are three parties: the lender, the borrower and the surety. What does each risk and what does each gain from the transaction? Does the law succeed in finding an effective and fair balance between their conflicting interests?

3 It is clear that the principle of *Barclays Bank v O'Brien* is to be applied to any surety whose judgement may have been impaired by reason of their sexual and emotional relationship with the borrower. The House of Lords made it clear that marriage was not relevant and that homosexual relationships would be governed by the same principle. Does this provide evidence of the judges being aware of and responding to social change? Can you think of other areas of law in which social change has, or has not, been addressed?

4 In *Barclays Bank v O'Brien* Lord Browne-Wilkinson commented on the need to balance the interests of wives and those of banks so as to ensure that homes remain attractive security, so freeing the capital tied up in homes for use in business. Having looked at these three cases, do you consider the law gets the balance right?

Write

1 'The relief is after all equitable relief. It is the substance that matters' (Steyn LJ). Explain this statement and, with reference to any other area of law, explain how the common law and equitable approaches differ.

2 You are the partner in charge of conveyancing in a large firm of solicitors. Write a memo to your staff explaining what advice should be given to a person proposing to sign a legal charge as surety for a business loan. You should explain *what* staff are to do and *why*.

Connections

If you have studied criminal law, can you draw an analogy between the distinction between actual and constructive knowledge and that between subjective and objective recklessness?

Illegality

If there is a general principle governing illegality, it would appear to be that the courts will not assist a party to an illegal contract. The cases tend to turn on their particular facts and whether the contract is illegal in its objects or illegal in its manner of performance. A lively case that gives some insight into the way judges view illegality is *Howard v Shirlstar Container Transport Ltd* [1990] 3 All ER 366. The plaintiff was a pilot who agreed to recover for the defendants an aircraft on which payments were outstanding. The aircraft was in Nigeria. The plaintiff got it out of Nigeria and flew it to the Ivory Coast but it was later returned to Nigeria by the government of the Ivory Coast. The defendants had thus not got their aircraft and did not want to pay the plaintiff. He claimed he was entitled to part of his payment because it fell due when the aircraft was out of Nigerian airspace. The defendants said they were not liable to pay because Captain Howard had breached Nigerian law in taking off from Nigeria without permission and the contract was thus unenforceable. Staughton LJ considered the issues:

> Counsel for Captain Howard accepted before the judge that, if performance by him involved illegal conduct in Nigeria, he could not enforce the contract here. In my view, it is necessary to be a little more precise when one is dealing with a contract which is not illegal in itself but involves illegality as performed, or is said to be tainted with illegality. In such a case the contract will not in general be enforced by reason of illegality in a foreign country in the same circumstances as a contract for performance in England will not be enforced by reason of illegality under English law.
>
> I turn then to the second point, the effect of illegality under a contract of English domestic law. This was dealt with in three propositions by Kerr LJ in the *Euro-Diam* case [1988] 2 All ER 23 [which concerned undervaluation of diamonds to avoid tax] . . . I can abbreviate them for present purposes. (1) The **ex turpi causa** defence rests on a principle of public policy. It applies where the plaintiff has been guilty of illegal (or immoral) conduct, if in all the circumstances it would be an affront to the public conscience to grant the plaintiff relief, because the court would thereby appear to assist or encourage the plaintiff in his illegal conduct or to encourage others in similar acts. (2) The main situations where the defence will prima facie

succeed are (i) where the plaintiff seeks, or is forced, to found his claim on an illegal contract or to plead illegality in order to support his claim, either in the **statement of claim** or in a reply; (ii) where the grant of relief to the plaintiff would enable him to benefit from his criminal conduct; (iii) where the situation is residually covered by the general principle in (i) above. (3) However, the ex turpi causa defence must be approached pragmatically and with caution, depending on the circumstances.

We were referred to *Pitts v Hunt* [1990] 3 All ER 344 . . . There Dillon LJ said that he did not find the 'public conscience' test satisfactory. One reason was that appeal to the public conscience would be likely to lead to a graph of illegalities according to moral turpitude. The difficulty of formulating a criterion for separating cases of serious illegality from ones which were not so serious was insoluble. However, Beldam LJ in that case recorded that in *Saunders v Edwards* [1987] 2 All ER 651 . . . the 'public conscience' test, first clearly set out by Hutchinson J in *Thackwell v Barclays Bank plc* [1986] 1 All ER 676, was approved. We do not have a complete transcript of the judgments in that case, nor do we know whether the *Euro-Diam* case was cited. In the circumstances, it seems right to me for us to follow the judgment of Kerr LJ in the *Euro-Diam* case.

In the present case it was, subject to an important point which will be mentioned later, illegal by Nigerian law for Captain Howard to fly the aircraft out of Nigeria without obtaining permission from air traffic control. Counsel for the defendants contends that it was also illegal by Nigerian law for other reasons, because there had been an order grounding or confiscating the aircraft and a decree grounding all privately-owned aircraft. The judge did not accept on the evidence that either the order or the decree had been made. Counsel for the defendants sought to challenge that conclusion. However, we did not hear him on that aspect of the case, since the second and third grounds of illegality would not, in our view, and in the particular circumstances of this case, add anything of significance to the first ground, which the judge did find established, that is to say contravention of air traffic control regulations.

If the case had stopped there, I would have no doubt that Captain Howard's claim would be unenforceable in an English court. To take off from a Nigerian airport in breach of regulations was central to his performance of the contract, as it was in fact performed. It was in no sense incidental illegality, like the example given by Russell LJ in the course of the argument in *Mackender v Feldia AG* . . . , or other examples which I gave in the *Euro-Diam* case . . . Counsel for the defendants concedes that it would not come within proposition 2(i) of Kerr LJ because Captain Howard would not need to plead or prove illegality to support his claim. Whether or not that concession be rightly made, the case would plainly fall within proposition 2(ii), as to grant relief would enable Captain Howard to benefit from his criminal conduct.

But there is another aspect of the case. Captain Howard and Miss Spalding [the wireless operator] gave evidence that, as time went by in Nigeria and during their conversations with Mr Odigwe [head of the Nigerian Federal Civil Aviation Authority], they were warned that their lives were in danger and that powerful people wished to prevent them taking the aircraft. There was much more in the same vein. Mr Odigwe's advice was that they should take off in the aircraft without delay. In addition, Captain Howard felt that it would be dangerous for him and Miss Spalding to attempt to leave Nigeria on a scheduled flight.

Staughton LJ considered the evidence at this point and continued:

There are then two problems to be considered. First, even if it was still illegal to take off in the aircraft, should the court hold that there would be no affront to the public conscience if Captain Howard's claim is enforced, on the ground that his conduct was not morally reprehensible? Second, did Captain Howard have an excuse in Nigerian law on the ground of **pre-emptive** self-defence, so that his conduct was not in fact illegal?

In answer to the first question, it is to be noted that proposition 2(ii) of Kerr LJ in the *Euro-Diam* case, dealing with the recovery of a benefit from the plaintiff's criminal conduct, is expressed to be an example of the main principle in proposition (1), that the court will not assist a plaintiff if to do so would be an affront to the public conscience. Can there then be circumstances where the public conscience is not affronted, even though the plaintiff does recover a benefit from his criminal conduct? In my judgment, there can be.

Staughton LJ referred to *obiter dicta* in *St John Shipping Corp v Joseph Rank Ltd* [1956] 3 All ER 683 in support of this proposition and continued:

If the court is free to take that view, as I think it is, this case is in my judgment plainly one where the plaintiff's claim should not fail, because the conscience of the court is not affronted. The offence, or offences, which Captain Howard committed were, on the judge's findings which are not now challenged, designed to free himself and Miss Spalding from pressing danger.

For the avoidance of doubt, I would add that I would have reached the same conclusion if a similar offence or offences had been committed in England under English law in similar circumstances. It would have been for the criminal courts to consider what penalties should be imposed, and I say nothing as to whether they should have been substantial or lenient. But if the offences had been committed to escape danger to life, I would not have held that Captain Howard was disqualified from claiming his fee in a civil action here.

Misrepresentation

Misrepresentations are untrue statements of fact that induce parties to enter into contracts. If there is a misrepresentation, the innocent party has the option to avoid the contract: so it is said to be voidable. A voidable contract is perfectly good until it is avoided, so if a person acquires goods under a voidable contract and sells them on to a third party before the original contract is avoided, the goods belong to the third party.

There are three types of misrepresentation: fraudulent, negligent and innocent. Each has particular consequences. In *Howard Marine v Ogden & Sons* [1978] 2 All ER 1134 the Court of Appeal considered a statement made by the plaintiff's employee about the capacity of two barges which were chartered by the defendants. Lord Denning MR said:

> . . . Ogdens claim damages for innocent misrepresentation under the Misrepresentation Act 1967. Section 2(1) says:
>
> > 'Where a person has entered into a contract after a misrepresentation has been made to him by another party thereto and as a result thereof he has suffered loss, then, if the person making the misrepresentation would be liable in damages in respect thereof had the misrepresentation been made fraudulently, that person shall be so liable notwithstanding that the misrepresentation was not made fraudulently, unless he proves that he had reasonable ground to believe and did believe up to the time the contract was made that the facts represented were true.'
>
> This enactment imposes a new and serious liability on anyone who makes a representation of fact in the course of negotiations for a contract. If that representation turns out to be mistaken, then, however innocent he may be, he is just as liable as if he had made it fraudulently. But how different from times past! For years he was not liable in damages at all for innocent misrepresentation: see *Heilbut, Symons & Co v Buckleton*. Quite recently he was made liable if he was proved to have made it negligently, see *Esso Petroleum Co Ltd v Mardon* [1976] 2 All ER 5. But now with this Act he is made liable, unless he proves, and the burden is on him to prove, that he had reasonable ground to believe and did in fact believe that it was true.
>
> Section 2(1) certainly applies to the representation made by Mr O'Loughlin on 11th July 1974 when he told Ogdens that each barge could carry 1,600 tonnes. The judge found that it was a misrepresentation, that he said it with the object of getting the hire contract for Howards. They got it; and, as a result, Ogdens suffered loss. But the judge found that Mr O'Loughlin was not negligent, and so Howards were not liable for it.

The judge's finding was criticised before us, because he asked himself the question: was Mr O'Loughlin negligent? whereas he should have asked himself: did Mr O'Loughlin have reasonable ground to believe that the representation was true? I think that criticism is not fair to the judge. By the word 'negligent' he was only using shorthand for the longer phrase contained in s 2(1) which he had before him. And the judge, I am sure, had the burden of proof in mind, for he had come to the conclusion that Mr O'Loughlin was not negligent. The judge said in effect: 'I am satisfied that Mr O'Loughlin was not negligent'; and being so satisfied, the burden need not be further considered: see *Robins v National Trust Co* (1927).

It seems to me that, when one examines the details, the judge's view was entirely justified. He found that Mr O'Loughlin's state of mind was this. Mr O'Loughlin had examined Lloyd's Register and had seen there that the deadweight capacity of each barge was 1,800 tonnes. That figure stuck in his mind. The judge found that 'the 1,600 tonnes was arrived at by knocking off what he considered a reasonable margin for fuel, and so on, from the 1,800 tonnes summer deadweight figure in Lloyd's Register, which was in the back of his mind'. The judge said that Mr O'Loughlin had seen at some time the German shipping documents and had seen the deadweight figure of 1,055.135 tonnes, but it did not register. All that was in his mind was the 1,800 tonnes in Lloyd's Register which was regarded in shipping circles as the Bible. That afforded reasonable ground for him to believe that the barges could each carry 1,600 tonnes payload; and that is what Mr O'Loughlin believed.

Bridge LJ took a different view of the provisions of s 2(1) of the Misrepresentation Act 1967 and the facts of the case:

The first question then is whether Howards would be liable in damages in respect of Mr O'Loughlin's misrepresentation if it had been made fraudulently, that is to say, if he had known that it was untrue. An affirmative answer to that question is inescapable. The judge found in terms that what Mr O'Loughlin said about the capacity of the barges was said with the object of getting the hire contract for Howards, in other words with the intention that it should be acted on. This was clearly right. Equally clearly the misrepresentation was in fact acted on by Ogdens. It follows, therefore, on the plain language of the 1967 Act that, although there was no allegation of fraud, Howards must be liable unless they proved that Mr O'Loughlin had reasonable ground to believe what he said about the barges' capacity.

It is unfortunate that the learned judge never directed his mind to the question whether Mr O'Loughlin had any reasonable ground for his belief. The question he asked himself, in considering liability under the 1967 Act, was whether the innocent misrepresentation was negligent. He concluded

> that if Mr O'Loughlin had given the inaccurate information in the course of the April telephone conversations he would have been negligent to do so but that in the circumstances obtaining at the Otley interview in July there was no negligence. I take it that he meant by this that on the earlier occasions the circumstances were such that he would have been under a duty to check the accuracy of his information, but on the later occasions he was exempt from such duty. I appreciate the basis of this distinction, but it seems to me, with respect, quite irrelevant to any question of liability under the 1967 Act. If the representee proves a misrepresentation which, if fraudulent, would have sounded in damages, the onus passes immediately to the representor to prove that he had reasonable ground to believe the facts represented. In other words the liability of the representor does not depend on his being under a duty of care the extent of which may vary according to the circumstances in which the representation is made. In the course of negotiations leading to a contract the 1967 Act imposes an absolute obligation not to state facts which the representor cannot prove he had reasonable ground to believe.

Bridge LJ then reviewed the relevant evidence and concluded that:

> . . . Howards failed to prove that Mr O'Loughlin had reasonable ground to believe the truth of his misrepresentation . . .

The third judge, Shaw LJ, agreed with Bridge LJ about the operation of the Misrepresentation Act.

Mistake

Generally speaking, the courts are unsympathetic to a party who says: 'I made a mistake and have not made the contract I thought I was making'. A mistake will affect the validity of a contract only if it is so fundamental that it robs the contract of any true agreement. If a mistake is held to be operative, then the contract is void. That is, the contract is of no effect at all and any goods which were supposed to have been sold will remain the property of the seller.

One of the situations that has arisen in many cases is that the seller of goods finds that he was not dealing with the person he thought he was dealing with. Sometimes the other party to the contract turns out to be a conman or, as the judges picturesquely put it, 'a rogue' who writes a worthless cheque then disappears, having sold the goods to an innocent third party. Such a case was *Lewis v Averay* [1971] 3 All ER 907 and the judge was, once again, Lord Denning MR:

The real question in the case is whether on 8th May 1969 there was a contract of sale under which the **property in the car** passed from Mr Lewis to the rogue. If there was such a contract, then even though it was voidable for fraud, nevertheless Mr Averay would get a good title to the car. But if there was no contract of sale by Mr Lewis to the rogue – either because there was, on the face of it, no agreement between the parties, or because any apparent agreement was a nullity and void **ab initio** for mistake – then no property would pass from Mr Lewis to the rogue. Mr Averay would not get a good title because the rogue had no property to pass to him.

There is no doubt that Mr Lewis was mistaken as to the identity of the person who handed him the cheque. He thought that he was Richard Greene, a film actor of standing and worth; whereas in fact he was a rogue whose identity is quite unknown. It was under the influence of that mistake that Mr Lewis let the rogue have the car. He would not have dreamed of letting him have it otherwise.

What is the effect of this mistake? There are two cases in our books which cannot, to my mind, be reconciled the one with the other. One of them is *Phillips v Brooks* [1918–19] All ER 246, where a jeweller had a ring for sale. The other is *Ingram v Little* [1960] 3 All ER 332, where two ladies had a car for sale. In each case the story is very similar to the present. A plausible rogue comes along. The rogue says that he likes the ring, or the car, as the case may be. He asks the price. The seller names it. The rogue says that he is prepared to buy it at that price. He pulls out a cheque book. He writes, or prepares to write, a cheque for the price. The seller hesitates. He has never met this man before. He does not want to hand over the ring or the car not knowing whether the cheque will be met. The rogue notices the seller's hesitation. He is quick with his next move. He says to the jeweller in *Phillips v Brooks*: 'I am Sir George Bullough of 11 St James' Square'; or to the ladies in *Ingram v Little*: 'I am P. G. M. Hutchinson of Stanstead House, Stanstead Road, Caterham'; or to Mr Lewis in the present case: 'I am Richard Greene, the film actor of the Robin Hood series'. Each seller checks up the information. The jeweller looks up the directory and finds there is a Sir George Bullough at 11 St James' Square. The ladies check up too. They look at the telephone directory and find there is a 'P. G. M. Hutchinson of Stanstead House, Stanstead Road, Caterham'. Mr Lewis checks up too. He examines the official pass of the Pinewood Studios with this man's photograph on it. In each case the seller feels that this is sufficient confirmation of the man's identity. So he accepts the cheque signed by the rogue and lets him have the ring, in the one case, and the car and log book in the other two cases. The rogue goes off and sells the goods to a third person who buys them in entire good faith and pays the price to the rogue. The rogue disappears. The original seller presents the cheque. It is dishonoured. Who is entitled to the goods? The original seller or the ultimate buyer? The courts have given different answers. In *Phillips v Brooks Ltd* the ultimate buyer was held to be entitled to the ring. In *Ingram v Little* the original seller was held to be entitled to the car. In the present case the deputy county court judge has held the original seller entitled.

It seems to me that the material facts in each case are quite indistinguishable the one from the other. In each case there was, to all outward appearance, a contract; but there was a mistake by the seller as to the identity of the buyer. This mistake was fundamental. In each case it led to the handing over of the goods. Without it the seller would not have parted with them.

This case therefore raises the question: what is the effect of a mistake by one party as to the identity of the other? It has sometimes been said that, if a party makes a mistake as to the identity of the person with whom he is contracting, there is no contract, or if there is a contract, it is a nullity and void, so that no property can pass under it. . . .

Again it has been suggested that a mistake as to the identity of a person is one thing; and a mistake as to his attributes is another. A mistake as to identity, it is said, avoids a contract; whereas a mistake as to attributes does not. But this is a distinction without a difference. A man's very name is one of his attributes. It is also a key to his identity. If then, he gives a false name, is it a mistake as to his identity? or a mistake as to his attributes? These fine distinctions do no good to the law.

As I listened to the argument in this case, I felt it wrong that an innocent purchaser (who knew nothing of what passed between the seller and the rogue) should have his title depend on such refinements. After all, he has acted with complete **circumspection** and in entire good faith; whereas it was the seller who let the rogue have the goods and thus enabled him to commit the fraud. I do not, therefore, accept the theory that a mistake as to identity renders a contract void.

I think the true principle is that which underlies the decision of this court in *King's Norton Metal Co Ltd v Eldridge, Merrett & Co Ltd* (1897) and of Horridge J in *Phillips v Brooks Ltd*, which has stood for these last 50 years. It is this: when two parties have come to a contract – or rather what appears, on the face of it, to be a contract – the fact that one party is mistaken as to the identity of the other does not mean that there is no contract, or that the contract is a nullity and void from the beginning. It only means that the contract is voidable, that is, liable to be set aside at the instance of the mistaken person, so long as he does so before third parties have in good faith acquired rights under it.

Check your understanding

Can you explain the meaning of the words and phrases in **bold** type? Are there any other words you need to look up in a dictionary?

Discuss

1 As the contract in *Lewis v Averay* was not void for mistake but was voidable for misrepresentation, what does the seller of the car have to do to avoid the contract and get his car back?

2 Lord Denning says in *Howard Marine v Ogdens*: 'Ogdens claim damages for innocent misrepresentation'. Does s 2(1) of the Misrepresentation Act 1967 deal with innocent misrepresentation? Is it possible that Lord Denning has not directed his mind to the change the 1967 Act made to the law?

3 Section 2(1) of the Misrepresentation Act 1967 does something very interesting to the burden of proof. Can you explain what?

4 What do you regard as Lord Denning's major ground for his decision in *Lewis v Averay*? Do you agree with his decision?

Connections

Contrast the firm line the law takes with parties to a contract who have made a mistake with the attitude to a defendant in a criminal case – see p. 127. Is the law inconsistent or should different rules apply in these two spheres?

6.6 INTERVENTION

The parties to a contract make a set of rules to govern a particular situation. The Victorian attitude to this was that it was right and proper to leave them alone – it was no one else's business. This *laissez-faire* approach has the disadvantage that a weaker party can be forced to accept terms he or she does not like and that there are times when making a contract is not really a matter of choice – one would have to make a contract with someone for the essentials of life and, if every supplier uses much the same standard terms, there is no real choice at all.

Intervention to protect weaker parties takes two forms. The judges have intervened to make rules about what is acceptable and, latterly, so has Parliament.

Intervention by judges

There are many cases in which judges have excluded onerous terms by holding that they are not part of the contract. It is important to note that, whilst most of the cases are about **exclusion clauses**, the principles apply to any term. An important case in this area, *Olley v Marlborough Court*

(1949), is referred to in the judgment of Lord Denning in *Thornton v Shoe Lane Parking*, below. In *Olley v Marlborough Court* the plaintiff had booked into a hotel. In the bedroom was a notice denying responsibility for guests' possessions unless they were handed to the management for safe keeping. A fur coat was stolen from the room and the plaintiff sued the hotel for its value. It was held that the hotel was unable to rely on the notice because it did not form part of the contract, having been brought to the plaintiff's attention after the contract was made at the time of registering at reception.

In *Thornton v Shoe Lane Parking* [1971] 1 All ER 686 the Court of Appeal considered a condition imposed by the owners of a car park excluding liability for damage to vehicles and injury to people. Lord Denning MR considered the law:

> We have been referred to the ticket cases of former times from *Parker v South Eastern Railway Co* (1877) to *McCutcheon v David MacBrayne Ltd* [1964] 1 All ER 430. They were concerned with railways, steamships and cloakrooms where booking clerks issued tickets to customers who took them away without reading them. In those cases the issue of the ticket was regarded as an *offer* by the company. If the customer took it and retained it without objection, his act was regarded as an *acceptance* of the offer: see *Watkins v Rymill* (1833) and *Thompson v London, Midland and Scottish Railway Co* (1930). These cases were based on the theory that the customer, on being handed the ticket, could refuse it and decline to enter into a contract on those terms. He could ask for his money back. That theory was, of course, a fiction. No customer in a thousand ever read the conditions. If he had stopped to do so, he would have missed the train or the boat.
>
> None of those cases has any application to a ticket which is issued by an automatic machine. The customer pays his money and gets a ticket. He cannot refuse it. He cannot get his money back. He may protest to the machine, even swear at it; but it will remain unmoved. He is committed beyond recall. He was committed at the very moment when he put his money into the machine. The contract was concluded at that time. It can be translated into offer and acceptance in this way. The offer is made when the proprietor of the machine holds it out as being ready to receive the money. The acceptance takes place when the customer puts his money into the slot. The terms of the offer are contained in the notice placed on or near the machine stating what is offered for the money. The customer is bound by those terms as long as they are sufficiently brought to his notice beforehand, but not otherwise. He is not bound by the terms printed on the ticket if they differ from the notice, because the ticket comes too late. The contract has already been made: see *Olley v Marlborough Court Ltd.* [1949] 1 All ER 127. The ticket is no more than a voucher or receipt for the money that has been paid (as in the deckchair case, *Chapelton v Barry Urban District Council* [1940] 1 All ER 356), on terms which have been

> offered and accepted before the ticket is issued. In the present case the offer was contained in the notice at the entrance giving the charges for garaging and saying 'at owner's risk' ie at the risk of the owner so far as damage to the car was concerned. The offer was accepted when the plaintiff drove up to the entrance and, by the movement of his car, turned the light from red to green, and the ticket was thrust at him. The contract was then concluded, and it could not be altered by any words printed on the ticket itself. In particular, it could not be altered so as to exempt the company from liability for personal injury due to their negligence.
>
> Assuming, however, that an automatic machine is a booking clerk in disguise, so that the old fashioned ticket cases still apply to it, we then have to go back to the three questions put by Mellish LJ in *Parker v South Eastern Ry Co*, subject to this qualification: Mellish LJ used the word 'conditions' in the plural, whereas it would be more apt to use the word 'condition' in the singular, as indeed Mellish LJ himself did at the end of his judgment. After all, the only condition that matters for this purpose is the exempting condition. It is no use telling the customer that the ticket is issued subject to some 'conditions' or other, without more; for he may reasonably regard 'conditions' in general as merely regulatory, and not as taking away his rights, unless the exempting condition is drawn specifically to his attention. (Alternatively, if the plural 'conditions' is used, it would be better prefaced with the word 'exempting', because the exempting conditions are the only conditions that matter for this purpose.) Telescoping the three questions, they come to this: the customer is bound by the exempting condition if he knows that the ticket is issued subject to it; or, if the company did what was reasonably sufficient to give him notice of it. Counsel for the defendants admitted here that the defendants did not do what was reasonably sufficient to give the plaintiff notice of the exempting condition. That admission was properly made. I do not pause to enquire whether the exempting condition is void for unreasonableness. All I say is that it is so wide and so destructive of rights that the court should not hold any man bound by it unless it is drawn to his attention in the most explicit way. It is an instance of what I had in mind in *J Spurling Ltd v Bradshaw* [1956] 2 All ER 121. In order to give sufficient notice, it would need to be printed in red ink with a red hand pointing to it, or something equally startling.

It is worth noting that the exclusion of liability for death or personal injury was forbidden by s 2(1) of the Unfair Contract Terms Act 1977. Much of what the judges achieved over the years in piecemeal fashion was reinforced or superseded by that statute.

There is something of a dilemma for the judges when they consider a contract made between businesses. Is it wise to assume that business people know what they are doing and contract on an equal footing? If it is, then it is logical to leave them alone and to enforce whatever they choose to put in their contracts. This was the problem in *Schuler AG v Wickman Ltd* [1973] 2 All ER 39. Wickman were to act as agents for the German firm, Schuler, selling presses, and also to be UK distributors for other products. The contract made very detailed provision for Wickman representatives to call on customers and provided that failure to make the calls in the specified manner would be breach of condition. This expression has a technical meaning and the majority of the House of Lords declined to enforce the contract with that technical meaning. Lord Reid explained why:

> In the ordinary use of the English language 'condition' has many meanings, some of which have nothing to do with agreements. In connection with an agreement it may mean a pre-condition: something which must happen or be done before the agreement can take effect. Or it may mean some state of affairs which must continue to exist if the agreement is to remain in force. The legal meaning on which Schuler rely is, I think, one which would not occur to a layman; a condition in that sense is not something which has an automatic effect. It is a term the breach of which by one party gives to the other an option either to terminate the contract or to let the contract proceed and, if he so desires, sue for damages for the breach.
>
> Sometimes a breach of a term gives that option to the aggrieved party because it is of a fundamental character going to the root of the contract, sometimes it gives that option because the parties have chosen to stipulate that it shall have that effect. Blackburn J said in *Bettini v Guy* (1876): 'Parties may think some matter, apparently of very little importance, essential; and if they sufficiently express an intention to make the literal fulfilment of such a thing a condition precedent, it will be one.'
>
> In the present case it is not contended that Wickman's failures to make visits amounted in themselves to fundamental breaches. What is contended is that the terms of cl 7 'sufficiently express an intention' to make any breach, however small, of the obligation to make visits a condition so that any such breach shall entitle Schuler to rescind the whole contract if they so desire.
>
> Schuler maintain that the use of the word 'condition' is in itself enough to establish this intention. No doubt some words used by lawyers do have a rigid inflexible meaning. But we must remember that we are seeking to discover intention as disclosed by the contract as a whole. Use of the word 'condition' is an indication – even a strong indication – of such an intention but it is by no means conclusive. The fact that a particular construction leads to a very unreasonable result must be a relevant consideration. The more unreasonable the result the more unlikely it is that the parties can have intended it, and if they do intend it the more necessary it is that they shall make that intention abundantly clear.
>
> Clause 7(b) requires that over a long period each of the six firms shall be visited every week by one or other of two named representatives. It

makes no provision for Wickman being entitled to substitute others even on the death or retirement of one of the named representatives. Even if one could imply some right to do this, it makes no provision for both representatives being ill during a particular week. And it makes no provision for the possibility that one or other of the firms may tell Wickman that they cannot receive Wickman's representative during a particular week. So if the parties gave any thought to the matter at all they must have realised the probability that in a few cases out of the 1,400 required visits a visit as stipulated would be impossible. But if Schuler's contention is right failure to make even one visit entitles them to terminate the contract however blameless Wickman might be. This is so unreasonable that it must make me search for some other possible meaning of the contract. If none can be found then Wickman must suffer the consequences. But only if that is the only possible interpretation.

If I have to construe cl 7 standing by itself then I do find difficulty in reaching any other interpretation. But if cl 7 must be read with cl 11 the difficulty disappears. The word 'condition' would make any breach of cl 7(b), however excusable, a material breach. That would then entitle Schuler to give notice under cl 11(a)(i) requiring the breach to be remedied. There would be no point in giving such a notice if Wickman were clearly not in fault but if it were given Wickman would have no difficulty in shewing that the breach had been remedied. If Wickman were at fault then on receiving such a notice they would have to amend their system so that they could shew that the breach had been remedied. If they did not do that within the period of the notice then Schuler would be entitled to rescind.

In my view, that is a possible and reasonable construction of the contract and I would therefore adopt it. The contract is so obscure that I can have no confidence that this is its true meaning but for the reasons which I have given I think that it is the preferable construction. It follows that Schuler were not entitled to rescind the contract as they purported to do. So I would dismiss this appeal.

Lord Morris of Borth-y-Gest supported this approach, saying:

Subject to any legal requirements businessmen are free to make what contracts they choose but unless the terms of their agreement are clear a court will not be disposed to accept that they have agreed something utterly fantastic. If it is clear what they have agreed a court will not be influenced by any suggestion that they would have been wiser to have made a different agreement. If a word employed by the parties in a contract can have only one possible meaning then, unless any question of rectification arises, there will be no problem. If a word either by reason of general acceptance or by reason of judicial construction has come to have a particular meaning then, if used in a business or technical document, it will often be reasonable to suppose that the parties intended to use the

> word in its accepted sense. But if a word in a contract may have more than one meaning then, in interpreting the contract, a court will have to decide what was the intention of the parties as revealed by or deduced from the terms and subject-matter of their contract.
>
> Words are but the instruments by which meanings or intentions are expressed. Often the same word has in differing contexts to do service to convey differing meanings.

Lord Wilberforce was not happy with this approach and gave a dissenting judgment. When the case was in the Court of Appeal, the judges had looked at the actions of the parties during the time the contract was in force. He began by explaining why he regarded this as an unsatisfactory approach to deciding what the contract meant:

> In my opinion, subsequent actions ought not to have been taken into account. The general rule is that extrinsic evidence is not admissible for the construction of a written contract; the parties' intentions must be ascertained, on legal principles of construction, from the words they have used. It is one and the same principle which excludes evidence of statements, or actions, during negotiations, at the time of the contract, or subsequent to the contract, any of which to the lay mind might at first sight seem to be proper to receive. . . .
>
> There are of course exceptions. I attempt no exhaustive list of them. In the case of ancient documents, contemporaneous or subsequent action may be adduced in order to explain words whose contemporary meaning may have become obscure. And evidence may be admitted of surrounding circumstances or in order to explain technical expressions or to identify the subject-matter of an agreement: or (an overlapping exception) to resolve a latent ambiguity. But ambiguity in this context is not to be equated with difficulty of construction, even difficulty to a point where judicial opinion as to meaning has differed. This is, I venture to think, elementary law. On this test there is certainly no ambiguity here. . . .
>
> [is it] open to the parties to a contract, not being a contract for the sale of goods, to use the word 'condition' to introduce a term, breach of which **ipso facto** entitles the other party to treat the contract at an end[?]
>
> The proposition that this may be done has not been uncriticised. It is said that this is contrary to modern trends which focus interest rather on the nature of the breach, allowing the innocent party to rescind or repudiate whenever the breach is fundamental, whether the clause breached is called a condition or not: that the affixing of the label 'condition' cannot pre-empt the right of the court to estimate for itself the character of the breach. Alternatively it is said that the result contended for can only be achieved if the consequences of a breach of a 'condition' (sc, that the other party may rescind) are spelt out in the contract. In support of this line of argument reliance is placed on the judgment of the Court of Appeal in

Hong Kong Fir Shipping Co Ltd v Kawasaki Kisen Kaisha Ltd [1962] 1 All ER 474.

My Lords, this approach has something to commend it: it has academic support. The use as a promissory term of 'condition' is artificial, as is that of 'warranty' in some contexts. But in my opinion this use is now too deeply embedded in English law to be uprooted by anything less than a complete revision. I shall not trace the development of the term through 19th century cases, many of them decisions of Lord Blackburn, to the present time; this has been well done by academic writers. I would only add that the *Hong Kong Fir* case, even if it could, did not reverse the trend. What it did decide, and I do not think that this was anything new, was that although a term (there a 'seaworthiness' term) was not a 'condition' in the technical sense, it might still be a term breach of which if sufficiently serious could go to the root of the contract. Nothing in the judgments as I read them casts any doubt on the meaning or effect of 'condition' where that word is technically used.

The alternative argument, in my opinion, is equally precluded by authority. It is not necessary for parties to a contract, when stipulating a condition, to spell out the consequences of breach: these are inherent in the (assumedly deliberate) use of the word [*Suisse Atlantique* case (1966)]. . . .

I would only add that, for my part, to call the clause arbitrary, capricious or fantastic, or to introduce as a test of its validity the **ubiquitous** reasonable man (I do not know whether he is English or German) is to assume, contrary to the evidence, that both parties to this contract adopted a standard of easygoing tolerance rather than one of aggressive, insistent punctuality and efficiency. This is not an assumption I am prepared to make, nor do I think myself entitled to impose the former standard on the parties if their words indicate, as they plainly do, the latter. I note finally, that the result of treating the clause, so careful and specific in its requirements, as a term is, in effect, to deprive the appellants of any remedy in respect of admitted and by no means minimal breaches. The **arbitrator**'s finding that these breaches were not 'material' was not, in my opinion, justified in law in the face of the parties' own characterisation of them in their document: indeed the fact that he was able to do so, and so leave the appellants without remedy, argues strongly that the legal basis of his findings – that cl 7(b) was merely a term – is unsound.

Intervention by Parliament

This problem was to a considerable extent resolved when the Unfair Contract Terms Act 1977 applied different rules, dependent upon who the parties to the contract were. If one party is a consumer and the other a business, there is very strict control over what the terms may be; if two businesses contract on the standard terms of one of them, then any exclusion clause must be reasonable; if two businesses contract on terms they have negotiated, the Act does not apply any restrictions on what they may agree. Judges still face, of course, the task of deciding what it was that the parties agreed.

The operation of the 1977 Act in protecting consumers is illustrated by the case of *Smith v Eric S Bush* [1989] 2 All ER 514. Note that this is not a contract case at all: the Act applies to the exclusion of liability in tort as well. The defendants were valuers who had carried out a survey on a house for a building society. Such surveys are, in fact, paid for by the intending purchaser of the house. This survey was negligently done, so that the house was worth far less than the surveyor said it was. The surveyor claimed that he was not liable because there was an exclusion clause on the application form signed by the plaintiffs:

> I/We accept that the Society will provide me/us with a copy of the report and mortgage valuation which the Society will obtain in relation to this application. I/We understand that the Society is not the agent of the Surveyor or firm of Surveyors and that I am making no agreement with the Surveyor or firm of Surveyors. I/We understand that neither the Society nor the Surveyor or the firm of Surveyors will warrant, represent or give any assurance to me/us that the statements, conclusions and opinions expressed or implied in the report and mortgage valuation will be accurate or valid and the Surveyor(s), report will be supplied without any acceptance of responsibility on their part to me/us.

So, the potential house-buyer pays for a survey. He or she cannot get a mortgage without agreeing to pay for a survey. Neither the building society nor the surveyor will be liable if the survey is completely wrong. The House of Lords, hearing appeals from decisions of the Court of Appeal in two such cases, applied the 1977 Act and decided that the surveyor *would* be liable. Lord Templeman first considered liability for negligent statements, then said:

> In general, I am of the opinion that in the absence of a disclaimer of liability the valuer who values a house for the purpose of a mortgage, knowing that the mortgagee will rely and the mortgagor will probably rely on the valuation, knowing that the purchaser mortgagor has in effect paid for the valuation, is under a duty to exercise reasonable skill and care and that duty is owed to both parties to the mortgage [the building society and the purchaser] for which the valuation is made. Indeed, in both the appeals now under consideration the existence of such a dual duty is tacitly accepted and acknowledged because notices excluding liability for breach of the duty owed to the purchaser were drafted by the mortgagee and imposed on the purchaser. In these circumstances it is necessary to consider the

second question which arises in these appeals, namely whether the disclaimers of liability are notices which fall within the Unfair Contract Terms Act 1977.

In *Harris v Wyre Forest DC* the Court of Appeal (Kerr, Nourse LJJ and Caulfield J) accepted an argument that the 1977 Act did not apply because the council by their express disclaimer refused to obtain a valuation save on terms that the valuer would not be under any obligation to Mr and Mrs Harris to take reasonable care or exercise reasonable skill. The council did not exclude liability for negligence but excluded negligence so that the valuer and the council never came under duty of care to Mr and Mrs Harris and could not be guilty of negligence. This construction would not give effect to the manifest intention of the 1977 Act but would emasculate the Act. The construction would provide no control over standard form exclusion clauses which individual members of the public are obliged to accept. A party to a contract or a **tortfeasor** could opt out of the 1977 Act by declining, in the words of Nourse LJ, to recognise 'their own answerability to the plaintiffs'. Caulfield J said that the Act 'can only be relevant where there is on the facts a potential liability'. But no one intends to commit a tort and therefore any notice which excludes liability is a notice which excludes a potential liability. Kerr LJ sought to confine the Act to 'situations where the existence of a duty of care is not open to doubt' or where there is 'an inescapable duty of care'. I can find nothing in the 1977 Act or in the general law to identify or support this distinction. In the result the Court of Appeal held that the Act does not apply to 'negligent misstatements where a disclaimer has prevented a duty of care from coming into existence'. My Lords, this confuses the valuer's report with the work which the valuer carries out in order to make his report. The valuer owed a duty to exercise reasonable skill and care in his inspection and valuation. If he had been careful in his work, he would not have made a 'negligent misstatement' in his report.

Section 11(3) of the 1977 Act provides that, in considering whether it is fair and reasonable to allow reliance on a notice which excludes liability in tort, account must be taken of 'all the circumstances obtaining when the liability arose or (but for the notice) would have arisen'. Section 13(1) of the Act prevents the exclusion of any right or remedy and (to that extent) s 2 also prevents the exclusion of liability 'by reference to . . . notices which exclude . . . the relevant obligation or duty'. Nourse LJ dismissed s 11(3) as 'peripheral' and made no comment on s 13(1). In my opinion both these provisions support the view that the 1977 Act requires that all exclusion notices which would in common law provide a defence to an action for negligence must satisfy the requirement of reasonableness. . . .

The government . . . recognises the need to preserve the duty of a professional lawyer to exercise reasonable skill and care so that the purchaser of a house may not be disastrously affected by a defect of title or an encumbrance. In the same way, it seems to me, there is need to preserve the duty of a professional valuer to exercise reasonable skill and care so that a purchaser of a house may not be disastrously affected by a defect in the structure of the house.

The public are exhorted to purchase their homes and cannot find houses to rent. A typical London suburban house, constructed in the 1930s for less than £1,000, is now bought for more than £150,000 with money largely borrowed at high rates of interest and repayable over a period of a quarter of a century. In these circumstances it is not fair and reasonable for building societies and valuers to agree together to impose on purchasers the risk of loss arising as a result of incompetence or carelessness on the part of valuers.

Check your understanding

1 Can you explain the meaning of the words and phrases in **bold** type?

2 Do you understand the mechanism by which a house is bought on mortgage? Which party is the mortgagor, which is the mortgagee?

Discuss

1 To what extent is it appropriate for judges to decide whether the parties to a contract should be bound by the letter of their agreement?

2 Do you think Lord Wilberforce would have been of the same opinion if Schulers were not a business, but a consumer faced with a standard term contract of a business supplier?

Write

Make notes on the Unfair Contract Terms Act 1977, outlining the circumstances in which (i) the Act does not apply, (ii) no exclusion clauses are permitted, and (iii) any exclusion clause must be reasonable.

Connections

1 '. . . no one intends to commit a tort', said Lord Templeman in *Smith v Eric S Bush*. What exceptions can you think of?

2 To what extent is the decision in *Smith v Eric S Bush* governed by legal rules, by principle and by policy? See the material on the judiciary if this distinction is not familiar.

3 Compare what Lord Reid says in *Schuler v Wickman:* 'The more unreasonable the result the more unlikely it is that the parties can have intended it . . .' with what was said in *Nedrick* (p. 102) about the relationship between what a person foresees and what he or she intends. Are courts engaged in similar exercises here?

4 In *Schuler v Wickman* Lord Reid reaches his decision by reading the contract as a whole. Judges use the same technique in statutory interpretation: see Beldam LJ in *Cutter v Eagle Star* at p. 27.

6.7 REMEDIES

Generally, the remedy available for a breach of contract is damages. There may also be a right to treat the contract as at an end (see p. 268).

Damages consist of a payment of money. The question of how much a plaintiff may recover is governed by the rule in *Hadley v Baxendale* (1854). The plaintiff had sent his mill shaft for repair. Whilst it was gone, the mill could not operate. He sued the carrier, who had delayed delivery of the shaft, for the money lost through delay. It was held that the carrier was liable only for loss that was either foreseeable by the reasonable man or 'within the contemplation of the parties', that is, foreseeable on the basis of facts known to both parties. As the carrier did not know he was handling the only mill shaft and the mill was out of action, he was held not liable for the resultant loss.

The question of how much should be paid was at issue in *Surrey County Council v Bredero Homes Ltd* [1993] 3 All ER 705. The Council had sold land to the defendants, who had promised to build a certain number of houses on the land. They later built more than that number and the Council claimed damages for the breach of **covenant**, claiming that they were entitled to the amount of extra profit the defendants had made as a result of their breach. The Court of Appeal looked at the principles involved. Dillon LJ said:

> The starting point . . . is that the remedy at common law for a breach of contract is an award of damages and damages at common law are intended to compensate the victim for his loss, not to transfer to the victim, if he has suffered no loss, the benefit which the wrongdoer has gained by his breach of contract. . . .
>
> Every student is taught that the basis of assessing damages for breach of contract is the rule in *Hadley v Baxendale* (1854) . . . which is wholly concerned with the losses which can be compensated by damages. Such damages may, in an appropriate case, cover profit which the injured plaintiff has lost, but they do not cover an award to a plaintiff who has himself suffered no loss, of the profit which the defendant has gained for himself by his breach of contract.

Counsel for the plaintiffs had suggested that, as it would be unjust to allow the defendants to keep the profit they had made in breach of contract, different rules should apply when there had been a deliberate breach. The Court of Appeal declined to change the law. Steyn LJ explained the principles:

> The issue in this appeal was defined by Sir William Goodhart QC for the appellants as the correct measure of damages in a case where the following three circumstances are satisfied: (a) there has been a deliberate breach of contract; (b) the party in breach has made a profit from that breach; and (c) the innocent party is in financial terms in the same position as if the contract had been fully performed. It is an important issue, with considerable implications for the shape of our law of obligations, and I therefore add a few remarks of my own.
>
> . . . An award of compensation for breach of contract serves to protect three separate interests. The starting principle is that the aggrieved party ought to be compensated for loss of his positive or expectation interests. In other words, the object is to put the aggrieved party in the same financial position as if the contract had been fully performed. But the law also protects the negative interest of the aggrieved party. If the aggrieved party is unable to establish the value of a loss of bargain he may seek compensation in respect of his reliance losses. The object of such an award is to compensate the aggrieved party for expenses incurred and losses suffered in reliance on the contract. These two complementary principles share one feature. Both are pure compensatory principles. If the aggrieved party has suffered no loss he is not entitled to be compensated by invoking these principles. The application of these principles to the present case would result in an award of nominal damages only.

Steyn LJ noted that there was a very restricted 'third principle' that protected reversionary interests and deprived the defendant of benefit gained from breach of contract, but he was not prepared to develop that principle further. He believed it was wrong to look at the motives of the person in breach:

> That is contrary to the general approach of our law of contract and, in particular, to rules governing the assessment of damages. . . . The introduction of restitutionary remedies to deprive cynical contract breakers of the fruits of their breaches of contract will lead to greater uncertainty in the assessment of damages in commercial and consumer disputes. It is of paramount importance that the way in which disputes are likely to be resolved by the courts must be readily predictable. Given the premise that the aggrieved party has suffered no loss, is such a dramatic extension of restitutionary remedies justified in order to confer a windfall in each case on the aggrieved party? I think not. In any event such a widespread

> availability of restitutionary remedies will have a tendency to discourage economic activity in relevant situations. In a range of cases such liability would fall on underwriters who have insured relevant liability risks. Inevitably underwriters would have to be compensated for the new species of potential claims. Insurance premiums would have to go up. That, too, is a consequence which militates against the proposed extension. The recognition of the proposed extension will in my view not serve the public interest.

This conservative approach to the measure of damages is also evident in the House of Lords' decision in *Ruxley Electronics & Construction v Forsyth* [1995] 3 All ER 268. The House of Lords held that Mr Forsyth was not entitled to the full cost of rebuilding a swimming pool that had been built a little shallower than had been specified in the contract because rebuilding would not be a reasonable course to take in the circumstances.

Specific performance

Sometimes damages are not a satisfactory remedy and then equity provides an order for specific performance, which compels the party in breach to do what they have promised and perform their contract. Courts grant specific performance in accordance with well-known principles, gathered from the cases over the years. The case of *Co-operative Insurance Society Ltd v Argyll Stores (Holdings) Ltd* [1997] 3 All ER 297 is interesting because application of the principles led the Court of Appeal and the House of Lords to different conclusions. The plaintiffs had leased a large unit in a shopping centre to the defendants, who operated a Safeway supermarket there. The lease contained a covenant by which the defendants agreed to keep the shop open during the usual hours of business. The plaintiffs heard that the defendants were considering closing the supermarket. As this could affect all the shops in the centre they wrote to Argyll, asking them to keep the store open until another company could be found to take an assignment of the lease and run a supermarket in the unit. Argyll did not answer the letter, closed the supermarket and removed the shop fittings. The plaintiffs brought an action for breach of covenant and asked for an order of specific performance which would require Argyll to reopen the supermarket. The judge at first instance refused specific performance. The Court of Appeal granted it. Leggatt LJ said:

> In my judgment this is a proper case in which to grant specific performance. It would do the court no credit if, in these circumstances, the court refrained from granting an injunction on the ground that it had become the practice not to do so. If this court were to follow that course, the result in practice would be that the common form words in this covenant would hardly ever, if ever, be construed as meaning what they say. If the parties want to contract that a failure to keep open will sound only in damages,

> they are quite at liberty to do so. But where a responsible and substantial company such as the respondents have undertaken to keep one of their stores open for a stipulated period, I see no reason why they should not be held to their bargain. That in recessionary times may entail trading at a loss; but it by no means entails that they will have to do so for the duration of the lease. In any event, there is provision made for **assignment** with the landlords' consent, and that may provide the defendants with an escape in this case. That they stripped out their store rather than respond to the landlords' cautionary letter was their own idea. They did it at their peril, and have only themselves or their legal advisers to blame for having done so precipitately.
>
> The plaintiffs would have very considerable difficulty in trying to prove their loss. An award of damages would be unlikely to compensate them fully; and the losses of the other tenants of the shopping centre would be irrecoverable, except in so far as they might be mitigated by reduced rents. The defendants have acted with gross commercial cynicism, preferring to resist a claim for damages rather than keep an unambiguous promise. This is not a court of morals, but there is no reason why its willingness to grant specific performance should not be affected by a sense of fair dealing.

Roch LJ said:

> Damages not being an adequate remedy for the plaintiffs, should the court nevertheless have declined to grant specific performance? There was nothing in the conduct of the plaintiffs which could lead a court to decline to grant this equitable remedy. The plaintiffs were not guilty of delay nor had they behaved in any way in which it could be said that they did not come to the court with clean hands.
>
> Was this an order which should not be made because it was either indefinite in time or an order the terms of which could not be sufficiently precise? In my view neither of those considerations represented in this case a reason for withholding the remedy. Specific performance would require the defendants to operate a supermarket at the premises until the year 2014 or until such time as they obtained a sub-tenant or assignee willing and capable to operate a supermarket at the Hillsborough Centre. Further, it is in my opinion possible to define with sufficient certainty the obligations which the order would enjoin the defendants to meet in carrying on the business of a supermarket; the order would simply repeat the terms of the covenants into which the defendants had entered. There has been no suggestion in this case . . . that the terms of such covenants were so uncertain that the covenants were void. Further, if the defendants are ordered to continue the operation of a supermarket at the premises, it is inconceivable that they would not operate the business efficiently. To do otherwise would damage their commercial reputation. Day-to-day supervision by the court or by the plaintiffs would be unnecessary.

Millett LJ gave a dissenting judgment. He said that specific performance should not be ordered because it never has been in cases of this kind. Legal advisers have always known that breach of this covenant will be remedied by damages. 'The equitable jurisdiction should not be exercised in a manner which would defeat the commercial expectations of the parties at the time when they entered into their contractual obligations.' The court should not order a person to continue in a loss-making business.

The House of Lords [1997] 3 All ER 297 agreed with Millett LJ's view and ruled that specific performance should not be granted. Lord Hoffman gave the only speech. The reasons for refusing specific performance were:

1 The court would not order a person to continue in business at a loss.
2 The only means of enforcement is imprisonment for contempt of court, which would be inappropriate, and 'the seriousness of a finding of contempt for the defendant means that any application to enforce the order is likely to be a heavy and expensive piece of litigation. The possibility of repeated applications over a period of time means that, in comparison with a once and for all inquiry as to damages, the enforcement of the remedy is likely to be expensive in terms of cost to the parties and the resources of the judicial system.'
3 There would be a need for constant supervision.
4 The loss A would make in carrying on in business might exceed the loss C would suffer from the breach of covenant. 'The purpose of the law of contract is not to punish wrongdoing but to satisfy the expectations of the party entitled to performance.'

Commenting on the Court of Appeal's judgment, Lord Hoffman said:

> Finally, all three judges in the Court of Appeal took a very poor view of Argyll's conduct. Leggatt LJ said that they had acted 'with gross commercial cynicism'; Roch LJ began his judgment by saying that they had 'behaved very badly' and Millett LJ said that they had no merits . . . The principles of equity have always had a strong ethical content and nothing which I say is intended to diminish the influence of moral values in their application. I can envisage cases of gross breach of personal faith, or attempts to use the threat of non-performance as blackmail, in which the needs of justice will override all the considerations which support the settled practice. But although any breach of covenant is regrettable, the exercise of the discretion as to whether or not to grant specific performance starts from the fact that the covenant has been broken. Both landlord and tenant in this case are large sophisticated commercial organisations and I have no doubt that both were perfectly aware that the remedy for breach of the covenant was likely to be limited to an award of damages. The interests of both were purely financial: there was no element of personal breach of faith . . . No doubt there was an effect on the businesses of other

traders in the centre, but Argyll had made no promises to them and it is not suggested that CIS warranted to other tenants that Argyll would remain. Their departure, with or without the consent of CIS, was a commercial risk which the tenants were able to deploy in negotiations for the next rent review. On the scale of broken promises, I can think of worse cases, but the language of the Court of Appeal left them with few adjectives to spare.

It was no doubt discourteous not to have answered [the] letter. But to say, as Roch LJ did, that they had acted 'wantonly and quite unreasonably' by removing their fixtures seems to me an exaggeration . . . There was no question of stealing a march, or attempting to present CIS with a fait accompli, because Argyll had no reason to believe that CIS would have been able to obtain a mandatory injunction whether the fixtures had been removed or not. They had made it perfectly clear that they were closing the shop and given CIS ample time to apply for such an injunction if so advised.

I think that no criticism can be made of the way in which Judge Maddocks [the trial judge] exercised his discretion. All the reasons which he gave were proper matters for him to take into account. In my view, the Court of Appeal should not have interfered and I would allow the appeal and restore the order which he made.

Check your understanding

Can you explain the meaning of the words and phrases in **bold** type?

Discuss

1 'This is not a court of morals', says Leggatt LJ. What *is* the function of equity in the law of contract?

2 The House of Lords regards an order of specific performance against a company as inappropriate because imprisonment for contempt of court is an inappropriate sanction against a company. Do you agree? Does this put companies 'above the law'? Consider the parallel with companies accused of manslaughter – see p. 148.

3 In *Surrey CC v Bredero Homes* Steyn LJ stressed the need for certainty as to what damages will be awarded for. In *Co-operative Insurance Society Ltd v Argyll Stores* Lord Hoffman stressed the need for certainty in awarding specific performance: 'The remedy for breach of the covenant was likely to be limited to an award of damages'. Why is certainty so important? Do you regard it equally important whether the remedy in question is common law or equitable?

Write

From the judgments in the Court of Appeal in *Co-operative Insurance Society v Argyll*, list the factors that are considered relevant to the decision whether to grant specific performance. Check your list against that given in a textbook.

Connections

1 In both contract and tort, insurance is an important issue. Judges do consider the insurance implications of their decisions both in terms of the effect on premiums and whether there will be compensation for injured parties, although some judges deny that insurance should have any impact on a decision. Look at the cases *John Munroe (Acrylics) Ltd v London Fire & Civil Defence Authority* (1996) and *Nettleship v Weston* (1971) for direct references to the effect of insurance. Undoubtedly, insurance is also a factor judges had in the back of their minds when deciding other cases in this book: can you discover some likely examples?

2 In *Co-operative Insurance Society v Argyll* Leggatt LJ argues that Argyll should be 'held to their bargain'. Compare this with the majority approach in *Schuler v Wickman*. This case turns on whether the covenant should be interpreted literally or given the meaning judges in previous cases have always given it – again, like *Schuler v Wickman*, it is an interpretation problem.

There are not many questions in this book that have one right answer. What follows, therefore, are suggestions to consider when you are stuck.

1.1 EUROPEAN LAW

Discuss

1 The rule that a litigant must have *locus standi* prevents people interfering in matters that are not their business and cluttering the courts with hypothetical cases. If a breach of law is anticipated, the Attorney-General sometimes brings an action to prevent it – but the Attorney-General is a member of the government. The question as to who might have had *locus standi* and be interested in bringing an action such as this is, therefore, very interesting.

2 This question asks how expressly Parliament has to word legislation that conflicts with the Treaties in order for the courts to give precedence to UK legislation.

3 Preambles give guidance as to what the legislation hopes to achieve; they are useful given the different style of interpretation practised by European judges.

4 Competition between states is distorted if the cost of employing labour varies widely between states. What makes this legislation controversial is that it affects the social conditions within Member States, as well as the economy.

1.2 PARLIAMENTARY LAW MAKING

Check your understanding

3 He is talking about the European Convention on Human Rights.

Discuss

1 One provides for the statutory instrument to become law *unless* it is annulled by Parliament, the other provides for the statutory instrument to become law only *if* it is approved.

2 Look for the evidence in what happens after each document is issued.

3 Consider first what kinds of changes to the law are generally made by statutory instrument, then think about what he is proposing.

4 There has to be a good reason for calling each other 'My honourable Friend' and not using people's names.

5 and **6** The evidence is all here; be patient and winkle it out.

1.3 STATUTORY INTERPRETATION

Discuss

1 Is he using the literal approach, the golden rule or the mischief rule, for example?

3 First, decide what Lord Diplock's approach to interpretation is, then take each case and apply that approach to the facts. Make sure you give reasons.

Write

1 Your own notes of cases are very important. Make sure they always contain all three of these elements. You can also include anything *obiter* that is interesting.

2 There is a whole essay here! Some would say the intentions of Parliament can be gathered only from the words that have been used, some would say you have to look at the background to legislation; the argument about whether Hansard should be used is also relevant.

1.4 JUDICIAL PRECEDENT

Discuss

2 The ratio of *Miller* is that a person who creates a situation comes under a duty to act, and that failure to act can then constitute the actus reus of a criminal offence. Everything else is *obiter*.

Write

1 What are the facts? What was the relevant issue of law? (There may be more than one.) What is the law on that issue or issues? How does that law relate to the facts? Was the defendant therefore guilty or not guilty?

2 Do this as many times as you need until it becomes second nature.

3 The examiner will have given you the facts. You have to decide what the relevant issues of law are. Explain the law, using cases and statutes as authority. Apply the relevant law to each of the issues you have identified. Come to a conclusion. Your conclusion may contain a series of 'ifs and buts': deal with all the issues, even though your decision on one of them might seem to make the others irrelevant.

2.1 THE JUDICIARY

Check your understanding

2 The 'fairy tale' is that there is a right answer waiting to be discovered, the 'Noble Dream' is that judges develop the law by identifying legal principles and the 'Nightmare' is that they make decisions that uphold the interests of the ruling class.

3 He expects them to consider the three factors at p. 43.

Discuss

1 Have a clear idea of what is meant by policy and principles before you begin. Policy is to do with what the law *should* be; principles are general statements about what the law *is*, gleaned from considering the rules applied in similar situations to the one before the court.

2.2 JURIES

Discuss

2 I consider this is a policy issue. It is about priorities in how public funds should be spent. I do not think this is an issue for a jury, but you may. The important thing is to have reasons for your conclusion and to recognise that there are good points on both sides of the argument.

3 and **4** Look at the start of Lord Woolf's judgment.

6 Think about the purpose of exemplary damages. Then consider the role of senior officers in setting standards for the force.

Write

A rule of law is a rule about what is legal or illegal; a rule of practice is concerned with how a dispute is dealt with; a guideline has no legal effect, but following guidelines is evidence of good practice. Employment law is a fertile ground for examples, but you could consider criminal law, particularly police powers.

3.1 CIVIL DISPUTE RESOLUTION

Discuss

1 The evidence would consist of comments received about proposals.

2 Proportionality here would refer to the amount of costs as compared with the amount of damages; ideally, the costs should be considerably less than the damages.

4 For example, it should be accessible, both physically and financially. This would raise issues about location of offices and, possibly, courts and rights of audience. There are lots of other issues.

5 You can find lists of advantages and disadvantages in textbooks. Try to think up your own before checking them against someone else's. First list the reforms proposed in *Striking the Balance*, then consider the likely effect of those reforms, then think about the likely effect of conditional fees, then come to a conclusion about which would be preferable.

Write

1 A summary can be written in continuous prose (sentences and paragraphs) or it can be a list. It depends what you want to use it for.

2 'Describe' involves some explanation. This would be the starting point for an essay about financing legal actions.

3.2 SENTENCING

Check your understanding

2 'triable either way' means triable either by magistrates or in the Crown Court. A trial on indictment is a trial in the Crown Court.

3 Sentencing policy involves consideration of the reasons why we, as a society, pass sentence on people and what we are trying to achieve. Sentencing practice is concerned with the way in which individuals should be dealt with. So, it is a policy issue whether and for what kinds of crime we use

imprisonment; it is a matter of practice as to what is taken into account in sentencing an individual.

Things to do

2 Flowcharts are really useful when you are trying to understand something complex. A flowchart regarding section 2 of the Act might begin like this:

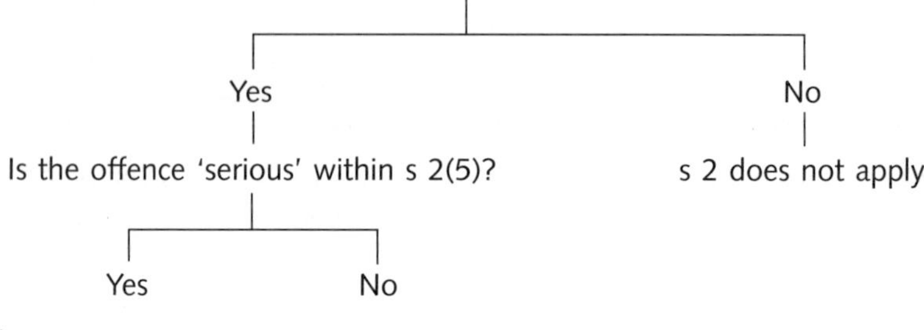

and so on.

Discuss

1 What are you going to do with people convicted of criminal offences? Why?

2 Now put the other side of the argument. When you have done 1 and 2, you have the material for a good essay.

4.1 THE SCOPE OF CRIMINAL LAW

Discuss

1 Policy: what the law should be. Public interest: what the law should be with regard to the best interests of society as a whole.

2 I consider this to be value-laden language – see p. 67.

Write

2 You should research more widely before writing an essay. Consider the Hart/Devlin debate on the proper scope of the criminal law, look at the report of the Wolfenden Committee, think about the wide range of the criminal law. You need to consider what is meant by 'harm' and 'others'. When you have completed your research, plan a structure for your essay. It is often easiest to begin by defining the words used in the question before moving on to discuss the different points of view. You are expected to reach a conclusion, but any well-argued conclusion is acceptable.

Connections

3 Consent is not relevant when it is not true consent – because a person did not understand the issues, for example.

4.2 ELEMENTS OF A CRIME

Things to do

1 You might, for example, have known that the window was likely to break but decided that you would go ahead anyway. That would be *Cunningham* recklessness.

Discuss

1 This is a criminal textbook job. One of the other situations in which a duty to act arises is where the defendant has a contractual duty to act.

2 At the time the fire started, Miller was asleep so he could not form any mens rea.

4 The '*Caldwell* gap' occurs when a defendant knows there is a risk, considers (wrongly) that he has taken adequate precautions and goes ahead.

5 Describe the two approaches clearly before you compare them.

6 Lord Diplock does not consider *Cunningham* recklessness – the defendant who recognises a risk but goes on to take it.

4.3 DEFENCES

Discuss

1 Look for the reasons given in the judgments in *Majewski*.

2 Find the justifications, then consider *Kingston*.

3 Make a note of the good and bad points about each decision, then decide which you prefer and why.

4 You need the reasons for Lord Edmund-Davies' decision and the reasons for Lord Diplock's.

5 Both cases involve facts that might arouse in judges, as human beings, distaste. Can you find evidence of the judges being influenced by such feelings?

6 First, you need to identify what the interests of victims, defendants and society at large are. Then find evidence of these interests being protected. Then consider what a satisfactory balance might be. Then decide whether the judges get the balance right.

Write

2 Remember that this is one of the most important functions of the Court of Appeal in criminal cases. Judges need to know what they should tell juries about the law. If the trial judge gets it wrong, the defendant could appeal against a finding of guilt.

4.4 STRICT LIABILITY

Discuss

1 I think they are very near to the same idea but that Lord Mustill is drawing a distinction between the existence of mens rea and moral blameworthiness. For example, if I kill a person I love who is in great pain I undoubtedly have the mens rea for murder but some people would argue that what I have done is morally right. Having the necessary mens rea amounts to being 'at fault' in a legal sense, though not always in a moral sense.

2 Think about the implications of this before making your decision and remember that you must always have reasons for your choice.

4.5 COMPANIES AS DEFENDANTS

Discuss

2 List the proposals, then apply them to the facts of the *Gateway* case.

3 Consider what you want to achieve in passing sentence on a company. Do the Law Commission's proposals achieve those things?

5.1 NEGLIGENCE: DUTY OF CARE

Discuss

2 Personally, I find it hard to see that these distinctions are logical in terms of principle. It is easier to view them as policy limits to negligence – though one still has to justify their existence.

3 The incremental approach is the step-by-step development of the law from one case to another, as opposed to recognition of new boundaries for negligence developed with regard to what is 'fair, just and reasonable'.

4 The relevant issue in *Frost* was that the police officers were employees of the organisation responsible for the negligence that caused their injuries.

5 Compare what Lord Keith said in *Murphy v Brentwood* with what he said in *White v Jones*.

6 What makes a satisfactory Court of Appeal decision? Presumably, a just outcome in the particular case(s) but also a clear view of what the law is, so that lawyers may advise their clients. Has this been achieved?

5.2 NEGLIGENCE: BREACH AND LOSS

Discuss

1 Reasoning by analogy, the standard to be expected of the medical student would be the standard of a competent doctor. That seems harsh, but what justification is there for it? Look at Lord Denning's justification for expecting a learner driver to be as competent as a qualified driver.

2 The fault principle means that a plaintiff cannot get damages unless he or she can find a defendant who is 'to blame'. The alternative is to have a system for compensating those who are injured or suffer financial loss, regardless of whether anyone is to blame.

3 The first test is to decide whether there is a duty to be careful. The second is to decide the scope of liability – how much of the loss a defendant should be responsible for.

5.3 OTHER TORTS

Discuss

1 *At the time it was made* is the important phrase here. What changed between that decision and the one in *Hunter v Canary Wharf*?

4 Sort out the objective (a reasonable man test) ones first and then the subjective (relating to the particular defendant).

5 Remember that this is about the constitutional relationship of judges and Parliament, not just your personal opinion.

5.4 DAMAGES

Discuss

1 The principle of insurance is that lots of people pay small amounts of money so that a person suffering a loss can be compensated from the fund thus accumulated. This means that every driver pays a contribution to the damages paid out to road accident victims, for example.

3 If a person has lost the use of his legs, the pain and the inability to walk cannot be accurately quantified in money.

4 Which is more likely to make employers change their systems?

6.1 FORMATION AND 6.2 CONSIDERATION

Discuss

1 Look at Professor Simon Lee on the judicial role (p. 40).

2 An objective approach means standing back and looking at what an observer would have thought the parties had agreed at the time the contract was made.

3 Three different rules here.

Connections

Equity developed a system of rules which are different from common law rules. They 'prevail' because Parliament decided that they should in the Judicature Acts 1873–75.

6.3 PRIVITY

Discuss

1 They were unable to change the law because the point was *obiter*. They might have been unwilling to make such a fundamental change to the law, regarding it as a matter for Parliament.

2 A straight yes or no will not suffice here. You *could* turn your answer into an essay! Make sure you have arguments both for and against.

3 A textbook job. Look at agency, for example. Think about the relationship between tort and contract and consider the decision in *White v Jones* (p. 167).

Write

1 So, in each case, what was the offer? what was the acceptance? what was the consideration?

6.4 INTENTION TO CREATE LEGAL RELATIONS

Check your understanding

2 He was a cousin of Oliver Cromwell. He is remembered for refusing to pay a tax imposed by the King, arguing that only Parliament had the right to impose a new tax. The relevance here is that he stood up and said: 'This is not right'. He was also making an argument about due process – the concept that there is a correct way to do things and a law or a decision is not valid if the correct process has not been followed.

Discuss

1 I think it is something to do with the principle of trying to give effect to the intention of the parties. The parties will often not have made it clear what their intention was – usually because they have not considered the issue – so the courts find it easier to make a broad assumption.

2 Following from the previous question, you would probably advise them to think out what they wanted and then commit that to writing.

3 Case dates are always interesting because the law changes as social attitudes change. I believe contemporary attitudes to separation and divorce had a lot to do with the difference in the decisions in these two cases.

Write

A collateral contract is one that exists alongside the main contract. It is really a judicial device, enabling judges to give contractual force to promises made on condition that the promisee enters into the main contract: 'if you sign this, I promise I will . . .'.

6.5 VITIATING FACTORS

Undue influence

Check your understanding

2 A person has actual notice when they know of a situation. A person has constructive notice when they *should* have known of that situation, usually because they have a duty to find out.

Discuss

1 The whole basis of undue influence is that a person made a bad decision because of improper pressure. If Miss Massey had simply been a bad businesswoman, she would have no defence against the bank. Her argument was that she did what she did because of Mr Potts' influence.

2 For example, the lender risks losing the money but gains interest payments and eventually gets the capital sum plus interest. Before you can decide whether the law gets the balance right, you have to decide what a fair balance might be.

Write

1 Equity is concerned with realities, rather than formalities.

Illegality, misrepresentation and mistake

Discuss

1 He has to avoid the contract *before* the car is sold to a third party. He could do this by telling the rogue that the deal was off. More realistically, he can do it by informing the police or taking other steps to demonstrate his avoidance of the contract.

2 Entirely possible. Have a close look at what he said and make your decision.

3 It shifts the burden onto the defendant, who must demonstrate that he had reasonable grounds for his belief. This is unusual, because the plaintiff usually bears the burden of proof.

4 Dig out what you regard as the *ratio* of the case.

6.6 INTERVENTION

Check your understanding

2 The person who is buying the house is the mortgagor. He or she gives the bank or building society a mortgage of the property, so making that institution the mortgagee. If the borrower fails to make payments to the lender, the lender can eventually obtain a court order for possession of the property and sell it to recover the amount of the loan and any outstanding interest. Any balance is then payable to the borrower.

Discuss

1 Put another way, should judges enforce what the parties wrote or what the judge thinks they meant? Can you see the parallel with statutory interpretation?

6.7 REMEDIES

Discuss

1 Read what a textbook has to say about the role of equity and consider the materials in this book on promissory estoppel and undue influence.

2 Do you agree that imprisonment is the only possible sanction? Do you agree that imprisonment could never be used against a company – given that a company has officers and directors?

Glossary

The words in the glossary are explained in the context they bear in the text. They may mean something slightly different in a different context so, when in doubt, use a dictionary.

A

abate	terminate, so a right of **abatement** is a right to terminate a nuisance
ab initio	from the beginning
abridgement	shortening
abrogate	avoid
absolute liability	criminal liability arising solely from the commission of the actus reus, even though the defendant's act or omission was involuntary – compare with **strict liability**, which requires a voluntary actus reus but no mens rea
absolve	excuse, release from blame, forgive
actuarial	relating to the work of **actuaries**, who calculate risks for insurance companies, so deciding what risks will be insured against and what premium will be charged
adage	a wise saying
adduced	produced or cited
administratrix	the person responsible for dealing with the affairs of a person who died without making a will. The male form is **administrator**. If a will is made, the job is done by an **executrix** or **executor**
adumbrated	indicated
adverted	referred
advice agencies	bodies that give advice, such as the Citizens' Advice Bureau
aetiology	cause
a fortiori	more so

agency an arrangement by which a person (the **agent**) transacts business on behalf of another (the **principal**)

alternative dispute resolution any kind of help with resolving disputes other than by a court or tribunal

anachronism something that is from another time

analogy similar case – so **analogous** means similar or comparable

anecdotal through stories or incidents

annulment making of no effect

anomaly something that is out of place or abnormal, so **anomalous relic** refers to something that is an abnormal survival from the past

antithesis opposite

appellants those who appeal to a higher court – the other side are then the **respondents**

arbitrator a specialist who hears disputes concerning his specialist area and gives a decision which is legally binding

arrogate to have pretensions above one's station

ascertaining finding out

aspirations hopes

assertion statement

assignment transfer of a lease to a new tenant

astute shrewd (the context is an odd use of the word – perhaps as a synonym for 'quick'?)

aught anything

austerity basic or harsh conditions

B

bench a collective term for magistrates sitting in court together

Bill a draft statute

brocard statement of a basic legal principle

C

candid honest

canonical authoritative

Case Stated the account of the facts of a case and the law applied which is given by a magistrates' court when an appeal is made to the Divisional Court

casus omissus Latin; something that is left out

causation the link between an act or omission and a consequence; the question as to whether

	they are closely enough connected for a defendant to be considered responsible for the consequence
caveat	warning
cf	compare
chose in action	an intangible piece of property, represented by a piece of paper such as a currency note, a cheque or a share certificate
circularity	an argument that is not conclusive because neither statement proves the other: if A, then B – if B, then A
circumscribed	limited or restricted
circumvent	get round, so **circumvention** means getting round
clandestine	underhand, secret
class interest	something that will benefit only a particular social class may be said to be in a class interest
clauses	the divisions of a Bill, which become **sections** when the Bill becomes an Act. **Sub-clauses** are divisions of a clause: cl 1(1) means clause one, sub-clause one
code of practice	guidance that lacks legal force. Following a code of practice is evidence of good practice
coercive, coercion	involving force or compulsion
cogent	convincing
cohesiveness	holding together; an argument that holds together well is **coherent**
Committee Stage	the process of considering a Bill in detail, carried out by a small group of MPs known as a Standing Committee
Community institution	the Council, Commission, Court or Parliament of the European Community
community sentence	a sentence involving a mixture of community service and probation or either one of them alone
commute	reduce or substitute
competent	capable, sufficiently skilled and/or qualified
compulsory third party insurance	the insurance which the driver of a vehicle must by law have. It covers damage or injury to other people
conceded	acknowledged as right
conceptual	relating to ideas
concurrence	happening together

conjecture	guesswork, an opinion formed on inadequate evidence
conscious volition	choice, free will
congeners	close relatives
consensual	by agreement
consideration	the money, promise or other thing of some value that is given by each party to a contract to the other party
constitutional	in compliance with the constitution, that is, with the rules governing the functions of different institutions of government
construction	interpretation
construed purposively	interpreted with regard to the purpose of the legislature in making the particular law
contemporary	at the same time, at present; things which are **contemporaneous** happen at the same time
contention	a point made in argument – so, **contentious business** means legal matters that are likely to go to court if not settled; **non-contentious business** is legal work such as conveyancing which is not generally concerned with a dispute of any kind
context	surrounding words
contiguous	adjoining
contingencies	things that may (or may not) happen
contravenes	conflicts with
convoluted	turned in on itself, going round and round
corporal punishment	literally, bodily punishment. Smacking children, flogging, birching, etc.
costs	the fees charged by solicitors. Sums paid out for barristers' fees, court fees, fees to experts and such like are **disbursements** but the word 'costs' is in some contexts, such as here, used to include both costs and disbursements
Council of Europe	nothing to do with the European Union. An older body, responsible for the European Convention on Human Rights
counsel	a barrister
covenant	a promise
criteria	standards for making judgments (singular: criterion)
critique	evaluation, academic criticism
crude	rough, unsophisticated
culpability	blameworthiness

D

damnified	caused loss
dearth	lack
declaratory powers	the power in a court to declare what the law is, as opposed to simply deciding the issue between two parties – the court makes a **declaration**
defer	give way
delegated legislation	law contained in statutory instruments, bye-laws or Orders in Council made by a body other than Parliament under authority given in an Act, which is known as the 'enabling Act' or 'parent Act'
deterrent	something that prevents a person doing something
detriment	harm or loss
dictum	saying, wise words
directly enforceable rule of Community law	a rule of EC law that is directly **applicable** is one that becomes law in each Member State automatically; one that is directly **effective** is one that can be used as the basis of an action by an individual. Both are thus directly enforceable because an individual can use them as a basis for court action
disconcerting	unsettling, upsetting
discretion	a choice
discursive	wide-ranging
dissenting	disagreeing with the majority

E

easement	a right over the land belonging to another
efficacy	effectiveness
efficiently, effectively	buzzwords of government! Efficiently means, in this context, giving good value for money; effectively means achieving objectives
electoral register	the list of local adults entitled to vote, from which potential jurors are selected at random
elicited	brought forth, gave rise to
embellishment	addition of detail
engendered	brought into being
enjoining	commanding or instructing
ensues	follows
enunciating	proclaiming, stating – so **enunciated** means proclaimed or stated
equable	even

erroneous	wrong
esoteric	secret, understood only by the initiated
estate	the property of a person who has died, handled by his executor if he left a will, his administrator if he did not
estopped	barred; an **estoppel** is a rule of evidence preventing a person attempting to prove a certain issue
esprit de corps	French; team spirit
exclusion clause	a term in a contract the aim of which is to exclude liability in respect of some obligation that one party would otherwise owe to the other
exculpate	remove blame; **exculpatory factors** are things which excuse or remove blame
exemplifies	illustrates
exhaustive	comprehensive
expounded	explained in detail
express	stated
ex turpi causa	Latin; abbreviation of the expression *ex turpi causa non oritur actio*, which means that a legal action cannot be based on wrongdoing
F	
fiduciary	based on a relationship of trust
First Reading	the start of a Bill's progress through a House of Parliament. A purely formal reading of the name of the Bill which informs MPs that the Bill has been printed and is ready for them to read
figurative	as opposed to literal – not really – metaphorically
fireman's rule	an American rule that someone who takes risks as part of their job cannot bring an action in respect of an injury suffered at work
fixed by law	a sentence that involves no discretion, or choice, on the part of the judge because Parliament has laid down the precise sentence always to be given for the offence
floodgates argument	'if we allow this plaintiff to succeed, there will be thousands of others who will then take actions'
fortuitously	luckily
fructify	bear fruit, produce

G

gratuitously	free of charge
gravitate	move downwards
Green Paper	a government publication, setting out proposals for changing the law. A consultative document
guarantee	a promise to pay as a security

H

headnote	a summary at the beginning of a case report, written by the publishers, so not part of the report itself, setting out the facts, decision and *ratio* in brief
hierarchy of courts	the courts viewed in terms of most authoritative (the House of Lords) to least authoritative (magistrates and county courts)
hypothesis	a theory offered as a basis for explanation; so a **hypothetical case** would consist of a set of circumstances that do not actually exist and a **hypothetical question** is one that begins: 'If . . .' and gives an opportunity to explore what might happen in a given situation

I

ibid.	Latin; in the same place (short for *ibidem*)
imminent	about to happen
implausible	difficult to believe
implement	bring into force. It is not uncommon for Parliament to pass an Act but to delay implementation. The law remains as it was before the Act was passed until the Act is implemented
implied, implicit	unstated, but to be gathered from surrounding circumstances
impotent	of no effect
impute	attribute
incanting	chanting
incapacitative effect	an effect of rendering people incapable (in this context, incapable of committing crime)
incarcerated	imprisoned
incidence	manner of occurrence
in credit	a bank account that has money in it is in credit in the accounts of the bank because the customer is thus a creditor of the bank; similarly, if an account is overdrawn, the

	customer owes money to the bank and is a debtor of the bank
incumbent	an obligation
indemnify	pay a sum of money owed by another person
indeterminate	unknowable, indefinite
inebriates	drunks
inexpedient	unsuitable
infer	imply or draw a conclusion, which is then known as an **inference**
inflation	the process by which the value of money falls over a period of time
inhibition	restraint
initiating	beginning
initiatives	a taking of steps, pursuing of an idea
injunctions	orders or instructions
integrated review	a review that looks at several related issues, rather than just one
intelligible	capable of being understood
interim relief	a remedy granted before a case has been heard – usually an injunction to prevent damage being caused
inter vivos	Latin; between two living people
in vacuo	Latin; by itself
ipso facto	Latin; thereby
ius quaesitum tertio	Latin; third party right

J

judicious	wise
jurisdiction	the things a court can do, the type of cases it can hear or a geographical area governed by a particular system of law
jurisprudence	legal theory or body of law (depending on context), so **jurisprudential basis** means theoretical legal basis

L

laconic	brief, concise
lacuna	a gap
Law Officers	senior lawyers within the government: the Attorney-General and the Solicitor-General
learned helplessness	a psychological condition in which a person is so demoralised as to be unable to make decisions
legal charge	mortgage
levitate	move upwards

licensee — a person who has permission, as opposed to a right, to occupy land

litigants — the parties to a dispute, those who are engaged in litigation

long title — a statement of purpose at the beginning of an Act immediately following the short title, which is the name by which the Act is known

M

mandatory — obligatory

manifest — obvious

margin of appreciation — a discretion to reach one of a range of decisions. This expression is used in relation to decisions of the European Court of Human Rights to describe their power to give a decision reflecting the culture of a particular state – so that the rules about what is acceptable may vary from state to state. In this context, the notion that a jury's award should be upheld by the Court of Appeal as long as it lies within a range that might be regarded as reasonable

mediation — resolution of a dispute through an independent third party, a mediator, whose job is to assist the parties to reach a solution satisfactory to them both

mitigate — to lessen or reduce; **mitigating circumstances** will tend to reduce the severity of a punishment imposed for a criminal offence

mutatis mutandis — Latin; having made appropriate changes

N

non est factum — Latin; it is not my deed. A plea that a signature to a document is not valid because the person signing did not know what he was signing

non-partisan — independent (so 'partisan' means a person committed to a particular point of view)

O

obiter dicta — Latin; words by the way, things said which do not have immediate relevance to the case in hand

objective — viewed from the standpoint of a disinterested observer

obloquy	disgrace
obtemper	to comply with (This is an unusual word, a new one to me. I found it in the massive and highly authoritative *Oxford English Dictionary*. It is, apparently, a word in use in Scottish law to signify obedience to a court order.)
obviates	removes
on notice	in a position of being aware of something
onus	burden
ordinary phlegm	ordinary courage, an expression from the older 'nervous shock' cases
orthographical	spelling
ostensibly	apparently, outwardly

P

palpable	obvious
parabolical	as in the parable
paradoxical	odd or absurd
paramount	the most important
parenthesis	by the way; a **parenthetical comment** is one made in passing
parity	equality
Parliamentary Counsel to the Treasury	lawyers who draft Bills for the government
parsimonious	mean
paternalistic	believing one knows what is best for others
pecuniary loss	loss of money
penalises	punishes, so **penal** means something to do with punishment
pernicious	destructive
perpetuate	continue, make permanent
per se	Latin; of itself
pertinent	relevant
pilots	trial studies, involving a smaller number of people than would be used in the final scheme
pleading	the formal document which sets out a plaintiff's case or the defendant's answer to it; the **pleadings** should reveal all the issues that are to be decided by the court
poignant	emotionally painful
policy	a view about how something ought to be, as opposed to how it is. Deciding what the law ought to be is generally thought to be a

	matter for politicians, although judges sometimes make policy decisions
poltroon	coward (in this context, a redundant word as 'coward' has already been used – although, arguably, this word conveys even more contempt than 'coward')
postulates	assumes
pragmatically	from a practical, rather than theoretical, point of view
precursor	something that has gone before, a forerunner
predatory	plundering, feeding on prey
pre-determined budgets	set sums of money, as opposed to a bottomless purse
predominance	domination
pre-emptive	action taken before, and in anticipation of, action by another
premature decisions	decisions made before all the relevant facts are known
prerequisites	circumstances which must exist before liability can arise
prerogative	power or right
presumption	something that is assumed to be the case; when there is a presumption the burden of proof shifts from the person who would normally have to prove an element in his case to the other party, who must prove it is not so
prima facie	Latin; at first sight
pro bono publico	Latin; for the general good. This phrase is also used to describe work undertaken by lawyers without payment, known as 'pro bono' work
procrastination	deliberate delay, so a **procrastinating ruse** is a device to avoid, or at least delay, making a decision
progression	in this context (progression of sentencing), meaning that a person who has reoffended, having been sentenced before, should receive a harsher sentence for the second offence than for the first
promisee	the person to whom a promise is made by the **promisor**
promissory estoppel	a rule of evidence that prevents a person who has made a promise claiming that he is not bound by that promise because it was unsupported by consideration

propensity	tendency
property in . . .	the legal right to something
proportionate	in keeping with, not excessive; so **proportionality** in sentencing means a notion that the sentence should equate to the crime
proprieties	what is proper
proscription	forbidding
prospectus	a document published by the promoters of a public limited company when it first offers shares for sale to the general public
pro tanto	Latin; by the same amount
proximity	closeness
public interest	for the general good; it is debatable whether there is any such thing as 'the public interest', as there are so many different interests within society that it would be difficult to find a solution to a problem that was best for everyone
punitive	relating to punishment

Q

quantum	amount
quasi	partly, not quite

R

radical	from the roots
ratio decidendi	Latin; reason for the decision in a case
rationale	reasoning
reasoning by analogy	a process of reasoning that rests on similarity: if case A is decided this way and the circumstances in case B are similar, then case B should be decided in the same way
recalcitrant	refusing to come into line or to obey authority
reciprocity	mutuality, give and take
recrudescence	relapse
remedial	designed to improve a situation
Report Stage	the process of a committee reporting back to the House of Commons on a Bill that the committee has considered in detail, usually with recommendations for amendments
rescission	an equitable remedy; the parties are put back in the position they held before the transaction was made

respondent	the defendant in an appeal – so plaintiff (or prosecution) and defendant become appellant and respondent
restitutio in integrum	Latin; put things back as they were
rhetoric	the art of argument
robust mechanisms	strong systems

S

salient	significant
scepticism	doubt
schedules	detailed provisions of an Act, often in tabular form, found at the end of the Act
Second Reading	the major debate on a Bill in either House of Parliament
sections	the divisions of an Act. 'Section one, sub-section one' is written as s 1(1)
self-selecting oligarchy	an oligarchy is a small group of powerful people. Self-selecting in this context means that new members are chosen by existing members
separation of powers	the principle that law making, enforcement of the law and adjudication of disputes are three separate functions that ought to be carried out by three different groups of people. If all these powers come into the same hands, there is potential for dictatorship. Note that the Lord Chancellor has roles in all three functions
session	here, 'Parliamentary session' – the time during the year in which Parliament is working
settle	agree a solution to a dispute before it is heard by a court or tribunal
sovereignty	power of decision making, especially the power to make law
specific performance	a court order obliging a party to a contract to fulfil his obligations under that contract, an equitable remedy
spurious	false, doubtful
Standing Committee	a committee of MPs that deals with the Committee Stage of a Bill
stare decisis	Latin; let the decision stand
statement of claim	the pleading which accompanies or follows a writ, setting out the plaintiff's case
statute	Act of Parliament

statutory bar a bar excludes a person; a statutory bar is an exclusion laid down by an Act

statutory instrument a form of delegated legislation, made by a government department under authority given by Parliament to a minister

stultifying dulling to the mind

subsidy a payment in support, a supplement

substantive something that confers rights or places obligations on people

susceptible open to

symbolic having an effect on people's perceptions or beliefs, as opposed to any measurable practical effect

T

take cognisance take notice of, take into account

ten-minute Bill a process by which individual MPs can bring a proposed Bill to the attention of the House. Theoretically, the Bill could become an Act but that is most unlikely

tertium quid Latin; a third thing

Third Reading the final stage of a Bill before each of the Houses of Parliament. There is no significant debate or change at this stage

tortfeasor a person who commits a tort

Treaty of Rome the Treaty signed by the original members of the European Community, often referred to in the context of European law as 'The Treaty'

triable either way criminal offences that may be tried in the magistrates' court (summarily) or in the Crown Court (on indictment)

truism something that seems obvious

trust a device by which the legal interest in property is held by one person and the equitable interest belongs to another, so that the person holding the legal interest (the **trustee**) has to deal with the property for the benefit of the **beneficiary**

U

uberrimae fidei Latin; the utmost good faith

ubiquitous present everywhere

unambiguous clear – something that is ambiguous could be interpreted in several different ways

unassisted opponents	parties who do not have legal aid, against parties who do
underwriters	the people who take on the risk and pay for losses under insurance policies
unqualified	without exception or limitation
utility	usefulness

V

verbatim	word for word
verbiage	excessive words
vetting	the process of considering whether jurors are suitable and removing those believed unsuitable
vindicating	upholding, defending
vis major	Latin; superior power – the same as the French *force majeure*
void	of no effect. A contract that is void was never a contract
voidable	effective until declared void by a party who has a right to make such a declaration
volition	choice, exercise of free will – so in the law of tort when one speaks of a person being ***volenti*** it means that he or she has chosen to be in a particular situation

W

warranty	a contractual promise
White Paper	a government publication giving details of firm proposals for legislation
Wolfenden Committee	a Committee that studied homosexual offences and prostitution and reported in 1957

Index